EVENTS LEADING UP TO MY DEATH

ST. MARTIN'S PRESS
NEW YORK

EVENTS LEADING UP TO MY DEATH

THE LIFE OF A TWENTIETH-CENTURY REPORTER

HOWARD K. SMITH

Book design by Gretchen Achilles

Map copyright © 1996 by Mark Stein Studios

Library of Congress Cataloging-in-Publication Data

Smith, Howard K. (Howard Kingsbury)
    Events leading up to my death : the life of a twentieth-century
reporter / by Howard K. Smith. —1st ed.
        p.   cm.
    "A Thomas Dunne book."
    ISBN 0-312-13970-5
    1. Smith, Howard K. (Howard Kingsbury), 1914–   . 2. Journalists—
United States—20th century—Biography.   3. Reporters and
reporting—United States.   I. Title.
PN4874.S562A3   1996
070'.92—dc20
[B]   95-40045
                                                                  CIP

First Edition: March 1996

10 9 8 7 6 5 4 3 2 1

TO BENNIE, JACK, CATHERINE AND DENNIS
AND ALEXANDER, GRAHAM AND LOGAN—
A SPRIGHTLY YOUNG FAMILY TREE WHERE LATE A LEAFLESS SAPLING STOOD

1946–1957

1957–1961

1961–1965

1965–1974

1974–1979

1979 and After

CONTENTS

ACKNOWLEDGMENTS

I want to thank my agent, Clyde Taylor, for placing this book with St. Martin's Press, Tom Dunne for welcoming me into his distinguished stable of writers (albeit with an occasional marginal explosion at my observations about his, the Sixties, generation), and above all Jeremy Katz for riding herd on the manuscript the whole way to publication and preventing such illicit marriages of metaphors as these. My love accompanies my gratitude to a wife who policed every word and to a small white cat named Lightfoot, who kept the whole thing from blowing away by conscientiously mounting the table and lying on it every time we sat down to edit. Withal, the result is wholly my work, and if mayhap there is approval as there surely will be dissent, the sole target must be . . .

HOWARD K. SMITH
High Acres
Bethesda, Maryland

1914–1937

CHAPTER ONE

1914–1918

It has always seemed to me appropriate that I, who was to become a professional observer of events, was coeval with the seminal bad event of the twentieth century. I was born in May 1914. The powder trail to the Great War was lit a month later in June 1914. After an interval for my growing up, the consequences of the two events intertwined in a combination that Neil Armstrong, the first man on the moon, might have described as a great experience for a man but nothing much for mankind.

I was born in Ferriday, Louisiana, a small dusty town just off the Mississippi River, one big bend above Natchez, Mississippi. Though numbering only a few thousand in population Ferriday claimed a high output of celebrities. A billboard in town recently advertised, "Ferriday, Louisiana, home of Jimmy Swaggart, Jerry Lee Lewis, Mickey Gilley and Howard K. Smith." For identification, Jimmy Swaggart is a magnetic evangelical preacher. His services, broadcast on television from Baton Rouge, Louisiana, to large audiences in many countries, brought him hundreds of millions of tax-free dollars a year in contributions from his far-flung congregations. Until a cruel blow fell: A competing preacher exposed, with pictures, Swaggart's patronage of a New Orleans prostitute. And she, suddenly made famous, sold her story to a magazine, again with pictures, illustrating nude poses she said the reverend liked most in their intimate hours. Like those who live by the sword, those who make a living by pictures may be undone by them; the most memorable vision the public has of the pastor is of his large, football player's face soaking in tears as he confessed his guilt to a television audience.

Jerry Lee Lewis is a flamboyant composer and singer of rock and country music, whose soaring career was brought low by the revelation of his marriage to his comely fourteen-year-old third cousin at a time when he had neglected to terminate a previous marriage. His career went on through a total of six wives and other rises and declines, till lately it enjoyed a climax of sorts as the subject of a Hollywood movie titled *Great Balls of Fire,* which is the title of one of his hit songs. The part of Jerry Lee is played by the actor Dennis Quaid. The third figure named on the billboard, Mickey Gilley, is also a composer and a singer but with executive flair. He operated a large nightclub in Texas. The fourth name is mine.

A lady in Los Angeles who wrote a book about Elvis Presley thought a book about the boys from Ferriday might fit the genre, so she asked me if I could think of a common thread in the lives of the four. Except that all four were communicators of one kind or another and all were marked by sin (though some were more public about it than others), I could not. Ferriday has been called the buckle on the Bible Belt, and their talents—preaching and singing—are in the air of the region. My life, proclivities, tastes, persona, whatever, seem to have no relationship whatever to them or it. I long puzzled over my seeming rootlessness, and some years ago I remembered an incident that may provide a clue. As a small child I awoke from surgery for circumcision and wailed to the doctor, what on earth had he done to me? He answered, "I've cut the Ku Klux out of you." And so it seemed; until I learned the basics of self-defense, or rather of masculine bluff, I was beaten up regularly in toilets and showers where my putative link to Jews and Catholics was visible. Till something more convincing comes along, that will be my working hypothesis for my lack of regional heritage. The old roots dried out, any fugitive faith in special creation eroded early, rendering me immune to the Ayatollahs of Southern evangelism and irretrievably loose in the broad vistas of skepticism and discovery in which I have roamed ever since.

Of course there is another possible explanation of the gap that separates us. They were genuinely talented—singing and praying seem to be in the water—while I had to labor at my kind of communication, had to be familiar with more than one book, had to gather and screen facts and respect them, had to puzzle over the nature of truth and had to make peace with confusion and uncertainty, all of which produce different results.

I was born in Ferriday because that is where my father's job stationed him at the time. My father was an almost fictionally perfect illustration of the declined fortunes of the southern plantation aristocracy. He was the scion of such a family and lived in a fine plantation manor house. It is still there as I write, at a crossroads called Lettsworth, north of Baton Rouge, and has been handsomely restored by a later owner. The family's financial decline had been in progress for a long time, with the final fall coming in my father's youth. He left boarding school—I think it was called Jefferson College—before finishing, due to shortage of funds. He took a wife, and to support her got a managerial job in a sugar refinery. (Its ruins are still there, too, on the Vermillion River just south of the city of Abbeville, used as a hunting and fishing lodge by the present owner.) When a tariff on Caribbean sugar was lifted in the time of President Grover Cleveland, the refinery failed. He then got a job with the Missouri Pacific Railroad as a conductor on local runs with a base in Ferriday. Meanwhile the Lettsworth plantation was taken over by a bank for nonpayment of debt. To outrun chronology, Dad lost his job in the 1920s, and we lived on small proceeds from odd jobs in my adolescent years. Thus did he descend from aristocracy to, so to speak, proletariat in half a lifetime.

My mother was a ravishing beauty and a child of misfortune. Her father was a Red River steamboat captain with the magnificent name of Christopher Columbus Cates, and her mother a Cajun with the family name of Enette— both of whom died at her birth in a yellow fever epidemic. She was separated from two sisters and handed around among relatives unable to care for her, until she ended up with a Cajun farm family by the name of Vignes across the Mississippi River from Baton Rouge. I have never been able to untangle the lines by which she was related, but it was a happy consummation. They were poor but loving, and the love extended through my generation. I spent wonderful childhood nights in the laps of my Cajun cousins in what would now be regarded as a backwoods shack, listening to stories of the swamps.

In her twenties my mother-to-be was somehow discovered by local society and invited to a party in the town of New Roads. Howard K. Smith met and fell in love with Minnie Cates and persuaded her to marry him. And she followed her husband from manor house to sugar mill to the railroad, creating three children on the way: my brother, a sister who died before I was born, and me.

My parents were very loving to me but not to one another. It was not a good marriage. To be forthright, it was a very bad marriage. I have no recollection of an affectionate word or gesture ever passing between them. There were no quarrels in my presence and in fact very little conversation of any kind, which suggests they had done with that stage and had given up on the relationship. I do not know why and never had the courage to ask. I surmised that religion had something to do with it. My mother was a devout Catholic; my father, a true believing Baptist. The state of Louisiana at that time was deeply divided along religious lines. The north was strongly Protestant, mostly Baptist, and the south strongly Catholic. This division affected every aspect of life; every statewide election then was a highly charged contest between a Catholic candidate and a Protestant one. Apparently it even affected love.

Beyond that, their personalities were too opposed. My father, born to aristocracy, became utterly plebeian. He addressed all new male acquaintances as "Cap'n," a term of high regard in river towns, and a way of assuring the addressee of your humility before him. When not leashed he sometimes appeared on the front porch in nothing but his union suit (a sagging piece of underwear in which top and bottom were sewn together, in union). He always bathed in his underwear, explaining that it saved trouble and soap to wash person and lingerie in a single operation. My mother, though out of backwoods poverty, had modest aspirations of class. Calling someone "common" was her worst aspersion. I recall my father being around the house as little as possible and my parents never sleeping in the same bed.

I suspect that my dear father, the doted-on youngest of his father's brood and the only boy, was simply not equipped by genes or upbringing to bear responsibilities. He married a poor but lovely girl who had distinct demands upon marriage that he could not meet. Later in life when we were all scattered by events, he married an undemanding seamstress half his age and seemed sublimely happy doing carpentry chores for the church, around which his life came to revolve, and distributing Gideon bibles to hotels and boarding houses.

My elder brother came to be very critical and hostile to my father as a bad provider and a slob. I have never been able to share his attitude. Most of our memories of him were from the Depression, and most men were poor providers then. And as the years accumulate I notice my father's younger son, increasingly, on hot days, moving around the house in his underwear and sometimes stepping out on the terrace in that state. But I do wear shorts, not a union suit, and I do take them off before bathing.

The life that began in these circumstances was, for most of it, spent trying to comprehend and make rational the events of the twentieth century. I have lived through most of the century and closely witnessed many of its high events—indeed, I calculate with some alarm that my life span has covered more than a third of the time the United States of America has existed—so I plan from time to time in this narrative to generalize and comment.

If there is a red thread running through the century, it is the breathtaking advances in science and technology without commensurate improvements in morals or wisdom. On the very first day of the century, January 1, 1901, such an advance was acknowledged in a most conspicuous way. In London, Queen Victoria's New Year's Honors list was published, and the most interesting name on it was that of Hiram Maxim, who was thereby elevated to a knighthood. Hiram Stevens Maxim was an American inventor whose name would be immortalized when attached to the means by which generations of gangsters and other assassins would rub out their victims: the Maxim silencer. At this point he was better known as the inventor of the most effective of several kinds of automatic or machine gun. This native of Maine had encountered insufficient interest in his machine gun in America, so he had moved to England and found a sponsor in the British Army. His gun was used to great advantage in mowing down Sudanese troops of the Mahdi in the battle of Omdurman in 1898. When the prospect of larger wars arose, Hilaire Belloc authored the lines, "Whatever happens, we have got/The Maxim gun and they have not." And that is how Sir Hiram Maxim became a "Sir."

In 1914 the nations of Europe engaged once more in their nearly ritual way of making history. Pursuing perceived interests, they fell into a pattern of conflict not essentially different from such patterns in the millennium before. As had often happened before, an incident of little moment fused the elements into a fight. And like many—not all, but many—such wars before, this one was not needed. The action of the German Kaiser set it off. Yet, had he been asked what he wanted from it, his only honest answer would have been, "More, sooner." For, as surely as water seeks its level, the German empire was drifting to preeminent power in Europe without war. In all its essential outlines the Great War was a garden-variety European conflict with all the features, a military historian has written, of "a moderate struggle."

What made it immoderate, horrible and epochal was the advances in the technology of war. Contrary to Belloc's assurance, all sides possessed the magic machine that sprayed death like water from a hose. And the breech-loaded, crucible steel, rifled, quick-firing artillery pieces, which fired bigger, more explosive shells farther, more accurately and more devastatingly than any before—these two made dug-in defense the only sensible operation. But traditional and romantic notions of war led commanders to order great offensives anyhow. Other technological advances cooperated to create the great human slaughter. The hygienic revolution supplied vastly more human lives than had been available before. The transportation and communication revolutions got them to the right altars for mass sacrifice in time to keep hell afire for four years.

The consequences of this great mass trauma shaped events long after—two consequences in particular. One, it allowed a small clutch of talky radicals in Russia to seize control of the world's largest country and clamp an iron ideological corset on human nature that did not fit. The Bolsheviks had little to offer, but one item of that little proved enough. They were the only party to promise the miserable Russian people convincingly that they would be taken out of that war. After another disastrous offensive mounted by the parties in power, enough soldiers sided with the Communists at just the right moment to allow them to seize control and become a main unsettling force in the world for most of the rest of the century.

The second consequence, the horror of it all, spread a vow of Never Again among all peoples of the western world. It was a pacifist mindset that opened the door of opportunity to the residue of people who did want to fight again. A catastrophic turn in the business cycle eventually brought that residue out from under the rocks and the back alleys of Germany and Japan and into power.

Of all this the central figure of this chronicle knew, at age three, only two things. Cousin Ulysse Goudeau of Pointe Coupée Parish was among the first called up because the U.S. Army needed French speakers for liaison. We would pore over his Kodak pictures of Ulysse and comrades in France years after they had yellowed. And there was a mindless ditty the three-year-old chirped to win applause from admiring elders: "Kaiser Bill went up the hill / to take a look at France. / Kaiser Bill came down the hill / with bullets in his pants." People who can discern the later man in the boy might note that the forthcoming observer of events was not naturally inclined to the journalistic ideal of objectivity, a flaw that would raise problems later in life.

CHAPTER TWO

The 1920s

In his volume on life in America in the 1920s the eminent historian Page Smith describes the vibrant changes going on in those years in all parts of the nation, save one. The changes, he writes, touched "the South hardly at all." He continues, "The South, still cherishing the 'Lost Cause,' stewed in the bitter brew of defeat and poverty." And he describes a region of desperately poor tenant farmers, ill-paid mill workers and Negroes living and dying in the terror of a Ku Klux Klan reborn and more vicious than ever.

His account is standard, and like the parson's egg, parts of it are all right. But Jack Smith, as I came to be called in childhood, living in the way-down deepest South, would have thought its characterization of that region the grossest calumny. In 1918 my father was transferred to Monroe, a town of 20,000 in northeast Louisiana; we found it a pleasant, untroubled place, and we spent the happiest period of our family's span there. Sixty miles east of Monroe was the region known as the Mississippi Delta, though it is far north of the river's real delta, one of the famous poverty areas of the nation. A hundred miles to the west was the city of Shreveport, which became a kind of regional capital for the Klan from which klaverns (as branch units were called) radiated out over the northern part of the state. Monroe, in between, had little trace of either ill. Neither in six years of schooling nor in overheard conversation of elders was I aware of any special interest in, much less obsession with, the famous Lost Cause. There was no Confederate monument in front of city hall. Life in the town was more typically American than specifically Southern—in no important way different from life in Salinas, California, or Salina, Kansas.

Monroe's equable social climate had in part a material basis. When oil was discovered in Louisiana, drilling was tried all over the state. Beneath Monroe exploratory wells found no oil, but great volumes of natural gas (which in one place pumped up the biggest, most marvelous saltwater swimming pool in the world). For a while the billboard outside town could claim with authority that it was the natural gas center of the nation. On their way north, enough of the proceeds leaked out into the community to make it moderately prosperous and a hotbed of social calm.

Another cause of the prevailing mood was a macabre drama played out north of the city in neighboring Morehouse Parish. There, as throughout the South and in the North-Central States, the 1920s saw a mighty resurgence of the Ku Klux Klan. It was due in the main, I believe, to the deep boredom of small-town life. The boredom was the greater because the nation had just had its emotions overinflated by its entry into the war against the Hun. Our part was relatively brief, and relatively few young men got to see actual combat, so there was lots of militant virtue swirling around with no cause to support. The reinvigorated Klan provided a cause or several. Its purposes were, to its constituents, altogether virtuous: to diminish intemperance by raiding and destroying stills that pocked the hollows in the years of prohibition (no contradiction was seen in keeping a flask of white lightning in a hip pocket to sustain the spirit of virtue); to keep the Romans, the Israelites and above all the Ethiops at bay by resorting to midnight warnings or bullets fired through windows or crosses burned on lawns; to protect white womanhood by carrying off and beating black men reported to have "looked too hard" at a lady on the street. It was all God's work, done in the most exciting way—riding the road at night, clinging to the running boards of chariots from Detroit while covered with white robes that flapped in the wind, wearing high peaked white helmets and white masks. Like little boys in treehouses they could see you but you couldn't see them. However dull his daytime drill, at night every Klansman was God's terrible, swift sword. Heroic action in the long hot nights provided lots to talk about in the long hot days.

In Morehouse Parish all places of power were soon filled by Klansmen. The Governor of Louisiana complained that the state had been divested of all authority there; Morehouse became Klaniana, subject to the Klan's whims, not the laws of state or nation. But soon absolute power did its work of corrupting absolutely; the Klansmen developed exaggerated notions about what they could get away with. Two bold young white men in the parish made jokes in public, calling into question the manhood of the white knights. One joke was that the reason they wore pointed hats was because they had pointed heads. One night, in 1922, the Klan blocked a caravan of cars returning from a social outing, pulled the two young men and their fathers and a fifth man out, took them to a clearing and beat them severely with leather straps. Three of the men were then released and allowed to wander back to the road. But the fourth tore the mask off one of his persecutors and shouted his identity within earshot of the fifth. So these two were not released. They disappeared.

The Governor ordered a thorough search for them. After weeks of hunting, a company of National Guard infantry found their two bodies, headless and mutilated, in a lake. It was determined that their bound bodies had been run over repeatedly and their bones broken while they were still alive. A grand jury inquiry and a special investigation by the Governor could not establish clear individual guilt that would support any criminal indictments, but public opinion was sickened and turned angrily against the Klan. Monroe elected a Jewish mayor, and Morehouse Parish a Jewish sheriff. The state legislature passed laws in 1924 requiring the Klan to publish names of all members and forbidding the wearing of masks except at Halloween and Mardi Gras. Another law declared that any threat made by someone wearing a mask would be deemed equivalent to aggravated assault and subject to harsh penalties. The white-sheeted terror withered in Louisiana and died in Monroe. Negroes in the city were no nearer to equality and dignity than in any other place; but the terror was off, and that was something. Monroe returned to being a progressive community whose citizens were at peace with one another and the world.

My father belonged to a strong union, the Brotherhood of Railway Conductors, and his income was modestly rising, so we partook of the good things. We bought (or acquired an affordable mortgage on) a home for the first and last time, a new little yellow bungalow at 1715 Jackson Street. We had access to an auto, a shiny new Durant, owned by Cuney Pritchard across the street. Cuney was a wizened old Yankee who owned the largest house on the block, with the largest yard and his own general store on the street behind. From his orchard I picked figs in season, paid him 25¢ per gallon bucketful and then hawked the harvest down the street for 50¢ a gallon bucket. In summer I worked for his store, going house to house soliciting grocery orders, then filling and delivering them in a horse-drawn cart. Cuney's store served as the polling station in elections. I was there for the counting of ballots after the primary gubernatorial vote of 1924. Hewitt Buonchaud, Catholic, lost to Henry Fuqua, Protestant. A young newcomer, Huey P. Long of Winnfield, came in third, losing an election for the only time in his life.

Cuney loved his Durant and kept it highly polished, but he could not drive it. He recruited my brother to do that. Every Sunday afternoon after church and lunch my brother would take us—Cuney and Mrs. Pritchard, my mother and me—for a wonderfully enchanting drive. Always the same route, out Jackson Street as far as the gravel lasted, then back and up north out to Riverside Drive till it ran out of surface. Beyond that was dust or mud so viscid that it was reputed to swallow little Durants whole.

But by far the most appreciated of the new urban delights were the moving pictures. There were two theaters: the classy Saenger, 15¢, where as I recall they showed only sigh and kiss movies that my mother liked but I thought were boring; and the barnlike Lyceum, 10¢, which usually featured westerns and, once a week, continued stories. I liked the latter most and remember most vividly Elmo Lincoln in *Tarzan of the Apes,* and a series starring the great heavyweight champion Jack Dempsey. My favorite has escaped all mention in histories of film. It was Charles Hutchinson in *Hurricane Hutch.* I sat frozen in admiration each week as Hutch swung from overpasses onto fast-moving trains or knocked three and four assailants down as though they were round-bottomed bowling pins, all without once taking off his coat or undoing his tie. Every Friday I would ride the tram home, glassy-eyed in fascination, then lock myself in the bedroom, put on my father's coat and tie and go before the mirror and duplicate and improve upon the feats I had just witnessed.

My formal education began. My first year, kindergarten, was spent largely in obsession with a very pretty little classmate named Nancy Pugh. My praises of her were so insistent that on the final day my mother gave me 50¢ to buy a box of chocolates to give her. After class that day I retrieved the box from a shelf where I had hidden it and went out to the steps of the schoolhouse to await her exit. Out she came, but holding the hands of her mother and father on either side. It had taken some courage to decide to approach Nancy; her formidable bodyguard cowed me into inaction. When all had gone I sat on the steps and in frustration opened the box and ate the chocolates.

For first grade, my mother enrolled me in the St. Matthew's Parochial School, fulfilling a promise she had made the Church on marrying a Protestant. It was a disastrous decision. All the teachers were newly arrived Italian nuns with accents so marked that I could not understand a word. My mother was about to dismiss her younger son as mentally retarded when she determined to try him out at the public Ouachita Parish school. There I immediately blossomed. I loved the school, the classes, the teachers and the kids, mostly the girls. I came to view as scholastic requirements falling in love with a new girl each class and harboring deep silent romances with pretty teachers.

The quality of sociability pervaded our life. I had neighborhood friends, school friends and relatives we dearly loved—mountainous Cousin Clemmy, who ran a boardinghouse for railroad men, and her two daughters, who were almost big sisters to me. My mother had weekly bridge meetings at our house, and occasionally a guest for dinner, and we knew and mixed with our neighbors. It sounds unremarkable, but in fact we never enjoyed it again and were to experience a kind of prolonged isolation after Monroe. Being intertwined with our community was a warm and remarkable experience to us, in retrospect.

My brother, Prescott, known to me as Bubba, was our prime social asset. He was a nearly perfect son—an athlete, the fastest runner, the best student and modest to a fault about it. He played quarterback on the Ouachita Parish High football team, which, in our small town, carried prestige comparable to that of being the star of a professional team in cities today. He ran the 440-yard dash on the track team. Our version of the Olympic Games was the annual Louisiana state rally; each summer the best athletes and students met in Baton Rouge to compete. In my brother's senior year in high school he returned from the state capital with a unique combination of awards, the gold medal for the 440 and the gold medal for debating. He put them away in a drawer. His little brother sneaked them out and went to school with them pinned on his shirt. I would have worn them out but for maternal confiscation.

I now introduce a figure of note in this narrative. I have told of the backwoods farm family, name of Vignes, who reared my mother. The son of the family was Clement Victor Vignes, a very tall, erect man of strong resolution. Somehow Victor, as intimates called him, made his way from the farm to Memphis. Somehow he put himself through a dental college there and, with his degree, settled in New Orleans. By skill and industry he developed a reputation and acquired respectable patients. He studied and transformed his Cajun patois into perfect French. He made an early practice of visiting Paris once each year. He won entry into refined French society in New Orleans and wooed and married a wealthy woman. She died and he married another. He became very wealthy, in large part by marriage. But it was his professional reputation that caused him to be named Dean of the College of Dentistry at Loyola University in New Orleans. When I later met him I saw a severe man, sharp and critical toward all humanity, especially little boys, a dark, oval face with austere lines running from the sides of his nose down to the corners of his sternly set mouth. His skin was very dark (the actor James Earl Jones was a close likeness), and my father once dared suggest to me he had Negro blood. My father disliked him, and he, a devout Catholic, disliked my father and had disapproved of my mother's marriage to a Protestant.

In my brother's last year in high school, when he was pondering what to do with himself, Clement Victor wrote my mother a letter and made a generous offer. He would finance a college education for Prescott in dentistry at Loyola and would allow my brother to live in his fine home in New Orleans for the duration; after that, if Prescott did well in his studies, Clement Victor would take him on as junior partner in his practice. This breathtaking offer was promptly accepted, and in September of 1926 we bade Prescott a tearful farewell as he, on a pass from my father, took the train for the city, probably, we feared, never to return.

Losing a brother—as if to death, I felt, for New Orleans was to hell and gone away, a strange, devouring place from which small-town emigrants never returned—from this tiny, already disparate family unit was a blow. A worse one followed hard upon. My father came home from a run, took my mother into the bedroom and they talked, with more purposefulness of manner than usual. She emerged wiping tears from her face. My father looked grim as I had never seen him before. It emerged in pieces over days: Dad had been fired from the Mo-Pac railroad. Why, they would not tell me. But many years later I found out.

One day when I was in my twenties and my mother was no longer about and my father thought I had attained a certain skill at putting words in sequence, he asked me if I would write a letter for him. The letter was to be addressed to the president of the Missouri Pacific Railroad, asking for restoration of Dad's job. He then told me: as a conductor on small runs between towns that often had no ticket offices, he pocketed some fares and did not hand the payments over at the end of the runs. An inspector posing as a passenger had found him out. Dad had the usual argument: it was petty stuff and most conductors engaged in it at one time or another. I'm sure his argument was accurate. His malefaction was I guess no worse than reporters' expense accounts I have okayed in times since. I had a hard time composing the letter, which amounted in my formulation to an apology and a promise never to do it again. Dad had wanted me to write a justification. My draft went unused.

Back to Monroe and 1927. My father traveled to St. Louis and then to New Orleans hunting for work. My mother suffered sleepless nights. After a few months a decision had to be made. Dad was going to stay in New Orleans in the belief that a bigger place was more likely to provide a job. My brother was also committed to staying in New Orleans. We could no longer afford to make payments on the house in Monroe. There was no way out. It was decided that my mother would move herself and me to the city to stay.

Often in later years I have wondered at the ease with which "army brats" move from town to town, following the assignments of their military fathers. For me this one move was traumatic. I begged to be left with Cousin Clemmy to continue school at Ouachita. My mother was firm: it could not be done. On a dismal day in late summer 1927 we shipped off a few sticks of furniture and boarded a train for the city.

My brother and I seldom exchanged confidences. Indeed he was the strong silent type who rarely spoke much to anyone. But decades later when I sat with him drinking tall drinks in his New Orleans home, the subject of Monroe came up. There was a moment of silence. Then from the fundament of his soul a moan, "Why did we ever leave that town? We were happy there. . . ." And his voice trailed off and he was silent again. I think he never regained that level of satisfaction with life. Nor did I, till my circumstances changed wholly in another time and in a distant country.

CHAPTER THREE

New Orleans

New Orleans was a hard city to feel negative about. It was peopled by lively citizens who mostly did not propend toward excessive exertion or haste or rigid moral codes. Symbolically the slot machine was at once forbidden and ubiquitous. Coming out of the train station one was greeted by odors of molasses and coffee (since displaced by fumes of natural gas and gasoline). The city possessed that trigger to the imagination, a past, richer and in brighter colors than any but a couple of American cities, with artifacts all about not yet polished and lacquered up for the tourist trade: the Cathedral of St. Louis, temple of its French rulers; the handsome Cabildo town hall, where its Spanish ones governed; the Chalmette battlefield, where a rip-roaring American frontier general whipped the daylights out of an invading British army; the riverside marts, where a gawky farmboy from way upriver, name of Lincoln, first got a look at the fault line running through American history, as he watched ebony humans being auctioned like bales of cotton. For architectural magnificence nothing in America matched St. Charles Avenue, a long valley of lovely high-ceilinged homes with generous porches built to the comfortable specifications of wealthy merchants (but lately decimated in favor of modern apartments).

It was a hard city to feel negative about, but I gave it a good try, and our circumstances favored the effort. Before we arrived my father rented us a house in what is called the Irish Channel, a poor white section of town. Ritually I was beaten up by local boys for being new and failing to have a Brooklyn accent (that is right: among several accents in the polyglot city one was identical to Brooklyn's). One of my mother's sisters and her two boys lived nearby. I mixed with them and at one point was taken behind the house and offered a draw on a crude butt of marijuana. Though only in their teens, those boys were well along toward becoming hard addicts and creating hell on earth for their widowed mother. My mother decided we would live elsewhere no matter what. She found us half of a double house in a really good neighborhood near the two universities—Loyola, where my brother was studying, and Tulane, which reputedly the swells attended. I do not know how we afforded it.

I sulked away two years, going to grade schools, making no friends and doing poorly in classes. As time approached to go to high school, Dr. Clement Victor Vignes made a deal with my mother nearly as generous as his arrangement for my brother. If I passed the eighth grade with an average mark of eighty, he would pay my way through the Jesuit High School, which was better than the public high school. It was not a stern test; eighty could be achieved with little more effort than was involved in showing up, and I had been doing far better than that in Monroe. But this time when the results were in, I barely made seventy-five, which was just above failing. The Apostate Angel was not dismissed from Heaven with greater finality than I from the furious presence of Victor Vignes. Since our settling in the city he had given my mother and her two sons a standing invitation to dine with him and his wife at his graceful home each Thursday. Henceforth, the younger son ceased to exist. I did not mind that much as I sat at the kitchen table eating meat and beans with my father (Dad cooked the way he bathed; since it was all to be mixed together in the eating, that is how he cooked it, everything together in one skillet). But I did suffer from the chilling silences of my mother and brother when they returned home every Thursday night.

I think that my real sorrow had degenerated into a juvenile peeve. In those same years I was reading at home for fun, oblivious to the fact that this was the kind of stuff they gave marks for in school. Somewhere along, Dad had bought a small library for nothing from a literate brakeman in financial straits. It included the famous "five-foot shelf" of Harvard Classics. The poems, three volumes of them, got me first; and first among them was "Locksley Hall," then "The Raven," then Longfellow's "Evangeline," an epic about my mother's people. You can tell that I liked rhythm in my rhymes. I liked "The Raven" so much that I drew an illustration and pasted it into the book. Then the prose: I thought Plutarch's ancient celebrities deserved portraits, so I provided some. Then into autobiography—Franklin, Cellini, Darwin on the *Beagle* (it tells you something that, in twelve years of public education in Louisiana, I never once read in a textbook or heard from a teacher's lips the words, "theory of evolution"). I was having a fine private time with literature while failing English Literature.

One feature of life began to draw me out of my sulk and into comradeship with other kids: sports. Living where we did it was inevitable. A couple of blocks away stood a string of sports facilities more spacious than any I have seen anywhere else. The academic buildings of the two universities were located side by side facing St. Charles Avenue, and behind these lay a total of seven large playing fields, two of them encircled by cinder tracks and three with gymnasiums alongside. (Most are now built upon.) Any day, two or three football or basketball games were to be watched. And no one seemed to care if kids organized pickup games on the fields that were idle. At the Loyola track, coach Tad Gormley, an Irishman with a Rockne-type broken nose and a torso that abhorred shirts, organized games for all in the city who wished to take part. Every Sunday after mass each runner was given a handicap yard, or several, over Gormley's Loyola stars, and a chance to beat them to the tape. In high school and college I rarely missed a chance to take part.

We were financially sustained, barely, by two talents of my father's that had not previously appeared to have economic value: a small skill at carpentry and generally fixing things around the house, and a genial disposition. His bent toward carpentry produced, out of Carnation milk crates and some used springs, a narrow, squeaky bed for me, which was the only bed I slept in for the rest of my young life in America. I grew, but it didn't, so until I was twenty-two I assumed that a crouch was the normal resting position for people. The bedroom was equally economical. My mother slept at night in the large bed near my cot; and when she arose in the morning, my father, back from a night-watching job he eventually found, climbed in and stole a few hours of sleep. The only other bedroom in the house had to be allotted to our shining hope, my dentistry-studying brother. Until he got the night-watchman's job, Dad's career in New Orleans followed a pattern. He would get into a home by means of the first talent, to free a jammed window or repair a table. Then he would be given longer-lasting assignments because he was easy to have around, never complaining or even frowning. He never drank liquor or smoked and would eat any leftover without discrimination—altogether trouble-free. Unless you were married to him and expected better.

His relationship with Mrs. Leathers was typical. She was actually Miss Leathers, the spinster daughter of the great T. P. Leathers, builder and captain of the steamboat *Natchez,* whose races on the Mississippi with the *Robert E. Lee* were a national drama. After the Civil War, Leathers transported the humbled Confederate President Jefferson Davis downriver on the way to his home. The foremost rebel took a liking to Leathers' tiny daughter and gave her a bottle of wine, to be opened at the birth of her first child. As she never married or had a child, she opened the bottle one day in the presence of New Orleans newspaper reporters and found only a residue of vinegar. Well, somehow she asked Dad to do a few handyman things in her house. He was so congenial that the lonely lady kept finding chores for him to do, until he became a kind of occasional companion. Mrs. Leathers was not wealthy, but it helped pay the rent. My mother thought there was an amorous element. I doubted it; Mrs. Leathers was seventy-five. I did not know at that time that advanced age is no cure for loving. Later Dad was called on to do some fixing in an enclave of homes of wealthy citizens. He made such a comfortable impression that they decided to keep him around as a night watchman. Those were the known sources of our upkeep. But I guessed, wholly without evidence, that Dr. Vignes gave my mother a quiet supplement when these incomes did not reach.

Over time I adjusted to the city, but I never quite came to terms with several deep-dyed features of this complex conurbation.

One, with apologies to the tourism industry, was the holiday of Mardi Gras. It is depicted and advertised as a festival of mass joy. I tried earnestly to get into the spirit or to find a high spirit to get into, but failed. I found it a long exercise in excess, an orgy to be tolerated only if one got solidly drunk and stayed that way. After several tries, in the week of that festival, my mother and I would pack a bag and flee to the farmhouse in Pointe Coupée Parish where she was reared, and return only when the detritus of the festival had been cleared from the streets and spirits.

Another objectionable feature was the excessive snobbism of an upper class that possessed few credentials but had constructed itself around the old Mardi Gras "krewes" with kings and queens and courts and balls and parades. Some people's whole year was made or ruined depending on invitations to the lavish balls. It may seem inoffensive play acting, but I came to know cases in which life's values were set by this structure, and a kind of incapacity to deal with the real world resulted.

A third feature was the quality, hard to nail down and define, that has given the town the sobriquet "the Big Easy." It ill behooves a teenage wastrel to complain, but when the wastrel sought to pull up, he found no handle to grab onto. There was a generalized lack of spirit of enterprise, a readiness to make do with mediocre effort and third-rate results. Later, when other Southern cities—Atlanta in the van—took off with energy and purpose, New Orleans seemed to lie back and let the century happen.

By one means or another the three men in the family were making their peace with the city, finding new interests and pursuits. The only total loser was my mother. She became housecleaner, cook, laundress and worrier for three men. The quality of sociability was lost. No bridge afternoons or guests to dinner. It took a while for the insensitive males, wrapped up in their own readjustments, to notice and comprehend, and for my brother to graduate and start helping. When he did, it was too late. The Depression swamped all.

CHAPTER FOUR

Depression

The Great Depression is judged by many historians to have been the second most traumatic experience in American history, surpassed only by the Civil War. Neither of the frightful modern wars that bracketed it left scars so deep on so many Americans. Indeed, it is a sorry fact that the biggest war, WW II, came to many Americans almost as relief.

The consequences of the economic crisis were great and far-reaching. The warlords could hardly have come to dominate the will of the Japanese had world markets for the goods they had to sell in order to live not dried up. Probably the monster Adolf Hitler could not have risen to power in Germany had there been no paralysis to rend so many people's ties to reason. It is anticlimactic to add that the economic collapse of the 1930s was a most powerful formative influence on the subject of this narrative.

The basic measures of the calamity are worth repeating. At one time around 14 million Americans were jobless. The equivalent in today's population would be about 30 million. The total of incomes of all Americans in 1929 was $87 billion for the year. In 1933, after three years of the Depression, it was $39 billion, less than half as much. We were a financially ruined people. Since unemployment insurance did not exist, 28 percent of Americans had no source of livelihood at all.

The blow did not fall as hard on the Smiths as on others. We were two years ahead of the nation in our descent from prosperity. Still, our standard of living fell. We began having more meals with red beans and rice and fewer with meat. Clothing had to remain in service longer, and we became shabby. Shoe soles with holes in them were reinforced each morning with a new inset of cardboard. It was painful only when we had to dress for an occasion, as for my graduation from high school. When we came up short with rent money, the real estate company decided to wait; they probably could not get other tenants who would come as close. The democracy of distress—there were few Joseph Kennedys who got rich on the times—was a great preventive of revolution. Had they existed in earlier times, two other preventives might have defused any revolution, even the Russian one: a flood of cheap escape movies, and rich entertainment every night on the radio.

For me individually one consequence was anguishing enough to be salvaging. It was the tonic effect Dr. Johnson attributed to knowing you are to be hanged in the morning. This awareness concentrated a mushy, diffuse mind wonderfully. I took a good look at my prospects in my penultimate year at Alcee Fortier High School and saw a void. I was fit for no job, which coincided with the circumstance that no job was to be had. I had worked occasionally in summers at one of the chain of Katz & Besthoff drugstores as a soda jerk. With better luck I had worked occasionally as a shipping clerk at the Haspel Brothers clothing manufactory. (I boasted that my weekly salary was in the high three figures: $9.98.) But with the Depression neither was hiring. College was out of the question. A terrifying feeling of emptiness within and without, of loneliness in despair overcame me. I had a sickening vision of a strong young man sitting around an unhappy house doing nothing or inefficiently helping an overworked mother clean the kitchen. I have never been suicidal but I did strongly feel that the life I was leading was not worth the few dollars I cost my poor disjointed family.

For effect I shall now skip to one year later, June 1932. That month I was graduated from high school, president of the senior class, editor of the school newspaper (which had just been awarded a huge silver trophy cup as the best student newspaper in the state), captain of the track team, holder of the public high school record for the 120-yard high hurdles, winner of the American Legion Award as best all around high school student, and—here was the power and glory—recipient of the Mayor's scholarship to Tulane University, then given each year to the public high school graduate with the highest academic grades. What a sharp look into the future had done for Ebenezer Scrooge, it had done for me.

The experience, incidentally, settled my future career. A decision to write was never made. I simply grew into it, rewriting Peter Rabbit to provide a happy ending at age eight; composing a hair-raising history of a band of carnivorous gorillas, shriekingly illustrated by me, at age eleven; writing fiction about football heroics for the school magazine at age fifteen. Now I considered soberly that one form of writing provided a weekly wage, and I went for it. I wrote some sports reports that a kind sportswriter named Harry Martinez published in the *New Orleans States* paper, sent items for a column in the *Times-Picayune* authored by F. Edward Hebert, who would later become a Congressman, and collected rejects for articles sent to the national popular magazine, *Liberty*. A straight line is the shortest path between two points, and I latched onto it, resolved on a life in journalism.

The material hardship of the Depression was made worse by ignorance. People could not see or otherwise identify the deadly beast eating away at livelihood and spirit. Montagu Norman, governor of the Bank of England, who was thought to know everything about such matters, said, "The difficulties are so vast, the forces so unlimited, so novel, and precedents so lacking, that I approach the whole subject not only in ignorance but in humility. It is too great for me."

In most minds the trouble was tied to the stock market crash in which share values, pumped up far beyond reality by speculation, were punctured and caused to collapse. Some saw a cause in Congress's raising of high tariffs—the infamous Smoot-Hawley act—to protect American markets for American business to exploit. The inevitable consequence was that all other nations raised their tariffs against American goods, and all, "like spent swimmers that do cling together and choke their art," went down together.

But I am inclined to see the central cause as the red thread noted in the opening chapter. In the 1920s, ever-improving technology caused output per worker to rise 43 percent while wages rose at a fraction of that rate. Came a time when incomes were so out of joint with the flood of output that output had to be curtailed, some plants closed, some workers laid off. Those without work bought still less, and down and around it went.

The trouble hit harder and lasted longer in the U.S. than in kindred nations of Europe. One reason for that is flattering: more intimately wed to invention, American producers met the Depression by cutting costs, and that was done by introducing a more labor-saving plant. But the result was, as the Depression seemed to ease in 1936 and producers began to produce again, they absorbed fewer workers, leaving too many people unemployed and still unable to buy. So in 1937 we headed right back into the depths.

The unflattering reason why America's purgatory outlasted Europe's is that the nations of Europe had long since created buffers to ease the pain of so-called business cycles. Beginning with Bismarck's social laws in Germany in the 1880s and on through the British Liberal Party's reforms in 1911, unfortunate citizens received something, however little, a dole, to fall back on in hard times and to keep the economy breathing a little. Typically in the U.S., when my father lost his job, there was nothing, zero. The American founders distrusted power so much that they composed a Constitution replete with checks that make it easy to prevent reforms and hard to initiate them, except under pressure of panic or war. In the early 1930s, panic allowed a new President to initiate action; and in the late 1930s, war solved the economic problem.

This may be the place to discuss a neighbor of mine whose activities somewhat eased the crisis for the whole state of Louisiana. My little home was on one side of the string of collegiate playing fields I mentioned. His was on the other side in an enclave called Audubon Avenue that one entered through a high grille gate. Since there was virtually no traffic on his street, kids of the neighborhood, including me, used to gather there, put on roller skates, shave the fronds that fell from the high palm trees into nicely curved sticks and, using a small block of wood as a puck, play lively games of roller skate hockey. He never complained about the ruckus. I saw him often, but I never met him, though years later in Washington, D.C., I came to know his son, Russell. Huey P. Long was a phenomenon, a wholly self-made politician, uniquely exempted from the need to favor either Catholic or Protestant to get along in politics. He won votes from both, and from black as well as white; and when he failed to win votes, he created them.

His economic method was simple. When he first became Governor in 1928, fruits of the state's abundant oil resources flowed straight up to the East. By tax and threat Huey redirected substantial largesse from these into the state treasury and used the funds (a) for public works and (b) to get reelected. He provided free school books, easing the scholastic path of the likes of me. He provided Louisiana with more paved roads than any state in the South. He repaved the streets of New Orleans, buckled and broken from too many floods, and provided the city with natural gas. He built its first bridge over the Mississippi River, and its first airport out over Lake Pontchartrain, which I remember with particular fondness: a big air show was put on to celebrate the opening of the airport, and I was paid three dollars a day as an usher. He converted Louisiana State University from a collection of buildings into a first-rate educational institution. My father worshipped him and my mother thought him vulgar, but none of us ever missed one of his broadcast speeches. He was the best entertainment there was.

Having conquered Louisiana, he became a U.S. Senator and set out to conquer the nation. His "Share the Wealth" program spread his fame like wildfire over a depressed, drought-parched country. He planned to run for President in 1936. Although he might not win, he might split the Democratic vote and bring in a Republican. And since the Republican could not, Huey calculated, cure the crisis, he might come back to win the whole thing in 1940. But he never had a chance to find out. One of the thousands of plain people who hated him assassinated him in 1935.

Huey was too rich for the nation's—any nation's—blood. If he was not a potential fascist he was as near to it as any American will ever be. His social plans would not have worked. His utter disregard for the civic rights of people would have led him into tyranny. He had no brown-shirt storm troopers, but there were thugs aplenty in our nation waiting to be recruited and favored with rewards.

Huey's son Russell subsequently became a U.S. Senator of considerable power as Chairman of the mighty Senate Finance Committee. We became good friends later in Washington. Back in the thirties, he had entered Alcee Fortier High School the year after I had left, so we did not meet, which was a pity for the health of our school paper, the *Silver and Blue.* I was a good editor and led the paper to win the award for best in Louisiana, but I could not make ends meet and left it in debt. On starting at Fortier, Russell joined the staff of the paper as advertising director. Had our tenures coincided, we would have been a great combination, for though he knew nothing about editing, he definitely knew how to make ends meet.

CHAPTER FIVE

Tulane

No one with a job to offer was impressed by my *annus mirabilis* in high school, so I spent an idle, impatient summer. On the appointed day early in September I went up the ancient steps of Gibson Hall at Tulane with a spring in my stride and nerves atingle at the prospect of four free years of higher education and a new life. I think I felt a little superior at being the only youth in the registrar's office without a check to hand over. When my turn came, I announced to a lady registrar that I was to be paid for by the City of New Orleans on the Mayor's scholarship. She retreated and whispered inquiries to a sister officer, which made me commence to worry. They both disappeared into another room and I began to sweat. A male officer returned with them and told me that there were records of the Mayor's scholarship in previous years, but there was no authorization for it this year.

The awful gasping sounds of my future dying filled my ears. The scholarship was everything. With it there were many, many possibilities. Without it nothing was possible. The void I had looked into long before was back now, smelling of a cadaver somewhere deep within. It made too much sense: with the Depression and the need to cut costs, the scholarship would be one of the first things eliminated. I went out onto St. Charles Avenue and took the streetcar to City Hall. I got as close to the Mayor's office as possible, but a policeman told me the Mayor was out doing things mayors do and would not be back today. Come back Tuesday or, better, a week from Tuesday, and I might have a chance.

I went to the Mayor's home and camped out across the street for hours. Cars came and went. After dark I crossed the street and pressed the doorbell. There were no guards, no police, no formalities. A girl I took to be his daughter came out and asked what I wanted. I told her, and she said, wait, and she went inside. Then the Mayor appeared. His name was T. Semmes Walmsley. He was a political enemy of Huey Long. Long's garish newspaper, the *Louisiana Progress,* always appeared with a huge cartoon on its front page, displaying his opponents in the most deleterious caricatures. I remembered that Walmsley was always labeled "Turkeyhead Walmsley" and was so depicted. My first impression of the Mayor was that his head did indeed resemble a turkey's. I stated my case breathlessly. He said he had never heard of it but would look into it, and he dismissed me. No trace of compassion or even of interest. I went home feeling desperate and in agreement on at least one detail with Huey Long.

Next morning I went back to the registrar's office. The lady registrar met me with a smile and told me that the authorization had arrived from the Mayor's office first thing. In a room suddenly filled with sunshine, I completed a form and was in. I make so much of this because it left a mark. In the twenty-four hours of deep disappointment I pictured myself as a penniless outsider, prying his way into an elite club where he did not belong. I felt warmly sorry for myself, as well as righteous in advancing so far, not like the other Tulaners by family, but by merit. Now, however, in a recent year, shortly before I sat down to commence writing this account, I received as an inheritance from a distant relative in St. Louis a fine big oil portrait of a handsome young man: Dr. Edwin Bathurst Smith, as he looked in 1837. Minimal research revealed that he was my great-granduncle, the brother of my great-grandfather. Dr. Smith studied in Edinburgh, practiced in New Orleans and later married and settled in St. Louis. He was one of several physicians who founded the Medical College of Louisiana, where he occupied the chair of Opera Medica. To this college the wealthy merchant Paul Tulane later offered his fortune, if it would adopt his name, which it did; and with his funds it expanded into a university. My fond recollection of being a poor but meritorious outsider has been damaged, if not destroyed, by the discovery late in life that I am in the family of the ultimate insiders, the founders.

Life on campus at Tulane produced a steep rise in my academic standard of living, although it would seem a Spartan existence to students there today. It was strictly an urban place for learning, nothing else: no dormitories, no student center except for the steps of Gibson Hall, not much of an auditorium, classrooms furnished with antique desks deeply grooved with initials and whimsical logos of generations past. But the climate consisted of students and faculty, and they were of a different order. Unlike students in public school, who attend because they are required to, these students were here to learn or at least to get some return on tuition, particularly in the Depression years. Teaching was quality. Everyone remembers one or two teachers to whom life-long debts are owed. One of mine was old John McBride, English Literature, who not only taught Shakespeare but also acted out all the roles and infected me with a fascination for the greatest wordsman that has only deepened with time. Another was young Mack Swearingen, History, who was at heart a news commentator and who always related what was in the books to what was happening today. Relevance was his unique contribution.

I wished to make Literature or History my major as a suitable background for journalism, but opted for Journalism itself instead. My reason was material. The local newspaper, *Times-Picayune,* offered an award of $100 to the best pre-journalism student of English Literature, and another $100 to the best Journalism student. Those were large amounts in those days. I wanted and got both. Then, for seniors, Elizabeth Gilmer offered $100 for the best human interest story by a Journalism student. Under the name of Dorothy Dix, she was author of a famous lovelorn advice column, universally syndicated, and she lived in New Orleans. I interviewed ragged WW I vets about what they planned to do with a bonus just voted for them by Congress, and won that prize. Carefully spent, the three awards paid much of the costs my scholarship did not cover.

Until my entrance to Tulane, such friends as I had were public school pals who ranked somewhat below middle on the social scale. Now I was surprised and rather uneasy to find myself "rushed" by a well-known social fraternity of youths located well above middle. This was the work of a much-admired figure whose name would have suited him to be one of the Sun King's generals— Calvert de Coligny. He was Tulane's star high hurdler. Because my high school team was permitted to practice on the Tulane track, we took to training together, and we became friends. It was he who persuaded his fraternity I had to be had.

By the time I was "pledged," that is, became a candidate for initiation, de Coligny had graduated, so my interest in joining evaporated. Toward the end of the pledge period I took the leader aside and told him that I wanted to reconsider; I could not afford the dues and did not have even a shadow of the sum to be paid upon initiation. There were meetings, and I was told to continue as a pledge, and perhaps something would turn up. So I remained an unhappy apprentice to the social elite for more than a year. By that time a university panel had presented me with the "White Elephant" award for the student deemed the outstanding freshman, so the fraternity elders resolved to have me no matter what. An anonymous New Orleans business figure paid my initiation fee and my dues. So, I was stuck in an organization I felt uncomfortable with but unable now to quit, lest I insult some kindly sponsor.

Relations did not improve when in the next "rushing" season I was asked to name some promising new recruit to be invited to a party and looked over. I named a young man who ran the mile on his high school team. When he had been looked over with other potential pledges, I was told he could not be considered. When I asked why, I was told that Jews had their own fraternities. I had not realized that he was Jewish, or that such a division existed in the fraternal world. For the next season I proposed a gentile youngster of Scandinavian descent who did the pole vault on his high school team (all my friends were from the little world of sports, my only social activity). He was rejected, and again I asked why. The answer was that he was the son of a workingman (his father was skipper of a cargo ship) and not suitable. I pointed out that I, too, was the son of a workingman, and even worse, an unemployed workingman. They said that was somehow different. I did not argue, but I never returned to the fraternity house.

I regretted the defection, for a fraternity had what I very much needed, a social life, with parties that girls attended. In an all-male high school of poor boys I had had too little of that. Since becoming a born-again superachiever, which takes a lot of time, I had had even less. Do not underrate the simple social graces. It lubricates life to feel at ease in a group of men wearing suits and ties, to be able to chat about nothing, to feel confident in the presence of girls. I lost this and sometimes feel I have never quite regained it.

The most painful lacuna in my life involved the feminine gender. I had never been without a sweetheart in Monroe. Now that glands I knew not of were maturing and making strange demands, the need for girls was greater than ever. High school had been all-male and Tulane was nearly so. Though Sophie Newcomb, the women's college, was part of the university, virtually no girls attended classes at Tulane; the only way to meet them was at fraternity parties, for which I had disqualified myself. In my case there was also an economic barrier: you could not take a college girl out on a date without money and a car, and I had neither. The few girls I forced myself to meet were surely put off by my awkwardness and silences and general social maladroitness. It strikes me as odd that, as a twelve-year-old in Monroe, I actually danced the Charleston with girls at school; in New Orleans I did not dance a step and have rarely tried since.

Suddenly a girl appeared in classes at Tulane, auburn of hair, pretty of face, lively of expression and most girllike. I composed some small talk and forced myself to address her with it. There was no cafeteria or student center to invite her to, so I took the leap and invited her to a basketball game. Luck smiled in the form of a fellow student who had access to a car and a second girl. We double-dated. It worked fine, that once. I sought to see her more often but ran up against rivals who were able to date her more regularly. Also, I wanted more than an evening of lively chat about nothing. Girls are designed to be embraced and to be kissed. Her evasive protections against such advances were practiced and perfect. She was, I began to see, one of that fabled kind, the Southern belle. She was cute, a tease. She milked her Southern accent, calling one of my double-daters named George by two syllables—"Jawidge." She was like the saying about Chinese food: you are still hungry afterward. My only college romance trailed off into nothing. I remained very hungry.

Aside from those drawbacks, my years at Tulane were rich. I felt that I learned a great deal, that my mind was better stocked and slightly more agile. My life in sports rose to a pleasing climax. I won a letter on the track team each year, and in the last year in the Southeastern Conference championships at Legion Field in Birmingham I ran second only to a tall, freckled power runner named Forrest "Spec" Townes. He broke the world record for the high hurdles on that occasion and later that year won the gold medal in the Berlin Olympics. I was not displeased to end my career running second in the collegiate South to the one who was first in the world.

Nearly half a century later, Miss Bea Field, the Alumni Director at Tulane, wrote to inform me that I had been handed a unique honor. My time for the 120-yard high hurdles had stood as the Tulane record for forty years. When someone finally broke it, university administrators decided to shift to the metric system, giving him the record for the 110-meter high hurdles. That left me the record for the 120-yard high hurdles—in perpetuity!

I kind of sleepwalked into college politics. Without being fully aware, I was elected class president two successive years. In the last year I became president of the student body. This time I wanted it and even had a platform. I recall only one plank: to replace those antique chairs, whose writing arms were so carved with generations of initials that you could not write on them. We took our platform to the home of the chairman of the Board of Trustees, Mr. Esmond Phelps, who was also head of the main New Orleans newspaper, the *Times-Picayune*. The competing *New Orleans Item* heard and assigned a reporter to go along with us. Phelps was humorless at his best, and now, with an *Item* man along to observe his embarrassment, he was ablaze; in quick succession he refused to accept our document and showed us the door. So nothing was done.

Many years later a new president of the university, Dr. Rufus Harris, confided to me that, the summer after I left, the old chairs were quietly removed and strong new ones installed. "And," he said, inviting me to follow him to a classroom, "I want you to see the nice new ones." There they were, deeply incised with initials, hearts and anchors of new generations and impossible to write on. I left Tulane that time with an honorary Doctorate of Laws, but with deep doubts about the efficacy of social engineering.

CHAPTER SIX

Germany

In my first months at Tulane, the great world was jolted out of wonted ways and onto new unmarked paths that would change it and all of its parts beyond recognition. Two months after I matriculated at the University, Franklin Roosevelt was elected President of the United States for the first time, and vigorous action to share the power of the economic magnates with the people at large began. Two months after FDR's election, Adolf Hitler was installed as Chancellor of Germany. In a remarkably short time he transformed weak, weary Germany into the strongest nation in the world and the terror of Europe. And in response, Roosevelt began an operation at least equally dramatic—changing the U.S. from the most isolationist nation to the most interventionist, from a country with an army smaller than that of Romania to one with, eventually, more than 2,000 military bases in thirty-two foreign countries.

There are many metaphoric ways to look at the drama of those events. One is to see it as a duel—one that grew intensely personal at times—between Hitler and Roosevelt for mastery of the world. When four years later I left the university, I had no way of knowing that within twelve months I would stand in the presence of each of these two giants.

Four good years in college ended in dismal swamp. Shortly before my graduation in 1936, my mother died. She had breast cancer, and in her last year physical pain deepened her disappointment at the wretched hand life had dealt her. I do not know how I pulled through examinations and a demanding track schedule. We were not only mother and son but sole companions. My brother rarely spoke, and my father was rarely there; with bridge afternoons a distant memory and not even knowing the names of her neighbors, she had only me with whom to chat and exchange gossip and views over our three meals a day together.

The weeks following were the most miserable of my life. I had no idea how busy college had kept me until it was over. When the last exam was returned, the last track meet over, the last meeting of the student council adjourned, I walked through a deserted campus past silent playing fields to a home that was now dark and empty, Dad staying away for days and my brother returning home after dark. I had scouted all the city papers and several by letter in other cities, but there was no job to be had. Then, when I had just about achieved a mood to make a bodily measurement of the depth of the river, surcease came from a completely unexpected source. Dr. Walker, lately my teacher of German, phoned me.

Heidelberg University in Germany was offering a tuition-free summer of study to qualified American students of the German language. He had casually entered my name. The German consulate informed him that I was accepted. Would I be interested? My first reaction was that it was unthinkable. European travel then was a diversion for the well-off. I had never even considered the possibility. But now, just for the hell of it, so to speak, I went to see the Lykes Brothers shipping company. I was told that it was quite thinkable; they would provide workaway passage to and from Bremen without cost or pay. I possessed Mrs. Gilmer's $100 prize, enough to pay my way inside Germany. My spirit caught fire. I procured the consulate's letter from Dr. Walker, and in a week I was aboard a ship and off on an adventure I had never thought possible.

The ship was old, cranky and arthritic, one of a series slapped together in WW I and christened by Mrs. Woodrow Wilson. The men in its crew were rough and ill-disposed to smartass college kids on an oceanic lark. They taught me to smile at such indignities as having the cook dump a plate of boiling soup on my lap. The experience was "character-building," that is, not the kind of thing you would do twice. But it got me there in fourteen days of scraping and repainting a rusty hull, my chisel often going right through to daylight on the other side.

From first sighting, Germany was captivating. Eyes used to the jungle banks of the lower Mississippi were delighted with the string of toy towns and beer gardens up the Weser River to Bremen. The streets of Bremen were incredibly clean and bright, like stage settings for a medieval play. Enchanted, I walked them all my first night, pausing occasionally for a stein of beer in taverns where they always seemed to be playing *"Du, Du Liegst Mir im Herzen."* I later discovered that the strongest walker with the most critical eye would have a hard time finding a slum in the cities of this orderly country.

With daylight and the peopling of the streets, uniforms became the strongest impression. Excepting Boy Scouts and policemen, I think I had never seen as many as ten persons in uniform in one place. Here in the port city the uniforms were naval. Along the train route to Heidelberg they were the field gray of the army.

I now recalled what I had noted only casually in a busy senior year. In the spring, German troops had marched into the Rhineland abutting France, and were still stuffing in reinforcements and supplies. It was a violation of the Versailles Treaty that ended the Great War, but Britain and France barely protested. Moreover, Hitler proclaimed his dedication to peace and offered to pull his troops back out if France would pull hers back an equal distance from the border. As that would have meant pulling out of their most expensive investment in self-defense ever, the Maginot Line, it was unthinkable for the French. Their refusal to agree to "equal terms" seemed to legitimate the German action. Hitler subjected his "peace policy" to a plebiscite and won nearly 99 percent approval. If the result was faked, it need not have been. There was no reason to disapprove of a leader who restored to dignity a Germany that had so long been an abject loser, who brought order back to the streets and who with his arms program was ending unemployment. In my summer with them, the German people were quite pleased with themselves.

Heidelberg was as charming as its light-opera reputation, and life in the city was easy for a student. I shared a room with two others at the *Studentenheim* for a pittance, and ate meals in the large student *Mensa* for fifty pfennigs a time. That left ample resources for beer sessions at *Zum Roten Ochsen* and evening plays in the wonderfully lighted ruins of the castle. Weekends offered opportunities for bus tours to the Black Forest or to the zeppelin hangars on Lake Constance. The purpose of showing Germany at its best to American youths was well fulfilled. Dictatorship seemed to rest lightly on the people.

Weekday mornings were spent in German language classes. Afternoons in a great semicircular hall we listened to lectures by eminent academics. It was in the amphitheater that the first worrisome doubts arose. The lectures were all of a theme: the surpassing excellence of Germans in art, sciences, music, whatever, achieved against machinations of hostile forces. A Dr. Schmitthenner stated it most purely. He was clearly a favorite with German students, for they thumped their desks loudly when he ascended the podium. He was dapper with a robin's-egg blue summer jacket and a smart bow tie. He removed his soft felt hat, brim at a rakish angle, as he acknowledged the applause.

Dr. Schmitthenner was professor of European history. He told us that in the Middle Ages, in the time of Frederick Barbarossa ("Redbeard"), Germans were ahead of all others in forming a nation, the most effective form of social organization. But the prospect of so much power in one people disturbed the Vatican, and it moved to make the imperial office elective among feudal lords. The popes, and later others, were able to manipulate elections and prevent a union of Germans. The great Bismarck created one Germany in 1871, but even he was not up to discerning and opposing the worst conspiracy of all, the one led by the international cabal of Jews. That had now become the mission of the greatest German, Adolf Hitler.

I had a mutual learning arrangement with a German student whereby we would discourse in German for an hour and then in English for an hour, several days a week. In such a session that day I expressed doubt about Schmitthenner's thesis. My partner smiled patronizingly and made a comment I was to hear a thousand times from Germans before their minds were changed in May of 1945. You Americans, he said, are incurably naive. He said we did not realize that America was dominated by Jews. Indeed, he said, the original family name of our President was Rosenfeld; it had early on been Dutchified for respectability to Roosevelt. And the more easily to control us, Jewish leaders were allowing America to become *vernegert,* negrified, debased, made simpleminded. Only the Führer and a revivified German nation stood firm against the spread of Jewish degeneration in the world. If there was a turning point for me, a moment when vagrant impressions of a summer's experience crystallized into a hard opinion, this was it. These people really believed this nonsense!

And they were preparing to act on it. One weekend I bicycled to Worms, a nodal town for the nearly arriving German army in the Rhineland. I found a room in a tavern that also provided quarters for young army officers. Evenings they made the restaurant blue with smoke and loud with song and chatter. Since they were about my age, I could not avoid making comparisons. They were all trained and ready for war. Probably most of my Tulane classmates had never fired a gun. As a nation, Germans were physically stronger than Americans. Sports in Germany were organized around the broad community, not the narrow college, and the government poured funds into stadiums, gymnasiums, courts and tracks. Approximately 60 percent of Germans of all ages regularly took part in competitive sports. I doubted if the number reached 20 percent in my country. They in their thousands and millions were prepared to march as one upon the order of the Führer. My fellow Americans had a loose general loyalty to their nation but were not prepared to do anything as one. I cycled back from Worms with a sense of fright that did not leave me for many years. Here was a powerful people, thoroughly trained and heavily armed, with a grudge against the world, prepared to act on the order of a single psychopathic genius with a special gift for inflammatory rhetoric. Far from thinking of preparing, my depressed country was not even aware that there was anything to prepare against.

After six weeks I received my little diploma, then entrained for a whirlwind tour of German cities. I reached Berlin in time for the Olympics but had run short of funds, so I walked around outside the stadium until I heard that Spec Townes had won the gold in the high hurdles. I had a slight sense of participation.

I reached Rotterdam, where my workaway home passage had been redirected, with a quarter dollar left of my original treasure. The ship, the *Meanticut,* took me to Tampa, where I had to switch to another tub to get to New Orleans. The old *Meanticut* then sailed out of Tampa, aiming for Tampico, Mexico, but broke in half and sank before it got there. No hand was lost, but all got very wet.

CHAPTER SEVEN

The *Item*

I ended my naval career at a wharf at the foot of Carrollton Avenue, and took a streetcar to a lodging house where my brother had moved us. Word had been left there of an improvement in my prospects. Mrs. Gilmer, a.k.a. Dorothy Dix, heard of my rejection by the New Orleans papers. She phoned the editor of the *New Orleans Item* and informed him that by turning me away he was passing up a chance to be an asterisk in history; I was so clever I would surely one day be a city editor on the *St. Louis Post-Dispatch* or something equally grand. So he reconsidered and left word that I should come and see him on my return from Europe. I was hired as one of three recruits to the reporting staff, with the understanding that after a month's trial only one of us would be retained.

The trial period was worrisome. Success depended on luck in getting worthwhile assignments. Most of mine were to social club meetings and rarely made it into print. There was one medium-grade crime, which I milked as long as I could: a young drifter eloped with the daughter of a well-off family and induced her to sign a couple of blank checks, then disappeared with the proceeds. That was all.

Then the assistant to an editor named George Coad told me he could no longer stand his boss and was leaving for an advertising job elsewhere. Coad was a features editor who had to have an assistant, so if I got the job I would be out of the chancy competition for last place on the news staff and into a writing job as secure as such things got. Coad and his assistant had the task of scouring the wires and out-of-state papers for stories that could be researched and rewritten and generally dolled up to help make the *Item* interesting. An advantage of the job was that you got to see a lot of your stuff in print. A disadvantage was that Coad was probably insane.

He was a wiry man with a bony nose that was always shiny. His hair was tonsured by a chainsaw that left the short hairs pointing out in all directions. His eyebrows were permanently arched as if in astonishment, but in fact, I discovered, in contempt of all people and things. He always made me think of *The New Yorker* cartoon in which the Paris taxi driver said to the female tourist, "No, lady, I am not anti-American. I hate everybody." When I applied for the job he looked away as though I smelled bad, and told me to be there at seven A.M. the next day.

Thus did I enter the George Coad school of popular writing, an institution known never to give anyone a passing grade. He began by handing me a Memphis newspaper on which he had ringed a murder story in red and told me to rewrite it and make it interesting to *Item* readers. The story was bare bones and didn't give me much to work with, but I spent half an hour shifting its focus and stretching it out. He looked at the result for about one second and handed it back and told me it was not interesting and to rewrite it again. Without knowing what he objected to, I had a hard time. After three rejections I asked if he could be clear about how he wanted the story changed. He began a tutorial that came in brief spasms and lasted several months.

First he asked me what was my aim in life. I said, to be a writer of some sort. He said, "Then you won't do in this job. I don't want someone who wants to be a writer; I want someone who wants to write." Having thus liquidated me, he proceeded over days with his lecture. In journalism school they teach you to pack all essentials into the first paragraph—what, who, where and when. His aim was to narrate stories, which is done differently. "What you do," he said, "is, make your opening sentence so interesting that the reader will want to read your second, and likewise with your third sentence. Build on that the same way for the rest of the story." That was nice to say, but I noticed that he did not realize it in his stories much better than I did.

He claimed to be a foe of adjectives. Don't say it was a dark and stormy night. Paint a picture that tells the reader it was dark and stormy, like "When pretty little Minnie Tibbs' lamp was blown out by the wind, she could not see as far as her two feet, as she stumbled across the farmyard." I objected, "That takes up a lot of space; adjectives save space. Besides, how do you know Minnie Tibbs was pretty and little? The story doesn't say how she looked." He said, "Phone the sheriff in Memphis and ask. Personal adjectives can be good adjectives." I phoned and the sheriff said he had never really looked at Minnie Tibbs, so she must have been homely. I wrote "plain Minnie Tibbs" in the story, and George crossed it out.

I did a lot of phoning and a lot of honing of verbal descriptions, and on many stories a lot of researching in the public library; but I was never able to meet his conditions, and George never indicated that anything I wrote was worth printing, although an awful lot got printed. He was a mean editor, but a good disciplinarian, and I never regretted the time I spent as his assistant. On the other hand, I never understood his hostility to everybody and everything. It added little to comprehension to hear, years later, that he had committed suicide.

Again in my new life, sociability escaped me. For survival I had leapt from general assignment, where reporters worked in close contact with the world, to a desk and writing job that was performed in virtual solitude. There were a couple of bars where people from the paper met after work for daily antitoxins, but my hours kept me from frequenting them. Coad came into the newsroom at about seven A.M. He wanted me to have the wire service stories tabulated in order of urgency for his attention and the papers scanned and marked. Since I was coming in early for him, the city editor suggested I come in early for everyone by turning on the wire machines and making a tabulation for the city editor, too. So, I arrived at three A.M., with no company in the big newsroom but the cleanup ladies, which made for an unaccommodating and unsociable daily life.

My pay was fifteen dollars a week, the highest regular income I had ever had. But when I added up my expenses, they came, no matter how I squeezed, to eighteen dollars a week. I went to Mr. Marshall Ballard, who was not in charge of personnel but whose editorials enjoyed prestige with those who were. He advised me to ventilate my troubles no further lest the bosses kick me out as an ingrate. There were people on the paper earning less than I, and they had families. My brother came to my aid. He had been elected president of the Loyola Alumni Association and was required to make a three-minute talk on radio (the Jesuits then owned WWL, the city's foremost radio station) once a week. He did not like writing and offered me three dollars a week to write his little speech for him. Thus did I balance my budget.

In tabulating story candidates for Coad to consider, I increasingly listed European items. He did not resist, for he was at least as concerned as I. He gave me a book titled *The Coming Struggle for Power* by the English author John Strachey, which he promised me would explain everything. It was the Marxist argument brought up to date with a theme Marx never dreamt of: the world faced a stark choice between going Communist or going Nazi. There was nothing else. It was a little too stark for me, but it was nicely argued. In later years I would meet and become friends with John Strachey and would present my doubts to him. To my surprise he told me he had changed his mind and now agreed with me.

I longed to get back to Europe to witness the drama beginning to develop there. I remembered that I had made desultory applications for several scholarships, including the Rhodes, when I left Tulane, and had won none. What about a shot at the Rhodes again? I went to see my old history teacher, Mack Swearingen, who had been a Rhodes Scholar himself. He had good news.

"You missed it by a hair," he told me. "I met one of your examiners recently, and he said that your record in student government and sports was superior to the others, and it was about equal in general education. The problem was, you gave Political Science as your major, yet you listed only four courses in that subject. I know that is all we have at Tulane; that department badly needs rehabilitation, and we are working on it. But it was too thin for the examiners to pass you as a scholar in Political Science. Why on earth did you give that as your major rather than Journalism?"

I told him that I felt that Journalism was looked on as a kind of trade school subject like carpentry or plumbing, not a recommendation for getting into the most elite of English-speaking universities. He said, "Nonsense! Every penny Winston Churchill lived on came from his journalism. And what about Charles Dickens?" He suggested that I apply again and make it clear that both my past training and my future goal were in journalism. Get sponsors who will write impressive letters. He, Swearingen, would write one that would make me seem a melding of Shakespeare and Einstein. In my own letter I should improve on my position, stating for example that I was taken on by the *Item* as a "special writer." Generally, try harder, he said, as if you really must have the scholarship.

I did all of the above, and to my surprise I easily prevailed in the state trials and became one of the two nominees from Louisiana. The finals, held in the Roosevelt (now Fairmont) Hotel consisted of long interviews by a panel of five former Rhodes Scholars who had become eminent academic and business figures. I asked leave of my editors to spend the day at the hotel for the occasion. They agreed, provided I saved them a reporter and made this an assignment: phone in the results to the desk when they were announced. I borrowed one of my brother's suits, a bit small but much more presentable than anything I possessed, and proceeded to the disputed barricade.

As in war, so in this endeavor the highest virtue after bravery was patience. I waited in the hall with the other nervous bright young men, as they one by one entered the dread conference room and much later came out sweating. I dealt with my turn as well as I could but was sure my answers to their questions had been maladroit and self-wounding. Late in the day I was called in a second time. When I was seated, one of the examiners asked what was the last event I had covered for my newspaper. I told him that this competition was it; I had to phone in the results as soon as they were available. The examiner said, "This must be the very first time a reporter has covered his own funeral and written his own obituary." For a moment I thought I was dead, but then quickly realized he would not have said something as cruel as this, unless I was safe. I had made it! The chairman of the panel said, "Mr. Smith, we have called you back in because we have had unhappy experience with journalists. As soon as they get to Europe, they become so entranced with politics and impatient with academic life that they leave Oxford and take a job. We want a pledge from you that you will stay the full two years." I gladly made the pledge and left the room walking on clouds with bands of angels singing in my train.

When the three other winners were named, I went to the phone. The city editor was tied up, so a rewrite man came on. I laid out the bare facts, the remarkable information that both Louisiana nominees had won scholarships, and waited for his questions. There were none, so I hung up and walked home the whole way, to meditate on what a wonderful life this was. The *Item* carried the news in a short story on the inside pages.

Next day the editors of the *Item* suffered a jolt. The old, unenterprising *Times-Picayune* appeared with the portraits of the two Louisiana winners filling three columns in the middle of the front page with a sizable detailed story beneath. My city editor was furious. "You made it sound ordinary," he said. "Why didn't you tell rewrite it was special? The *Picayune* has blown us out of the water on our own story." I had no ready answer to why I hadn't told a veteran rewrite man that I was to be given special treatment, and why I hadn't suggested that the *Item* run my picture on the front page. But I could not be induced to get mad at or even reproachful toward anyone. I did not even mind when George Coad said, "You got off yesterday; you'll have to stay a couple of hours more today to catch up."

The picture of me the *Picayune* used was from a college annual, all character air-brushed out of the face, making me look like a well-embalmed corpse. Marshall Ballard was deeply impressed with the story, without recognizing the person in the picture. He wrote a moving editorial along this line: it is a signal honor for two young men from our state to make it at once. But now these two lads will go away to England. And the probability is, they will not come back to Louisiana. They will go elsewhere to make lives and fortunes. Why? We must ask ourselves why our best leave us never to return.

I was so deeply touched that I knocked on his office door and went in, and roughly the following colloquy ensued:

"Yes?"

"Mr. Ballard, I liked your editorial. I was particularly moved by it."

"Yes. Of course. It helps when one feels strongly about something. Well, thank you for your kind comment. Is there anything else?"

"Yes sir. You ended it with a question."

"That is right. It is a question Louisianians should give some thought to. Thank you again. Now I must make some calls."

"Well, sir, I thought you might like to know the answer to your question."

"What do you know about it?"

"I am one of the two, the one on the left. Smith."

"You are?" (He picked up the paper from a corner of his desk and studied it briefly.) "It doesn't look like you."

"No sir. I think it is not meant to. It is a picture from the Tulane Annual. They touch them up to make you look better. But it is me, all right."

"My God. And you have been working here all the time?"

"Yes sir, and the answer to your question is, three dollars. The difference between fifteen and eighteen dollars a week. That's why I am going away; and you're right, I am not coming back."

I got out the door just before something, I think it was a dried-up inkwell, hit the place on the wall where my head had just been.

CHAPTER EIGHT

A Conversation with Franklin Roosevelt

I felt like a poor relation suddenly come into an unexpected rich inheritance. I could leave the *Item* any time. And I almost did, but something remarkable turned up. The White House in Washington announced that President Franklin D. Roosevelt was coming to visit our town. As Louisiana was a set-in-concrete Democrat-voting state, Presidents had never found it worth their time to look in on us. I dared not miss this unique occasion.

The circumstances making for his visit were these: As Senator Huey Long of Louisiana intensified his attacks on the Roosevelt Administration, it began reducing the flow of federal patronage to the state, to the dismay of our more orthodox politicians. By 1936, the state was on starvation rations. Then Long was assassinated. Immediately, the surviving political lords of our realm put out feelers to see if peaceful relations could be reestablished and the flow of loot resumed. They could, and the President agreed to pay a personal visit to New Orleans to seal the deal.

In my order of worship, Roosevelt was separated from God only by Abraham Lincoln. Decades later, very nearly the same verdict came from American historians; asked to list Presidents in order of "greatness," they voted Lincoln first, Washington second and F. D. Roosevelt third. But one could only be amazed at his provenance. He was a thorough mama's boy, a spoiled patrician child, wholly conformist, pretty without depth. Mother dominated his growing up and even his marriage, to the sadness of his wonderful young wife. He proved not to be very good in business or law and supported his family pretty much on what he inherited from Mother until late in life, when a public source of income became considerable.

Then what a flowering there was. The transformation is popularly attributed to his adjustment to being crippled by disease, but I suspect there were genetic combinations in his DNA that proved special under pressure. That shallow college-boy smile became just the robust good humor a people in distress needed to see in a leader. He had, as Justice Holmes said, a first-rate temperament, but also great instincts. Grasping the unused weapon of government, he began practicing Keynesian economics three years before Professor Keynes published the book giving birth to that doctrine. Under the name of public works he began building what was later called an "infrastructure" that would change the fortunes of a great war. His biggest mass program was the CCC (Civilian Conservation Corps), made up of city youths housed in rural camps engaged in the rescue of some 10 million acres of overused and desiccated lands, the planting of millions of trees and much other ecological repair. In 2,000 camps more than 1.6 million youths were employed. FDR gave the mission of organizing and overseeing the program to the long-neglected U.S. Army, superbly preparing it for the vital mission no one knew was coming: the mobilization for a world war. To cure maldistribution of wealth and to make wealth grow he created laws strengthening labor unions and their power to bargain for a larger share of industry's fruits. When the smoke and dust of mid-century turmoil subsided, his monuments were the world's richest national economy and in time its only military superpower—that and a people terribly prone to spoliation.

The *Item* assigned half a dozen reporters to cover the President's day at places along the route of his tour. I accumulated passes for all. The great experience began at the Illinois Central railway station at the foot of Canal Street near the river. I was one of a clutch of reporters and photographers allowed to wait outside the observation platform of the President's special car, which, shades drawn, had been parked at the rail platform in the small hours. To the Washington regulars from the big papers, who followed the President wherever he went, this levée was a nothing, and they congregated instead in the old French Market next door to have doughnuts and the most authoritative coffee (with chicory) in the world. But we locals clung to the base of the observation platform of the car like hungry peasants hoping for crumbs from the lord's table.

After daybreak, people—secret service agents probably—began to come and go. A ramp was placed so that it connected the side of the special car's observation platform to the station platform. An open touring auto was driven up onto the station platform and parked next to the ramp. From the door of the special railway car, a man who looked just like FDR appeared, smaller but with the same pince-nez eyeglasses, a similar face and the same fedora uptilted at the front and back. He looked around for a moment, then straight out at us, then disappeared down the ramp. I felt sure it was the President's double, whose abrupt appearance and departure was meant to confuse possible assassins. Someone said, no, it was just one more agent. I liked my story better and stuck to it.

Then, with agents standing at the corners of the observation platform, Roosevelt came hobbling out, clinging to the arm of another agent, head down, wholly absorbed in the difficult and apparently painful labor of moving out to the rail of the car and getting a grip on it. When he was fully positioned, an agent nodded to us, and the scene came alive. The President's look of concern for his physical movement vanished. His large face burst into a wide, happy grin, warming as sunrise on a good day, and the grin graduated into a hearty Rooseveltian laugh as he lifted his hat in salute to an imaginary crowd of voters out beyond our little group. For a minute or so flashbulbs flashed, as photographers captured the image of the President greeting the hordes of admiring New Orleanians in the empty station. Then the agent lifted his arms in signal again. The flashing stopped, the grin vanished, the President put his hat back on his head, and the look of concern returned as he faced the ordeal of being carried down the ramp and placed on the back seat of the touring car.

It is hard to believe, even now as I write, that I did not know until that moment that the President was a nearly helpless cripple. His great bull-like torso stood on lifeless legs. But press and photographers in a respectful conspiracy refused to mention or to display his physical disability. One day a few years later in Berlin I thoughtlessly violated that discipline. An angry Nazi foreign office spokesman said in a press conference that America was governed by "a tyrant crippled in mind and body." I thought the remark shocking enough to quote it in a radio broadcast that day. Minutes after the broadcast I received a telegram from my boss in New York: "NEVER REPEAT NEVER MENTION THE PRESIDENT'S DISABILITY ON RADIO AGAIN—WHITE."

Now, back in New Orleans in 1937, I established permanent claim to a seat in the lead press car in the motorcade that followed the President, first to a federal project, where he made a little speech; then to City Hall, where post-Huey peace was settled and reconciliation photos taken; then at noon to Arnaud's most famous restaurant for an elaborate lunch. I had never been inside Arnaud's before: for one in my station the menu was invisible—that is to say, the prices were out of sight. But with the city of New Orleans paying the freight I was able to verify that its reputation was soundly based. The President, whom I kept always in view from my seat, seemed to agree. He and Mrs. Roosevelt were reputed to run a tightwad cuisine in the White House. I guessed that his nutrition was maintained by having many of his meals on others, as now. Most enjoyable, both of us seemed to agree, was a spinach-laden confection called Oysters Rockefeller. Years afterward I had to order a small repast for the Rockefeller then current in the news, Governor Nelson A. of New York, and I asked him what he would like. "Anything," he said, "but, please, not Oysters Rockefeller; I've had them up to here." I told him that FDR had loved them. In a comment appropriate for a Hudson Valley squire in the money about a Hudson valley squire who merely made President of the U.S., Nelson said, "He would."

After lunch the President vanished. I saw him one moment; an instant later he was not there. Secret service sleight of hand had arranged for him to disappear for an hour of rest, one knew not where or how. After that came a meeting with state officials. The public day ended with a parade through cheering throngs out Canal Street to the river, where a destroyer was tied up waiting for its commander in chief. The President remained sitting in the big open car, parked on the wharf, and presided over an informal press conference. The big-time journalists from Washington knew the drill and nearly monopolized the space immediately around. But when I saw how things were forming, I grew sharp elbows, and maneuvered into a position right next to the car, not three feet from the cynosure.

Roosevelt clearly enjoyed these little sessions, parrying questions, giving answers that said nothing or providing a demonstrative laugh that indicated there would be no answer at all. As things proceeded, it occurred to me that the regulars were putting cosmic-type questions to FDR about the Supreme Court or sitdown strikes in Detroit, with not a word about this momentous visit to our town. So the thought came, why not launch my career as a national-class journalist now by intervening? My other New Orleans colleagues were beyond easy communication on the outskirts of our small group. I seemed to debate the daring thought several minutes, but I am sure it was barely seconds before someone left a microscopic space between the end of an answer and the beginning of a new question, and I blurted out, louder than I intended, "What have you got to say about your day in New Orleans—and the second Louisiana Purchase?"

I felt that all eyes focused on this scabrous, unauthorized interloper, this impudent intruder, this small-minded local yokel, who had broken the order of things with a question of interest only to the New Orleans Chamber of Commerce. The President's eyes certainly did. I turned red. The instant turned into long minutes in my imagination. At length, he laughed out loud, then purred, "It's been splendid, simply grand," and he added a cliché or two about the beautiful city on a crescent. I floated meters up into the air. The great man had answered me. I had shared a moment in history. I did not settle back on the planks of the wharf until the President was carried by two strong men up the gangway of the ship, stood up against a railing and provided with a cigarette and a martini. He continued exchanging banalities with shore-bound reporters for about fifteen minutes until the destroyer cast off and began to float down the river.

Quietly elated with my little coup, I got into a car with some other locals. Herman Deutsch, the *Item*'s foremost political correspondent, sat next to me. "Good touch," he said, "nice little quote for the last edition." I was horrified. Deutsch wondered at my silence. "You did phone it in?" I swallowed and went pale. Every newspaper in the world might have my little exchange if it wished, but not my own. While others were on the phones to their papers I was floating happily above the river. Had it been important, the editor would have fired me. And he would have been right.

CHAPTER NINE

And So Farewell

"There is a magic place somewhere between the United States and the Caribbean, but belonging to neither, called New Orleans," a lyrical visitor to the city once said. A distant day when all members of my immediate family were gone, I would return to the city and, with all personal ties dissolved or forgotten, see it objectively. Then, as an outsider, I would understand for the first time its fascination, color, mood and personality, and would agree that it was one of only three extremely distinctive American cities, the other two being New York and San Francisco. But now, in 1937, I wanted nothing more urgently than to get out and get it behind me. Absolutely all that I thought of with satisfaction was contained in the big rectangle enclosing the two universities and their playing fields. When I was through there, I was through with the place and everything about it.

There was nothing to hold me, no friendships of quality, no girl to be left behind, no scope for getting somewhere in my profession. I retained a native affection for my remnants of family, but that tie, too, had grown tenuous. Hard times had strengthened my brother's Catholicism and my father's Baptist faith. I had gravitated to the opposite attitude toward formal religions, apathy. We no longer spoke the same language. There was not enough common experience to sustain more than a minute or two of conversation. My departure now would be, I expected—and so it turned out—the most complete break with the past in my life. The childhood breach with Monroe was not comparable. And nothing in my future, not even the intrusion of Armageddon, was as complete a cutoff.

There was little to pack, and I had few loose ends to tie up. Yet, when this little was done, I still had a gnawing feeling that something important remained undone. One day my brother came back from the office and told me what it was. "After all these years," he said in a tone of triumph, "Dr. Vignes would like the pleasure of your company. He invites you to join me for our Thursday dinners at his home."

That was it, and I was relieved by the invitation. A reconciliation. That would please the shade of my mother. In a glow of good will restored, I accompanied my brother to the doctor's home the next Thursday.

My notion of a reconciliation proved to be a howling misconception. Clement Victor was prickly from the moment I stepped inside his screened porch. He shook my hand tentatively as though expecting that I had a trick buzzer in it. As we sat in rockers and received martinis from an attendant, it was left to me to do any talking. He simply observed me with a manifestly critical eye, as though inspecting a particularly bad piece of dental work. My brother's silence was expected; but the silence of Victor's friendly, usually talkative, French wife told me that, far from reconciliation, he had let her know this was to be some manner of confrontation.

I quickly exhausted the weather and the view from the verandah as topics. There was a pause. No one filled it. After awhile the doctor cleared his throat. We all sat back awaiting a declaration. At length it came. "I see," he said, motioning to the floor beneath me, "you don't wear garters." All four of us looked down at my socks, loose on my ankles. I felt the stuffing escaping from me like air from a punctured balloon. I began to feel like what I often feared I was but hoped I wasn't: a disheveled, tobacco-stained, third-rate, underpaid reporter with heels worn round, humps in the knees of his pants and last night's alcohol on his breath. It was a confrontation all right, and I had just had my testicles cut off. I found myself able only to smile wanly, as he launched a monologue on public affairs of the day, whose message to me seemed to be Ring Lardner's famous line, "Shut up, he explained."

How to explain his behavior? I could only think that our meeting at his request served the purpose of reasserting his dominance of the family of Pointe Coupée Parish and its later offshoots, of which the Smiths were one. It was important to him, as a man without family, to be seen as the patriarch and the most, the only, successful member of the tribe, to be addressed and spoken of with a certain respect if not awe. My defection became serious only when I gave a sign of succeeding on my own. He was simply angry and wanted me delivered to him that he might vent his anger. I could see no higher reason in his calling me into his presence after so many years.

I begged Prescott to let me off future Thursdays. But my brother was insistent. "No. Please nurse the relationship. Beginnings can be rocky. He will mellow." Prescott had an unarticulated need for family. Bringing these estranged remnants together meant a lot to him.

Victor's news commentary that first Thursday was standard conservative dogma, mostly praising General Franco's holy mission in the Spanish Civil War, no more offensive to me than my liberal prejudices in favor of the Spanish Republic were to him. The second Thursday he escalated into the more emotional topics of race and conspiracy. The growing reach of the Jews, symbolized by the assumption of the premiership by the Jew Léon Blum, was weakening his beloved France. At home, Roosevelt was half-way to dictatorship. The Supreme Court, dominated by appointees of past Republican administrations, was the line of last resistance to him, declaring one after another of his New Deal laws unconstitutional. Now Roosevelt broached his plan to increase the number of justices on the court and appoint enough of his own men to bring the institution into subjection. Meanwhile, the auto workers, carrying out their revolutionary new "sit-in" strikes, were being prepared to serve as his storm troopers to run the nation's economy.

At that second meeting I was at least forewarned and no longer smiled, even wanly. I stared down at the table and grimly took it. In the car going home I told my brother I would have to call in sick next Thursday. I could take no more. Prescott pleaded that it would be my last trial; I was leaving for Europe after that.

The final dinner proved to be one Thursday too many. I had lost patience and the capacity to be intimidated. Somewhere amid the martinis Victor made some reference to FDR's "well-known homosexual tendencies," and I blew. "Bullshit!" The expletive came out of me like a shot from a gun, so unpremeditated that I shocked myself, so loud that I think the neighbors must have heard it. Victor's face turned dark red and he was on his feet, and I was on mine. He was angry but looked strangely relieved. He had at last gotten a rise out of me. I felt a good deal better too. In fact, Victor and I were the only satisfied people present; his wife was now in tears and Prescott was near them. We exchanged a couple more brief but strong unpleasantries and somehow got into religion. I recall only his reference to my defection from Sunday mass and a prediction that, without the Church to guide me, I was condemned to hell. I exited the screen door he held open with a remark to the effect that if we two ever met again that is where it would be. I departed elated with a discovery. I had always thought of him as being very tall so that I had to look up to him. In fact, when we stood there, glower to glower, our eyes were nearly level. I was quite as tall as he or perhaps a little taller.

I tried to persuade Prescott that the old man had been provoking me with intent and that he was pleased with himself and the outcome. My brother would have none of it. On my sleeping porch next to his room in our boarding-house I heard him sobbing in the night. This time I decided I would simply have to tough it out. Victor's behavior was not to be countenanced, and there was something unmanly about my allowing it. The next day—my departure day—I planned to take the streetcar to the wharf alone. But Prescott showed up, back from his office, as I was about to leave and insisted on driving me to the ship. There he saw me aboard. This time, with a loan from him, I was go-ing as a passenger on one of those same rickety old ships. The ship cast off shortly after I settled in, and my brother and I waved goodbye.

At the end of my first year at Oxford, Prescott came a-visiting. After he en-joyed an idyllic few days at the college, I took him on a brief tour of Europe, climaxing in Austria, which Hitler had just occupied and annexed. Prescott had agreed to go anywhere with me, provided that we ended up in Paris. When we did I found out why he had insisted. Victor and his wife were there and wanted us both to have cocktails in the Hotel Lutetia. We went. The greeting was warm. Victor did much of the talking, about the weather and the view. There was no mention of politics or religion or past encounters. When we returned to our hotel I said, "I wonder what happened to the old man since last we met?" Prescott said, "I think he must have gone to confession."

·

1937-1939

CHAPTER TEN

Back to the Future

By any measure my return to Europe was eventful. All in one season I got a handle on a future dream job as a foreign correspondent, was arrested and jailed by the Gestapo, worked my way into the presence of Adolf Hitler, saw Paris for the first time, and found a home in the oldest university building in the world in a 700-year-old college in Oxford. All this I experienced in an oddly schizoid mood. Everywhere the forces of Good, or just of Adequacy, retreated, and those of Evil, or just of Disadvantage, advanced. America, after a blip upward, redescended into Depression. The governments of Europe went whole hog for appeasing Hitler, and his prestige at home and abroad soared. There were no grounds for hope of improvement. Yet the subject who witnessed the melancholy scene was bright, eager, excited at being assured a front seat for the Apocalypse.

My seat was good for two years. My first act on arriving in Bremen was to stake out a claim on a longer tenure in Germany, a reservation on a future place as a foreign correspondent. I went to Berlin. The United Press bureau in Berlin was headed by a native of New Orleans, Frederick Oechsner. The previous year I would not have dared approach his offices on Unter den Linden; I was without cachet, a mere aspirant to the profession, shy, unimpressive, with a personality that automatically went flat in the presence of people I wished to impress favorably. Now I was a newsman of some experience, writing for a newspaper he knew and respected, and bearing a letter from the publisher, who was a friend of his. Moreover I was a Rhodes Scholar–elect. I felt qualified to notify him of my casual interest in a job I would have cut off an arm to get.

Fred was extremely handsome, patrician in manner, with a Marine recruiter's eye for a few good men. The six reporters on his staff were, like him, sharp, bright, personable and clearly equal to any situation that might arise. I was much impressed by one good-looking man named Richard Helms, who had recently had the rare—now unique—experience of meeting and chatting with Hitler, who had just about decreed a stop to meetings with American journalists. Within another year, Helms grew tired of being an observer and returned home to seek out another career, a search that ended a quarter-century later in his being named America's number one spy, the director of the CIA. I asked Oechsner about my chances of landing a job in his office when my two years at Oxford were over. He seemed favorably inclined. After a few days I left Berlin for an adventure that practically assured me of getting the job.

In Heidelberg the previous summer I had met a German medical student on holiday named H. G. Schaefer, called Hah-Gay by his German friends. He was highly intelligent and strongly anti-Nazi and was able to inform me about aspects of life in Germany I could not have learned from others in this land of enforced conformity. We had corresponded during the year, and I had agreed to spend a few weeks with him at his digs at the University of Kiel, in the far north of Germany on the border with Denmark. From Berlin I repaired thereto and spent two weeks, both happy and instructive, with a small band of German medical students who, it turned out, were not well disposed toward the Nazi government and were full of evidence to justify their judgments.

Among his other attributes, Hay-Gay was an impoverished gourmet, a combination that enabled him to concoct marvelous meals with scraps and scrounges from nearby food shops and delicatessens. I complimented him several times on our dinners, and on one occasion toward the end of my stay he asked if I would like to experience a culinary paradise? Naturally I said yes. Then, he said, we shall go to an earthly heaven called Denmark, a short hitch-hike across the border. In a day we were in Copenhagen. It was and is one of the most beautiful cities in the world, with a unique skyline of green-patinated copper towers, steeples and roofs. The food was wonderful, as advertised by Hay-Gay, and the people who prepared and consumed it were the handsomest in Europe. Had I known that somewhere in the suburbs there was a tall, fifteen-year-old girl with flaming red hair, for whom I would one day be prepared to lay down my life, I would have stayed and hunted. But I did not know, and at that time of my life I was absorbed not by lovely peaceful countries but by the ugly play of big mean nations around the fringes of war. So I took leave of Hay-Gay (his mouth stuffed with Danish pastries even as I informed him) and returned to Germany, where I planned to wait for him. Unable to speak Danish I decided not to hitchhike but took the train, for a few Kroner. Unable to read Danish I stuffed my pockets with German-language newspapers to read on the way.

When the train stopped at Flensburg on the border for entry formalities, a large, young officer of the *Geheime Staatspolizei*, commonly shortened to Gestapo, studied my passport and me with what seemed excessive interest and finally said, *"Kommen Sie, bitte, mit."* In a small room in the Flensburg station I was stripped and searched. The newspapers were found and confiscated. While I was putting my clothes back on I saw my train, next stop Kiel, pull out, and I became thoroughly scared. The young officer was impervious to questions. I was taken in a small car from the station to the Flensburg jail. While I was being booked, and my shoelaces, belt and pocket contents taken from me, I asked what I was being arrested for. The booking officer said, "You will be told." I asked if I might phone a friend or the American consulate; I was told no, and don't ask any more questions.

There were three objects in my cell, a cot folded flat up against the wall and latched there, a straight hard wooden chair wide enough for one buttock and a half, and a tiny wooden table. I unlatched the cot and lay down on it. The cell door was thrown open and a guard came in and ordered me to fold the cot back where I had found it, no lying down till nightfall. So I alternated sitting and thinking with calisthenics. I called out through the peep slot in the door for some writing materials; at least I would write my brother a letter. The guard said absolutely no. But it was clear he was interested in me; you got all kinds in the Flensburg jail but rarely Americans. So he found me a book to read and handed it to me. It was titled *Auf der Mississippi* von Mark Twain. I thanked him. It really helped. Mark Twain reads well in German, especially in jail. Mornings I was given a mop and made to clean the floor. It was dull but not bad except for worrying about the unknown. What was I in for? How long? Would there be a trial? Could I simply be transferred to the dark entrails of a concentration camp and forgotten? After all, no one knew I was in jail. Hay-Gay might assume I had decided to go on to Paris, as I told him I intended to do eventually.

On the third morning, at last, I was taken into what appeared to be an interrogation room and sat down facing a kind of tribunal of three men. The middle man, the highest ranking officer, displayed one of the newspapers found in my clothes. It was titled *Freies Deutschland*. It was, he told me, the organ of the banned German Communist Party, so I was guilty of bringing forbidden enemy propaganda into the country and was subject to severe punishment. However, investigation into my background showed no inclination on my part to political or other crimes, so he assumed my innocence and released me. I was given my clothes and a bill for my food (thirty pfennigs a meal) and was shown the door.

A city cop was driving to the station and invited me to come along. In the car he told me what had happened: I was observed living with German students known to be cool to the New Order. The Gestapo had all it needed to know about the German students, but it knew nothing about me. So a subordinate officer at the border decided to take me in on suspicion of he knew not what and find out something about me. Inside the jail the Communist newspaper was found and he was sure he was onto something worth pursuing. Then the superior officer arrived—he rode circuit around a circle of north German prisons dealing with arrests—and took up my case. He opened my passport; Fred Oechsner's professional card fell out; the superior was furious. He scolded the officer who had arrested me for not noticing that I was in contact with an eminent foreign journalist—something the Nazis still worried about—and he had me brought in to be released.

I phoned Oechsner about my adventure. He had one of his men write it up and put it on the wire. I took the next train to Berlin at his bidding and wrote a light little first-person piece on How I Spent My Incarceration by the Gestapo. At home the *Item* ran it on the front page with an uncommonly ugly picture of me under a big bannerline, "Tulane Star Jailed by Nazis." For a day or two I toyed with the notion of writing a letter of thanks to the overzealous Gestapo underling who arrested me—it got Oechsner's attention and I got a pretty sure foothold on a future job in Berlin—but I managed to suppress the impulse.

Within weeks of seeing Franklin D. Roosevelt I found myself in the presence of the other great duelist of the twentieth century, Adolf Hitler. I was on my way out of Germany to France, but I stopped off for a day in Munich to see a highly advertised exhibit of Nazi-era art—or rather to see its most talked-about entry. It was a very large canvas depicting Leda and the Swan at the climax of their encounter. Leda was red-haired, nude, prone and tremendously salacious, and Jupiter in the form of a swan was agitated. It was realistic to the point of bits of light reflecting moisture on Leda's pubic hair. The purpose I guess was to make Germans want to go home to bed to create more Germans. After that I paid a visit to the foremost political sight in the city, the Brown House, the cradle and still the headquarters of the National Socialist German Workers Party. Lo, from a mast on a high balcony the standard of the Führer was flying, indicating (as with royalty) that the Leader himself was in residence. I waited on the street with others hoping to get a glimpse. Then someone told me Hitler was in town to attend the opera that night. I raced to the opera house and bought one of the last tickets in the highest balcony.

That night, the royal box remained empty until the lights went out and the curtain rose. Then all on the stage paused, and the audience stood to salute Hitler, who at that point entered the box. I could see none of this from my seat near the planet Mars. I squirmed in my distant place through the first act, until I guessed the interval was near. Then I left my seat, went down to the level of the boxes. The doors behind the royal box were guarded by black-uniformed SS men of the Death's Head unit, the personal bodyguard. I stationed myself at the door to the very next box to the royal one. When the lights went up, I summoned boldness and opened the door and went in. I expected to be thrown out, but the occupants were all at the rail getting what I sought, a view of the great one. Boldness encouraged boldness. I eased my way through the occupants of the box now bunched in the corner nearest the royal box, saying under my breath *"Entschuldigung, bitte, Sicherheitsdienst."* Assuming I had something official to do with security they gave way, and I soon held the utmost corner position, mere yards from Adolf Hitler in the next box. He stood at the rail smiling and giving his patented little Hitler salute—flopping his open palm back over his shoulder—to the cheering audience below. He was wearing tails. I don't know why. I never saw him out of military uniform again. Possibly it was just to make himself at one with the upper-middle-class opera-going audience, which was not his original lower-middle-class constituency.

It lasted only a few minutes. He did nothing special, and nothing noteworthy happened. But it was mightily impressive to see that the powerful, raucous, commanding voice one trembled to hear when he spoke on radio was encased in a very ordinary, mild-looking person. It was quite thrilling to see in the flesh the figure to whom the best educated, most capable and—if Leda had her effect—most numerous people in Europe had surrendered their wills. FDR might express a wish that some action be taken, and it would be debated, possibly rejected, at best amended before becoming law. Then its force would be weakened by people carrying it out only partially and without enthusiasm in the slovenly way of democracy. But this man I was looking at could express a wish for action, and all opposition would fade to nothing. And it would be carried out with precision and enthusiasm by all. It was frightening to see the single plain figure who possessed all this power.

I have often thought that, had Hitler been assassinated as he stood there at that rail in September of 1937, historians (and not only German ones) would have set him down as a great, constructive leader of a great nation, deserving of general admiration. That year, 1937, contained none of the bold military actions that so frightened Europeans, including the German people: no scary march into the Rhineland as in 1936, no seizure of Austria as in 1938. It was still possible for apologists to say that the Jewish Thing was merely a way to get votes and would wither by neglect as a policy. While economic depression clung like a sick cold and a headache elsewhere, it was a bad dream of the past in Germany. When Hitler came to power in 1933, 6 million Germans were unemployed; at this moment in 1937, the number was under 1 million. Pride matters deeply, and the pride, rubbed raw, of the German people was greatly salved by the bloodless reoccupation of the Rhineland. Far from being alienated, famous foreigners came to praise. Lord Halifax was sent by the British government and reported back favorably. Lloyd George, who led the coalition against Germany in the Great War, visited Berchtesgaden and called Hitler a great man. Mussolini of Italy was proud to be received. The most popular private American citizen, Charles Lindbergh, came and reported that Germany would be invincible in war. Germans cheering and saluting Hitler in the opera house in Munich that night were probably representative of most Germans in feeling that this was very nearly the best of times, and that Adolf Hitler was their author.

Abroad, this seemingly quiet year, 1937, marked the transformation of the European strategic situation from one unfavorable to one wholly favorable to Hitler. Intimidated, the King of Belgium backed out of a mutual defense pact with France. Italy signed the Axis alliance with Germany. The tide of civil war in Spain turned in favor of Hitler's little friend, General Franco. Thus, France found itself suddenly hemmed in by unfriendly nations.

The morning after my night at the Munich Opera, I took the train for my first visit to the capital of that beleaguered country.

CHAPTER ELEVEN

Paris

Paris seen for the first time is for poets, not reporters, to describe. Even before seeing the broad boulevards and great edifices, I was captivated just emerging from the railway station. The air was pellucid, the colors subtler, the sidewalks broader and sunnier, the street scene livelier than anywhere else I had been. I felt exhilarated for no particular reason beyond just being there. People seemed attractively unself-conscious, and the trait was contagious. Walking wide-eyed from the Du Nord station I soon felt I could disrobe in the middle of the street and no one would notice. I stopped at a corner bistro with a slate outside chalked "Prix Fixe" and had *choucroute garnie* and a small carafe of *vin ordinaire*. Then I applied my cajunated French to find out how to reach the Porte d'Orleans and the Cité Universitaire near it. The fast way was by underground metro. I opted for the slow way, standing on the rear platform of transfer buses where I could look at faces and places along routes on which all faces were interesting and every street corner a tableau.

I had written ahead to reserve a room at the Cité. The dormitory was spacious, almost luxurious, with an elegant library and a downright sumptuous cafeteria. How different from my accommodations in Heidelberg. I met a wild Welsh student who wore a red star in his beret and said he was a Communist. Together we metroed most evenings to the Place de l'Opéra where he was forward (as I was not) in descrying foreign students and engaging them in endless seminars around the little tables of sidewalk cafés. One night we met three Canadian students who puzzled me. Whenever my turn to say something came around they listened in respectful silence they accorded no one else. I wondered why. Then late in the evening I found out. One of them asked me, "Did you have no one else to help you carry the presses across the German border?" It dawned: They had somehow heard the story of my arrest for carrying an anti-Nazi newspaper into Germany—probably from my imaginative Welsh friend at a moment when I had left the table for some reason—and assumed I was transporting the whole works needed to print an opposition journal under Hitler's nose. The vision of being thought a Scarlet Pimpernel was very pleasing, and I gave a moment of serious thought to let it stand. But my prosaic side took over, and I clarified the story and watched their respect disappear.

We did not spend all our evenings in intellectual intensity or constructive endeavor. We devoted two nights exclusively to getting seriously drunk, and others to visits to two fancy houses that were considered musts for young unattached newcomers to the city of light. But politics, deep profound politics, was so heavy in the air that summer that it was impossible not to breathe it in long draughts and give thought to how France got into its unholy fix, and what was going to happen next. The Popular Front government of Léon Blum had just collapsed, the Spanish Civil War was going badly, and the Depression was hurting more than ever.

The Paris World's Fair was on, and Picasso had just completed his great painting of *Guernica* in honor of the Spanish town that the Germans had bombed out of existence. I was in the crowd that lined up at the Spanish Pavilion for the unveiling. Riots had been anticipated, but in fact there was no trace of disorder, demonstrating that the French people were not of two minds: all but a tiny minority favored the Spanish Republic, so there was no one to riot against. Which made one wonder: why had the Popular Front government of France forbidden aid to the Popular Front government of Spain, when 95 percent of Frenchmen wanted to help the Republic, and when France's potential enemies were pouring troops, tanks and planes into Spain in the service of the Fascists?

The French Communist Party held its annual convention in the suburbs of Paris, and we attended. Usually these were rather austere assemblies, to which only proven comrades were welcomed. This year it was a bright fair with games and prizes, and speeches interspersed, to which all were invited. It was a reflection of Stalin's shift in global political strategy. Hitler was on the march, with Russia as the proclaimed ultimate destination. In response Stalin ordered his foreign branches to abandon the previous line of surly isolationism and instead seek alliances—Popular Fronts—and friendships wherever they could be found.

For balance we attended a fascist meeting. The great braggart and Mussolini-mimic Jacques Doriot spoke. He ordered the public address system turned off to demonstrate that his mighty voice needed no artificial amplification. He had not spoken minutes before cries arose that people could not hear. Doriot shouted, "You cannot hear me? Well you will hear me!" And he resumed with increased volume. In a moment the cries resumed. Rather than yield and turn the amplifiers back on he spoke louder still. And so it went until after ten minutes the Hercules of the podium had lost his voice altogether.

Political attractions abounded. But more than anything else I enjoyed the hours-long bull sessions around tiny café tables. France had to be talked about. Paris was a joy. But Paris was also a mess. Out from under the city's magnificence and gaiety one caught unmistakable whiffs of decay. For six centuries France had been the pivot of European history. Its language was the language of world diplomacy. Yet it was now allowing itself to be encircled, dressed for sacrifice, by a nation it had joined in defeating a few years before. At home in this rich, Edenlike land the Depression seemed only to grow worse. And the elected politicians whose function was to determine what was wrong, to formulate plans to make it right and to enact them into law, had in fact become a Babel of irrelevant rhetoric.

One clue to what was wrong was omnivisible. Above specified rows of seats in every metro coach, public bus and railway carriage sad little signs announced, *"Places reservées aux mutilés de la Guerre."* France had lost 10 percent of its male population in the Great War, but the *mutilés* who lived were a multiple of that. Four of every nine combat soldiers had been killed or wounded. In gratitude and sorrow, governments voted extensive benefits of all kinds for veterans, the bill to be paid with reparations exacted from defeated Germany. But by definition defeated Germany was poor and unable to provide money, even though France decided to put her troops back into the Rhineland to force payment. So France effectively saddled itself with a condition of big, permanent, unmeetable debt. Also, a slaughtered generation produces few offspring. The year before my first visit, the young population had supplied the armed forces with 240,000 conscripts. From then on the number declined till in 1940 the number was 120,000—half the norm set for defense of the nation.

The French Parliament, supposedly elected to face problems like this, was made up of a Senate structured to prevent change, and a Chamber of Deputies chosen by the people to legislate. Its failure to do so is generally attributed to something inexplicable: a strain of excessive individualism that somehow inheres in every Frenchman's DNA. It is said that a French politician's definition of the ideal political party is himself plus the number of voters needed to elect him to the Chamber. Multiplicity and scatteration of parties produced coalition governments with insufficient support to formulate distinct policies. To suit all members of the coalition, bills had to be compromised down to nothingness. And it produced unstable governments. The average duration of governments between the wars was four months, enough time to locate the men's room but little else.

Another feature thought to be peculiar to the genes of Frenchmen is contained in André Siegfried's famous aphorism that Frenchmen keep their hearts on the left and their wallets on the right. Thus the Chamber occasionally passed pieces of much-needed social legislation, but then stubbornly refused to appropriate the moneys needed to carry the laws into effect. That in turn led to the final and ultimate preventive of decent government: the *mur d'argent*, or wall of money. A premier would go to the banks to borrow the money to achieve some public goal, and the banks would either offer the money at usurious rates that made the incurred debt unbearable or sadly inform the first politician of the realm that there was no money—it had flown to richer borrowers abroad. In the 1930s capital flight was chronic, preventing essential legislation and depriving lagging French industry of the means of catching up with the world.

In 1936, the year before my first visit, there was a burst of hope that this could all be changed. Fascist organizations, stimulated by the apparent success of their models in Germany, Italy and Spain, launched a great riot that threatened to end constitutional government. Both plain people and leaders of the regular parties were alarmed. However disgusted they were with one another, they did not want to lose their freedom. The three leading parties, Radicals (read liberals), Socialists and Communists, went into elections as one bloc, a Popular Front. They won the election in a landslide, and Paris exploded in joyous celebration.

The premier was Léon Blum, an intellectual, lawyer, literary critic, and head of the Socialist Party. He fashioned a program similar to Roosevelt's in America and called it the "French New Deal." Early momentum got some proposals through, but then the built-in brakes—the Senate, the bureaucracy, the banks—put a stop to legislation. Stagnation at home and limp-wristed foreign policy encouraged popular dissatisfaction with Blum. The Spanish Civil War began. At first, Blum supported the Popular Front government of Spain against that country's Fascist rebels. Then the British persuaded him to join them in a policy of nonintervention, giving aid to neither side. As the Nazis and the Italian Fascists continued to pour in troops and tanks and planes to help the Spanish rightists, the policy became a mockery and discredited Blum with his own followers. After a year, Blum resigned the premiership. He remained in the cabinet, and the government was still called the Popular Front, but in fact the last best hope for France in the interwar years had died.

I have given the standard explanation for the failure of government in France: the ideological one, the right-wing Senate and the moneyed classes of finance. In fact, French students insisted to me, the real problem was not in the realm of ideas, but was simply inertia elaborately created over centuries. In ancient Roman France, roadways ran roughly north and south, and east and west, generally following rivers. As the monarch in Paris established his rule over the unruly in the Middle Ages, control over France ran in ripples out from Paris creating the spiderweb shape of roadways today. Power moved in the same form, from Paris outward. No part of France ruled itself; all its ninety departments were run by prefects appointed from Paris. No local initiatives to build bridges or sewers were settled locally; permission had to be got from Paris. Even the marketing of France's wonderful produce could not be done locally. All had to go to the central market of the nation at Les Halles, a teeming few blocks of Paris, and then be shipped from there back to the provinces, often to locales a short distance from where it originated.

All this power was wielded by the King's advisers, almost independently of him. They grew into a permanent body that did not change essentially despite political events. The *noblesse de robe* of the kings grew rather smoothly into the *grand corps d'état* of the republics. The great French revolution changed the names but kept the same types of bureaucrats in the same institutions as before. In modern times, the central bureaucracy, the Conseil d'État of 150 members remained self-coopting and self-perpetuating. It received acts of the legislature and "reinterpreted" them to prevent change. It made use of never-repealed acts dating back to the Middle Ages to justify its tangles of regulations by which new legislation was nullified. Its financial counterpart, the Inspectorate of Taxes, did the same with the state's finances, reinterpreting the budgets passed by Parliament and often turning their intent backward. It even used, through the 1930s, quill pens and ledgers as under the Capetian kings. Politicians might play-act in the spotlight and enjoy accounts of their heroics in the papers, but the tenor of events was settled behind the scenes by these institutions, on the ground that they supplied stability and continuity to a political scene of unstable, ever-changing cabinets.

Thus was Léon Blum's Popular Front government, elected by a landslide, emasculated, and his "French New Deal" legislation to end the Depression negated. Feeling unable to control its own destiny, increasingly surrounded by enemies, France followed the British lead in trying to keep Hitler at bay by appeasing him. I spent some of the summer and a margin of the fall in France, and made a transition from exhilaration on arrival to gloom at departure.

CHAPTER TWELVE

Oxford

When I was a small child a teacher exercised the wonder of our class by telling of an old sailing ship that was dry-docked each year for replacement of boards and sails, as they wore out, and then putting the question, when did it cease to be the old ship and become a new, different ship? I don't remember the response or whether it mattered, but I recalled the story and felt that it applied to me in the few years after leaving the U.S. I felt that the elements of my young persona were tired, worn out, or in tatters from depression, both economic and spiritual, and that they were being replaced to such an extent that I sometimes had difficulty remembering the boy in the young man. Once, early in my residence in Europe I recorded an interview speaking German. Years later when I replayed it I was astonished at the change in my very sound. I had learned German when I had a Southern (U.S.) accent, and that was the only way I could speak it—though I no longer spoke my own tongue that way. I did not develop an English accent, but by magnetism or some such, my accent drifted to approximately the Mason-Dixon line, and perhaps a little offshore. An American friend said he discovered my origins only by my pronunciation of the one word—"police." In the way of my fathers I gave the two syllables equal weight, while the rest of the English-speaking world stresses only the second one. But the sound was merely the outer sign of a whole change. I had always had a tendency toward self-sufficiency and independence. Now with opportunity and means I become completely so, with no feeling of indebtedness to or dependence on anyone or any time past. Sheilah Graham, lover of F. Scott Fitzgerald and a writer herself, made it on her own so completely that she said, *"Je suis mon ancêtre."* I felt and behaved as if I, too, was my whole ancestry. My family tree began with me, and for several years I was all there was of it.

The change, not noticed till much later, began when, in the autumn of 1937, I crossed the threshold of the great gate beneath the statues of medieval benefactors and into the patinated world of Merton College. It was a crossing no less amazing than Alice's through the looking glass. Merton College is at this writing 735 years old. Its qualifications for being the oldest Oxford college are impressive. Its core quadrangle, called Mob Quad, is the oldest collegiate structure in the English-speaking world. Its gray stone walls and pointed arches are thus the models, by many removes, for the hundreds of gothic college and high school buildings that went up in America in the first half of the twentieth century, a burden the little old original bears with grace lent by age. After a stay in new buildings, I got quarters in Mob Quad, in the very room where legend located the medieval scholar John Duns Scotus. Directly contiguous to my rooms was the old, very old, library with its rows of huge vellum-bound books filled with words written by scriveners before printing was invented. Directly across the quadrangle I looked out on the rooms once intimidated by Lord Randolph Churchill, father of Winston.

In these surroundings I had many adjustments to make, most of them pleasant. It is odd to me even this late in life to record that I now had the first bedroom to myself in my life, with an ample sitting room attached. I had a servant called a "scout." But I had to adjust to the truth of the famous student colloquium: Q.—What do American students do in Oxford? A.—The same thing they do in America but with inferior plumbing. Every morning my scout woke me up with a small can of very hot water to be poured into a crockery basin and mixed with cooler water for washing face and hot spots, and he took my chamber pot out to empty. That was the extent of daily ablution. To get really clean was adventurous. You descended the stairs, walked through rain or cold across the quad to another quad where there was a kind of brick shed with two bathrooms that featured bathtubs and running water. Next to Godliness, perhaps, but surely nearer to pneumonia.

Happiest of adjustments, I had money. Each quarter year, the Warden of Rhodes House presented each scholar in his charge with a check, or cheque. He advised that scholars might have to eke things out from private resources. Having none and being unaccustomed to having even this quantity of pelf at my disposal, I found it ample, indeed generous. And I received advice on how to spend it from a young English student who shared my staircase. Seeing me writing out checks to pay for purchases, he stopped me and said I had it all wrong. Do not pay immediately, he said; desist from paying as long as you can. Shopkeepers forget you immediately if you pay. But if you do not pay, and your bill mounts, they remember you, and your each entrance into a shop becomes an event. They memorize your every whim and wish and fall over themselves to please you. Micawber was dead wrong about debt. It is the only ticket to distinction and honor and happiness. He told me the story of the celebrated Claud Cockburn. Whenever Claud received a third or fourth dunning notice he mailed a form letter to the sender: "I think you should know that once a year I put all my bills in a hat and stir them vigorously with a stick. Then I take out two and pay them in full. If you importune me just once more, your bill shall be removed from the competition." I listened intently and even put his advice into practice on a couple of experimental runs, but in the end my temperament failed me, and I returned to paying bills as they came in. I simply had no compelling ambition to be famous with shopkeepers.

Sociability, which I have hitherto emphasized because I had had so little of it, ceased to be a concern in a tight little corporation where some two hundred contemporaries dined together in a great hall every evening and, as the gates were locked at nine P.M., forgathered in one another's rooms for argument or wassail long into the night. Having heard much of English class consciousness, I expected to run into cool receptions or even rejections. But the opposite was the case. At that time England had not been inundated by millions of Americans in uniform or thousands flying in as tourists. All they knew of Americans was what they saw in American films. About us in the flesh, therefore, they were curious—befriending and watching each of us with the expressions of people at the zoo observing a panda, waiting for something extravagant to happen.

I watched them in wonder, much as they regarded an ex-colonial. It was a joy gathering in rooms after Hall and listening to just about the best English you could hear off a stage. English youths at Oxford were three or four years younger on average than the Americans, and in many ways they showed it. But they were, at least in comparison to me, much better read. They were easy conversationalists from homes, you could tell, where talk flowed smoothly and plentifully around dinner or tea, and where bookshelves contained books, not vases and photos of relatives. I could not but take special note of their cultivated little awkwardnesses and hesitations occasionally in conversation. I soon learned that these were protective devices against slipping into error and being called on it, giving the speaker time to think of the next remark, hedges against overhasty commitment. These were after all members of the uncommitted generation when the Oxford Union voted not to fight for King and Country, much to the satisfaction of Adolf Hitler. This generation did not know it yet, but it was on the brink of a wrenching change of attitude on this subject, and I was going to help push them over the edge.

At the height of British accommodation to the visiting scholars were arrangements for young Americans to take substantial whiffs of the rarified air of the uppermost classes. Thus a number of us received invitations to the Goldsmiths Ball in London, a traditional annual event of great pomp and glitter. Before the ball we were farmed out for preprandial sherry to different notable families. I felt myself very lucky to be chosen for the home of the Right Honorable Leopold Amery. He seemed only about five feet tall but was considered a giant of Parliament. Harrow and Oxford, correspondent for the London *Times* in the Boer War, Minister in Conservative cabinets since 1922, but now on the outs with his party leaders. I dared in a roundabout way to ask why. He said unhesitatingly, foreign policy. Later, in war, it was he who stood in Parliament and applied the words of Oliver Cromwell to the appeasement government of Neville Chamberlain, "You have sat here too long for any good you have been doing. Depart, I say, and let us have done with you! In the name of God, go!'"

On another occasion, a Canadian friend asked me to go with him for a weekend with a titled family with whom he had developed a friendship. It was the home of the widowed Lady Mander and her daughter in Staffordshire. We spent a most enjoyable several days there, but it opened with an embarrassment so personal as to be still painful. With my new wealth I was slowly re-outfitting my wardrobe in stages. First, the outer things people could see, like jackets, trousers and shirts. The intimate invisibles could wait. When we arrived at the Mander mansion, my little suitcase was taken to a bedroom by a servant, while I stayed downstairs beside a giant fireplace for a cozy chat with our hostess and her friends. Before dinner I went up to brush up and found my miserable underwear and socks and pajamas, all literally ragged, carefully laid out on the bed! Only the remembered warmth of my hostesses rescued me from horror and a brief flirtation with suicide as an alternative to going back to dine.

In a couple of important respects my Oxford experience was a falling off. I studied less than was my custom, and sports became a low priority. In a word, achievement ceased to be the all-consuming purpose it had become in New Orleans. Oxford's tutorial system, so widely praised, never took hold of me. My tutors were less interesting than my best classroom teachers at Tulane. I went out for running at the Iffley Road track so casually and intermittently that I failed to make the team that first year. For the latter failure I tried for awhile to blame English eccentricity: for one accustomed to running in blazing hot Junes and Julys, it was surprising to find that the Oxford–Cambridge relays competition was held in frigid December just before Christmas. And to one accustomed to the universal quarter-mile track it was disconcerting to train on the track at Iffley Road, which, for reasons I could not divine, had been made one-third longer than a quarter mile, making it approximately one third of a mile in length. However, a few years later, Roger Bannister became the first human to break the four-minute mile on that very track, so my excuse was a poor one.

With honesty I recognize two genuine explanations for my defection. One was a reaction to a Spartan adolescence. I relaxed. I learned to drink. My supreme athletic achievement was to climb the twelve-foot ornamental grille fence near my rooms after hours and go to the Wheatsheaf Inn nearby for some serious imbibing before climbing back in and going to bed, this almost every night.

The other explanation for my decline was a beautiful woman.

CHAPTER THIRTEEN

The Raven

At Oxford the school year was divided into trimesters that added up to six months in the University and left six months for vacation. The three vacation periods were meant to be spent largely in traveling and studying elsewhere. I was unhappy about my defection from discipline and so was determined to spend my first, deep winter vacation studying. I packed a load of books and planned to go to Munich, seek out a nearby snow-bound village, hole up in a cozy Gasthaus and catch up. I told friends about my plans, and two of them, a Canadian studying at the London School of Economics, and an Indian school-mate from Merton, asked if they might come along and do the same. I was de-lighted.

The day we arrived in Munich and took up temporary quarters in a railway station hotel, the papers announced that former Field Marshal Erich Luden-dorff had died in the village of Ludswigshöhe not far away. His funeral promised to be a bit of history one dared not miss. When the Great War began, every single corps in the German army was commanded by a titled nobleman. This stiff-necked, pop-eyed commoner fought his way up through their ranks and by midwar was de facto commander of the whole army. In the last year of the war, while the Kaiser and old Field Marshal von Hindenburg were figure-head leaders, Ludendorff was in fact the dictator of Germany. He was thus a principal strategist in the biggest disaster of the century (up until then), and in the 1920s he compounded his erratic reputation by sponsoring the unknown Adolf Hitler. So, the morning after our arrival in Munich we took a local train to Ludswigshöhe to see what could be seen.

A large crowd swarmed the cottage where his body lay. After an hour of gentle elbowing we got about five yards from the door. We could hear a high-pitched female voice wailing inside. It seemed to be some kind of prayer or fu-neral poem doing honor to the German soul and to the old man's soul in particular, for I made out the word "*Seele*" in different contexts several times. Questioned casually by someone in the crowd who noticed that we three were speaking an alien language to one another, I casually answered that I was an American. Word was passed that I was an American admirer of Ludendorff. The rumor enlarged to report that I had come all the way from America for the occasion. And when it moved across another layer of humanity outward, it asserted that I was leader of an American delegation that had come to honor the Field Marshal. Finally, when it rippled back to me, it averred that I had come to make a funeral oration on behalf of the Volksdeutscher community in America. Alarmed at prominence unearned and unwanted, we wriggled back out of the crowd and took the train back to Munich.

Resolved to let nothing further delay our plan to find a place to hibernate, I told my friends of a postcard-perfect hamlet in the nearby mountains an hour's train ride away, where I had a friend. Now, with snow falling, it would probably be enchanting. We agreed to go and inspect it immediately, and if it was judged right for us we could move in that afternoon.

We climbed aboard the train; and there in the same third-class compartment, on the seats facing us—I remember it as a blinding flash giving way to a heavenly vision—sat the terminator of all my plans. Her name was Ruth Raven. She was twenty-one. Words fall short in describing her: cream complexion, jet black hair, long lashes over eyes whose pupils appeared to be made from blue diamonds, a splendid mouth capable of smiles that made the male onlooker weak in the hams. She was quite simply the most beautiful girl I had ever seen. I would learn that my judgment was widely shared. When one entered a room at her side one noticed all heads, male and female, turning in her direction as if magnetized. Half a century later I ran across an old colleague and asked him if he remembered when we had first met. He answered, "How could I forget? You were escorting the prettiest girl I ever saw. I even remember her name, Fräulein Raven, Ruth Raven."

She sat there smiling. On one side of her was a pretty American girl named Mary; on the other, Ruth's handsome sister. They were in ski togs for a day in the mountains, farther out than our village. Mingling began almost before we were seated. Names and telephone numbers were exchanged. A time was set, tomorrow noon for lunch at the Café Luitpold. A nice symmetrical three of them and three of us.

My comrades and I found the village we visited as enchanting as ever we had hoped, but we were transfixed by prior enchantment and could hardly wait to get back to Munich. Lunch at the Luitpold led to dinner at a beer tavern which led to ice skating the next day and tea, hours of tea, in the English Gardens the next. Ruth and her friends and her mother went for a week in the little mountain ski town of Reit-im-Winkl. We followed. Snow being infrequent in the swamps of Louisiana, I could not ski, so I had lots of talks with Ruth's handsome mother. (I have a record, short but impressive, of winning the mothers and losing the girls, as happened with my Southern belle in New Orleans.) I was now wholly in love and sternly resolved to get the girl, too. Somehow I did, but I do not know how. My two companions were both handsomer and more charming than I, Brahmins both—one from Bombay, the other from Toronto. But as Bagehot said in another context, do not let light in on magic. Ruth, not very good at skiing herself, began to displace her mother and take walks and have talks with me, too. They led on the last night in the mountains to my bedroom at the inn. When we returned to Munich, we had a relationship stronger by many factors than I had ever known with a woman.

Ruth lived with her mother and sister in a large well-appointed apartment overlooking a main residential avenue in Munich. The husband and father had died and left a legacy, but not quite enough. They boarded a few American students. I spent much of the rest of my time visiting the apartment (careful to agree to dine there only once; I was Depression-sensitive to having her mother pay for my courtship). I took Ruth to the English Gardens nearby and to restaurants every day.

Yet there remained something mysterious about this family. I never met any Germans in their presence. There seemed to be a deliberate disassociation. They were bitterly anti-Nazi, less for political reasons apparently than for reasons of class. They referred to Nazis as *Lumpen* or trash. Once at the opera when a busload of workers arrived to be given seats—part of the *Kraft Durch Freude* (Strength through Joy) program of cultural events for the lower classes—Ruth fulminated at them so angrily that I took to defending the right of Nazis to go to the opera, till I realized what I was doing. What puzzled me most was that no Nazi official made a play for this ravishing German girl. There seemed to be some kind of wall isolating her from the all-pervasive Nazis. Later when I ran across cases in which Nazi officials with their unquestioned power and perquisites simply took possession of good-looking girls of my acquaintance, I was the more mystified. She was to all appearances untouchable, sharing with the new Nazi elite only a mutual abhorrence.

A friend hinted knowledge that her late father was a Jew, and that was why she was left untouched. I considered the possibility; she was certainly in the rank of beautiful Jewesses—I think for example of Hedy Lamarr. But Jewishness was a punishable offense in this hideous society. Jews were being thrown out of desirable homes even this early. And in the war they were moved out of Germany altogether. But the splendid Raven was faced with no extraordinary hardships and traveled freely even during war. I never found out why. She did not volunteer information, and my affection was too strong to let me push questions; they sounded too much like a prying for credentials she did not need.

As my vacation neared its end, my infatuation graduated into a passion. My mates from England had gone back, but I stayed on for a week alone and spent every waking moment with her. In her arms I could hear, as if a theme of our affair, the voice of young Marlene Dietrich in the *Blue Angel:*

Ich bin von Kopf zu Fuss
Auf Liebe eingestellt.
Das ist meine Welt,
Sonst gar nichts.

Like the seductive young Marlene, she was from head to foot made for love making; it was her whole world, nothing else existed. But it made for a love affair too hot to be entirely happy. And I could not but note that, except in actual embrace, the heat was on my part; uncoupled, I remained urgent and ardent but she was wholly at ease and capable of seeming indifferent to my presence.

Back at Oxford I was consumed by memories of her. I considered making a proposal of marriage. I had stunning photos of her, which I placed about my room where books should, figuratively and actually, have been. I wrote every evening and picking up her little blue envelopes at the Merton gate became the peak of my day. Passion was no longer as good a description as obsession. I paid scant attention to a note from a friend in Munich warning me that those lovely blue eyes did not imply innocence. "Take care!" it said.

In the spring vacation I whisked her from Munich and took her, with her friends and mine, on a journey due south, stopping each night in a new, enchanting Italian town until we settled in Taormina, Sicily, for a week, then back up the ladder to Munich. It was a memorable holiday, seeing beautiful sights by day, making love by night. But midway through the trip doubts began to gnaw. Out of bed, there was little to do. She did not volunteer much conversation, and I noted an absence of those fond little pecks and pats indicating affection. On the train we had little to say. On the last lap back to Munich I found myself observing her critically, against my will, as she sat in the compartment, munching chocolates and wholly absorbed in a magazine of pulp literature called *Wahre Geschichten*—"True Confessions."

A wise man would have recognized in these doubts the beginning of the end of the affair. But back at Oxford in the final term of the university year absence did its perverse work and I longed to be with her.

It was then that my brother came to visit. He arrived the day the term ended and students were leaving. I secured him an emptied room in college for a couple of nights. Things conspired to let him see Oxford and England the way they appear in the movies—a couple of days of most unusual sunshine; students in boaters and blazers having tea with crumpets and scones (or "strumpets and crones," in student idiom) and delicate watercress sandwiches on incredibly green grass; a languid evening of punting on the Cher. I then escorted him to Munich to meet the person whom I had begun to speak of as my betrothed. She had never been to Paris, and I had written her promising to take her there with us.

We arrived in Munich in the evening. I managed to have one night alone with her before we left for our tour. After we made love, the emptiness of our relationship was laid bare. She settled into bland indifference, and I into irritation. From then on I watched her more critically than ever.

Showing her and my brother around Paris, I became wholly intolerant of the lethargy that was her normal expression. I had noticed it before, but now it became clear: whenever a new man appeared anywhere in our purview, she instinctively flashed the lovely smile, her blue eyes caressing all who looked in them; but a moment afterward she lapsed into her dead-eyed apathy. The fact—so simple to the sighted, but I had been blinded—was that within a wonderful wrapping of beauty God had created a very dull girl. The last line of Marlene's song, "Sonst gar nichts," said what I had resisted comprehending: aside from sex there was nothing.

We had carping little arguments over irrelevancies, the arguments all started by me. The situation became flat and clear to me. Had I looked on our relationship as a pleasant flirtation, a bubbly little night music, an affair, as she did, it would have been a marvelous small experience. But I inflated it into a dream of a lifetime companionship that was never possible. I sought a devoted wife in a *Mädchen* who was suited only to be a mistress. I wanted one woman; she wanted a variety of men. Later a fellow scholar told me he had dared to try her defenses and was surprised to find her pleased and compliant.

Feeling that I had to put an end to my obsession, I settled on a way that still assails me with shame half a century later. I told my brother about my condition. If I stayed in her presence I would continue to make love to her at night and roil in anger that she was not a different person. I admitted that I had no grounds for anger. She was innocent, had given me all she had to give and had promised nothing beyond it. I felt that I had to make a clean break without argument and with a minimum of explanation. I begged his permission to disappear in Paris. He would take her on one promised last tour of the city, then put her on a train back to Munich. He agreed. I wrote her a short note thanking her for her many kindnesses, but saying that nonetheless we were not compatible and that I could think of no other way of ending our relationship. I should have seen her off on the train myself, but I was not entirely rational then and urgently needed to cut this tough emotional knot cleanly. Prescott gave her the note. She seemed sad but did not blink. When he put her on the train, she was dead-eyed and shed no tears.

When she had gone, I rejoined Prescott only to see him off at the St. Lazare station. I felt that my wound was deep, and it went on hurting for weeks, but only for weeks. There were other passionate things going on in the great world and I soon lost myself in them.

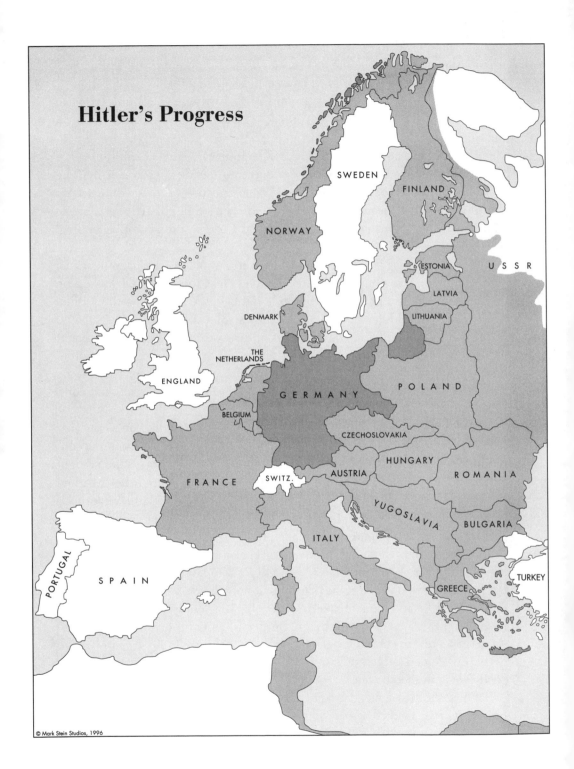

Hitler's Progress

SWEDEN

FINLAND

NORWAY

ESTONIA

LATVIA

U S S R

LITHUANIA

DENMARK

THE
NETHERLANDS

ENGLAND

G E R M A N Y

P O L A N D

BELGIUM

CZECHOSLOVAKIA

HUNGARY

FRANCE

SWITZ.

AUSTRIA

ROMANIA

YUGOSLAVIA

BULGARIA

ITALY

PORTUGAL

S P A I N

GREECE

TURKEY

© Mark Stein Studios, 1996

CHAPTER FOURTEEN

On the Brink

I settled in Paris in a tiny attic room in a small hotel near the *Folies Bergères* and resolved to use the balance of the summer break to get up to speed in my studies. But again I was interrupted—as was the rest of the world—by another seduction in Munich, this one involving the Prime Minister of Great Britain.

Early in 1938, Hitler took advantage of the pacifist mindset of the time by seizing Austria, without opposition or even much verbal criticism. Now in late summer of the same year, he moved on the finest prize in central Europe, a nation with high morale and a sizable army, an arms producer (Skoda) that equaled Germany's own Krupp works and fortifications in its Sudeten mountain border that were as strong as France's Maginot Line—Czechoslovakia. Hitler could move neither east nor west with that restraint in his groin.

At the annual Nazi Party Rally in Nuremberg in September, Hitler screamed that his patience with Czechoslovakia—allegedly mistreating its German minority in the Sudeten mountains—was at an end. He implied he would attack. That would bring France and Russia into war to fulfill their treaty obligations, and Britain could not stay aloof in a general European war.

The war a generation swore not to fight was at hand. Blank terror gripped France. It happened that the most moving antiwar film, Jean Renoir's *La Grande Illusion,* had its première at a cinema down the street from my digs. For several evenings I watched audiences coming out, pale, drained, eyes red. They appeared ready to pay any price to avoid sending another generation to slaughter.

I decided I had to be near my base and returned to London. Prime Minister Chamberlain had flown twice in eight days to Germany to plead with Hitler, offering generous, appeasing terms. But the Führer was implacable. The worst war scare of the century followed, more emotional than that announcing World War I, greater than the one accompanying the actual outbreak of WW II a year later. I tried to get into the House of Commons to hear the debate but was hopelessly far back in line. So, what does one do when the world ends? I went to the movies, to see Cary Grant and Katharine Hepburn in *Holiday* at the Odeon on Leicester Square. That night I joined a friend to listen on the radio to Chamberlain speaking to the nation: "How horrible, fantastic and . . . incredible it is that we should be digging trenches here because of a quarrel in a faraway country between people of whom we know nothing."

The next day around noon I was on a platform at Paddington Station watching the train for Oxford switching into place. The platform was alive with parents shepherding children to whom place labels had been attached, preparing to send them off to towns less bombable than London. The public address system came alive with an announcement: A breath away from the outbreak of war, Mussolini had persuaded Hitler to agree to one last conference of leaders in an effort to avoid conflict. Prime Minister Chamberlain was flying immediately to Munich where the conference was to be held. There was hope. Drawing on Shakespeare, Chamberlain would tell the House of Commons, "Out of this nettle, danger, we pluck this flower, safety."

People on the platform broke into cheers. Some wept and embraced others they did not know. I admit that I felt some relief too, such had been the tension. But by the time I reached Oxford I was of a mind that it was all an indecent charade, designed to induce the British and French peoples to accept what, the next day, would be the most famously outrageous, immoral and stupid sellout in the history of diplomacy: Czechoslovakia was excluded from the Munich conference, but bullied into dropping its arms and letting Hitler take what he wished, which was possession of the only defenses that made the little nation viable—and the last physical bastion by which a German conquest of Europe could have been prevented. There was an agreement to guarantee the new defenseless borders of the country; but this, predictably, proved mendacious. And Chamberlain brought back and waved to crowds a piece of paper signed by Hitler promising "peace for our time."

I cannot resist an urge to repeat some facts we now know about the great sellout, confirming what some of us then thought. Years later at the Nuremberg trials, Field Marshals von Manstein and Keitel in separate testimony said the Germany army was not at that time strong enough to pierce the Czech fortifications. The Czechs might have won a conflict by themselves. Had France come in, Hitler would have been in a hopeless position; General Jodl said at Nuremberg he had only seven divisions left on the French border to face a hundred French ones.

A large reason people supported the sellout was fear of the unknown new factor in war, bombing from the air. A perfect terror of air raids had taken hold. A film based on H. G. Wells's story, "The Shape of Things to Come," then drawing full houses all over Britain, seemed to justify it. The Left Book Club, which supplied a new socialist-inclined book to 60 thousand subscribers each month, also did its part. It commissioned a volume of surmise by the well-known leftist scientist J. B. S. Haldane, titled simply *A.R.P.* (for "Air Raid Precautions"), which became the last word. Influenced by Haldane's book, the official estimate of the casualties German bombers would inflict on Britain in sixty days of air raids was 600,000 dead and 1.2 million injured. A. J. P. Taylor in *English History 1914–1945* contrasts these with the actual figures. In six *years* of war the actual toll was 60,000 killed and 235,000 injured. The truth was bad enough, but fear had magnified it by a fantastic factor.

Carroll Quigley in *Tragedy and Hope* cites another set of statistics that tell something of the time: Colonel Charles Lindbergh's expert figures on German air power, much cited in the Munich period to discourage any challenge to Germany. The American hero emerged from Germany saying Hitler possessed 8,000 planes ready for attack. Later facts set the figure at 1,500. Lindbergh also said German industry produced 1,500 airplanes a month. The true figure was 280.

CHAPTER FIFTEEN

Appeasers

My late colleague and contemporary, the English journalist Henry Fairlie, acquired immortality with his name graven in the *Oxford English Dictionary* for creating a new definition of the word "Establishment." It was, he was the first to write, the collection of eminences who set British policies and effectively ruled the country regardless of election results. Fairlie formulated his thesis after World War II. But it is entirely convincing as a description of British society in the prewar, Munich period when a remarkable lot of intelligent, highly placed Britons from a wide variety of callings marched in lockstep into a pit where the sign clearly read: Here Be Monsters.

All the categories he prescribed for a mighty Establishment were then represented. The public-spirited wealthy, like Lord and Lady Astor; the very clever and willing, typified by Lord Lothian, later to be Ambassador to the U.S. for the crucial destroyers-for-islands deal; the editor of the *Times*, Geoffrey Dawson; the Warden of All Souls College Oxford (equivalent to the Princeton Institute for Advanced Studies) governed then by H. A. L. Fisher, leader of the "History is just one damn thing after another" school of historians as opposed to the Arnold Toynbee "It is all cycles and patterns" school; the archbishop of Canterbury, at that time Cosmo Gordon Lang; heads of the Civil Service, like Sir Horace Wilson; and the ex officio leader, the Prime Minister of the day.

The propositions they put together were simple and reasonable. One, Germany had been maltreated by the Versailles agreement in a way likely to cause, not prevent, instability in Europe. Two, Bolshevism was a threat to Western values, especially in times of economic trouble, and must be more effectively contained. Thus the policy to grant Germany concessions, restoring her to an equal place in Europe, thereby creating a strong bastion of anti-Communism in the way of Russia.

This might have become a sane and fruitful course, but two factors made such an outcome unlikely. One was the displacement of democratic government in Germany by Adolf Hitler, a messianic racist, in whom the normal capacity for human feeling was obliterated by a raging paranoia, not to be appeased. Had appeasing concessions been made to the German Republic before Hitler, the history of Europe and the world might be different.

The other was the accession to the prime ministry in Britain of Arthur Neville Chamberlain, whose talent was that of an accountant and whose virtue was skill at dealing with mundane domestic affairs like slum clearance and widows' pensions. A colleague likened him to a conscientious chambermaid, "He was good at tidying up." His speeches, Aneurin Bevan said, "were like a visit to Woolworth's, everything in its place and nothing above sixpence." He acquired a mighty self-confidence as a successful Lord Mayor of Birmingham. Complete assurance of his rightness plus ignorance of history and foreign affairs made him a dangerous man in the complex, explosive late thirties. I had the impression that he moved farther and more rapidly into appeasement of Germany and Italy than the rest of the Establishment felt comfortable with. When his foreign minister, Anthony Eden, indicated he was going too far, he forced Eden's resignation from the cabinet. When the permanent civil servant who ran the Foreign Office, Sir Robert Vansittart, indicated the same, he was promoted into functionlessness.

The policy of appeasement was said to have been given its shape by the "Cliveden set," the Establishmentarians who met in long weekend discussions at Cliveden, the palatial home of Viscount Astor and his more famous wife, Lady Nancy Astor, formerly Nancy Witcher Langhorne of Danville, Virginia, U.S.A., daughter of a horse auctioneer. She married Vincent Astor in 1906. When he was elevated to the peerage, she ran for his seat in the House of Commons, won and became the first woman member of Parliament. Her energies were fierce and aroused enmities along with admiration. The famous story is told that she one day addressed her special nemesis, Winston Churchill, "Mister Churchill, if you were my husband I would give you poison," and that he answered, "If I were your husband, milady, I would take it."

Capitalizing on her role of an ex-American with special ties, Lady Astor had all American journalists in London motored out to Cliveden for a day in

1937 to have the policy of appeasement explained to them. The next year she made an investment in the future by busing all American Rhodes Scholars to the great Thamesside manor for the same purpose. She was a middle-aged woman striking less for her appearance than for her energy and aura of authority. She announced that we were going to have a tour of the grounds, a vast garden down several levels. She grasped the arm nearest her, which happened to be mine, and away we went. "Son," she said, "where you from?" I said I was from Louisiana, which seemed to please her. "Do you know," she said, "I think we Southerners get along better with these English people than we do with the Yankees in our own country, don't you?" In my best Southern I lied, "Yessum." Of the rest of the tour I remember only one remark because of its eminent vividness. In respect to some sight she was exhibiting, she said, "They didn't know where to bury the old man [her father-in-law, Astor]. I told them to stuff him and stand him up in the hall as a hatrack." I suspected that the remark was an illustration of a woman learning to get attention in the presence of so many dominant males (the Tory leaders who weekended, not us) by such tricks as making outrageous statements.

Afterward we assembled in the drawing room, most of us sitting on the carpets, for a few remarks of welcome from Lord Lothian. Before he succeeded to the title as eleventh Marquess of Lothian, Philip Kerr was already known as an ardent and reasoned proponent of a federal union of America and Europe. At this moment he was an exponent of appeasement. But it was a soft sell and unimpressive. Our ensuing questions got mushy answers. I was encouraged by the skepticism displayed by my fellow students in their questions. Years later in recollection I would realize that the appeasers themselves were growing skeptical; Hitler was as bellicose after Chamberlain's free gift of central Europe as he had been before. But at the time I considered appeasement simply an absence of character in those who created this dreadfully wrong policy. Afterward we had tea, and fellow student Walt Whitman Rostow sat at the grand piano, and there was a kind of sing-along. When we left Cliveden in our bus, all raised fists in the Spanish Republican—or was it Communist— salute. It was not an expression of conviction, just overage naughty schoolboys wishing to be as outrageous as the lady standing in the drive and waving us goodbye.

Throughout the first term (called the Michaelmas term; the ensuing terms were called Hilary and Trinity) I hung onto the attitude of the reformed scholar, shunning strong drink and long evening powwows in favor of sober hours alone with books. I even trained for athletics seriously and made the Oxford team sent to relay competitions in Cambridge in December. But early in 1939 the world seemed to come apart. In February, the Spanish Republic began to collapse under the blows of Italian- and German-supported offensives.

In March, Hitler, having been given the border defenses of Czechoslovakia, moved in, dismembered the country and declared the main portion a German "protectorate." His press turned up the volume in its attacks on Poland for the now standard sin of misteating a German minority.

Though his peace paper, bearing Hitler's signature, was now confetti, Chamberlain said in Parliament, "We must not be deflected from our course." (I began to hate Chamberlain almost as much as I did Hitler. The point was confirmed to me a few years later when I sat in the Berlin Sportspalast watching Hitler deliver a mighty tirade. At one point Hitler began berating Chamberlain, and I began cheering along with the storm troopers, until I caught myself and fell into ashamed silence.)

I had no trouble fitting these events into the long trends of history. From the pit of the Dark Ages there had been a slow, staccato progress, with frequent fallings back, toward winning some rights and making rulers both representative and accountable. It was registered in tectonic movements: the Renaissance, the Reformation, the Enlightenment, the Parliamentary civil wars in Britain, the eighteenth-century revolutions of which the American one, as improved by Jackson and Lincoln, was a pro tem summing up and consolidation. Now had arisen the severest menace to that progress ever, not just a setback but a resolve to halt and to cancel it all in favor of a way of life nearest to that of some social insects, divided into ruler-warriors and degrees of subservience for the rest. I felt that all I identified myself with was being surrendered, without much protest. I had taken part as a kind of precinct worker in a British Parliamentary by-election campaign the previous autumn, the main issue in which was the Munich agreement, and my side had lost; pro-appeasement won. I now felt more strongly than ever that I was settling into being part of the whimper with which my world was ending. Almost suddenly in the early spring of 1939 I threw aside books, abandoned sports and devoted my energies wholly to the only form of action available in that time and place.

CHAPTER SIXTEEN

The Eve

The Munich trauma caused in my time at Oxford a strange, brief contortion of student life. Mine was called by an eminent contemporary "the most political generation ever at the university." There were three political clubs representing the three British political parties, called clubs, not parties, in order to enjoy a degree of university status and some advantages in such matters as renting halls for meetings. The Conservative and Liberal clubs numbered a couple of hundred members each, mostly passive members who did not attend meetings. Due to the Munich issue, the Labour Club had more than a thousand dues-paying members, out of a total undergraduate enrollment of 5,000 students, in the years 1938 and 1939. It easily bested the Oxford Union and the various sports as the biggest extracurricular institution at the University. Its foremost assets were two. It came into early and sole possession of the burning issue of the times, appeasement, and brought in outstanding speakers to debate the policy. And it had outstanding leaders in Denis Healey for the undergraduates, and Lord Pakenham for the dons. I was an ardent member and was elected to succeed Healey as its leader for the second of the two great years.

Denis Healey was a classics scholar at Balliol. Descriptive adjectives of him that come readily to mind are bushy-browed, exuberant and brilliant. His was, indeed, about the sharpest mind I have ever known, with an eloquence to give it expression. With what appeared enviable ease he would win a "first" in his studies. In Labour governments of later years he served as Defense Minister, then as Chancellor of the Exchequer, and then, out of power, as his party's "shadow" Foreign Minister. His agile mind, never bested in debate, won him these places. But it was probably the same gift that kept him from rising to Prime Minister. Healey argued with zest. With no malice whatever, he felt it part of the game never to leave an opponent any avenue of escape. He took no prisoners, left the earth in his path scorched, sought not just to get the better but to leave his adversary devastated. He was called a "verbal Rottweiler." His high cabinet places were appointive by prime ministers needing a brilliant subordinate. But the prime ministry was elective, requiring the votes of his fellows. Too many of them had had their egos battered at his hands to accept him as leader. But even those who opposed him agreed with the description widely given him as "the best prime minister Britain never had." In 1938, at crowded meetings of the Labour Club at the Co-op Hall in Oxford, with Tory students present in force and heckling, his qualities were exactly those needed.

Frank Pakenham I remember as a caricature of a professor, a tall, lanky, young man with sprouts of hair on either side of a balding head. He too was an outstanding debater. He was a descendent of the British officer who lost the battle of New Orleans to Andrew Jackson, and who died on the battlefield, Major General Sir Edward Pakenham. The Pakenham Oaks on the New Orleans battlefield were named after him. Our modern Lord Pakenham became in later life Lord Longford, famous for his campaign against pornography in Britain, and for the gifted pens of his womenfolk, wife Lady Elizabeth Longford, biographer of Queen Victoria et al., and daughter Antonia Fraser, biographer of Mary, Queen of Scots, et al.

I joined the Labour Club soon after my arrival in Oxford. After Munich it was my only relief from despair, and I began writing for its periodical. The events of early 1939 led me to make the organization my consuming interest, to the detriment of studies and sports.

As the year progressed, I wrote more for the Labour periodical. I joined in organizing a demonstration on the streets of Oxford, and addressed it. I led an Oxford delegation to London, to be part of a mile-long parade to Number Ten Downing Street, where a document of protest against appeasement was presented. There was a convocation of students from all over, and I was assigned to make a speech stating Labour's case. The statement was well received. A Conservative student from Cambridge protested to the Chair that I had spoken beyond my allotted time. The Chairman, a don, said that the Chair had the right to extend the time for particularly interesting speeches, a dubious statement but one that pleased me no end. I was assigned to do more speeches, and in a short time a consensus seemed to crystallize that I should be Healey's successor as leader.

The local Communists were the most ardent spirits supporting us, since their mecca, the Soviet Union, was Hitler's stated ultimate target. My curiosity to see that place deepened. I arranged to spend my early spring vacation on a tour. Two friends and I went by boat and train across Scandinavia, still under snow, and reached the Russian border through southern Finland. A rickety wooden arch, with red cyrillic letters faded pink by the winter's blasts, welcomed us to the land said to function under the proletariat's dictation. The sight beyond was a jolt. One could see that Leningrad had the substance of a beautiful place but badly needed pointing up and a universal coat of paint. That mild complaint was not suited to Moscow. The street scene there was just this side of squalor. Apartment buildings completed last year were crumbling. Nets anchored around their outer walls jutted out over the street to keep falling debris from injuring passers-by. People were ill-clothed and walked the streets looking like prisoners without hope of release. I had brought along an old suit—the one I had won the scholarship in, now grown shabby—and took it out on the street. In five minutes I had that many offers from prospective buyers. I accepted the highest bid and pocketed enough rubles to finance the rest of my stay.

As the end of the third term and of the university year approached in June, I gathered courage and went to Dr. C. K. Allen, the Warden of Rhodes House (an accomplished barrister and friend, in no way deserving the smartass student sobriquet, "the Rodent of Ward's House"), and, confessing that my political activities forfended my taking a degree now, asserted my wish for a third year. He was justly displeased and only begrudgingly agreed.

I then attended a dinner inaugurating me as head of the Labour Club. I made an acceptance speech, the substance of which I have forgotten. Edna Edmunds (later to be Mrs. Edna Healey) was present and years later related a story that I had used to ease into my remarks. It seems I had an Uncle Henri, a cajun who lived in the swamps of Louisiana. One night he awoke to see two large mosquitoes, each 2 feet high, seated on bedposts, contemplating his prone form. One said, "Shall we eat him here or take him down to the river and eat him?" The other said, "We better eat him here. If we take him down to the river, those big mosquitoes will come along and take him away." I have forgotten what my point was.

My accession to student office was smooth. The actual vote had been unanimous. In fact there was one impressive dissenter. Indira Nehru, daughter of Pandit Nehru and a contemporary student at Oxford, considered the election of an American to a prominent British student office inappropriate, and said so, but there was nothing to be done about it. It is my impression that Miss Nehru saw Americans with their mere two hundred years of history as rather vulgar upstarts, and in a way as competitors of an India soon to be free and sure to be a world leader. Much later, when she was Indira Gandhi and Prime Minister of a free India, her anti-Americanism was transparent. She came to Washington on a state visit, and I was one of a half-dozen reporters invited to breakfast with her at Blair House, the official guest house. At that time, India was being flooded with refugees from a disaster in poor, contiguous Bangladesh. We asked her if foreign help with foodstuffs and medicines was adequate. She answered, "The small nations do their duty, but, as we have come to expect, the big nations hang back." I dared not call the prime minister of the world's most populous democracy a liar. But when I checked the facts in my office later, that is what she turned out to be. The U.S. had donated by far the most to India. As a state gift, President Lyndon Johnson presented her with a painting of a rose, her favorite flower. I suggested that he borrow it back and have a thorn painted prominently on the stem.

Even zealots need a holiday. With the term over, and in an interval when the world crisis seemed to be on hold, I took my bike across to France and joined three friends for a wonderful tour of the Loire Valley. From there we took a train to the Côte d'Azur, playground of the rich and famous. We found reasonably priced lodgings in the hills above Cannes and studied awhile. We saved on other expenses in order to treat ourselves one day to buffet lunch at Eden Roc, the utmost of the most. Two memories remain vivid. First, Marlene Dietrich was there, in shorts. Let others enthuse about the bluest of blue waters swishing between great boulders at the base of the pavilion. The perfect shape of two famous female underpinnings will ever fill my memories of travel among the celebrated. The second incident was that the U.S. Ambassador to Great Britain, Joseph P. Kennedy, was there with part of his brood. Having met him when he came to speak to us at Oxford the year before, we dared to go to his table and say hello. Present was a gangling, good-looking boy about our age. Years later my casual handshake with him would have been marketable. The boy's name was John F. Kennedy.

Then one friend, Karl Price, and I repaired to a peasant hostel in Brittany on the coast, opposite one of the wonderful sights of the world, the fairy islet of Mont-St.-Michel. We studied and we ate and drank. A shot of Calvados and a large glass of hard cider made every meal a junior Bacchanal. We cycled the effects off in the afternoons, and as we cycled we talked. I had but one note: at any and every cost we must stop Hitler. My friend felt that the time for that had been let pass. "The consequences of war with modern technology would be too horrible to contemplate. I don't think anyone dares resist Hitler," he said. One day we cycled across the peninsula to the cliffs overlooking the coast of Normandy, where we stopped and sat and talked, looking out to sea. Had there been a ghost of summers future, it could have told us that a few years hence my fellow student would be a captain in the 82nd Airborne Division, overflying that coast full of conviction that Hitler could and would be overcome.

1939-1941

CHAPTER SEVENTEEN

A Stand at Armageddon

I gravitated somewhat toward the Indian student community at Oxford and, when in London, stayed at an austere rooming house they had virtually made their own at Number One University Place. On returning from France in August 1939 I settled there, thinking it as good a place as any to monitor the distant, rising drumbeat of Nazi press and radio attacks on Poland and to wait out the decision on war or peace.

I acquired reading-room rights at the nearby British Museum to prepare a chronology of events of the year. In retrospect things seem to follow one another logically, but, living through the time, I found that events seemed to tumble over events in a most confusing way. The previous school year the Labour Club's meetings at the Co-op Hall in Oxford had been turbulent. We dared believe that one of them—which turned into a kind of mass cancellation of the Oxford Union's "We won't fight for King and Country" resolution in 1933—may have influenced Chamberlain to throw away a prepared speech he was making in Birmingham and to make his first public utterance critical of Hitler. At the meeting Healey and Pakenham spoke brilliantly, overcoming a jeering squad of Conservative students. The tumultuous occasion was reported in the national press. Since most members of any British cabinet were graduates of Oxford or Cambridge and always followed events there, it may in fact have had the influence we boasted. If there was now to be no simplifying outbreak of war, the coming student year was going to be more turbulent. I wanted to be very sure of my facts before diving into it.

Also I wanted to prepare an argument to make a big change in our policy. When Chamberlain, getting worried at last, introduced conscription to create an armed force of size, we—from the depths of student irresponsibility—opposed it. We said you couldn't trust a Tory government to do anything, even if it made sense. In the dead of one night back then I took a pot of paint and a brush and spelled out "Conscript Wealth Too" on the sidewalk in front of the Oxford police headquarters. An agile friend scaled three stories of the Westminster Bank on High Street, and we passed up for hanging on its facade a large sign with the same silly message. Thus did we propagate the thought that Hitler must be fought, but without troops. By the end of August 1939, I was resolved to change that policy.

In London, meanwhile, preparations for possible war were going on with a kind of dogged deliberateness and without the fright of the previous autumn of Munich. In parks, gray, elephantine carcasses of barrier balloons lay flat on the earth waiting to be inflated and raised on cables to inhibit low-level bombing. Trenches were dug in the parks. Schedules for standing in line to receive free gas masks were published. High above the commercial signs on Piccadilly Circus was a huge billboard expressing futilely the wish of many: "CHURCHILL PRIME MINISTER."

One morning the landlord, who never performed services, performed one for me. He appeared in my room with a cup of tea and a newspaper. The previous night he had worried to me that Britain was stumbling toward war alone with Germany, and I had reassured him that Britain could always count on Russia in any anti-Nazi encounter. As Hitler's announced ultimate target, Russia simply had to fight. Now he displayed to me the newspaper headline: "Hitler Stalin Sign Alliance Pact." I needed something stronger than tea. He said, "There's your Russians for you." Leaving the room he threw back, "Bloody Russian troops aren't no bloody good anyhow."

The tremors of that shock had not fully settled when, on September 1, the intermission in Europe's Thirty Years War came to an end: the Germans invaded Poland.

Under pressure from public and political outrage following Hitler's swallowing of the rest of Czechoslovakia earlier that year, Chamberlain had announced a British guarantee of Poland's integrity. Would he now somehow use the Soviet defection to back out of the pledge? At first it seemed that he would. He did nothing the long first day of the attack on Poland. He appeared to be seeking another Mussolini initiative and another Munich conference. The next day he temporized in the House of Commons. The members grew impatient and unruly. When Labourite Arthur Greenwood rose to demand that Britain keep its word, the Conservative Leopold Amery shouted across the room, "Speak for England, Arthur!" Late that night, Chamberlain's cabinet met and insisted that he declare war.

At eleven A.M. on September 3, the landlord's kitchen was crowded to hear the Prime Minister announce on radio that Britain was at war with Germany. I was surprised that he had really done it. He was dead set against fighting and it would soon show. French and British troops would sit on the border indefinitely with no thought of undertaking an offensive to relieve some of the pressure on Poland. Still, this was the watershed. A decision to confront the Antichrist had been made for the first time. Churchill was brought out of the political attic and made First Lord of the Admiralty.

Now, at 11:30 A.M., September 3, in London the dread air raid sirens sounded almost as soon as Chamberlain stopped talking. With people from the streets, we poured into the cellar of the Tottenham Court Road dance hall across the way, awaiting horror. But only the Poles were to know horror for a while. The all clear sounded, and the radio announced that the warning had been a mistake.

I went to Fleet Street immediately, to the United Press office in Bouverie Street. A man named Harry Flory saw me and heard my application for a job. He put me on hold outside until I could be seen by the UP's star reporter, Webb Miller. In my habit of likening people to movie actors, Miller was Spencer Tracy, only more handsome. He had authored a marvelous book, *I Found No Peace,* about his travels in the awful 1930s. He asked me if I could speak German, really speak it? I said I could, even in Gothic print if he wished. He left me to Flory who signed me up. When the dust settled, I would be sent to Germany, but for now I would work in London. Twenty-five dollars a week.

I was given one day to clean up my affairs in Oxford. I went to see the Warden of Rhodes House, Dr. Allen, to say I would not take my extra year after all. At Merton College I packed all my belongings I couldn't wear and left them in the college cellar. Then I sat in my room for the last time and wrote a careful note to my second in command in the Labour Club, resigning from office just as my active term was about to commence. A civil war was already beginning in the Club. Breakaways from it, opposed to the Communists, formed a Social Democratic association and attracted much of the membership. One of its leaders was Roy Jenkins, who later became Chancellor of the Exchequer, an author of note and ability and Chancellor of Oxford University. By the time the struggle for the Club's body and soul reached a climax I was a warring side away.

CHAPTER EIGHTEEN

From London to Berlin

The British Ministry of Information took over the largest building of the University of London as its new headquarters. With nothing going on at the front, the only action was there. In its ample lobby press conferences were held, daily military and naval communiqués were issued, and reporters were provided with tables for their typewriters and telephones. The United Press was given a very long table, as it had many reporters to accommodate. I surmised that the table had magical qualities. Unless someone watched it through the long, eventless nights, it would presumably fly away. I could see no other reason for my being assigned to sit at it, or lie on it, every night from midnight to eight A.M. During the period of the Phony War, or the Sitzkrieg, little happened in daylight and nothing at all at night. On arriving each night I would phone the Bouverie Street main office to let them know I had the table under control. Then I would read German novels, keeping my syntax pure for the coming assignment in Berlin, until I fell asleep on the table. One of the novels, by Hans Fallada, described Berlin at the outbreak of the Great War, when masses of Germans filled the streets, shouting and singing for joy. Reports from Berlin about the outbreak of this one, the Greater War, told of a people turned glum, silent and worried.

I was relieved at eight A.M. by another ex-Oxonian who had resorted to the UP for employment. He was Charles Collingwood, a handsome—silent-film handsome—figure with wavy blond hair and a profile that commanded attention. He was always impeccably attired and favored the manner of an eighteenth-century dandy; he even kept a handkerchief crumpled in his cuff and retrieved it from time to time to dab at his nose. Of all the Charleses I have ever known, he was the least likely to be called Chuck. But the manner was misleading. He had a keen mind and level head and became an outstanding reporter. Much about him was as illusory as his manner. For example, he loved to regale us with stories, eminently believable, of his conquests of women, giving an impression of inconstancy in love. Yet, his later marriage to the film actress Louise Albritton seemed very successful. From the first moment, Charles and I became good friends and were to have nearly identical careers. When those long careers finally debouched into television, a medium specially created for Charles Collingwood, I expected to see him become a dominant figure. Instead he was rather passive about it. One of his marked traits was unambition: he did not want to let life become a fitful fever and did not strive to compete.

The idleness of most of the UP London staff in the early months of the war was deliberate. Flory was hoarding reporters for fear of being understaffed if and when the Sitzkrieg ended. Oechsner in Berlin became impatient. He was not sitting or waiting. He had a real, live Blitzkrieg on his hands and not enough men to meet demands. The military campaign was over quickly. Polish resistance was dead after twenty-two days, and the Russian Red Army joined hands with the Wehrmacht over the victim's twitching body. But the campaign had been a brand new kind of warfare, and reporters would be digging for months for details to explain it. There had been a tendency to believe that this war would be a continuation of the last one, gainless slogging between trenches, long artillery duels, small advances at great cost. We stood over the telex and pondered an early dispatch from Germany that began, "The German army went over the top at 4:30 A.M." "Over the top" was a relic term from the previous war, describing how offensives always began, with attackers climbing out of trenches and rushing forward. It was as outdated as muzzle-loading muskets, but no one could think of what to say to replace it. There were no trenches in the new warfare. From running starts, tanks and troops made sudden swift penetrations by focusing immense power—masses of tanks on the ground and dive bombers in the air—on single points in the enemy front till there was a gaping hole; then, not waiting for additional troops or supplies, they shot arrows of armor through and encircled opposing troops before they were fully aware that fighting had begun. From frozen stasis war had changed to quicksilver movement. The pendulum of war technology had swung from all advantages lying with defense, to all advantages lying with offense. Was this way of war applicable to opponents more formidable than the Poles, like the French? Warsaw was the first victim of massive bombing; was it as horrifying as everyone had feared? How were relations between the two totalitarians? What signs of Hitler's future plans? This was the overloaded agenda of the Berlin office. Oechsner insisted, and in late October shook me free for transfer from London to Berlin.

I journeyed from one warring capital to another by a narrowly prescribed way: from Harwich, England, aboard a Danish vessel, to Esbjerg, Denmark, and thence by train to Copenhagen and by ferry south to Germany. No one dared sleep crossing the North Sea. But for a narrow passage, it was filled with mines and warships programmed to sink anything that moved. There was no Sitzkrieg on the water. Thirty vessels were sunk in those waters the month I crossed. I relearned prayer that night.

In Copenhagen I stopped off for the night to exchange greetings with the lone UP reporter stationed there. I shouldn't have. He informed me that the Russians had just attacked Finland, and I was to remain with him in Copenhagen till further notice. The next morning the great Webb Miller flew through to Helsinki to cover that conflict. I volunteered to go and be his man Friday. I was told I was badly needed in Berlin; they were sending two reporters from London to help Miller. But I was clearly not needed enough in Germany; I was ordered to stay in Denmark, relaying copy from Finland until they could find someone else. It was not till the end of December that I was told to proceed as planned.

In the long Scandinavian nights I talked with reporters there, and others passing through, and discovered I had a serious financial problem. My colleagues told me I should be proud that, though I was new to the business, I was already owner of a superlative: I was the lowest-paid American reporter in Europe. I was on expense account in Denmark, but once I was settled in warring Germany with no expense account, my twenty-five dollars would vanish well before each payday. I sent a message to Flory in London asking for a ten-dollar raise. Back came the response: "DONT WORRY UNIPRESS NEVER LET REPORTER STARVE YET REGARDS—FLORY." Reassuring, but of no help to my household economy. Years later another UP alumnus put it well. "You can't run these big news businesses without money," said David Brinkley, "but you've got to give it to UP—they tried."

I arrived in Berlin on the night of January 1, 1940. Familiarity with the terrain enabled me to make my way through the blackout to the Continental Hotel near the Friedrichstrasse station. Next morning I went to the UP office. It was high in a building on Unter den Linden, the broad avenue that had been designed to be the main street of the city, but had later been overtaken and passed in popularity by the Kurfürstendamm, sparkling with shops and cinemas, in the west end of Berlin. Fred Oechsner introduced me to my five colleagues, as they checked in throughout the day. One of them, Richard Hottelet, was assigned to escort me to each of the two press conferences the working day was built around. They were held in the Wilhelmstrasse, the government street, which joined Unter den Linden at our corner.

The noon conference was held at the Foreign Office and was presided over by Dr. Paul Schmidt, a big, bovine, aggressive figure who sought by his pronouncements less to convince than to intimidate. He looked upon every question as hostile until proved innocent, causing some reporters from small countries to fear asking him questions at all. He was young and clever and managed to brazen his way unscathed through the war and later through war crimes trials, eventually becoming a popular lecturer on anti-Communism.

The second daily conference, in the early evening, was held across the street in Goebbels' propaganda palace, with Dr. Karl Böhmer presiding. Böhmer was trim, blond and intelligent. He was a star propagandist until the war in Russia turned bad. Then he was overheard expressing doubts about the Führer. He was promptly drafted into the army as a common soldier and sent to a combat unit on the Russian front where, as was intended, he was killed. However, the Böhmer I knew in 1940 was a slick and loyal dispenser of the Leader's line.

In the Sitzkrieg period there was little news to be had at these conferences. But one day early on my watch, the Böhmer conference blew up, the disturbance created by nothing Böhmer said but by my esteemed boss, Frederick Oechsner. A terrible thing had happened. The Russo-Finnish war ended, and our Webb Miller returned to London. One morning, Miller's dead body was found next to the tracks in a rail yard near a London railway station. Immediately it was a headline mystery in London as in America. But to Dr. Goebbels it was no mystery. His headline, all across the front page of the main newspaper, *Völkischer Beobachter,* screamed "Political Murder by British Secret Service!" The ensuing report told of Miller's book *I Found No Peace.* It quoted copiously from a chapter Miller wrote about his stay in India, in which he criticized the British roundly for their misbehavior in India. Skipping over Miller's chapter on Germany, which was scathing, the Goebbels story developed its thesis: in war the British feared that this honest, highly regarded journalist would tell horrid truths about warring Britain, as he had in his chapter on India. That would turn the Americans against Britain. So the Secret Service received orders to waylay and murder Miller when he was alone on a suburban train. That handy old standby "well-informed sources" was cited to support the story.

The next day at the press conference Böhmer was asked for further details. He answered that he would announce them as they became available. Whereupon Fred Oechsner stood in the audience of journalists and said, "Dr. Böhmer, as you do not know the latest news, and my colleagues wish to know it, I shall make the latest facts available to you." And he proceeded to read a coroner's report: There was conclusive evidence that Miller, exhausted from his Finnish assignment, took a drink at a pub before boarding the train to his suburban home. The coach was one of those whose every compartment had a door to the outside. Miller, alone, opened the door of his compartment, as the train moved out of the station, and stood on a running board and sought to relieve himself. A lurch, a stumble, a missed hand grip, and he fell down and hit his head on a switching lever, which fractured his skull and killed him.

When Oechsner began, Böhmer called him to order. Fred disregarded the summons and continued reading. Böhmer looked about for an assistant to go and stop Fred. Those present were enthralled listening to Oechsner and paid no attention to their boss. Böhmer then leapt from his table in the front of the theater, and ran to the row in whose middle Fred stood. He was blocked by the knees of reporters taking notes. Fred finished. Böhmer returned to his table, his face as red as a tomato. He scolded Oechsner from a distance, but his scolding had a tone of futility to it. The lie had been dealt a death blow in the presence of the press of the world. After that there was never a follow-up on the original story or any further mention of it in the German press. We were overjoyed. You didn't win successes like that very often in a country in which opinion was totally controlled.

About this time, Jack Fleischer arrived from America to join the staff. He came from a German family in Wisconsin and spoke German. I had been apartment-hunting in a feeble way till then. We joined forces and found a comfortable small apartment on the Wittenberg Platz near the social center of town, the Kurfürstendamm, and lived with some contentment amid the unpleasantness for most of two years of war.

CHAPTER NINETEEN

Living and Reporting in Berlin

Since sitting bug-eyed and horrified, aged seven, through *The Four Horsemen of the Apocalypse,* starring Rudolph Valentino, there was one thing about war I was sure of: it involved physical danger and want. It was a little deflating now to have left placid warring London and to arrive in placid warring Berlin. I did experience a mild discomfort in moving from the groaning restaurant boards and bright lights of ever-wonderful Copenhagen to the blackout and tight rationing of Germany. But one got used to the blackout amazingly quickly, and a half-dozen arrangements put hunger at a far distance. Our home offices diverted a few dollars of our pay to a firm in Portugal, which in return sent us weekly parcels of bacon, butter and coffee. The Propaganda Ministry maintained a posh restaurant for the foreign press on the Leipzigerstrasse in town, and the Foreign Office another on the Fasanenstrasse in the west end. And the expensive private restaurants, like Horcher's, the Taverna and Tusculum, were not subject to rationing at all.

I note in passing that this privilege was enjoyed only by the luxury restaurants. Diagonally across from my apartment on the Wittenberg Platz was an ordinary restaurant with an extraordinary name—"Alois," after the name of its owner, Alois Hitler. I lunched there occasionally for economy and to keep in loose touch with what the masses were getting. Let the record show that the Führer allowed no wartime favors to his half-brother: the helpings became smaller, the fish smellier and the potatoes spottier as the war progressed. Having introduced him to this chronicle, I should add that I never saw Alois in person. The story was that, during the 1936 Olympics, visiting journalists swarmed about him as the only available Hitler, asking his views on everything. Adolf grew worried that his sibling might be considered an authorized spokesman. So, when in 1939 war began, and new swarming was possible, the Führer gave Alois a personal subsidy and an order to disappear from view and run his enterprise as an absentee.

The only category of rationing that hurt the foreign guest was clothing. German textiles in the war were composed of imperfect synthetic materials, suspected by the populace to be predominantly wood fibers. They were adequate for one or two wearings only if you did not sit or walk in the rain. The cartoon magazine *Simplizissimus,* which was allowed within limits to be funny, displayed a strip cartoon of a man promenading happily in his new suit, then caught in rain, then nonplussed at seeing twigs and leaves beginning to sprout from his cuffs. My stay in Germany launched me on a period of ever deeper sartorial poverty, till by the end of the war I possessed mainly uniforms in a world sick to death of uniforms.

The most welcome mitigation of the hardships of war was a raise in salary, courtesy of the German Foreign Office. Colleagues advised me that if I took my twenty-dollar paycheck (after five dollars were diverted for food parcels) to a particular office in the bank, as they regularly did, I would be given an exchange rate more favorable than the standard one, magnifying my twenty to almost thirty dollars in spending value. I did so and chanced upon a discovery of some moment. To the teller I spoke well of a law that allowed this favor. With peculiar lack of guard he said, "Oh, it is probably not legal." I expressed astonishment. He said, "This special rate is by law available only to employees of foreign governments, diplomats and so on, not to private people like journalists. By word of mouth we were once told to let you have it too, 'till further notice.' But the written law still excludes you." With a cheery smile he confided, "So you are probably in violation of currency laws. If anyone high up comes to disapprove of you, he will know how to get you." I would discover that there were other little laws one was violating just by living in Germany. Your criminality would become effective when the Gestapo decided to make it so.

In this foremost warring nation, and in what was to be the bloodiest and costliest of wars, that risk—of having the authorities land on you for some hoked-up civil misdeed—was the nearest a war correspondent could get to danger. There was no getting close to shooting at a military front. Travel was restricted and access to military areas nonexistent. When German military campaigns were on, against Poland and later against others, leading reporters were taken on tightly organized tours, but only after victory, to defenses overrun or cities captured. As I was the lowest figure on the UP's eight-man totem pole, I was rarely assigned to such outings, and then only to the least important.

Interviews with high officials were just about impossible to come by. Hitler disappeared from public view for long periods, showing up only for formal speeches and occasions. Göring was unapproachable. Goebbels, the foremost communicator, allowed one interview to my knowledge; the remaining members of the political power structure were way off-limits. Once I thought I was getting close to a talk with Himmler, but it proved not to be close enough. I was assigned to cover the arrival of the Italian foreign minister, Count Galeazzo Ciano, Mussolini's son-in-law, at a secondary Berlin airport. It was considered a minor occasion, and I found myself walking unnoticed out to the grass beside the runway in the midst of the official reception committee. Himmler then showed up to serve as chief of the reception party and positioned himself about a yard in front of me. The first torture-master of the world looked like a pale office drudge, a deputy assistant keeper of accounts, pleased to be out of doors for the lunch hour. He bantered and joked with the other waiting officials, who knew to laugh, and was altogether the life of the little party. I told myself this opportunity would not arise again, and besides, all he could do was say no. So I tapped his sleeve and introduced myself and drew my breath to ask a general question about the state of things. Someone in the group muttered, *"Amerikanischer Journalist,"* and Himmler froze. A couple of SS uniforms moved between us and shoved me back. I got no interview but a few minutes later captured an unforgettable vision, a tableau of the handsome sun-bronzed Ciano exchanging embraces with the pale little man who would eventually arrange to have him shot.

There was one category of information available for risk-takers, but the risk to the sources of it became almost impossibly great. That was news of the Jews who remained in Germany. After the Kristallnacht pogrom of 1938 most of the wealth of German Jews was confiscated as a mass fine, so buying their way out of the Reich was no longer possible. Now they were required to wear the yellow cloth patch in the shape of the Star of David over their breasts and to carry internal passports with the large letter J stamped on every page. In shops they were required to stand aside and let every gentile who entered be served ahead of them. All Americans I knew—and indeed most foreigners from non-Axis countries—declined the privilege, though it frequently led to quarrels culminating in the shopkeepers' refusal to serve either the foreigners or the Jews.

One of the apartments on the landing above mine was occupied by two Jewish women who spoke perfect English. In a few conversations I discovered that they had come from wealthy families, and that their husbands had been arrested and disappeared in the horrors of the Kristallnacht. They begged me not to continue any form of relationship, for their fate was precarious. How precarious I found out after a few months. One day when I came home from work, the *Hauswart,* or janitor, told me there had been excitement on the floor above mine. I climbed the stairs to their landing and found the door of their apartment sealed with strips of tape on which was stamped, "Do not enter. Closed by order of the *Geheime Staatspolizei.*"

I could not imagine what had happened to them, but I acquired a close idea a short while later. I was coming home on the U-Bahn subway. Across the aisle from me sat a dowdily dressed young man with his hat brim pulled down to his eyebrows. He seemed to study me. At a stop he moved across and sat next to me. He had been sitting sideways. Now next to me the star of David patch on his breast pocket was visible. He asked me if I was a foreigner. I told him I was an American journalist. He asked me if I knew what was happening to Berlin's Jews now. I did not. He told me Jews were being picked up, a few at a time, in no clear order, sent in passenger trains to collection centers, of which the one in Berlin was the largest, and there packed into cattle cars and sent east, undoubtedly to concentration camps. At the time this was not generally known. The terrible "final solution"—mass executions of all Jews—had not yet been formulated at that famous meeting of Nazi chieftains in the mansion on the Wannsee Lake in Berlin. My informant asked if I would like regular installments of information, and I eagerly said I would. We agreed to meet on a designated subway platform every two weeks and take the same train. He would not tell me his name or address or anything about himself. We met in this way twice. After that he did not show up again.

I was unsure what to do. It had become clear to me by this time that my career in Germany would end with my being expelled for some reason, but I was, after a few months, not ready for it yet; I did not know enough. So I did not hazard sending a story out by telegraph. I went to the American Embassy, but was told that they knew all I did and more. I composed a "mailer"—an article with no time urgency, sent to the home office by mail—and sent it off unsigned. The story remained difficult to pursue for moral reasons. The Nazis were choosing victims at this time for some reason, and in my two cases I feared the reason was me. Jews were watched, and reporters were too. When contacts between the two were observed, the Jews subsequently disappeared. I did not feel easy being the unwilling finger man for gangsters in control of a government.

Generally, information was hard to come by in wartime Germany. William L. Shirer, whom I thought to be the most knowledgeable of the Berlin correspondents, and who worked then as a CBS broadcast reporter, wrote later, when the documents were opened after the war, "It is surprising how little we who worked in Germany knew." Acquiring that little called for two talents: keeping antennae ever extended and sensitive to catch little passing clues or a momentarily flickering shadow, and a lively intuition to guess what larger event those little clues and shadows portended.

That sounds simple, but I had yet to learn the mechanics of it. One day in the spring of 1940, in my fourth month in Berlin, I was walking down Unter den Linden and spotted a soldier approaching in a uniform I had never seen before. He wore a billed, woolen cap with side flaps that buttoned on top and, when unbuttoned, became ear muffs. He wore hobnailed boots that clacked sharply on the sidewalk. The brief mystery was settled when he drew close, and a badge in the shape of an edelweiss mountain flower on his lapel became clear. Over the next several days I saw more of these alpine *Jäger* in ones and twos near the Anhalter station, which received trains from the south. I was casually curious as to what mountain troops were doing coming from the Bavarian Alps to flat Berlin. I surmised that they must be in town for some ceremonial purpose, for there were no mountains near Berlin or north of it.

My languid imagination, made lazy by the Phony War since the conquest of Poland, failed to tell me that there were indeed mountains north of Berlin—in Norway. A little excogitation might have reminded me that Germany received its iron ore, a life-and-death resource in wartime, from Sweden by ships that descended the coast of Norway protected by Norwegian territorial waters. I should have remembered that, since the Russo-Finnish war, the British navy had been playing around those waters. A daring Winston Churchill, First Lord of the Admiralty, might well be tempted to mine the waters and interrupt the flow. And a daring Adolf Hitler would not sit by and let that happen.

Early on April 9, reporters were called to the Foreign Office in the Wilhelmstrasse and told that, indeed, Churchill had set out to mine the waters, and even to land troops and occupy Norway. For once the Nazis told the truth about their motivation for an aggression. Germany, it was announced, was beating the British to it, invading Denmark and landing troops at a half-dozen towns in Norway. I had seen clues to this in the strays from the Anhalter station all that week and had acted on that conspicuous evidence with the alertness of a mental retardee.

For an hour I considered resigning as unsuited for journalism. Then I remembered that other, more gifted reporters had missed as badly, and even the British, with the advantage of clear aerial observation of gathering German warships in the north, had failed to see what was afoot. Everyone now knew that the Sitzkrieg was over; watch out for the Blitzkrieg.

CHAPTER TWENTY

All Over on the Western Front

May 10, 1940. I was awakened by a phone call from the office just before dawn. "Fred wants all hands in the office faster than awhile ago. The radio is playing Wagnerian music with an interruption every five minutes to say an important communiqué is coming." I turned my set onto the BBC on shortwave to hear us scooped on our own story. The newsreader cited reports from Holland and Belgium that German troops had crossed their borders. I switched back to Berlin Radio. While I was shaving, the music stopped, and a thunderous silence prevailed. Then the full press fanfare, to become familiar several times a day. Then the portentous voice: "*Das Oberkommando der Wehrmacht gibt bekannt. . . .*" The High Command of the armed forces announced that after twenty-two years there was no longer quiet on the Western front. Before dawn that day German troops had begun an offensive the length of the Allied front and in Holland and Belgium. There was good progress. In ten more minutes I was in the office, standing about with six others, watching the seventh and eighth trying to find fresh words with which to rewrite the official communiqué. We were war correspondents a long, long way from the war, with less information to impart about what German troops were doing than the BBC was providing from the other side.

But on fields where Germany had suffered defeat a quarter-century before, triumph now trod on the heels of triumph and the Wehrmacht wanted witnesses, so foreign reporters were soon welcomed in frequent groups to admire the acquisition of each trophy.

Of all our correspondents far from the war, I, the newest employee, was the farthest. But I chanced upon a way to get a little closer. As the caboose on the UP train I was given the trivial assignment of going to the Propaganda Palace's theater each week for a preview of the next week's newsreel, to see if it contained anything worth reporting. The same department offered the week's batch of "*PK Berichte*"—reports from the scene of operations written by German Propaganda Kompanie reporters attached to the armed forces. The reports were generally mere propaganda puffs, and the foreign press disregarded them. But with the war on again, the PK reporters competed with one another to be more vivid and informative in order to get printed—that way lay promotion—and their efforts were now offered daily and hourly, not weekly. I began collecting and studying them closely.

I was on the night shift that week, which meant that I was therefore responsible for writing each evening's "night lead." Usually this bit of copy was simply a rewording of the day's main news for American papers that needed fresh language for next editions. I was able to assemble my crumbs from the PK reports to make the night leads fresh, informative stories. For example, several reports described the taking of an unnamed strongpoint. From details it was clear to me that the target was Eben-Emael, the famous Belgian fort I had read about in WW I literature. Other fragments described the first use of airborne troops, without stating where they were used. I dared to report that Eben-Emael had been taken by parachute troops. I was even able to recount how a mere seventy-eight soldiers had landed on the casemates, deposited explosives in the gun slits and locked the Belgian soldiers inside, effectively ending Belgian resistance. I was delighted at being accused by Captain Sommerfeld, Goebbels' military analyst, of scooping the military censors. I reveled in being mysterious and in not telling him that my stuff had come from handouts issued by his own office.

My scooplets got the facts right but their meaning dead wrong. I thought that the taking of Eben-Emael was decisive. I, and most of the world, thought that Hitler intended to use some variant of the old Schlieffen Plan to defeat the Allies. But instead of swinging like a sickle through Belgium and down the French coast—Schlieffen plan like—to seize Paris from the unprepared south, the Germans snipped through the Allied line at the handle of the sickle and encircled and eliminated the best Allied troops around Dunkirk. Lacking effective defenders, Paris fell without the Wehrmacht's firing a shot within its walls.

I sat covering the war from a desk in Berlin, envious of my seniors as they went one by one out to the fronts. At last one day, Oechsner called me in. "Get your Richard Harding Davis clothes on," he said, "You are going to the war, or what is left of it."

What was left was pretty rich. We were flown to a military airport on the Rhine, and there bused across a pontoon bridge to what appeared to be a garden of recently slain, half-buried super dinosaurs or parts of dinosaurs—rounded, boulderlike, dark green surfaces bulging out from the earth. These were the casemates and pillboxes of the amazing Maginot Line. Deep in the earth below were barracks and mess halls for thousands of troops, huge storerooms, elevators to move ammunition up to guns, all air-conditioned and strung together on hundreds of miles of underground railways.

As we bused down the supply roads in the rear, this line of apparitions seemed to go on forever; but as everyone now knew, the flaw was that it did not go on far enough. The line ran from France's Swiss border to its border with Belgium. There it stopped short. The idea was, when war came, Belgium would join France in defending the rest of the way to the coast. In fact, when the Nazis were able to reoccupy the Rhineland in 1936 without France's taking action, Belgian faith in France collapsed, and the Belgian government declared neutrality; it would not help France or anyone in a war. The French then hesitated to build the line on to the North Sea, lest they appear to be shutting out a Belgium that might favorably change its mind in a crisis. Or so it was said. But I think the main deterrent to finishing the line was a failure of the French will to go on building this extremely expensive and uniquely elaborate fortification.

We were at length led to the heart of the matter: a section not half a mile long, where the massive reptile's surface was terribly broken into huge fragments, some of them perhaps ten feet across, and we looked through twisted and broken reinforcing rods into the dark interior of the beast. The message, delivered by Captain Sommerfeld, was that the Wehrmacht had taken the Maginot Line, not from the rear, as all were saying, but in a mighty frontal attack.

It was an impressive feat, burnishing—as was intended—the prestige of the German armed forces with the thought that nothing could withstand their ferocity, not the mightiest fortification ever conceived, and certainly not (if the thought should cross someone's mind) eighteen miles of English Channel.

That night I wrote out my piece about the day's experience, pretty much accepting what we had been told, and sent it off to Berlin. Later, sipping wine at a French inn, I began to wonder. Next morning we were driven back across the pontoon bridge to look at German fortifications, called the Siegfried Line by the British, and the West Wall by the Germans. The pillboxes seemed small by comparison. Their surfaces were smooth and unscarred. The ground around them was, as far as sight could reach, without a single crater or other mark. Now, it was reasonable to think that, if the Germans had attacked, the French with their mighty guns would at least for a while have responded with fierce fire, in which case there should have been scratches or gouges or worse on the German side. In fact there were none. Back on the French side we took a long second look at the blasted French fortification. A German captain of Pioneers (engineers, sappers) stood by to answer questions. I maneuvered him out of earshot of the others and asked, "You must have had to truck in a tremendous load of explosives to get this job done?" He, a good engineer but new to the propagandist art, said, "Many loads. It was the biggest demolition job I have ever done." So, the hole in the Maginot Line had been blasted the easy way, after it had been isolated from the rear and emptied, and not in the course of a German frontal attack. Later I wrote a corrective story, but it was subject to the established journalistic injustice that a correction never catches up with the original error.

So, what many saw as Europe's twenty-six years' war was over, beginning in 1914 and ending—after an interval—in 1940. Of course Britain remained, but her situation was hopeless. It was only a matter of time before she withered on the vine or was casually plucked. This was said all over Germany and most of Europe as an accepted truism. No one spelled out exactly how this withering or plucking would happen. It turned out, when the facts were known, that Hitler had not thought things out beyond this point either. For the moment, no matter. Hitler was at the high-water mark of an awesome career.

A bizarre small episode made this hiatus personally memorable. One deep summer afternoon, when I had completed my shift at four P.M., I decided to walk home from Unter den Linden, turning left into the Wilhelmstrasse, the government street, down it until just past the Reichskanzlei, the Chancellery where Hitler lived and worked, then right into the Voss Strasse, which formed the long side of the building, and thence into the great Tiergarten Park on the way to the west end of the city. When I made the right turn into the Voss Strasse, I walked on the other side of the street from the Chancellery. There was a single door, a kind of French window, in the side of the great building, about ten feet about street level. As I walked, it opened, and out stepped Adolf Hitler. He took two steps down the ledge below the door and looked down the length of the structure in an interested way, as though there was something specific he wanted to see that could only be observed from here.

It was Saturday and summer, and not a soul was around to check impressions with, just the conqueror of Europe and I, about thirty yards apart. I froze in my place. Could it really be Hitler, or was it a double? Later research revealed the existence of no double. None of the tremendous documentation discovered since has revealed the existence of any. He wore black trousers and a jacket of a special hue of light brown, famous as being the uniform reserved for the Führer alone. His gestures were Hitler's: as he observed, he casually rubbed his hands together in a kind of hand-washing gesture, often seen in films of him at ease in his eyrie in Berchtesgaden.

I knew that Hitler, the painter of houses, was absorbed by monumental architecture. He had given Albert Speer, his architect (and designer of monumental displays that made the annual Nazi rally in Nuremberg so impressive and frightening), the mission to build this new Chancellery, allowed him only two years to complete it and was immensely pleased with the result. I surmised that some detail of the structure had been discussed over lunch, and the great one had seized upon a safe moment of an idle afternoon to open a door and take a good long look at whatever that feature was.

This train of thought took seconds. I crossed the Voss Strasse and headed for him, resolved to say something to him even if it was only hello. As I approached the foot of the building, he saw me, turned, mounted the couple of steps and reentered the building, and the door closed behind him. I paced about for a few minutes, thinking there must be something I should do, but finally deciding there was nothing. The incident has no moral and no point. It simply tickles my fancy to think that the least of America's journalists and the conqueror of the world stood face to face, maybe ten yards apart, for one moment at the peak of his fortunes.

The incident comes back to me especially sharply, for not long ago I revisited Berlin for about the tenth time, this time specifically to take a nostalgic look at the Voss Strasse, in what was then the Communist sector of Berlin. It was still there, but the Wilhelmstrasse it joined was renamed the Grotewohl Strasse after the Communist German leader. And of the massive Chancellery there was no trace. Lest someone in the future seek to make a shrine of it, the Russians had left not a stone or a fragment of one. It was a vast area of arid earth with not a blade of grass on it and no indication that there was ever any structure there. The plain rose very slowly to a rather low apex, where a metallic stopper, as for a manhole, forbade entrance to what long ago was a bunker to shelter the Führer. There was no indication, no plaque, no sign to say the words, and it is not in the desert, yet the spirit of the words was there:

"My name is Ozymandias, king of kings:
Look on my works, ye Mighty, and despair!"
Nothing beside remains. Round the decay
Of that colossal wreck, boundless and bare
The lone and level sands stretch far away.

CHAPTER TWENTY-ONE

The Not Quite Victory

My first six months or so in Berlin, doing at last what it seemed I had spent forever preparing for—foreign corresponding—kept me in a condition of excitement that precluded depression about the state of things. Reporting about the invasions of Scandinavia, the low countries and France was sports reporting. One focused on technique and it was beautiful. But this frame of mind could not last. My own small role in covering these events was too minute for technique to continue to be absorbing. And the dark meaning of the string of triumphs for the Prince of Hatred became insistent. He was no longer just one figure in history; he alone was in control of it.

My old miseries advertised their continued existence with the fate of my few Jewish acquaintances. Now, in the autumn of 1940, with the fascinations of the fast decisive ground war over, the new terrors dealt by the Nazis to my late home, Britain, brought the miseries back in force.

We returned from our trip to the Maginot Line by bus. At one place we were delayed for an hour by a strange congestion. A big river vessel, a coal barge mounted on sets of wheels and towed by two tractors, filled the road. When it first came into sight, Sommerfeld leapt to his feet in the front of the bus and declaimed, "No cameras. Take no notes. Whoever mentions this in a report will be drawn and quartered!" This was the first evidence that an invasion of Britain was being planned. The barge was being towed from one river to another that could float it down to a Channel port. The barge nearly filled the roadway and had to be edged to the shoulder before we could pass.

This incident illustrated how little Hitler had planned beyond the conquest of France. He soon learned that he was in no way prepared to launch a seaborne invasion. The craft for carrying troops to land on beaches had not yet been invented. (When they were, the British invented them, the U.S. Army Corps of Engineers designed them, and Andrew Jackson Higgins of New Orleans, Louisiana, a maker of pleasure craft, made them.) Canal barges were laughably inadequate and sank or broke up in tests in the ever-unruly waters of the English Channel. Anyhow, the German Navy was not nearly strong enough to protect its invading craft from the mighty British Royal Navy. Hitler's attempt to take control of the air over Britain began in late July 1941. In August and September the attack intensified and ran into a resistance that could be called a battle, the Battle of Britain. The R.A.F. proved surprisingly strong, so that aspect of invasion had to be abandoned, too. The Luftwaffe was ordered to switch goals from winning mastery of the air to, in Hitler's words, making terror attacks on the population, mainly of London.

This was something new under the sun; a battle of airplanes and support for airplanes, to be decided wholly in the air and by the morale of the civilian victims below. Reporting it was very frustrating for a correspondent in Germany because there were no clues to be sensed. We were wholly dependent on official communiqués, and they told only of the wreaking of perfect hell on the cities of Britain. Day after day and night after night, the rain, the cloudbursts, of bombs on London continued and intensified. With no other information, one had to think Britain was finished. Its armed forces had been chewed up beyond early repair in France and Belgium. Its supply lines were hemorrhaging more each day in another battle we had little useful information about, the U-boat war on shipping, now made more effective by Germany's acquisition of submarine bases from the Arctic to Spain. The pressure being brought to bear by Germany was altogether too much.

There is a problem about learning what really happened by reading history. The trouble is, we know beforehand how each chapter turns out, and therefore the outcomes seems inevitable. Rising generations since WW II tend to see Hitler's defeat as certain, because that is what happened. Well, it was far from inevitable. In the fall of 1940, Britain was surely going to be bombed and starved out of the war. Europe would belong to Hitler. America would be courted and soft-soaped, isolationism would be nurtured by well-financed German-American cultural societies and business wooed with contracts. Russia, already terrified by Germany's triumphs at arms, would be intimidated into inaction until Hitler was ready for it.

For me the result was deep depression. I had acquired some standing as a frequent drinker and carouser in Oxford. I won tenure in those pursuits in Berlin. With no way to get a handle on reporting the air war or the war at sea, I began to lose my edge in my work. I became passive. I rewrote communiqués with the usual disclaimers, but I made no effort to get information on my own. The Hitler mystique was beyond analyzing. It was a fact. There was magic about the man. The gods or Luck must be totalitarian, for They or It loved this man. He never lost. He was predestined to win. Or so it seemed.

Late in August, a pinpoint of light in the darkness. Air raid sirens sounded, the first time I had heard them in Berlin. I thought it was a false alarm; to reach Berlin, British planes had to fly five times as far as German planes did from French airfields to London. I did not think they could carry bomb loads that far. A distant sound of thumps announced that they had made the distance, but the bomb load was indeed tiny and the aim was not very good. They damaged a shack in the far suburb of Babelsberg. Still, the impertinently aggressive spirit was heartening.

In September sporadic British attacks on Berlin damaged somewhat more impressive targets. One night in September, when I was working the deadman shift, a bomber came deafeningly close to the ground. I ran up the stairs to the roof and took a place at the parapet just in time to see another plane illuminate Unter den Linden with a string of firebombs dropped right down its middle for about a mile. The bomb that landed in front of our building gave me the immediate incentive and enough light to make it back to the roof door in a single bound, whence I descended six flights of stairs as though they were a chute. Once on the ground floor, I ran out toward the fizzing and blinding firebomb display, turned to the sky and shouted, "More! bigger! more! bigger!" then ran back into the shelter of the building. The janitor who appeared from the cellar told me I was verrückt.

Three developments were changing the atmosphere radically in Berlin that long winter of 1940–1941. One, the Germans were bitterly disappointed. They had won the war as it was formatted twenty-six years before, yet the damned British refused to face the fact and clung on like the remnant of a bad case of flu. Two, to everyone's surprise, the British air attacks, though far from seriously wounding, were weekly more effective. Newspapers in England were even saying the Battle of Britain had passed its climax by the New Year and had become the first battle lost by Hitler. Officials we reporters dealt with lost their composure and became increasingly irritable. Three, the U.S. was becoming a factor. When France fell, Roosevelt commenced an enormous buildup of the U.S. Navy. As the Battle of Britain neared its climax, FDR announced the deal to provide Britain with fifty U.S. destroyers. At the same time, selective service was legislated, the beginning of the creation of an American armed force of wartime size. As the year ended, Roosevelt announced a plan to provide Britain with what it needed to fight the war through a so-called lend-lease arrangement. American reporters in Germany, once carefully wooed, were that winter converted very nearly to enemy status. FDR was transforming the U.S. from the sulky backwater I had left to a country boldly assuming responsibilities for the condition of man in the world.

At first we were allowed to report the British raids freely. UP kept an open line to Zurich, our relay point to New York, and one man sat at the telex writing descriptions sent down by another on the roof and phoned in by others from the streets. Then the Propaganda Ministry ordered all communication with the outside world broken the moment a British raid began. We could do no sight-seeing of bomb damage on our own; all foreign reporters had to move together in a bus supplied by the Propaganda Ministry. Finally even the bus was discontinued, and we were allowed to report only the text of the official communiqué about a raid. Anything further would be considered espionage.

Later in the year 1941, as the raids became more effective, German officials decided to do something drastic about a feature of the city that made it easy for bombers to orient themselves and find their targets with accuracy— the so-called East–West Axis, a very broad miles-long boulevard running through the middle of the conurbation. It was to be camouflaged to appear from the sky to be a network of streets leading nowhere. Over months, square miles of netting were erected on tent poles over the area. Just before the massive work was completed, a rare windstorm hit the city and, in a few hours, made a ruin of one of the greatest works of gargantuan art since the hanging gardens of Babylon. At least the god of weather was not a totalitarian.

Early in 1941, German sensitivity about the raids, and growing German anger at America, came to a head in an incident that I happened to be in the midst of. I was working the all-night shift, trying to doze on a cot in Oechsner's office. At about 5 A.M. the door opened, and a dozen large men entered the room and made for the desks. I asked the one who appeared to be their leader what this meant. He drew from his watch pocket a metal disk on a chain and held it up to me: "*Geheime Staatspolizei*" it read. He shoved a chair against a bare wall and, for the first time, spoke: "Sit there and keep still." I asked again for an explanation and he said to shut up. For about an hour the silent search continued, the only sounds being those of shuffling papers and an occasional whispered communication among the raiders, as all the contents of each desk were carefully examined and placed in neat piles.

I accumulated moral support. The cleaning lady came in and was ordered into a chair beside me. Then one of our "Eurocont" editors—one of the Ger-

man staff who sold and distributed UP's world service to German newspapers—appeared and had to take a place with us. Oskar Reschke came in. Oskar, our star German reporter, had been called up and was now in uniform,
assigned to the signal corps. He wanted to borrow twenty marks till payday. I
gave him the money and whispered for him to get the hell out of there if he
could; this was the Gestapo. Oddly, none of our visitors paid any mind to the
one figure to whom suspicion might be attached: a German in uniform working in the Wehrmacht's communication department, now seeming to share
confidences with an American journalist. Oskar moved silently to the door and
disappeared.

About two hours later the shuffling silence was broken by the telephone
ringing. The leader told me to answer it, but to speak only in German, not one
word of English. On the line was Dorothy Oechsner, calling, I learned later, to
tell me Fred would be coming in late this morning. The following colloquy
took place:

"Good morning, Howard."

"*Guten morgen.*"

"I wanted to tell you . . . what did you say?"

"*Ich sagte bloss guten morgen.*"

"*Guten morgen,* yourself. I . . . why don't you speak English?"

"*Das darf ich nicht, gnae' Frau.*" The chief was leaning over my shoulder.

"Why in heaven's name not?"

"*Auch das darf ich nicht sagen.*"

"Oh, I think I see!"

She hung up. The main man saw his order did not work. But any reason
for secrecy soon ceased to be. The antiquated little tape machine next to the
copy desk, providing German official news to us, began to wheeze and cough.
In a moment the words formed, letter by letter: "On suspicion of espionage
Richard Hottelet, an American journalist for United Press, has been arrested."

Dick Hottelet was of German origin, had done graduate work in Berlin
and spoke German better than most Germans. His anti-Nazism was fierce, and
he made no effort to hide it. When the ban on reporting the results of air raids
took effect, he disregarded it, and went bicycling all over the city to see what
had really happened. That was the public reason for the Nazis' arresting him.
The real reason, I believe, was that the FBI in New York had recently arrested
two German journalists on well-grounded charges of espionage. The Nazis
locked up Hottelet to make an exchange of prisoners. Later in the year the exchange was made, and Hottelet went home. Fate compensated him for his ordeal when he was recruited to the most desirable news staff in the war, that of
CBS News. Years later, as the war was winding down, he became the first
American newsman to drive into the German capital.

CHAPTER TWENTY-TWO

Play Time

One did not work all the time in wartime Germany, just almost all the time. The way I filled my little free time during my two years there underwent a marked moral deterioration, paralleling that of the nation's life in general. At first I did commendable things, went to the theater or the opera some nights, and out to the Olympic stadium other days. The stadium was open to the public; I had brought my track shoes along and had osmotic satisfaction running in the footsteps of Owens and Towns. I even leapt the same hurdles Spec Towns had crossed on his way to the gold.

As weariness, more spiritual than physical, set in, I spent more time in the company of bottles, in bars or restaurants or at home. With our special imported luxuries to barter, Fleischer and I were able to keep the house supplied with drink. And also with girls. For a young bachelor that metaphor of earthly heaven applies, being a child locked up all night in a sweets shop. The men were gone to the armed forces. The women were restless. I was needful. Particularly as the war looked like dragging on after the British refusal to quit, the spirit of the time and place became that of *après nous le déluge,* a mood that loosens morals and inhibitions like nothing else. Because my romantic adventures were a large part of my life and well describe the tone of the time, I shall dare some details.

My dolce vita began, oddly, not with one of those most abundant, a German girl, but with an unusual outlander, a girl most English. I was dozing at the desk near midnight when Edward called. That is not his real name. He was and is a prominent, altogether married colleague who will be allowed to sort out his love life without my narrative adding to the problem. He said, "Howard, be a prince and help me. I am sitting here at the bar of the Hotel Eden with a lovely little English girl. She is blonde, fresh and, I think, willing. But it is a double date. Her friend is a German girl. The German girl's male escort has had a spat with her and just walked out. So I have two girls on my hands. The German girl is very charming and pretty. If you could come over here and make a bonding with her, it would free Peggy and me, and well, you know, you'd have a friend for life."

I did know, and when my shift ended, I went to the Hotel Eden. But the German girl had acquired a new escort and departed. Edward and Peggy were nuzzling one another alone at the bar. Having arrived, I felt it only polite to sit with them and have one drink before going home. Peggy was all Edward said, including willing. In addition she was tipsy. She transferred her attention to me on her other side, put her hand on my thigh, asked where I had been all her life and began to cuddle. Edward made it clear that his lifelong friendship promised me had ended. I felt that the honorable thing to do was to go, which I did, but with a chit of paper bearing her phone number that Peggy had slipped into my pocket.

I phoned the next day, and on my day off we met. At her request we met on the Wittenberg Platz just outside my apartment house; she would never tell me where she lived. She wore a brimmed felt hat almost on the back of her head—the kind English schoolgirls often wore, the brim turned down in the front. Her face was a bright little girl's face, and her expression was sweet, happy, blue-eyed, blond innocence. It misrepresented the lady within. I recognized her character almost instantly. A fellow Mertonian from a few years before me, named Christopher Isherwood, had spent time in Berlin and written a novel about his experiences titled *Goodbye to Berlin.* After the war, the central story became a very good play, *I Am a Camera,* then a musical show and later a memorable film by the name of *Cabaret.* The leading figure was Sally Bowles, but it might just as well have been Peggy Brock, who met me in the square.

Peggy had come to Germany on a school outing and been charmed by this *gemütliche,* orderly country. She was charmed also by handsome young men in sleek uniforms and was at just the right stage of development to be captivated. One of them besieged her, slept with her and impregnated her. On her return to England, her parents were outraged and virtually disowned her. She fled back to Germany and gave birth to a baby girl in Berlin. Peggy was miserly with details, but these few were coaxed out of her. The man was an SS officer. She found reason to become disgusted with Nazis generally, and with him in particular, and refused his offer of marriage. War caught her in Berlin. His family begged to be allowed to take care of the child, and in return paid for an apartment plus an allowance for Peggy. I don't know exactly how she decided to dedicate her life to pleasure, but it seems not a difficult transition for people to make. Anyhow, I became a willing way station in the progress of a lovely young female rake.

From the square we went up to my apartment for a drink. Half-way through the drink this little girl stood and began quietly taking off her clothes. She saw my astonished look and said, "Don't be shy about it. You know what we are here for." In a moment we were both naked. Afterward we dressed, had another drink and walked to the Ristorante Roma for dinner. We returned and went to bed for the night. At about 8:30 A.M. Fleischer arrived home from the all-night shift and found in his kitchen the foundation of a wonderful dream, a pretty little blond girl, nude but for shoes and a kitchen apron that covered little, preparing breakfast. "Holy whatever!" I heard him say, "I must have done something right." From my bedroom I warned him that he was addressing my property. I allowed him to have breakfast with us.

It was a fling and not meant by either party to last. When it died away, the beautiful Ruth Raven arrived from Munich. She had seen in some paper a list of American reporters stationed in Berlin, and sent a note suggesting that I visit her. I could not, so she visited me. We cohabited pleasurably for a week. I was relieved to find that she was a pretty girl I could take or leave; obsession had vanished.

In periods of drought my roommate Fleischer rendered aid. He had a way of drinking heavily at dinner in a restaurant somewhere, charming some lonely *Mädel* into coming home with him, then passing out and leaving me to provide hospitality. His most spectacular delivery was "Lilo of the Legs." Lilo (the name is short for Liselotte, which is short for Luise Charlotte) was a waitress at Goebbels' restaurant for foreign correspondents. She was tall, statuesque, with startlingly shapely legs, which she displayed to advantage by wearing ridiculously short skirts and carrying trays the long way through and around the tables to ensure a maximum audience. Her silken pins were well described by the words of a Broadway play, "Only the floor kept them from going on forever." She was also flighty and carefree about distributing her favors. Well, one night whom should Fleischer deposit on the sofa facing me—handsome legs crossed, knees a short distance from my chin, skirt high up her thigh, with a look on her face that said, "I've come all this way; what are you going to do to amuse me?"—but Lilo.

I remember making a gross beginning; I placed my hand on the patch of thigh above her stocking. I then thought to myself, "That is really crude, Smith." So I removed my hand. Lilo worked up a pretty little frown and said, "Put it back, I like it." After exchanging favors in bed, she said to me, "You are so polite, so gentlemanly, you don't make me do all those mad things my Polish boyfriend likes." She shouldn't have said that. I spent the rest of the night learning things Polish boys know that American boys don't. She reminded me of the saying of a famous American comedian: "Sex is dirty only when done right."

Not all my adventures were amusing or provided grist for male bragging. There was Giselle, an English girl, a dancer who did not believe war was going to break out and, like Peggy, woke up one morning to find herself a hostage in a hostile country. For some reason she was released from internment early, creating suspicions among diplomats about her patriotism. She too was English and blonde. She was dainty and cultured. Her figure was closer to perfection than any I had seen since Dietrich at Cannes. I first saw her in a bathing suit at a swimming place on the Wannsee Lake and was breathtaken. Her taste in clothing made her always and in whatever look beautifully got up. She shared an apartment with two German showgirls. She was very lonely for the company of her kind, and American was near enough to it.

I forget how we met; I think it was on a double date. Then I took her to dinner alone, and what I regarded as a fluffy little affair developed. It grew to full size, alarmingly to me. I was still in a mood for flings, but she wanted the real thing. After a month I began to back out. I had not meant for her to take me that seriously. I stopped calling her. One of the German girls who lived with her came to see me to tell me that I was cruel to leave Giselle in loneliness. Worse, an American priest residing in Berlin asked me to visit him, and he told me she had come to see him about rescuing our relationship. I phoned her, and we met again for a dinner, but it only confirmed that neither of us was enjoying it. Our date was not healing but blamatory. I decided that my only course was to break off clear, which I did. Nonetheless, I am still immersed in guilt every time I think of her. After the war I asked about her and was told that she had died in an air raid.

Like a child in a candy shop, I found that excess began to cloy. Children with no discipline are unhappy, and so it was with this moral child. I began to crave substance and durability in a relationship. I had no idea I was close to finding it.

CHAPTER TWENTY-THREE

New Departures

Hitler and I made radical decisions to change our luck at about the same time in the spring of 1941. The Führer saw he could not invade Britain or bomb it into submission under the stubborn new management of Winston Churchill, so he decided to strangle the island by methodically severing its supply lines. In WW I German U-boats had almost accomplished this from limited North Sea bases. Now, with bases ranging from the Arctic to Spain, Hitler thought he would surely succeed. Meanwhile he turned eastward to establish his ownership of all continental Europe and also to seize his once and always goal, Russia, as a source of oil, raw materials and slave labor for the long haul.

The Hitler magic was still there. He intimidated Romania and Bulgaria into admitting his troops. When Yugoslavia bridled, he attacked and went through that country like a purgative, then into Greece, which he soon seized, throwing the British out.

My own (to me, far-reaching) decision was to seek other employment. Salary was a factor, but not the only, or even the decisive, one. I wanted scope. On a large staff I got only about 10 percent of the opportunities offered for covering the war. A lone correspondent, say for the *Chicago Tribune,* got all 100 percent. War, bloody war, a horror for mankind, is horror plus opportunity for reporters. I wanted more of it.

The New York Herald Tribune had closed its office. I phoned the editor in New York and offered to reopen it on a string basis: I would be paid a small retainer, then a fee per article. He thought it over and decided against it. Then something most unexpected turned up in my favor.

Bill Shirer of CBS had made a habit of calling me at the UP office just before a broadcast to get the latest news. When he left Berlin, CBS sent a correspondent named Harry Flannery to replace him, and Flannery took up where Bill left off. Flannery had a fine radio voice but no experience as a reporter; he could not speak German and knew little about Germany. At his suggestion we met, lunched and over time grew rather close. He needed the background I could provide.

The Propaganda Ministry, which understood the power of radio from having witnessed Shirer's immense success at using it, sought to win over Flannery from the start. He was given tips on breaking stories. When the Germans landed in Crete, they flew him to the island and set up facilities for him to conduct an exclusive interview with their prize paratrooper, the boxer Max Schmeling. They also let him have an exclusive interview with a fine old innocent who had chanced into their hands, the author P. G. Wodehouse. Although Flannery abhorred Nazism, he failed to notice that some of his broadcasts were taking on an unintended slant.

His boss in New York, the famous Paul White, was not pleased with Flannery's output. Harry showed me a telegram saying his broadcasts were too "wooden" and suggesting he "take a leaf from Shirer's book." One day Harry told me White had suggested he hire an assistant with stronger background to share broadcasts and advise him. Would I be interested? The pay would be $100 a week. I agreed then and there, but asked whether a voice test would not be required. He said, "Have you ever heard Bill Shirer? Next to his squeaky voice yours would be considered mellifluous."

Oechsner was enraged. He said UP had made a big original investment in bringing me to Europe, and it was immoral for me to leave after little more than a year. I said it cost UP nothing. I was already in Europe, and the investment, making me the lowest-paid American in Europe, was not impressive. But it was no use arguing. When he told me he would have me blackballed by every news organization in the U.S., I stopped talking and left his office.

About that time, Guido Enderis, Berlin chief of *The New York Times,* called me in. He had heard of my switch and offered me a job that would dovetail with my CBS position. Together the two jobs put my value at $160 a week, more than five times what UP was paying, which put an end to all argument with Fred. I had a genuine affection for him, so I am pleased to report that, when we met a couple of years later, he conceded that I was right. He himself had left journalism and spent the rest of his working life in the State Department.

For a while my news broadcasts were a sometime thing. Harry did almost all of them himself. I watched from the control room at the transmitter in the cellar of a building on Adolf Hitler Platz. I sympathized. His ego had been bruised, and he felt his career was threatened, so he clung to every chance to rescue his reputation—to no avail. He was told to give the assignment entirely to me and to come home. Much later, when he was working in public relations in Washington, we resumed our friendship.

I was alarmed at suddenly having top responsibility in a warring capital for a great network. When we knew one another better, I asked Paul White how he came to have faith in an unknown. He said, "I knew you were well brought up, from a top school." I said, "Oxford?" He said, "No, United Press." That year and next, he hired Collingwood, Hottelet and Bill Downs, all from UP. Where did Paul White himself get his start? You need not ask.

Broadcasting to America twice a day, I first came to hear the voice of the champion, Edward R. Murrow, from London. Unlike White's other charges, Murrow had never worked in news. He was a bright, handsome young man on the executive ladder at CBS. As European director, he had the job of arranging for famous people, like Winston Churchill, to speak on CBS. When prewar news grew exciting, he arranged for well-known newspaper reporters to do occasional broadcasts. One night, when all reporters were busy with their own work, he did a report on a session of Parliament himself, and a blinding star was born. He had a talent for finding the essence of things, describing it in thrifty but fine prose, in a voice said to be "the way God would sound if He were Edward R. Murrow." It was intimidating to follow his handsome contributions on the air with my puny, censor-riddled efforts from Berlin.

My dual job made an interesting combination. UP had trained me to write with the utmost compactness to save on cable tolls. My first story for the *Times* was written that way. Enderis handed it back to me and said, "Spread it out. Take your time. Loosen up." I rewrote it in ten paragraphs rather than five, and it did make for an easier read. Then I would take the same material out to the radio building and drastically retighten it. A minute and fifteen seconds was the limit for a broadcast, space for a sonnet and a half.

But my main problem soon became putting substance into my radio broadcasts. There was no direct censorship of print news reports—if a print reporter overstepped bounds too seriously or often, he was simply thrown out—but a script written for radio had to run a gauntlet of three censors, one each from the Propaganda Ministry, the Foreign Office and the High Command of the Wehrmacht. In the Shirer era they had been relatively lenient. But they felt badly burned when Shirer's book, *Berlin Diary,* came out in America and became the basic document of anti-Nazism. Then their large investment in his successor, Harry Flannery, proved a failure. Any last fugitive hopes of favorably influencing American opinion were dashed by President Roosevelt's stern actions. In January of 1941, lend-lease, designed to provide Britain with anything it needed to fight the war, was introduced in Congress. The bill establishing it passed the House in February and the Senate in March. In signing it, the President said it marked "the end of the compromise with tyranny." In April, American troops were installed in the Danish colony of Greenland, and America's "national security zone"—the area patrolled by U.S. ships and planes, which reported the locations of German U-boats to British convoys—was extended to near the middle of the Atlantic. In June, Roosevelt froze German assets in America. And in July he increased the area patrolled by the U.S. again, to within 400 miles of the British Isles. The question arose, how deep can you get into a war without getting in it? Ever deeper, I hoped. And the censors knew I hoped it.

The battery of three vultures I faced twice a day grew resolutely negative. It became hard to put anything into a broadcast beyond official communiqués and quotations from German newspapers. Day after day, with minutes left till air time, the censors would return to me a sheet of paper that looked as though it had stepped on an anti-personnel mine; every line had holes cut into it or blue-penciled out. I had to improvise connections between sentences to have any text at all. If Flannery's scripts had seemed wooden, I feared that New York would think mine termite riddled. But Paul White remained compassionate.

CHAPTER TWENTY-FOUR

A Turning Point

June 21, 1941, was the longest day of the year and also the first anniversary of Hitler's conquest of France. I took note of both in my midnight broadcast, then went home to bed. After a couple of hours the phone rang, and an official told me to be at the Foreign Office by five A.M.; there would be an earthshaking announcement. No transportation was operating so I half-walked, half-ran through empty streets to the Wilhelmstrasse.

The handsome room where Bismarck once planned the creation of the German nation, now the site of the daily news conference, was bright with lights for cameras and full of sleepy reporters. Officials, usually in mufti, were standing around in uniforms. As cameras whirred, in walked Foreign Minister von Ribbentrop, natty in his uniform resembling Hitler's—brown double-breasted jacket, black trousers. There were Nazi salutes. Then that most arrogant member of the cabinet read out a declaration of war on the Soviet Union, together with a brief justification. An hour previously 4 million German soldiers had attacked an even more numerous Red Army in the biggest clash of arms on one front in the history of warfare.

There had been signs. In my small orbit, the first came in a bookshop on my square next to Alois's restaurant. With the onset of good relations with Russia in 1939, German publishers had begun translating a few Russian books for publication. One was a book of delightful short stories titled *Schlaf Schneller, Genosse*. The title story was about a railroad hotel in Russia where over the bed in every room hung a framed sign that said, "Sleep faster, Comrade, another Comrade is waiting for this bed." In the spring of 1941, weeks before the invasion of Russia, I went in to buy a copy for a friend. I was told that it and the few other Russian books available had been ordered off the shelves.

One evening well before the invasion as we sat waiting for the regular daily press conference to begin, I happened to mention my little adventure to Ivan Filipov, the Tass correspondent in Berlin. I was surprised at how shaken he appeared. A few days later he invited me to lunch in a hotel and asked if I had seen any further odd signs. I had not. He then told me of rumors reaching him of very large troop movements over several days on the Soviet border. A week later the blow fell. Stalin's least employee in Berlin knew what Stalin refused to believe, even when told by high-ranking British and American diplomats.

The number of months before winter being well known, and a protracted two-front war being abhorrent, Hitler evidently expected a quick victory. In the news I broadcast to America in the next weeks it looked as though he was getting it. In the first month the Wehrmacht took 800,000 Russian prisoners and destroyed or captured 12,000 tanks. Surely no nation could survive such blows. During that time, Germany conquered 600,000 square miles of Soviet territory, two times the area of Germany. I had very little trouble with the censors in that period. The military censor had my number. "Poor Mr. Smiss," he said, "he is in ze news business, yet he hates ze news."

After acute unhappiness at the British refusal to quit, Germans were now back on a high. At the big round table in a corner of Goebbels' press club, officers attached to his ministry spoke of Russia becoming Germany's India, only richer. An architect present told of germinating plans to build an autobahn highway from Berlin to Kiev and to stud it with colonies of Germans who would direct the work of the plantations by the Slavs. From Kiev the road would go on to the Crimea, to become Germany's Mediterranean holiday shore. My mood was the obverse. Roosevelt had grown bold too late. With an empire from the North Sea to the Urals, Germany would have all the resources needed to beat off, then later conquer, the world.

Triumph followed upon triumph through August and September, never seeming to approach an end. In October a strange succession of events occurred in Berlin that I can only attribute to Goebbels' propaganda instincts. On the verge of the third war winter, he apparently felt that the German people badly needed to see light at the end of the tunnel. Hitler had disappeared from view; now suddenly, on October 3, the Führer appeared in Berlin to speak at the Sportspalast. I was in a party of foreign reporters bused from the Propaganda Ministry to the rally. I thought the Führer looked pale and haggard, and indeed later news told of a bad attack of dysentery in his eastern headquarters in the Ukraine. But his message enlivened him and overjoyed his audience. He listed the breathtaking statistics of the war in Russia so far, and each was met with a louder roar of approval than the statistic before: 2.5 million prisoners taken; 18,000 tanks captured or destroyed; 14,000 airplanes destroyed. He said, "I declare today, and I declare it without any reservation, that the enemy in the East has been struck down and will never rise again."

There was a week of silence, no communiqués, while the final offensive was presumably in progress. I relied on incidental scraps for my broadcasts: a newspaper published a poem titled *"Ostland"* ("Eastland") about Germany's need to adjust to the blond man's burden in Russia. My bookshop displayed German–Russian grammars for those who wished to prepare to operate in the new colony. Walter Funk, the finance minister, made a speech about the need for German industries to prepare to set up in Russia. It was published in the papers under the heading, "Europe's Economic Future Secured." Had anyone noticed it, there was also an ominous item saying the first snow fell on German tanks in Russia on the night of October 6, a tad early.

Six days after Hitler's visit the silence about military operations was dramatically broken. On the morning of October 9, we were summoned by phone to be in the Propaganda Ministry Theater by noon. Again lights for cameras blazed upon bureaucrats usually in civilian dress, now in uniforms for a big occasion. In came Dr. Otto Dietrich, Hitler's press chief, fresh from the Führer headquarters in the Ukraine. Hands flapped all around in Hitler salutes, and smiles wreathed all faces. A curtain was drawn to reveal a huge map of European Russia. Dr. Dietrich recounted details of the final offensive. The *last remnants* of the Red Army were locked in two steel German pockets before Moscow and were undergoing swift, merciless annihilation. He said, "For all military purposes Soviet Russia is done with. The British dream of a two-front war is dead." On the stage before us, handshakes and some embraces were exchanged, before Dietrich left and sped back to be present for the kill. The news was reported in the evening papers under ecstatic headlines: "The Veil over the new Offensive is lifted." "Dietrich: Campaign in East Decided." "The Great Hour was struck! Army Groups of Timoshenko, Voroshilov encircled— Budyenny Army Group in Dissolution."

The German propagandists lied often, but rarely so disadvantageously to themselves. They had put the Wehrmacht out on a high, long limb, and it promptly began to crack. A week later, after sensational headlines, the best Hitler's *Völkischer Beobachter* could do on its front page was "Operations in East Proceed According to Plan." And the next day, in smaller print below the fold, "Operations in East Proceed as Foreseen." That day, the main headline was "Speedboats Sink British Freighters." In little more than a week after the greatest military success ever, the demise of two more enemy merchant ships was more important than the biggest military conflict. The Russians simply, surprisingly, held outside Moscow, and the Germans began to freeze in the relentless Russian winter.

Life in Berlin soured badly that fall. The food in Alois's restaurant was inedible to one able to afford better. As the weather grew cold, a nationwide campaign was launched by press and film to induce people to give up warm things, old overcoats, sweaters, warm underclothes, woolen socks, for the soldiers who were still wearing summer gear in Russia.

Hitler for the first time mentioned the possible existence of serious internal opposition to him. He returned from the East for his annual November speech to old comrades in the Loewenbräu beer cellar in Munich. He said, "Should anyone among us seriously hope to be able to disturb our front—it makes no difference where he comes from, or to which camp he belongs—I will keep an eye on him for a certain period. You know my methods. That is always the period of probation. But then comes the moment when I strike like lightning and eliminate that kind of thing." Hitler had never spoken of opposition to him before to any audience, and it was shocking that he would feel a need to say it to old die-hard Nazis.

Life for the few remaining Americans became very hard. Roosevelt extended the lend-lease program, initiated to help Britain, to Soviet Russia. German officials were blind with rage. Paul Dickson, the Mutual Broadcasting Correspondent, was arrested by the Gestapo, then released with no explanation. I returned home one night to find my papers rifled through and scattered all over the floor. Oechsner had suggested that all his UP men join in a mass burning of notes to stay out of jail. I took all my papers to his office and joined the exercise. At the radio station I was ejected from my usual workroom and issued a typewriter with one key missing and the others arthritic. I often had to write scripts in longhand.

One night in November, as I struggled with a script in that room, the Foreign Office censor came in and handed me a document. It was a criticism of President Roosevelt written by the Press Office. "We expect you to use this in your broadcast tonight." I was shocked that he would think it possible to order me to say anything. I told him I could not possibly comply. He left the room in a rage.

I knew that some kind of ugly confrontation was imminent. It happened the next day. I was used to getting my scripts back from the censors savaged by blue pencil. Now there was something new: I found two paragraphs handwritten by someone in the middle of my script. A conversation of the kind one does not easily forget ensued.

"What is this, this handwriting?" I asked.

One of the censors said, "You will find that those lines exactly compensate for what we have cut out of the rest of the script."

"You wrote them?" I asked, knowing he had.

"Yes. They are needed to make your report balanced."

"Sir, with all respect, that is ridiculous. I cannot possibly read as my work something someone else has written."

He could no longer stifle his fury, "You have gotten away with writing whatever you wish too long. We cannot allow you to use our facilities and our time and effort to make hostile broadcasts. We are fighting for our lives. You Americans think you own the world."

"This is beyond argument. I simply will not read what you have written."

"Then you will not broadcast from Germany."

I asked studio technicians if they would pass on a message to New York explaining my absence. The answer was no. I met the correspondents for the other two networks in the hall. To my relief they had had the same experience. We tried to send a joint telegram to New York. It was not accepted for transmission. I went home and phoned New York. The Germans had forgotten to block phone calls. The next day I received a telegram from the director of the Reichs Rundfunk formally forbidding me to broadcast from Germany again. Paul White phoned me and suggested I get on a train to Switzerland. "I have a notion the air in that city won't be good for your health," he said. I applied to the Foreign Office for a permit to leave the country. There was no response. I returned each day for a week and made the same request. Finally one day I was told there would be no such permit for me.

I don't think that I have ever been so chilled in my life as at that time. I was functionless, but unable to leave the country, a hostage, susceptible to being thrown in a concentration camp, whenever authority invented an ad hoc broken law, never to be heard from again. Thus does the imagination gravitate to the worst possibility in a dire situation. Our two governments despised one another, so the worst was entirely possible.

CHAPTER TWENTY-FIVE

True Love

Disemployed by the censors, and given lots of time to worry and something to worry about, I took a good look at myself for the first time in a long while. The view was discouraging. My wardrobe on leaving Oxford was adequate, just. But after two years in Germany, with no additions or replacements, I was shabby. When Stephen Laird of *Time* left Berlin he was moved by my appearance to leave me his tweed jacket. Though secondhand and a little tight, it was by far the best piece of apparel I possessed. For one rolling in wealth—by my standards—I appeared a pauper. At least I was well fed and well watered, if mainly with the water of life. Our apartment suited my personal state. We had sublet it from an American who left his furniture with us. Now he was leaving and had sold his furniture out from under us. What remained were a few packing cases and two cots.

In desolation a flower bloomed, amid aggravation arose hope, near to despair I had an angelic visitation. She was very tall and slim, her hair a flame-burst of red. She had warm brown eyes and a willowy form. Her gaze was level, calm, assured, as if she had tested the world and felt she would be equal to anything it threw in her way. She was nineteen.

I was first introduced to her months before I knew her, in Goebbels' restaurant for foreign journalists. She was introduced as "Frøken Traberg." I ran down my short list of national appellations and decided that she was Danish. She had come to the bar to fetch drinks for two friends at a table. She smiled at the introduction, but did not so much as look at me. She just took the drinks back to the table without a word. I was enchanted.

At that time I was leaving UP and breaking in as a radio reporter, twin stresses that took up a great deal of my nervous energy, but I was determined to add this new excitement. On inquiry I learned that her primary assignment was to cover the noontime Foreign Office press conference presided over by the domineering Paul Schmidt. I resolved to attend and find a way to force myself into the range of those warm brown eyes. But then CBS sent me a full schedule of daytime broadcasts, all to be done at noon, which frustrated that design. Now, nearly idle, I returned to it with resolve.

The authorities did not notice, so I continued to write for the *Times*, signing Guido Enderis's name to my dispatches. I did so mainly as an excuse to look in at the noon news conference and seek out the flame-haired Dane. I watched her intently for a couple of days and thought I saw her give me an encouraging look as intent as my own. Later I found out she was nearsighted and teen-aged vain about wearing glasses, so she looked that way at anything that moved. Although generally accompanied by a couple of males, she one day left the conference alone. I got next to her and engaged her in conversation about nothing until we reached her office. By that time a dinner date had been arranged. I took her to the Taverna, a fine restaurant much frequented by the foreign press and by the department of German intelligence that kept an eye on us. The tables were alleged to be bugged, but as I had no secrets to impart I did not mind. Early I noticed that I had begun to talk too much, which is a sure sign of falling in love, as the movie *Marty* would later illustrate. So did she, as we rushed to tell and to find out everything about one another.

What I found out from her account in a winning Danish-accented schoolbook English, was that she was the daughter of a prominent Danish country lawyer, head of the poultry farmers' association, which is very important in a country economically dependent on exports of high-grade foods. She had always determined to be a journalist, and when war fever grew high, she left Copenhagen University in her second year to take a job procured for her by her father as an apprentice reporter on a newspaper. The paper was the *Berlingske Tidende,* which means "Mr. Berling's Times." It is the oldest newspaper in the world, and the only European paper that published the American

Declaration of Independence when it was issued in 1776. She started in the newspaper's Berlin office as a gofer and utility reporter, but a bright talent had led to her promotion to writing regular daily dispatches. She was about to leave, having been transferred to the Stockholm office as a full-fledged correspondent. I had found her in time's nick.

After dinner at the Taverna, I took her to a night spot called the Jockey Club, a place where late into the night people sat around the piano singing boozy songs. We held hands on the way. In the informal lounging around at the Club I dared a kiss which was received and returned. When I kissed her good night at the door to her apartment house on the Kurfürstendamm, I was lost in love, with a rather strong feeling that she was, too. This one I resolved I was going to keep. It was not one more Berlin affair. It had to be managed with delicacy and respect.

From that moment my life was markedly changed. A city grown dark and scruffy took on a bright sheen. I woke up to pleasant thoughts, grudges forgotten, and looked forward eagerly to days I would have apprehended with mixed boredom and fear the week before. Fleischer wanted to know why the hell I was humming when I shaved.

Our relationship was born in an atmosphere of acute crisis. She was to leave in a few days for Denmark, and then move on to Stockholm. I expected to go in the other direction, south, but didn't know whether it would be to Switzerland or to Dachau. Something in the air suggested that some kind of break in the war was imminent. Winter had overtaken the Wehrmacht in Russia. The failure to win quickly was hurting. On the other side of the world, America was daily becoming bolder, an insufferable irritant to Hitler, patrolling the seas in blatant support of British convoys. Something, one could not guess what, was going to snap. My girl and I felt urgency; we had very little time. Things moved rapidly under intense pressure.

Yet, the next several days were among the happiest of my life. We did not care where we were, as long as we were together. She dined with me three nights in a row. Days, I walked her to and from her office, waited for her and took long walks with her, talking, talking, talking, in the big Tiergarten park. Among other things I complimented her on her legs. She said it was the silk stockings: "If my stockings are right, I feel right all over." They were right and she was right all over. The fourth night I prepared dinner for her in my apartment. That was an unlikely exercise for me. I am weak on domesticity and, in the realm of cuisine, able to boil an egg only by following directions. The prologue to this rare occasion was this: The American embassy maintained a well-stocked commissariat for embassy employees. The chargé had begun to think that, with the U.S. now a great manufactory of arms and food to keep both Britain and Russia fighting, U.S. relations with Germany were going to suffer some kind of interruption—possibly a simple breaking off of relations. So he decided to deplete stocks by allowing American reporters to have shopping privileges. Thus was I able to prepare an hors d'oeuvre of carciofini from a jar, an entrée of spaghetti with canned tomato sauce made noble by emptying a jar of smoked oysters into it, and at last a dessert of succulent pears from still another tin. All was improved by candlelight and a bottle of Mosel wine that I had acquired in exchange for coffee beans. She was impressed. So was I.

A little earlier that day sensational news had come from the embassy. Long ago, President Roosevelt had withdrawn the American ambassador from Berlin in protest against the Kristallnacht horrors. Since then the embassy had been run by a series of chargés d'affaires, the latest of whom was a young man named George Kennan. In a subsequent era he formulated a policy for saving the free world, called Containment. Now he limited himself to working out a policy for saving me. He told me that he had noticed that CBS had not been banned from working in Germany; only I, individually, had. It had been suggested to CBS in New York that the network appoint a new Berlin correspondent—whether or not it actually planned to send him—and I might be released. So, CBS formally asked the German Foreign Office to accredit a new CBS man. Our stringer in Switzerland was named (but was never sent). Sure enough, the Foreign Office relented. Satisfied that it would have a hostage against my misbehavior, it had an official notify me that I would receive an exit visa when he got around to it. It would stipulate, I was told, that I must be out of the country within forty-eight hours after receiving it.

So, I had no time to lose. I looked at my love of four days' acquaintance and decided I could not live without her. Ten years before it was composed, I was moved by an imperative from a song—once you have found her, never let her go. As we sat on packing crates in my apartment after dinner, I confessed my thoughts and asked, what would she say if I asked her to marry me? She did not answer. She smiled and cuddled deep in my arms. In later years I reproached her for not having answered my proposal. She pointed out that I had never made one. I had only said, what if?

Anyhow we acted as if the matter was settled. We had about a fortnight before we had to separate. She would turn down the *Berlingske* job in Stockholm. But if she was going to join me for marriage in Switzerland, a trip home to Denmark was more urgent than ever. As a legal minor she had to have her parents' written permission to marry. We mounted an elaborate campaign to persuade her father that he should consent to assigning his daughter's future to a man, a foreigner, he had never met and knew nothing about. Her boss in Berlin, Helge Knudsen, a respected journalist in Denmark, wrote Jens Traberg a letter commending me. Another colleague was induced to send a news item to the paper, announcing the engagement of Frøken Benedicte Traberg of Store Heddinge, Denmark, to an American journalist of whom nothing really bad was known. The editor in Copenhagen cooperated: it was published in a box on the front page. Our hope was that, with congratulations coming in from friends, Jens would find it hard to say no. Overcoming modesty, I wrote him a letter in which I failed to deny the good things being said about me and even hinted that they might be true. It included a brief story of my virtuous life that an American would have known was inspired by Horatio Alger. As Churchill once said, he knew history would do him justice, since he was determined to write that history himself. Jens received it—carried by a courier who was a friend—the same day he read about us in the paper.

The last days were filled. Knudsen and his wife gave us an engagement party, a rare bright celebration in a dark, depressed city. Colleagues joined us at lunch to congratulate. Only Fleischer hung back. Like all bachelor roommates, he thought his roommate was not the marrying kind. I told him separating from him would be sad, but with a pretty girl wife I thought I could endure it.

On December 1, 1941, I saw her off to Denmark at the Lufthansa office. It was rather an emotional parting because I had not yet been given that official permit to leave. Bennie did not confess to me till much later that each night in that period, when we said goodbye at her door, she worried whether that would be the night I would be picked up by the Gestapo, and she would never see me again. But five days later I was called to the Foreign Office, and the liberating document was stamped in my passport. I immediately reserved a berth on the night train to Basel, Switzerland. The UP boys improvised an alcoholic farewell party, then took me to the Anhalter station and poured me onto the train. That was December 6. I was so pleased with the celebration and so happy at the favorable turn my life had taken that I considered partying on for a day longer and leaving Berlin on the second night of my forty-eight hours, which would be December 7, 1941.

I shudder to think how events might have transpired, had I done so.

1941-1944

CHAPTER TWENTY-SIX

Switzerland and Pearl

Those abstractions, Peace and Freedom, acquire impressive content when one crosses from a country that has neither to a country that has both. In the ordinary course of things, civil life demands and receives a lot of maintenance. The absence of it in a warring country lets the color of everything—houses, clothes, buses, faces—drain out, and grayness sets in unnoticed. After Germany, Switzerland, a country almost excessively normal, seemed a riot of color. Emerging from customs was an experience like the sudden transition in the movie *The Wizard of Oz,* from black-and-white in Kansas to bright technicolor in Oz. Likewise civility. One does not realize how it gives way to universal irritability in a community under wartime stress and tyranny, until one enters a place at peace. There was no great friendliness or exaggerated courtesy at the Swiss border; people, customs officers, waiters, conductors, bellboys, were simply normally civil, and it seemed an extraordinary thing.

From Basel on the border I took the *Schnellzug* to Berne, the capital, a train arrow-fast, clean and bright, needing no repairs, lacking the smell of being excessively used. Across the square from the Berne station I went to the Schweizerhof Hotel, probably the best hotel in Europe at the time. Elated at the rise in my standard of living I gave the concierge a large tip. In recompense, he phoned my room a half-hour later. "Mr. Smith, you may want to know that a short while ago the Japanese bombed Pearl Harbor." For a while I didn't get it. Briefly we debated the location of Pearl Harbor. I thought it a place south of Long Beach in California; he thought it an American island in the Pacific Ocean. Either way, America was in a war. I was directed to a room with a radio, and listened stunned and excited at once. I returned to my room and wrote my girl in Denmark a superfluous caution to come at once; this could get complicated.

The Schweizerhof bar had become the mart where transient reporters and locals gathered to exchange fictions about their scoops, and commentaries, rational or silly, on events. I went there and joined in. There was fear—how could great America have been so easily blindsided by a country not as big as California? Had ten years of Depression really drained the stuff out? Relief: at last and at least the bonds of neutrality were burst; no more hypocrisy about not fighting in foreign wars. No more limitations on belonging to a humanity desperately struggling for its heritage. Dismay: we were sucked into the wrong war across the wrong ocean just when it seemed at last possible to brake the breathtaking progress of Hitler in the right war.

Four days later Hitler himself came to the rescue. He summoned his Reichstag and declared war on the U.S., bringing us into the right war. That solved the geopolitical problem, but it created a serious personal problem for me. Bennie and I were now separated by Germany in an unforeseen war. German occupation officials in Denmark had surely taken note in the Danish papers of the engagement of this Danish girl to an American. They were unlikely to give her a visa to improve the life of one who never was very friendly and now was an enemy. Without their transit visa, she could not take one of the few civil air flights still able to operate in warring Europe: that from Stockholm, via Copenhagen, across Germany, to Zurich. I wrote her a letter urging her to lie about the purpose of her requested visit to Switzerland and to hurry. I went to the bar and enlisted multilingual colleagues to translate my English letter into French, German and Italian. I signed each with the appropriate translation of Smith—Marechal, Schmidt and Fabbri—and sent four letters hoping one would get past the censors. In fact all did. The doleful answer came back: the German officials were indeed sitting on her application for transit. I would have to settle down and wait.

Waiting meant finding a convincing function. The little country was a tiny vessel in a turbulent sea and could not accept idle passengers. I tested the job market and found that one of Pearl Harbor's tectonic effects was to shift advantage in the job market from employers to reporters. *The New York Times* offered me seventy-five dollars a week to start at once. Stephen Laird of *Time* telegraphed a better offer from London. But sweeping all else aside was a call from Paul White signing me up permanently for CBS and ordering me up for a broadcast the night of his call. White was the creator of what to my mind was the greatest event in informing people since movable print, the CBS World News Roundup, gathering an ever-larger audience as war proceeded. I was overjoyed.

I appeared at the Berne studio just before midnight with a script. The director took me to his office and told me, politely but beyond appeal, that Switzerland's survival depended on keeping neutral. While America was still neutral, American reporters had been allowed to use Swiss broadcast facilities. Now that America was a belligerent, it was no longer possible. I phoned White. The Swiss had already informed him. I confessed to my romantic problem. He said to sit tight a while and see what happened. Meanwhile send telegrams.

So began a series of idle and troubled days. I spent them around two locales: the Schweizerhof bar, to keep informed; and the arcaded streets of the old city, to keep sane. Chiefly I walked one course, down a street with four names, commencing beside the railway station as the Spitalgasse, continuing in stanzas as the Marktgasse and the Kramgasse, and ending as the Gerechtigkeitsgasse two miles downhill to a sharp turn in the Aar River. It was cobblestoned all the way, punctuated at intervals by horse troughs in the middle of the street. For a city without horses, these were very fancy horse troughs, carved of stone, with a stone pedestal in the middle and on top of the pedestals handsomely carved and brightly painted medieval figures. One was a stone knight with a conspicuously swollen codpiece. I felt that a few weeks without woman and I would comprehend how a man could be that way after standing alone for centuries. The tramlines and bus routes swerved wide on either side to give each splendid monument plenty of room, as well they might.

But the principal attraction of this unique thoroughfare was the arcades—altogether six kilometers of streets on which you could dwell lifelong and walk, shop, window-shop, go to the dentist, the doctor, the hairdresser, in storms of rain or snow without ever a drop touching you. Above the arcades were small apartments occupied, it was my impression, mainly by bachelors. I had occasion to visit Swiss colleagues in several, and first saw the feature common to all dwellings in the land, and essential to Switzerland's existence: inside an armoire was an army uniform and a rifle and a railway pass to a preordained destination. Every male who could walk, be he bank president or trash collector, was a soldier on call. When the balloon went up, each donned the uniform, took the rifle to the railway station and was transported to the assembly point on the ticket. Within hours a professional army of thousands became a garrison army of a million. The garrison was a concentrated area in the middle of the country containing all the mountain passes, called the National Redoubt. Its periphery was a great circle of gun emplacements, built into the Alps. The nation contained industries that manufactured the best big machines (turbines, locomotives) and the best small machines (watches) in the world. The Germans could have access to these essentials, but only if they did not attack. Though wholly surrounded by Hitler and Mussolini one felt curiously secure walking down the protected way to the bridge over the Aar.

The city's claim to fame, however, was sustained less by anything military than by a signal event of recent times. Early in this century, half-way down the Kramgasse stanza of the old street, dwelt a young man whose principal physical features were a thick aureole of disobedient hair and an amused expression. Up near the top of the old street, near my hotel and the telegraph building where I began carrying daily telegrams to New York for transmission, stood the Swiss Patent Office, where that young man worked. From home to workplace he rode a tram. He rode the back of the tram and watched the town clock, called the *Zeitglocke*, receding in the distance. The experience contributed to his working out his Theory of Relativity, or so he suggested to me years later. By then, when the war was a mere memory, I was a journalist who traveled often to New York. He phoned me from Princeton and asked me to visit him. I did, and he read to me from a book I had written about the nations of Europe. He was particularly amused by my description of the Swiss, which read, "It is said that the Swiss can be very noisy in church, but on entering a bank they take off their hats and talk in respectful whispers." He laughed aloud at that. In the course of conversation I asked the inevitable question about how one thinks out a great theory, and he responded with the tram story as one possibility. I told him that it must have been something else, because I too had ridden that tram and watched that clock receding, but it had not done a damn thing for me. Among my most prized possessions is a photo of himself that he sent me, inscribed "Your loyal and grateful listener, A. Einstein."

On my second morning in Switzerland, I walked about half-way down the old street, turned left and found the Predigerstrasse, Preacher Street. There, at the city administration building, I filled out a long form with vital statistics and swore to their truthfulness. Every morning after that for a while I was able to read on a bulletin board outside the building that Howard Kingsbury Smith, Jr., of New Orleans, U.S.A., would be legally authorized to marry Benedicte Traberg of Store Heddinge, Denmark, unless substantial objections were made known within a fixed period of time. I went by every morning and watched the document, called "the banns," crinkle with snow spots and gray with the air of the city.

CHAPTER TWENTY-SEVEN

Love's Labor's Won

In about the second week of nocturnal strolling beneath the arcades, watching the snow fall on the streets just outside, I, like Einstein, was seized with an idea, though on a humbler level of endeavor. What about using this time to write something of higher moment than anything I had attempted up till now? After all, I had just completed two years of life in the foremost warring capital, among the most feared rulers in the world, in an imperial state threatening to be more successful in conquest than any since Genghis Khan's. Why not—

dared I be so bold—write an article and try to sell it to *Life* magazine? The notion thrilled me. I had turned down *Time*'s offer of a job, but I now cabled Stephen Laird, who had sent it to me, and asked whether a market existed for such an article, and how best to frame it. A few days later, Laird responded that he had a better idea. A publisher named Dennis Cohen of Cresset Press in London had heard of me and wanted me to write a book about my time in Germany. The thought electrified me. Somewhere in the back of my brain was an assumption that, when I was middle-aged and big with experiences and enjoyed some standing in the profession, I might try my hand at a book as an act to crown my career. But now, barely out of the journeyman class, the notion seemed presumptuous, brazen. But think of it I did, and of nothing else, all night. The next day I cabled Laird that I would begin. Then for six long weeks I lived the life of an impostor, pretending that I could produce a whole book, harried by fear that I could not.

I took quarters in an ancient home in the Junkerngasse, parallel to the Marktgasse, equally arcaded and beautiful, but strictly residential, no shops. I had destroyed all my notes in Germany, but I had a plan. Soon after my arrival in Berne, the British Military attaché had invited me in and spent two hours "debriefing" me, asking me about every aspect of German life and taking full notes. In return now I asked a favor of him. He kept in a storeroom copies of the main Nazi newspaper, the *Völkischer Beobachter*, for every day since the war had begun. I asked to borrow them all—stacks of newspapers, each four feet high. I got them to my digs and, using them to make a chronological skeleton, each joint of which brought back memories, I began writing and rewriting. I wrote all day with breaks for lunch, an afternoon nap and a walk on the streets late at night. I smoked far too much, and as fatigue accumulated in the marrow of my bones I began drinking, which rapidly became too much, too. Abuse demanded its payment; in my fifth week I was hit badly by flu. I still worked at intervals. In my sixth and last week came a remedy for all that ailed me—to be recounted in a moment—and with that in hand I completed the book. I sent it off in the British diplomatic pouch to London. There was no thought of sending it to America as well; I did not think it could find much of a market anywhere. Isolated in Switzerland, I heard little about it except that it had made a bit of money, and what should be done with that? I suggested giving it to Mrs. Churchill's relief fund. The publisher thought better and saved the money, taxes paid, in a special account. On returning to the real world two years later I was pleasantly shocked to learn that it had been a bestseller in both Britain and America and in several other countries besides and had made me a considerable pot of money. In occupied Denmark it had been duplicated on an office machine and passed from hand to hand. The British had translated one chapter into the languages of some of the countries Hitler occupied and reprinted it in tiny match-box-size booklets bearing the title *"Un Té-moignage"* and dropped tens of thousands of them from airplanes. Twentieth Century Films bought the title, improving my financial condition, and hired Harry Flannery—he who had hired me—as consultant and prepared a script for a film that designated Gary Cooper for the role of the reporter. It had little to do with what I wrote and eventually was abandoned. I was given the script, which was pretty poor. Later in the war, Bill Shirer, author of the celebrated *Berlin Diary*, came to see me, and with mock irritation told me, "A pretty little WAC met me at the airport and said to me, 'Oh, Mr. Shirer, I so enjoyed your book *Last Train from Berlin*. I thought it the best book written in the war.'" Forty years later, in 1982, on the anniversary of Hitler's rise to power, a German publisher bought it, translated it and published it as written four decades before with only a new preface by me.

The most pleasing comment came from Willy Brandt when he was mayor of Berlin well after the war. I went to Berlin for a première showing of the movie *Judgment at Nuremberg*. At a preshow cocktail affair I chatted with Brandt and complimented him on his wartime correspondence from Stockholm for *The New York Times*, when he wrote under the name Herbert Fromm. He asked me about some of the American reporters in Berlin during the war. One of them, he said, showed special insight into Germany and the Nazis. I suggested Shirer. He shook his head. I named several others. No. Then we sat down in the theater, I in the row just behind him. As the lights went down, he turned his head and said, "His book was called *Last Train from Berlin*—I can't recall his name."

Meanwhile things were happening in Store Heddinge and Copenhagen. Jens Traberg did not really have the power to decide whether his younger daughter might marry. He knew that, when her heart was that set, she was as unopposable as an avalanche. When she wept uncontrollably over the stonewalling of the Germans, he searched his considerable experience for a stratagem. And he came up with one. With the prestige of his standing in the poultry business—he had been decorated by the King—he made a formal appeal to Queen Alexandrine of Denmark. She was touched by the story and summoned the German Ambassador. She told him it was her wish that Miss Traberg be given the permissions needed to fly to Switzerland. The German occupiers, still hoping to keep the Danes compliant, had to accede. But they expected to make the permit meaningless: it was valid only for forty-eight hours, and all places on planes to Switzerland were booked for a month to come. But the Germans had not reckoned with the adage that had made a fortune for Hollywood: all the world loves a lover. A travel agency got in touch with Stockholm, where the flight that mattered originated. The story was told to all those who had seats for the next two days. One, a Swedish businessman, decided that his mission could wait and surrendered his seat, and so Benedicte Traberg was enabled to fly across Germany to her lover.

The lover was in pretty miserable shape. I had heard nothing of all this. Someone from the Danish Legation in Berne phoned to inform me that my bride would arrive the next night in Zurich. I was stunned. I asked the caller if he could send her instructions on how to get from Zurich to my bedside, where I lay with a high temperature, in a pool of sweat. If I got out of bed and went into the winter air in this condition, her first experience in marriage would be widowhood. With the negativism that seems to afflict small people in governmental office, he said rules did not permit. So I had to wait until Bennie had actually arrived in Zurich and phoned me to tell her to take train and taxi to my—our—address.

The next night, she phoned, and I told her what to do. Two hours later she burst through the door, and we met in an embrace not less prehensile than that of a man hanging from a tall building, as though if we let up we might never touch again. My recovery began immediately. Wiving it proved much happier than even my dreams foretold. Not only did her presence restore me to the outer fringes of health, but she also helped me with my last stages of typing and writing. Overnight we were almost as though we had always been one. Only one detail had been neglected. After three days, my landlady, a handsome old Bernese noblewoman with a commanding presence, invited us upstairs to her rooms. After thimbleful of sherry she got right to the point. "It was my understanding, Mr. Smith, that you brought this young lady here to marry her?" I apologized for the oversight and the next day arranged for us to take two witnesses to the city hall and get married.

The ceremony took place in a government office with dark red curtains, reserved for weddings and funerals. Presiding was an official in a dark swallow-tail coat who looked like an undertaker doing spadework for the future. He pronounced his lines in Schweetzer Dootsch, so we understood not a word. When prompted, we said, in turn, "I do." Then, at what sounded final, I embraced my lady and we kissed. The official was upset. *"Noch nicht!"* he said, *"Nicht jetzt!"* ("Not yet!"). We stood still for a minute more of speech, then he looked kindly at us and said, *"Jetzt."* And he motioned that we might clinch. We returned to my place for a wedding lunch, after which I went to the typewriter, and my bride took a walk through picturesque old Berne, alone. We slipped into married life as easily as one of those sea lions on the Carmel coast slips from a rock into the water.

Shortly after her arrival, my lady had occasion to use the telephone and found it dead. With sure instinct, she looked at the debris on my desk, and found a notice from the phone company that I had not paid my bill. There were also several unopened envelopes from New York containing salary checks. That enabled her to bring up the one cloud that she said hung over our relationship. It took her a little while and some screwing up of her courage to tell me: "I have only one sad memory of my mother and father. It is of my mother having to beg my father for money." I told her to keep the checks, and all others that arrived would be hers. I would ask when I needed money. So it has gone, and in her care our finances have prospered.

I loved and love this lady, so any description of mine may fairly be considered biased. But as I would have you know her, I shall quote from the description of another. After serving his nation in the highest places, Denis Healey recently wrote his memoirs, entitled, *The Time of My Life.* He said:

> My closest friends throughout my years at Transport House were not in the Labour Party, nor even British. They were American. Howard K. Smith, who had preceded me [a small error: I didn't precede, I followed Healey, which I consider to have been heroic—HKS] as Chairman of the Oxford Labour Club in 1939, had settled in London as the CBS correspondent following Ed Murrow. He . . . brought with him an exceptionally beautiful Danish wife, Benny, with long legs, silky auburn hair and a milky complexion—the soldier's dream of a [George] Petty Girl from *Esquire* magazine. She was also deadly serious, had no eyes for anyone but Howard, and had the capacity to do anything she chose after reading the relevant book. During treatment for tuberculosis in Switzerland she taught herself to paint with academic efficiency. Back in Washington many years later when Howard was under a cloud . . . she decided to earn money herself. So she bought a book on growth stocks and before long was making more than her stockbroker.

And on it went, with the kind of flattery I find myself able to absorb with no sign of getting spoiled.

CHAPTER TWENTY-EIGHT

Birth of Hope

We remained in Switzerland longer than we intended and than was good for us. Bennie had developed appendicitis in Denmark but would not consent to an operation lest a chance to leave should arise while she was immobilized in a hospital. During her first month in Berne it became acute, and after the operation she had to be confined to bed for a while. When she became mobile, the long strain on my health demanded full payment, and I too, had to go into the hospital. When I was upright, we took a needed holiday.

Soon after that the Allies invaded North Africa, and the Germans in response marched into Vichy France, effectively closing the borders of Switzerland. Until then it had been possible, with some difficulty, to get through unoccupied France and Spain. Now it was impossible for a citizen of an Allied country to leave.

The year 1942 was the watershed year in every theater of war. Early that year, probably a majority of people in Europe believed that Hitler and the Japanese were going to win the war. Now the German army recovered from its first winter disaster, drove an incredible 1,000 miles deeper into the U.S.S.R. to the city of Stalingrad on the Volga, and, moving south, occupied the prize of prizes, the oil fields of the Caucasus. In North Africa, after back-and-forth fortunes, Rommel made it far into Egypt, pausing only to draw breath before, it was feared, going through the Middle East to join hands with his compatriot armies in the Caucasus. In Asia, Japan appeared invincible. The Japanese won a watery empire in the Pacific nearly as extensive as Hitler's on land and, in the west, reached the border of India. A logical continuation of momentum would permit Germans and Japanese to link armies somewhere in Southern Asia, and, like a python that had swallowed a goat, digest Eurasia at leisure.

When 1942 ended, all had changed. A German army was encircled and being destroyed at Stalingrad. Another had been forced to retreat from the oil fields lest it be cut off and destroyed. The German Afrika Korps had retreated and would soon be expelled from North Africa. At Midway Island in the Pacific, a smaller U.S. fleet had delivered a Pearl Harbor–size defeat to a large Japanese fleet and turned the sea war in the Pacific around 180 degrees. For the first time, a majority of people in Europe began to think that the Allies were going to win the war. Among the consequences of this change of fortunes that history will not note was that I acquired a journalistic function in Switzerland.

For me, now stuck in a small neutral country, finding something useful to report about a war getting farther and farther away had seemed an insuperable problem. One morning the *Völkischer Beobachter* suggested a solution. It appeared with the headline, "Peoples of Europe Pray for Germany's Victory." The story beneath told of a rash of V signs, just the two-stroke V in red paint, appearing on walls all over occupied Europe. The *VB* called it a "remarkable demonstration of spontaneous solidarity with the Reich against the Bolsheviks and the Imperialists." There were photos of crude V's splashed on walls in Paris and in Prague. The problem for Goebbels was that the German word for victory (*Sieg*) did not begin with a V. He got around that by explaining that the European demonstrators were displaying pan-European solidarity by using V for the universal Latin word *Victoria*.

The purpose of the Goebbels report was, of course, not to boast about support for Germany, but to explain away a bold expression of opposition to Germany that was becoming so widespread among conquered peoples as to be worrisome to the conqueror. The BBC always began its radio reports to the continent with the rendition of the Morse signal of V for Victory from Beethoven's Fifth Symphony: three quick musical dots and a dash. As the months of bad news in those reports began to give way to good news from all fronts, people all over Europe began painting that sign of hope everywhere—it only took the subversive graffitist two quick strokes of a brush before running back into hiding. So, opposition to Hitler was beginning to awaken and to organize in countries next to or near Switzerland's borders. I decided that would be my journalistic quarry.

I sought out useful individuals. In Locarno I found Otto Braun, prime minister of Prussia till Göring displaced him. He had contacts and was willing to share information. I made contact with the court of Spain, which was established in Lausanne around Don Juan, the Pretender, whom I interviewed. Dr. Ernst Lemmer, a German and Germany correspondent for the Swiss *Neue Zürcher Zeitung*, came often and I made sure to see him. Lemmer later became Minister for All-German Affairs in the postwar cabinet.

Far the most pleasant contact, which became a lifelong friendship, was with Ignazio Silone, the Italian author. His first book, *Fontamara*, won him worldwide fame. Now he lived in Zurich and was a leader of the Italian resistance. As Fascist Italy's fortunes worsened, Mussolini complained increasingly about Silone's activities, so the Swiss felt it prudent to keep the author under close surveillance. I first interviewed him on assignment from *Time*, for whom I began writing on the side. I got the interview thanks to meeting his friend, who was to become his wife, a beautiful Irish girl named Darina. In writing it up I earned a dose of professional ridicule it took a while to live down. *Time* was in love with colorful adjectives, like "porcine" Hermann Göring, or "moose-tall" Charles de Gaulle, and I was asked to manufacture one to fit Silone. I thought of the dark areas around his ever-doleful eyes and, in a moment that will live in infamy, wrote "panda eyed." Darina saw it and exploded in laughter. (It was ridiculous, but not quite as bad as the magazine's eventual grand champion, the application to Jane Russell of the adjective "hypermammalary.")

The last American to make it into Switzerland before the Germans decided to police all Swiss accesses and shut the gates on us was Allen Welsh Dulles, who set up office in Berne as America's foremost spymaster and who was in every way the most important American left on the continent. In our related functions as seekers of information we gravitated to one another. Indeed at one time, CBS and he agreed for me to work for him, but I begged to remain on my own. I went often to his handsome home on the Herrengasse, which became a magnet for underground leaders from everywhere. The scene could on occasion become ridiculous, as these secret leaders met secretly with Dulles in a large, conspicuous house where the Swiss police could stand on the curb and check off who was visiting and for how long. On one occasion I became involved in what might have been a scene in a Marx Brothers comedy. Dulles met me in his entrance hall and asked, "Can you speak Italian?" I lied (reporters always do in response to that question) that I knew enough. He said, "Go into that room and keep the Italians busy while I get rid of the Greeks in the drawing room and the Romanians in the pantry." I went into the appointed room, where the Italians engaged me in perfect English.

I kept up a sequence of pretty good reports from underground Europe, far the best being a series about Yugoslavia. That country consisted of six nations that did not much like one another, stitched into one. Hitler went through the country in days, too quickly, leaving caches of undiscovered weapons and large pockets of soldiers with hurt pride. Many of them crystallized into a Serbian guerilla force under Colonel Dragoljub "Draza" Mihailovic. The Yugoslav government-in-exile in London promoted him to general and named him Minister of Defense. Then began a campaign to romanticize him. *Time* made him its man of the week, but, having no photos of him, had an artist drawn an idealized portrait of a guerilla fighter. The British broadcast daily communiqués "from General Mihailovic's headquarters" about daring assaults on Nazi occupiers.

Enter in Switzerland an emissary from someone in Yugoslavia called Tito. He told me that Mihailovic was a fraud. The mountain warrior was not warring, except against his own people. He was a Serb nationalist who was preserving his forces intact to make the country into a Greater Serbia after the war, with the other nationalities made subordinate. The real fighting against the Germans was being done by Tito's partisans of the National Liberation Army.

My informant turned my radio on to the proper wavelength, and we listened to a scratchy transmission of the daily communiqué from Tito's headquarters. A while later he tuned in the BBC, and we heard the same communiqué but now said to come from "the headquarters of General Mihailovic." The government-in-exile was simply hijacking the exploits of the Tito partisans.

I told my visitor that I needed more substantiation. He produced a giant of a young man named Latinovic. The giant had fought in Spain, caught tuberculosis in a French refugee camp and fled to Switzerland, where he was in a camp but was allowed to go out to a doctor one day a week. He was using that day to come and tell me that he was the head of the Swiss unit of the Yugoslav partisan structure, and that he had regular couriers moving from and to Yugoslavia every week. They would provide further information.

I told Dulles about all this, and he asked to meet Latinovic. I arranged a meeting, not at Dulles' home but, at his request, in my apartment. I brought the two together and left the room. Even outside I could tell that they were arguing in French. At one point Dulles' voice rose up in a declaration that *"mais je suis socialiste aussi."*

I acquired a mass of information and began sending it to my several clients. The Partisans were a creation of the Yugoslav Communist Party. The name of Tito had been heard of, but I think my cables were the first public identification of him. He was a Croatian communist named Josip Broz, whose previous *noms de guerre* were Comrade Walter and Engineer Tomanek. He had been in the Austrian army in WW I, was captured by the Russians, converted to Communism and had fought in the Russian Civil War and, in the 1930s, in the Spanish Civil War.

Broz had created a bigger and more active guerilla army than Mihailovic's. His Communist cadres simply organized better. Also he had the acumen to make his army mainly a peasant army. To peasants in the Balkans the town was the enemy, the home of the tax collector, the requisitioner, the police given to arbitrary arrests. Tito exploited this hatred. On entering a village he would win the peasants over by making a public bonfire of local tax and debt records prepared in the towns. The country's biggest problem throughout its existence was the "nationalities" question. Tito won the educated by promising equality of all peoples in the Yugoslav federation, an end to the trend toward domination by the Serbs, the most numerous people. Working with this base, he created a very large underground army, and in continuous war tied down fourteen German divisions.

I piled report upon report for CBS and *Time*. A tabloid New York newspaper asked, via CBS, for a series on the subject, and I supplied it. It stirred quite a controversy. An early reaction to my reports was that of Eric Sevareid, then back in New York: "We thought you were off your rocker with your story from Ruritania about a man with a name out of Gilbert and Sullivan." Among the diplomats in Berne my reports were deemed weird. One of them said to me, "If all this were true, you may be sure Churchill would know it, and would act on it. You must think he is a fool."

Churchill did know. His son was dropped into Yugoslavia as an envoy to Tito. On September 17, 1943, Churchill announced that Britain was accepting Tito's partisans as the only Allied force in Yugoslavia, because they were fighting the Germans, and Mihailovic was not. (The giant Latinovic later became Yugoslavia's chargé in Moscow and helped engineer Tito's break with Russia in 1948.) I was relieved to be certified normal by Winston Churchill.

The shift of fortunes to the Allies was accomplished, as victories generally are, by courage, intelligence and skill. But courage, intelligence and skill were able to reach and pluck the fruits thanks to standing on a platform of continually rising industrial production, while that of their foes declined. Two technological miracles were in progress.

First, there was a Soviet miracle. Before the war the Russians began moving factories to the Urals for security reasons, but progress was slow. With the spur of invasion, the plan took off. Every train bringing soldiers west to fight the Germans went back east loaded with machines torn out of factory floors. In the first three months of war, 1,500 factories were moved, resettled and put back into operation. How the Soviets, who gave planning a bad name, did it can be explained only by that terrible motivation that alone seems to make all humans perform beyond their normal limits: war. Hence came to Stalingrad the thirteen fresh Soviet armies nobody knew existed.

The other act of magic was done in America. Little that is good can be said about American's Depression, but foremost of that little is that it devoted ten years to creating (in order to provide jobs) the best, slickest infrastructure in the world. The Russian armies that moved back westward wore 13 million pairs of winter boots made in the U.S., and moved on 450,000 tons of American steel rails with 2,000 American locomotives and half a million Detroit-made trucks. By the end of the first year of the war, the U.S. was producing 40 percent of the arms turned out by all the nations in WW II.

Bennie and I developed a lively private life, deliberately cutting ourselves out of the main social activity of the Swiss capital: the endless round of small-bore diplomats having parties for one another. Self-exclusion left us time to do some things that proved wholesome as well as fun. Both our educations had been heavy on arts, and light on science. So we bought a microscope, borrowed some textbooks, bicycled to neighboring lakes and fields for specimens and acquired a pretty good primary education in biology. The clear bright mountain nights were fine for star gazing, so with observation and books we became decently familiar with astronomy. We read a lot of books, generally out loud to one another. Among our few social contacts were a delightful English businessman turned wartime intelligence officer named Peter Jellinek, whom I had recruited as a witness for our marriage, and Allen Dulles. We came to know well Alice Leigh-Smith, a physicist of note, married to a British diplomat. Through her we met Irene Curie, Nobel Prize–winning physicist, wife of co-Nobelist Frederick Joliot-Curie, and daughter of the more famous Nobelist Marie Curie. From her we heard of the fantastic notion that tiny atoms could be burst in sequence to create a monstrous explosion, a fascinating topic for after-dinner conversation—but clearly not one to be taken seriously.

CHAPTER TWENTY-NINE

Redemption

In the game of nations, as played in neutral Switzerland, reporters were light players—in the "game" strictly for fun and profit. But there were also heavy players, for whom the risks of information-seeking were a matter of freedom or prison, or even of life or death. They were the operatives of the warring nations, the spies. As an ardent light player, who stuck his nose into everything, I am surprised in retrospect that I did not intrude into the territory of the heavy players more often and get hurt. One of my near-serious encounters was scary enough.

I was moved to it by that most durable of American traits, a mighty propensity to feel guilty. It was a mindset thought to have been carried to the New World by a few boatloads of English Puritans; but it seems to have been just as pervasive among their opponents, the English Cavaliers, who settled Virginia and moved out the Natchez Trace to populate the lower Mississippi Valley—and who incidentally were my people, the landed colonels and captains who lost the English Civil War and begot descendants who lost the American Civil War. Down the generations the virus of guilt was carried till I saw it active in both my parents. Part of the grip of Catholicism on my mother, as on most Catholics, was the offer of periodic liberations from the scourge of blame by purging it, washing it away, in confession and the saying of a few penal Our Fathers and Hail Marys. The famous Protestant evangelical Brother Swaggart of Ferriday positively wallowed in guilt.

I myself have not been free of it. Fits punctuated childhood and adolescence. The man I most admired, my role model, Ed Murrow, was saturated with it. Now, noting that I was happy amid a terrible, brutal war, guilt made periodic assaults on me. In numbers of lives snuffed out and tortured or maimed, this was undoubtedly going to be the biggest tragedy ever. How had I reacted? I have told how I greeted the outbreak of war in 1939 with relief. And in 1941, when America was brought into the carnage, I responded with outright enthusiasm. Early in life I decided that what I needed most were two things: love and a fulfilling job. By accident of timing I acquired both at the same time and blessedly early—someone to hold onto and to hold onto me, and the respect of my peers and bosses. I was enjoying the happiest of consummations, being wanted by lover and editor alike. This at a time when Hell was opening up for fellow humans—Jews, Slavs, dissenters.

The Swiss Red Cross administered a plan whereby one could support a specific child in occupied France, and Bennie and I had done so. One day we received a chilling notice: "Our foreign delegation informs us that the child you have sponsored, Emil Dortort, has unfortunately been deported, so the continuation of this sponsorship is no longer possible." This incident triggered another attack by the virus of guilt. I asked myself: why should you be happy and safe on one side of the border, when just on the other side, in France, people are suffering hunger and torture?

In response to an irrational question I gave an irrational answer: I must at least risk the fate of those in France. I must try to get there and see them, and tell the world about them from personal experience. For weeks I laid out lines and made contacts. Finally one came through. He was a Frenchman, living in Lausanne, operating an irregularly published underground newspaper for distribution in occupied France. He said he could deliver me to a forested place on the border, where soldiers from the main underground force, the *Forces Françaises de l'Intérieur*, would take me in hand, show me their mission, let me talk to some people, then return me, with a fair probability of safety. But I would have to ski. I did not know how to ski, but I promised him I would be a quick study.

In Adelboden in the Bernese Alps stood a camp for American fliers who had escaped the Germans and made their way to Switzerland. I had wanted to write something about them for some time. Bennie and I rented a chalet there, and I learned to ski, following the mad American fliers down the slopes. Back in Berne, I phoned my guide in Lausanne to say I was now ready, but there was no answer. After a day of fruitless calls I went to Lausanne to his apartment. It was empty. Back in Berne I asked around and was told that he had been arrested. He was an agent of the *Milice*, the French arm of the Gestapo. It took me a few days of strong drink to recover from the thought that, had I been able to ski, I would have ended up in a German concentration camp, never to be heard of again. The thought bade the dogs of guilt to lie down and keep silent for a while.

Later in 1944, Bennie and I did get into occupied France, not entirely safely, but under more reliable sponsorship. This was the train of circumstances: Life for an American in Switzerland changed for the better in 1943 and 1944. The Allies swept North Africa clean, took Sicily and landed on the Italian mainland. As the Supreme Court is said to follow the election returns, so the Swiss followed the battle reports. The main Swiss newspaper, the staid *Neue Zürcher Zeitung,* had never recognized the Russian Revolution and made a point of calling Russia's second city Sankt Petersburg. As the Russians pushed the Germans back and looked like coming to Western Europe, the paper switched appellations to Leningrad. And the Swiss allowed me to broadcast again, by telephone from my apartment, for which they would not feel responsible. When the name of the Allied commander became known, a Swiss canton promptly claimed Eisenhower as a descendant (a claim that was disputed by the Germans after the war). For the rest of the war, Swiss and Americans were practically old buddies.

On a great day in early June, we joined a world glued to the radio to hear the voices of Roosevelt, Churchill and Eisenhower announcing the longed-for invasion of Fortress Europe. Sounds of battle were still rising when there came a rumbling nearer by. German and French guards disappeared from the border crossing south of Geneva, and hirsute irregulars appeared. Shooting could be heard at night. The Maquis, the underground fighters who lived in the Savoy mountain forests and bushes, had lost patience and decided to liberate themselves. They attacked a border post and occupied it.

I went to Geneva and took a tram to the border at a crossing spot called St. Julien. The Swiss would not let me leave without a passport. (On entering Switzerland one had to surrender one's passport and could get it back only by submitting a note from the Treasury that one had paid up all taxes.) I returned to Berne and set Bennie to work getting my passport. She did so only on condition that she come with me. "If Europe as we know it is about to disintegrate, we must stay together," she said. When she had rescued our passports, we took them to the French consulate in Geneva. The office, manned by Vichy

French officials, had been visited that day by Free Frenchmen from over the border and been told to get right or get out. They got right and were glad to prove it by giving entrance visas to an Allied journalist and his associate (my official designation of my wife), something they had not had occasion to do for several years.

Late that same afternoon we walked across the Swiss border. Colleagues were sitting on the barrier like crows on a fence, denied permission to cross by the Swiss police, wondering how we got through so easily. I did not share our deep secret: we had a French visa in our passports. A hundred yards on the other side we met two French partisans. Tourism was not on their training agenda, so they did not know what to do about us. They used the phone to a command post for the first time, and it worked. We were told to walk on down the lonely country road, and we would be met. About a mile into the woods there was an inn, the *Lion d'Or,* and a kindly looking Frenchman in a disheveled business suit greeted us. He was Jean-Henri Morin, one of the sweetest-tempered men I ever met, a lifelong friend. He was a reporter for a Paris newspaper soon to be named *Libération.* He had been on the *Milice's* death list, so he fled Paris, but was arrested and jailed in Upper Savoy. The Maquis then attacked and freed him and, feeling journalism must have something to do with intelligence, made him their one-man security officer. He cleared us as friendlies and took us into the restaurant. Thus began a week of pure adventure behind German lines with a people's army too keyed up to wait for the Allies. Later my report appeared as an article in *Life* magazine.

The inn was milling with young fighters with guns, in various stages of eating. The unit commander was a Jewish merchant from Paris named Boule, about thirty years old. A place for us was cleared, but it was a nervous meal. The youngster jammed next to me had come into possession of a German potato-masher hand grenade and was eternally spinning it, hitting it on the table and tossing it from hand to hand.

The next day we proceeded to the beautiful provincial capital, Annecy. For some reason, Boule insisted I ride shotgun next to him on the front seat of a tiny Citroën, holding a tommy gun, my generic name for all that sort of weapon. The windshield was knocked out to improve my vision. I told him I had not fired a gun since childhood. He said there was not much science to it. "If you see a German, don't wait to see if his intentions are friendly. Just flick the safety catch and pull the trigger and try to keep it pointed at him."

Annecy resembled a disturbed antheap, everything in motion, everyone excited. German occupiers, hopelessly surrounded, had surrendered to an overwhelming guerrilla force during the night. When the city-wide public address system, set up to give German orders, blared out the *"Marseillaise"* in the early hours, the people knew their men had won and began a celebration in the streets that never stopped. I went to the football stadium to interview some of the hundred or so German soldiers held there as prisoners. Five SS Gestapo soldiers had refused to surrender unless allowed to drive themselves to the stadium prison camp in their own open car. To avoid bloodshed it was agreed. But when they reached the gate to the stadium, the five stood in their car and poured tommy-gun fire into surrounding partisans, killing about twenty. The celebration turned into an angry, city-wide search for Germans and collaborators that nearly embraced us.

We settled in a hotel that was half burned out from an earlier affray. It was after curfew, and we were very hungry. Morin sneaked us out through empty streets to a bistro that appeared closed but opened at his bidding. We sat down to a meal of bread and soup and wine. Suddenly the door burst open and four or five soldiers of the FFI entered with guns pointed at us. Bennie had gone to the toilet, which consisted of a hole in the floor, and was captured in the awkward position the use of it required. She, Jean-Henri and I were taken outside, where the soldiers, augmented by an ever-growing mob, debated whether to shoot us there or take us to the town hall and try us first. Finally, they decided on the town hall and marched us through dark streets with the mob escort shouting curses at us and windows opening as we passed to let households shout, "*Salauds!*" Insofar as I could think, I thought this must be a replication of scenes from the French Revolution, lacking only tumbrils and guillotine.

At the town hall, police and some of the mob squeezed us into a room and gave us an hour of chaotic misery. No one noticed in the brouhaha that Morin had escaped. He soon returned in triumph. The doors to our room swung open, and in strode a body of guards making way for Morin and a good-looking young man of a little below medium height in rough mountain clothes and a beret and with a German Lugar pistol strapped to his side. He extended his hand, and Morin introduced us. He was Commandant Nizier, commanding the Maquis for all Upper Savoy. He was a professor of biology in his other career.

He took us into an office where Hitler's picture was turned to the wall and explained. Since the SS murders, the town was in uproar hunting for the chief French collaborator, who had disappeared. He was known to carry a false passport. The American one I carried established my guilt: it was deemed counterfeit, for it was known that the Americans were far away in the south. But the clinching fact was that he traveled with a red-haired mistress. For a couple of hours, on Liberation night, Bennie and I were the most famous people in Annecy. We were overjoyed to be relieved of the honor.

In recompense, Nizier made the town ours the next day. We went to the municipal jail, where they held thirty or forty young women, charged with having given pleasure to the Germans. They ranged widely. One was a long-lashed temptress who had arranged to be incarcerated wearing a gossamer blouse, through which nipples of nicely formed breasts told the onlooker that she was carefree and generous. She would not stay in restraint long for she offered what moved men, German or French, to forgiveness. At the other end of the scale was a proud, nice-looking girl who said, hell yes, she slept with a German soldier. They loved one another and were married and had a child, to which she wanted to return as soon as possible. All were subjected to a head shaving, then were paraded through the streets, then turned loose.

On to the provincial prison. The night of the transfer of power, the German jailers opened the cell doors, handed the prisoners the keys to the prison and then took their places behind bars. The abjectness did not seem to help. Some of the ex-jailers were badly beaten. One of two fell on their knees before the visiting American and begged me for support. Morin said to me, "If you could see the abominations they committed, you would not feel that surge of compassion I see overcoming you." Bennie took a lot of pictures and was planning to send them to *Life*. But later, when we were back in Berne, Morin phoned from the border and begged us not to let them be published. Nizier was seeking to induce the nearby Germans to treat captured French partisans as prisoners of war in accord with the Geneva conventions, and our photos might set back his effort. So we did not send them off. As matters turned out, the Germans refused and continued to execute all captured guerrillas; so Nizier ordered the German prisoners I had interviewed shot.

One night we joined a column of trucks winding up the mountains to the Plateau de Glières. The Germans might counterattack at any moment, and the partisans were desperately short of weapons. The RAF had promised to drop two planeloads of arms. Fires were built at the designated landing areas, ready to be lit when the plane approached. We waited all night, but the planes did not come. The following night, after Bennie and I had gone back to Switzerland to write and transmit my reports, the partisans returned to the plateau, and one plane, not two, dropped a cargo of arms. Now came a crisis. There were two underground armies on the plateau, the French Communist FTP (*Franc-Tireur Partisans*) and de Gaulle's FFI (*Forces Françaises de l'Intérieur*). The latter were twice as numerous as the Communists, so the arms were to be shared two to one in favor of the FFI. There was a mountaintop conference: the Communists demanded that, since there was only one planeload, the weapons be distributed equally. Else, said the Communists, we forget the Germans and fight it out here and now. Nizier, in uneasy command of all, finally agreed.

The German counterattack did not materialize. With the Allies penetrating ever deeper into France, they had other matters to worry about. Back in Berne, I phoned Paul White and told him that I thought I could, with the aid of the Maquis, get to Paris. It might ease my way if he could send me a telegram certifying me as a CBS war correspondent. Within an hour, the telegram arrived.

1944–1946

CHAPTER THIRTY

To Paris

"I think I have got it figured," my son said to me. We were sitting on our terrace overlooking the Potomac having long summer drinks thirty-seven years after the time at the end of the last chapter. "Figured what?" I asked. "Figured out how I came into existence," he answered. "I thought I had explained all that to you when you were about seven. I think I showed you X-ray pictures," I said.

"No," he said, "I have often wondered why, after waiting a couple of years you two decided to have me when you did." Bennie and I could but wait for his conclusions. "It was St. Lô," he said, "the breakout at St. Lô. I have back-counted nine months from the date of my birth, and it comes out at about the time the invasion of Europe ceased to be a bridgehead, and the Americans blew a hole in the German lines at St. Lô, and it became a real second front." (I remembered the St. Lô story for another reason. It was a New Orleanian who commanded the breakout, General Joseph Collins, nicknamed "Lightning Joe," commanding the VII Corps.)

Jack continued, "I can see you two there in Switzerland, breathing a great sigh of relief. The future was going to belong to the descendants of Roosevelt and Churchill, not Goebbels and Himmler. I can almost hear you saying, 'Honey, let's go naked tonight,' and I became a real possibility."

His reasoning was surely right; I do not remember that we were that clear-cut about it. Anyhow as the summer of 1944 waned, and Bennie was very pregnant, American troops coming up from the south reached our friends, the French Maquis in Upper Savoy. When Paris had been liberated by the troops who broke out at St. Lô, I told Bennie that, even though there was still fighting in between, I had to get to Paris. I proposed that she remain behind and have the baby in Berne. I might as well have ordered Niagara Falls to go back up.

A Norwegian businessman in Switzerland with a car wanted to drive to Marseilles and sought my advice about safety. I assured him he could get through partisan territory all right. Could he take Benn and me as far as Lyons? There we would try to persuade an American pilot to fly us over the German lines and still-occupied France to Paris. He could. I bought a stack of dollar bills, we packed belongings to be stored in Berne, and off we went.

The trip down was eventless. The FFI had been left to occupy its own country all the way down to the big city. But Lyons was crawling with uniformed Americans. As I spoke their language with minimal accent and showed my certifying telegram from Paul White, I had no problems. With my precious green dollars we had no trouble getting dinner and a hotel room.

But the next day was a form of hell. Bennie was now very pregnant, and terribly sick to her stomach. It had begun raining in the night, and continued raining all the next day. No matter, we went to the airport, which was milling with American soldiers; only military planes were operating there. Nobody seemed to be in charge. A friendly sergeant looked at my telegram and told me my only recourse was to stand out on the runway, in the rain, and go from plane to plane, as each landed, and flash my telegram and ask the pilot if he was flying to Paris, and if he would take me. My wife would probably have to stay out in the rain with me, because as these men were in a war, and took off when they had to take off, I probably wouldn't have time to go back and get her. I followed his suggestion, sat Bennie down on a suitcase, and went from one just-landed plane to another.

This went on from nine in the morning until about four or five in the afternoon when at last a pilot, about to enter his cockpit, looked at my telegram and thought maybe he might be carrying a potential Hemingway to Paris and said, hop in. When I produced an obviously pregnant wife, soaked through and looking quite ill, his face dropped and he began groping for words to call it off. But I had lifted her and stuffed her through the door before he succeeded. The cargo space was empty but for us. The trip was exciting. The pilot hedge-hopped low to the ground the whole way to avoid being shot at by the Germans. Bennie had dreadful nausea. When the craft dipped to land in Paris, she let go and her vomit hit the metal floor with a splash and ran in a rivulet the length of the plane. The navigator was so disgusted that I thought he was going to turn the plane around and take us back to Lyons. He settled for giving me a short, burning essay on what he thought of a man who would take a wife in that condition into a theater of war. At a little makeshift army airport outside Paris we had little difficulty getting places in one of the many Jeeps going to and from the city.

We were let off at the hotel taken over by the army for the press, the Scribe, around the corner from the Place de l'Opéra. I phoned upstairs to Charles Collingwood's room. A hearty voice told me to come on up. Of all the embarrassments I have ever subjected Bennie to, this was the worst; but I feared that if I left her alone in the lobby a fussy concierge might have put her out on the street. In her first appearance before the single most fastidious American in the world her lovely red hair was a dirty rust, and in form rather like dead seaweed cast up on an untidy beach. Her face, uncontaminated by cosmetics for a long day, was sallow with sickness. Clothing plastered to her body by wetness all day had now begun to wrinkle and fray. I was at least as unpresentable, but I was not a female or pregnant or making a first impression.

What made the situation really miserable was the state of the one on whom the impression was being made. Charles was clothed in a red silk dressing gown over red silk pajamas. His wavy hair appeared to have been secured in place one hair at a time. He sat propped up in bed on pillows. A touch of flu, he explained. He smoked from a cigarette in an ivory holder six inches long. On one side of the bed was a bucket with a bottle of champagne in ice; on the other, seated on the side of the bed, a fluffy blond nymph looking upon him with blank admiration and caressing his cheek. He whispered to her, *"Jusqu'à ce soir."* She whispered back, *"Ce soir,"* and pecked his cheek with a little kiss and smiled us all a goodbye. Around the chair rail of the room were propped five or six cartoons. "Picassos," Charles explained. He said he had won them in poker games, which apparently filled free hours in the hotel. High-power poker games.

For all the impression of effeteness, Charles was deadly serious about essentials. He called the proper officer and had me a room in the Scribe in moments. He called another proper officer and got me lined up for accreditation the next day. That would open all else to me, in particular, the restaurant (now disguised as military by being dubbed a mess) and the post exchange; the former would supply me with comestibles, the latter with uniforms. He proposed an engagement for cocktails and dinner. We turned down the cocktails and dinner, thanked him, and went to our room to clean up and rest. Later we went around the corner to a small restaurant for a quiet meal, then to bed, pleased to have made the transfer to a whole new life at the cost of only one day of solid misery.

CHAPTER THIRTY-ONE

Americans in Paris

Charles accompanied me to the offices that bestowed accreditation. His presence hastened the process. Charles had become a figure of moment in American journalism. He had been hired by Edward R. Murrow at about the same time I was hired by Paul White. Immediately, in his first year, he had won the Peabody Award, roughly the radio equivalent of the Pulitzer Prize, for his broadcasts during the London blitz. He wore a handsomely tailored British officer's uniform, which mattered. It was intimidating to U.S. Army bureaucrats, for it said, "I was in this war two years before you, including the year we, Britain and we happy few, faced Hitler alone." With this person on my side I acquired in hours what would have taken me, acting alone, days: dog tags to stay around my neck till the war was lost and won, and a little brown folded card stating that I was accredited to the U.S. Army and had the "assimilated rank" of captain. It was the highest military rank I would have until the Governor of Kentucky made me a colonel. Neither promotion strained my resources. With that precious I.D. card I took off to the biggest PX in Paris and in another hour was in uniform. It was American off the rack, and not as becoming as Charles's, but I was elated.

For my first few days I was assigned to SHAEF, Supreme Headquarters Allied Expeditionary Forces, located at Versailles outside Paris. The work was ridiculously easy for one used to having to scramble for stories. You simply stayed in the SHAEF press headquarters, which was the Scribe Hotel. It was possible to remain in bed till eleven A.M., get to the noon briefing in the ballroom, go up to the workroom and write it up, then go up another floor to broadcast it to the U.S. at one P.M., leaving you free to have an elaborate Parisian lunch and take your girlfriend/wife walking in the Bois in the afternoon, or to go back to bed. Evenings seemed to be one long party for journalists in newly liberated Paris. "I gave my man an unlimited expense account," complained one boss, "and he exhausted it in three days." The Puritan in me saw possibilities for wonderful stagnation. As soon as opportunity offered itself, I asked for and got assignment to an army in the field.

While waiting I began to meet people in the profession, an unfamiliar activity after beginning my career in all-night solitude in London, being isolated with a few fellows in Berlin and even fewer in Switzerland. Oechsner was there, in uniform as an officer in the Office of War Information. He introduced me to his British counterparts, one of whom, R. H. S. Crossman, became a long-time friend. Charles Wertenbaker, chief of correspondents for *Time,* invited us to drinks and regretted my decision to leave his staff and work full-time for CBS. I exchanged drinks with a number of celebrities including John Dos Passos, William Saroyan, and, always at the Ritz bar when not trying to get killed at some disputed barricade, Ernest Hemingway.

One day I did one of those noon broadcasts just to stay in practice, and immediately afterward Collingwood told me that I was summoned to the George V Hotel, where William S. Paley was at that moment awaiting me for lunch. He was the wonder executive who created the CBS network, turning a fortune into a bigger fortune and himself into a man of influence. He was now serving as a colonel in the psychological warfare branch of the Office of War Information. I was nervous. I had never met a big business executive before, particularly not one whose dog tags were done in silver by Cartier. Six or seven of his staff, mostly ex-advertising people, were standing around the private room having drinks. When he saw me at the door, he walked right through them and shook my hand. "At last we get to see what you look like," he said. He was in his midforties, good-looking, unassuming, and he immediately put me at my ease. He was impressed by my book and by my discovery of Tito. He admitted to thinking I was crazy at first, but noted that very few reporters get their scoops confirmed in the end by Winston Churchill.

The next morning I was led to a room where all of CBS's field reporters had assembled, and met them for the first time. Then I found out why they had come together. In walked the most impressive male person I was ever to know. (The most impressive female person I ever met I married.) The boss, the Chief European Correspondent, Edward R. Murrow, had flown over from London and wanted to talk with us. I did not think it possible, but he was more suave than Charles, very tall, very slim, very dark and handsome and wearing an at least equally handsomely tailored British officer's uniform. It was hard to believe that this natural aristocrat was born in the impoverished hollows of the North Carolina Appalachians and worked in his youth in the logging camps of the Northwest. He sounded the way he looked, elegant, commanding attention. He had no special message, just praise for reporting done up to the German West Wall and a wish to stay in close contact. I dared to think that his purpose may have been to size up the newest member of his staff. He asked me what I wanted. I said I hoped to be assigned to an army at the front, unless all such missions were taken. He said he knew of a fresh army in the line, headquartered in Holland a stone's throw from the German border and rumored to have the mission of taking Berlin, the U.S. Ninth Army. I leapt at it.

Murrow's impressive presence was enhanced by his reputation. He was that rare phenomenon, a reporter who had a direct influence on the war. Along with Ernie Pyle and William Shirer he was one of the three outstanding journalists of WW II. Millions waited on his broadcast word each day. His reports on the British, under fire and alone, surely helped move Americans from neutrality to the angels' side. Whenever he returned to the U.S. for a short spell, he was called to the White House for consultation with Roosevelt. He was probably even more popular in Britain, where his pieces were rebroadcast and were a factor in sustaining morale. Churchill, himself a master of language, was an ardent listener and called him a master of language. Once just after the war I had occasion to watch the making of a Murrow broadcast, hoping to learn something about how to do it. It was his farewell broadcast to the British. He did not write, he walked about the room and smoked and dictated in short bursts to his secretary. As I heard those shaped, immaculate, glowing sentences I knew that this was something you did not learn, you had to be born with it. A radio reviewer for the *Daily Express* wrote the next day, "When I hear a broadcast like that I want to give up and throw my typewriter away."

His forte was descriptive, rather than analytical, journalism. His description of a North African desert battlefield before a battle, seen through binoculars, was a classic exercise in painting a picture with spoken words. One night he improved on a description of people scurrying to shelters at the outset of a bombing raid by holding the microphone at ankle level on the street. Destined to become a part of every anthology of writings for the ear was one of his descriptions of a bombing raid on Germany seen from the bomber. It was distributed as a booklet with the title, "Orchestrated Hell," a term taken from his text. Among others it contained the famous description of flak shells bursting around the plane as resembling "a handful of rice thrown against black velvet." He would be the first American correspondent to enter a liberated concentration camp—Buchenwald—whence he wrote and spoke a terrifying description. He was not above using that marvelous voice for tricks. His most famous one was speaking in short sentences, separated by silences just long enough to make you want to beg to hear more. At an army camp I sat with about twenty reporters on the edge of our seats, listening to his reports on Buchenwald: "'You won't want to go into the next room,' my guide said . . . 'Why not?' I said . . . 'You won't be able to keep your food down' he said . . . 'Where's the door?' I said . . . 'There' he said . . . I turned the handle . . . the door opened . . . I went in . . ." A bit corny, but very effective. A colleague summed it up, "With that voice, he could say 'Twenty-eight' and it would sound like the most important utterance you ever heard."

Remarkably, he had never been trained in journalism and had never had any intention of becoming a reporter. Trained reporters, Elmer Davis wrote, "are faintly scandalized that such good reporting can be done by a man who never worked on a newspaper in his life . . . he has the habit of going around town in an open car to see what is being hit. That is a good way to get the news, but perhaps not the best way to make sure that you will go on getting it."

The day after Murrow had come and departed, the Scribe was put under heavy guard for an hour, and General Eisenhower appeared to brief us. The regular-guy charm of a clearly superior guy came through. An unknown lieutenant colonel when war began, he gave the impression that he felt his swift rise was too much for him. It lent him a becoming manner of modesty. "You guys are going to crucify me yet," he said with a laugh in response to one too probing question. (Never missing an opening to be critical, a couple of reporters dared to wonder in their dispatches whom he was comparing himself with in his reference to crucifixion.) His main message to us was that the present breathing spell after the dash from Normandy to the German border would not last. "I'm not going to sit in a hole with a blanket over my head this winter," he said. I felt that I should get to the front as soon as possible.

But first I had to look to the two main members of my family: wife and embryo. Their situation at the Scribe Hotel was paradoxical. A young major in charge of assigning rooms asked me to come see him. "The red-haired girl with you," he said, "I have been told that she is your wife?" I said that was right, moreover she was a pregnant wife. He shook his head sadly and said, "She will have to go. It is strictly against all rules for her to be here." I said, "But if she were a girl I picked up on the street, she could stay?" "That's right," he said, "we could overlook her. But we can't overlook a wife. We aren't allowed to provide family quarters." I could see the ineluctable logic there. We had no recourse but to adjust and get out.

We found a small hotel. On her own Bennie later found a better place, a pension called Le Nid de Verdure, "the Verdant Nest." It was a place of assignation for wealthy Frenchmen and their mistresses, so it had good black market connections and good food for those who could pay. She had a hard, cold, war winter to endure, but Jean-Henry Morin and his Irish wife, Leibh, for friends. I would return as often as I could get leave. My heart stayed with her, but the rest of me bade her goodbye.

Bill Downs had reserved a Jeep and driver (reporters were not allowed to drive themselves) to return to his post at the First Army headquarters in Belgium. I would go with him as far as he went, then find transportation northward to Holland and the Ninth Army. Nobody in those armies would spend the coming winter in a hole with a blanket over his head. But it would not be Eisenhower who decided that; it would be Hitler.

For seven years I had lived and dwelt almost entirely with foreigners—the British in Britain, the Germans in Germany and all kinds in Switzerland. In Paris and on the western front I was back again with my own people. It was a reintroduction to Americans, and how they had changed! Having been one of them, I remembered how desolated they were by the Depression when I was last among them. They were supernumerary, unwanted, an embarrassment to society in their large useless numbers. No wonder they took to the new name given them in the army: originally the equipment given them was labeled "Government Issue," and so, once uniformed and trained, they too were GI. But now, what a switch! They had suddenly been recognized as persons of worth and value, each individually wanted and needed; the hope of the world reposed in them. Huey Long had not made every man a king, but the war made every American boy a hero, celebrated in multicolored ads for everything in the slick magazines, and in hundreds of movies about everything from stage door canteens to fighting fronts. And how their nation took care of them.

Leonard Shapiro described an American invasion operation with exaggeration but with a certain insight: first wave, GI's; second wave, tanks; third wave, movies and chocolate bars; fourth wave, Bob Hope and Marlene Dietrich and the Rockettes to make sure they know we love them. I would spend the rest of the war reporting what it cost them to be important once more.

CHAPTER THIRTY-TWO

Once More, the Western Front

After a long day's ride we reached Spa, the little Belgian town whose name became over centuries the generic name for all European watering places. In the Great War, Spa had been headquarters of the whole Imperial German Army and became the scene of one of the high political dramas of the century. In a dark week in 1918, Kaiser Wilhelm took refuge there with his highest officers, hoping for surcease from demands that he abdicate. The officers, however, reinforced the demands. His soldiers would no longer fight under his command. The victorious Allies would not negotiate with a Germany identified with him. As a major cause and a complete symbol of a terribly failed war, Wilhelm had to go. In the silence of night his special train pulled out of Spa carrying him into the Netherlands and out of history.

Now, in the winter of 1944–1945, Spa was the headquarters of the American First Army, dedicated to trying to drive a new German emperor out of history. It was the only break on my way to my assignment, and I was thrilled at the stopover. I delight in visiting places of high history and imagining what happened; as when I sat alone in the Roman Forum one night (my plane to leave Rome at three A.M. was delayed five hours on that occasion, so I took a taxi to the foot of the Capitoline and climbed the fence and communed with the ruins) watching Mark Antony utter the words composed for him by his gifted amanuensis, Shakespeare; or spent a solitary evening in Lincoln's parlor in Springfield (we had set up lights for a TV interview with Carl Sandburg the next day) hearing Republican moguls propose that the resident run for President. There was no solitude to be had in teeming Spa, but at the Hotel Britannique I had no trouble seeing in my mind's eye the departure of Kaiser

Wilhelm, history's personified warning that inferior people in high positions are more dangerous than dens of rattlesnakes.

I stayed in town that night, and the next day joined other reporters in a trip to the Hürtgen Forest, where a battle was raging. In sidling up to the Siegfried Line—the name the Allies gave the German West Wall—the First Army had cut into those woods and got engaged in a bloody contest I imagined to be something like the Wilderness Campaign battles in the U.S. Civil War. We parked our Jeep in the forest, then walked deeper in to a command post, diving often for cover from "tree bursts" that turned stands of trees into instant kindling and spread hot shrapnel democratically around. It was my first experience in combat, and I was mighty glad when it was over, and we were back out of the woods.

I stayed on part of the next day, when advised that there was to be a top-level briefing. At the appointed hour about thirty reporters were led into a map room. The commander of the First Army, General Courtney Hodges, and the commander of his assigned air force, called the Ninth Tactical Air Command, General Elwood Quesada, met us. I had trouble matching Hodges with the role of aggressive warrior; he was dumpy, inarticulate and looked and behaved old for the job. Quesada was more the war type, of Spanish derivation, but 150 percent American, and all youth and energy. In time, he would become a good friend, treasured for, among other things, his store of humor. He told me that in midwar he had been called back to the U.S. and found the armed forces lodged in a brand new, giant structure called the Pentagon. He said to his taxi driver, as they approached the monster, "Wonder how many people work there?" The driver said, "Oh, about half." A favorite story was of the German general assigned to govern newly occupied Paris, who ordered that a lady of the aristocracy be provided to share his bed the first night. The French obliged. The morning after, he said to his bedmate, "I must tell you my dear, in nine months you may have a little boy. You will have my permission to call him Adolf." The lady responded, "I think I must tell you, mon General, that in a week you may have a little rash and you will have my permission to call it measles." In a high-tech war, Quesada invented an elementary instrument of command in air actions. For quick reference, he mounted over his instrument panel a grapefruit studded with matchsticks, indicating where all around him the airplanes of his command were located, and (by deduction) whether any were missing.

The two generals revealed details of a planned operation to push the whole front across western Germany to the Rhine River, the last geographical barrier before victory. I rushed on northward to my assignment, the Ninth U.S. Army, headquartered in the Dutch city of Maastricht. I arrived in time to be present for a similar briefing there. The briefer was the commanding officer, Major General William H. Simpson, a very large, lean Texan with the head of a bald eagle. His face wore a perpetual smile, as did his disposition. He seemed altogether too gentle, gentlemanly and sweet-tempered to command expeditions of mass killing.

Unfortunately, the offensive to the Rhine they were all foretelling was not going very far that winter. The Ninth advanced about eight miles and was stopped cold. I got a driver who knew the terrain to take me to a good lookout point over the Roer River, atop a slag heap. I had found a primitive recording machine at First Army and brought it with me, and now I wrestled the bulky apparatus up to my lookout, hoping to describe the scene. Beyond there was not the lazy little river I had been told to expect, but a raging torrent, broad as my native Mississippi River.

We had a problem. All the Allied armies north of France were paralyzed by interlocking obstacles. The British were the farthest north and were assigned to make the biggest assault, over the north German plain to (presumably) Berlin. They had to move across soggy Dutch soil, so they went very slowly and had to have us move alongside to shield their flank from murderous German counterattacks. But we could not move, because in front of us ran this little river, about twenty-five yards wide, but capable of swelling to a quarter mile's width in hours. That variability was achieved because the Germans controlled seven Roer dams high in the mountains and could open the spigots to drown our men or to cut off those who made it to the other side of the river. Here was a circumstance all our planning had not foreseen. We could not move till the dams were seized. But the dams were in the region of the First U.S. Army, on the edge of that same Hürtgen Forest, south of us. The First was trying, but the Germans were holding on tenaciously. The dams would not be taken until February of the next year.

So, though I had come to report a Blitzkrieg, I began to adjust to covering a war of attrition. Press accommodations were the work of the fabled Major Barney Oldfield. Blond, good-looking, always cheerful, Barney was what God meant when he allowed the term "PR" to be coined. Resolved despite everything to have a happy camp, he had requisitioned a good hotel and acquired a good local cook, a band and a pretty girl to sing or just sit and be looked at.

I spent my days sharing Jeeps with other reporters and touring segments of our front. It was cold business. Jeeps were required to stay uncovered in order not to be surprised by low-flying planes. On all-day drives in the freezing wind, snow and rain, one got numb. One also got a happy lesson about the limitations of our smallest enemies, bacteria and viruses. You never caught cold or pneumonia, a wonderful boon to one like me who catches cold at every hiccup in the weather. In the icy, ever-fresh gale the little beasts simply could not get

a hold. Often you found a warm company command post in the cellar of a ruined house and stayed the night under fire, less for the experience than because it was too damned cold to drive back. Utter joy was finding a field
hospital. They did wonderful things with medicinal ethyl alcohol and canned
pineapple juice. If you had to go to bed without a warm body next to you, a
belt of liquor was next best.

You found out things about yourself too. One day I sat with an artillery observer in the fragmented remains of a second floor of a ruined house. At one
point he said, "Here, you direct fire," and he moved aside. Through the glasses
I saw a German soldier rise from what appeared to be a trench and walk away
from it. As directed, I gave the coordinates and the order to fire. In a moment
the soldier disappeared in smoke, and when it cleared he was not there. I was
startled, "My God," I said, "I am afraid I killed him!" I was horrified, and must
have showed it. My GI friend looked at me with utter disgust. "You guys!" he
said or something like that, "What the shit do you think we are in this war for?"
It took a long night for me to recollect that I was the Oxford man who had proposed war without, apparently, thinking that it would involve killing people.

On another occasion I had a crisis of ethics and international law, and
didn't come out too well. On a sub-subartic day I was walking back from a
wrecked front-line village along the Roer and reached a line of forest. On its
edge several GI sentries were easing the pain of cold by nursing a wood fire in
an oil drum. I had about a mile more to walk to my Jeep but stopped a few
minutes to store up some warmth. Then across the flat field I had just tra-
versed we saw three bundles moving toward us. They turned out to be an
American soldier with a rifle, delivering two German prisoners from a captured scouting patrol.

The American was a sergeant with the habit of command. "You guys get
these Krauts back to battalion. The major may want to interrogate them."
There was no response, just a cluster of looks that said, "Who? Me?" Getting
angry, the sergeant said, "Okay, you, you with the dumb look. You escort these
prisoners to battalion CP, starting now. Git, or I'll give you some reasons to
wish you had never been born!" Dumb Look muttered, then pointed his gun
at a road through the trees, then at the two men, and all three moved off. A
few moments after they had disappeared into the woods, two shots rang out. A
moment later Dumb Look was back, warming his hands at the fire. "Tried to
escape," he said. "Bastards tried to kill me."

I felt something ought to be done about a bum killing two people so he
could stay near a fire, but I didn't know what. One of the other sentries read
my mind and said, "War Correspondent, if you are thinking about making
something out of this, you better think about something else. You got no witnesses and Dumb Look's got two—us." I mentioned it to the major back at

battalion, but he had a war on his mind. I still do not know what should have been done.

A superb army, superbly equipped and trained, that did little but sit and watch a changeable little river run in front of it did not provide a wealth of good copy. I did not get out to the big green van in the woods that was our transmitting station often enough. When I did, I was not pleased with my copy. To go way ahead of chronology, when the dams were taken, and we launched our big offensive across the river, I spent the day and night with a company assigned to lead the assault. It was a good story, my best opportunity yet. But I was dissatisfied with my broadcast reports on it. Then, it occurred to me that it might make a good short magazine article. I rewrote it with that in mind, and it read well. I sent it to Murrow's office in London, and asked that if be offered to an agent. Two days later I got a telegram from Murrow himself telling me *Liberty* magazine had grabbed it and would publish it under the headline, "Over the River," making me $3,000 richer. Murrow added the sentence, "Why don't you do some of that kind of writing for us?" His comment troubled me. I was simply not writing for radio and the ear; I was still tied to the printed page and the eye. I would try harder, but I am not sure I ever fully succeeded.

Back now to our slow war of attrition. It did not last. One day in December of 1944, we were warned by a briefing officer to avoid roads south. Some of our Ninth Army divisions were leaving us and moving south to help the First Army, and the roads were almost impassable to other traffic. Something very big was going on down in First Army territory.

CHAPTER THIRTY-THREE

The Bulge

It was very big indeed. It comes as a surprise to most Americans to learn that the greatest battle Americans ever fought anywhere was the Battle of the Bulge, which took place in the Ardennes mountain region of Belgium from mid-December 1944 to mid-January 1945. No battle in our bloody Civil War or our part in two wars in Europe was as big in numbers or expanse. More than 600,000 American soldiers took part, and they suffered 81,000 casualties. On the other side, about 500,000 Germans were involved, with about 100,000 casualties. Late in the battle the British provided 55,000 men and took 1,400 ca-sualties.

The location was a long but very thinly held sector of the U.S. First Army front, well south of the Roer dam fighting, deep in the Ardennes mountain forests where the Allies had been sure there would be no further action. Four American divisions, unready for combat, were hit by a surprise German attack. They would later learn that the attackers were more than twenty German divi-sions, led by elite SS Panzer units, the best Hitler had. So great was the sur-prise that it was a while before the Americans considered it anything more than a local operation. Communications lines from some American front-line positions to their divisional HQs were cut, so division commanders were un-aware of the severity of the attack and reported to Spa, First Army headquar-ters, that the situation was well in hand.

With inadequate information, General Hodges in Spa concluded that the operation was a long-expected German counterattack against his divisions, which were trying to take the Roer dams. He felt he could handle that with troops at hand. Not for twenty-four hours did the Americans realize that this was no mere local attack but a great new offensive by three Ger-man armies, with 1,500 tanks and tanklike guns, against the four American di-visions in this sector, designed to turn the tide and win the war for Hitler. The magnitude of the offensive was made clear to First Army reporters when, jeeping out of Spa to go to the front, they found that the front had come to them. They ran into German tiger tanks eight miles from town and Hodges' headquarters.

Farther north we at the Ninth Army had even less reason to know that anything important was happening, until we saw our divisions being stripped from us and redirected south to help the First Army. When we decided to take Jeeps and go down and see, the dispatcher informed us that passwords were suddenly *de rigueur;* we couldn't get past the corner without knowing the password of the day. We got it and took off.

But passwords were not enough. We were stopped every few miles by GI roadblocks and subjected to a barrage of questions designed to certify our Americanism.

"Who is Betty Grable's husband?" I said Jackie Coogan, which was out of date; it was now Harry James. But I got passing remarks for knowing the pre-vious one; a German infiltrator would not have known.

"Who is Blondie's husband?" This was a good one. Every American would know, no German would.

"Who won the World Series?" I drew a blank, but enough of our party knew to keep me from being shot.

"Who is Charlie McCarthy's boss?" I had philosophical doubts about which of the two figures in the act was boss, but this was no time to quibble. Edgar Bergen.

Just outside Spa, MP's stopped us. The First Army was moving its HQ and was not at home to visitors. We followed the parade to a place near Liège called Chaudfontaine, designated to be the new HQ. There amid chaos I found Jack Frankish of the UP at a typewriter and begged for information. He said to beware of wild rumors of mass American desertions, of massacres of Americans taken prisoner. We were falling back, but in fair order. I raced back to Maastricht to broadcast. My informant's reassurances lost some conviction when I heard that, half an hour after I left him, German planes attacked Chaudfontaine, and he was killed. That night, First Army reporters appeared at our camp, theirs having been disrupted. They were full of those rumors, but now at our place they ran into a new and savage army censorship that sheared their dispatches down to the bone. Then came an official announcement that suggested the worst: Hitherto all American armies in Europe had been under American command all the way to the top. We had been part of General Bradley's 12th Army Group. Now, Eisenhower announced, our Ninth U.S. Army and the besieged First U.S. Army were being placed under British command, to be part of the northernmost Army Group under British Field Marshal Montgomery. Since Ike hated Monty, this must mean we were in serious trouble.

As soon as it was clear that the Germans had made a big breach in the front, everyone assumed that Hitler's goal was to retake Paris. In Paris, Eisenhower was nearly suffocated by the dense guard assigned to protect him. I thought briefly of leaving the front and getting to Paris as soon as possible to take my wife southward to safety.

But Paris was not the goal. To ease narration, I shall now go fast-forward to tell what our leaders were trying, with too little information, to comprehend and what we reporters were puzzling out with even less. Ingeniously, Hitler had put together about twenty divisions in the impenetrable Eifel Mountains of Germany facing the weak First U.S. Army sector. On December 16 at 5:30 A.M. he attacked. The target was Antwerp, the biggest port in Europe, west of us. The move was designed to cut the British (with a couple of U.S. forces) in the north off from the bulk of the Americans in the south. Then he planned to destroy the British, as was tried around Dunkirk in 1940, then offer to negotiate with the Americans. He would offer, as bait, to turn all his force eastward and prevent a Soviet occupation of Europe.

I thought that the idea of dividing the Americans from the British and dealing with them separately was an absurd hope for Hitler—till some facts emerged later. Montgomery had always wanted Eisenhower to ascend to a figurehead overall command, but cede real command of all Allied troops in Europe to him. When Ike, for convenience of communications, gave him American troops north of the bulge, leaving those south of it to U.S. General Bradley, the pompous British general saw it as a confession of U.S. failure. In talking to reporters he publicly depicted himself as the savior and proposed more brazenly than ever that he be given all. Ike blew. He wrote out a demand that his civilian superiors choose between him and Monty. As they were sure to choose Ike, Monty, facing the end of his career, apologized and backed down. Throughout this period of acrimony the London press conducted a vicious anti-American campaign. We were nearer to a split than even Hitler supposed.

This, the biggest failure of American intelligence since Pearl Harbor, occurred because the Germans observed strict radio silence (so we could not use our amazing Ultra decoder) and because air observation was impossible due to a cloud ceiling so low you could touch it from a sitting position. The Allies also suffered from a cocksure conviction that the Germans were no longer strong enough to mount a major action. The Germans instilled panic on top of surprise when they sent German soldiers in U.S. uniforms and U.S. Jeeps behind U.S. lines to sabotage and confuse. Thus the need for passwords and tests on Americana at roadblocks. After the battle, when all the information was in, this last Hitler scheme of putting mock Americans behind our lines proved to be ridiculously ineffective. But some incidents that were initially dismissed as wild rumors turned out to have degrees of truth. There were no desertions, but some U.S. regiments, surrounded and rendered defenseless, did capitulate in the biggest American mass surrender—7,000 men at once—since Bataan in the Pacific. And a spearhead of ruthless SS troops did perpetrate massacres of American prisoners.

The positions of troops changed by the hour. But I was determined to get close to some unit and at least acquire some first-hand notions of what was happening. The only reserves Eisenhower had were the two airborne divisions resting in France. They were rushed to the bulge, the 101st to the town of Bastogne on the southern side of the incision, and the 82nd on the northern side. I found out that the 82nd was headquartered near the town of Werbomont. It had recently been called by the British General Dempsey "the best division of troops in the world today." I headed for Werbomont as fast as clogged roads and mud and snow would permit. I was delighted to find there my old Oxford college mate Karl Price, with whom I had innocently surveyed Normandy in student days. He was a captain on the staff. Then he had doubted that Hitler could be stopped by war; now he was stopping Hitler at the point of highest cost. I asked if I could see the commanding officer, Major General James M. Gavin. I was told, "You can if you can catch him." He was almost always out in his Jeep, or, rifle in hand, loping from one front line unit to another. I got the temporary location of a battalion command post and took off in my Jeep in the direction of gunfire, scared but determined.

After a drive of about a quarter-hour we came upon an incongruous sight: a homey little snow-covered bungalow in the forest, so placid and untouched by war that you expected to see children playing in the snow and a housewife sweeping the steps. Instead the family had fled, and an American soldier, his vehicle on the roadside, stood guard. The soldier said, "We were informed you were coming this way. We are laying out something to eat for the General inside. General Gavin would like for you to join him."

A tiny peripatetic staff was apparently expert at anticipating his moves and concerned not to have their commander become mistake-prone because of undernourishment. They searched out this empty home, got word to his driver and waited. Soon he rolled up in his Jeep equipped with radio, driver and bodyguard. For the role in the film *The Longest Day*, Robert Ryan was chosen. Actually, even with Hollywood's special requirements, Jim Gavin fit the role better. Tall, good-looking, slender (as his nickname "Slim Jim" indicated), his face smooth-shaven and unlined with cares, he walked into the spotless little dining room like a man who had spent the morning casually reading a book, not out in a war dodging bullets at the front, to which he would soon return. He suited the cliché, a soldier's soldier, having risen from the ranks to West Point to become now, at age thirty-seven, the youngest division commander in any army in World War II; and he would become a lieutenant general in time. A better cliché might be Renaissance man, for after the war he became a successful business executive and author, and served President Kennedy as ambassador to Paris—a post one had to be very rich or very able to fill, and he was not rich.

We were seated in the small family dining room, where everything was spotless and just where it ought to be. The table shone as if freshly polished, and so did the china. The war was never out of mind due to the thunder of nearby artillery and the rattling of the china. Over clear soup and a plate of Spam greatly improved by the GI cook, I learned that the big arrow Hitler was pointing toward Antwerp was the Sixth Panzer Army commanded by Colonel General Joseph "Sepp" Dietrich. He was a Hitler favorite, once Hitler's chauffeur and bodyguard. The 82nd was now trying to stop the sharp arrowhead Dietrich had sent out, detached from the rest, to break through to the goal. It was called *Kampfgruppe Peiper*, named after its commander, fanatical young Colonel Joachim Peiper, and it consisted of a string of armored vehicles fifteen miles long. The rest of Dietrich's army was being slowed badly by the stubborn refusal of American units to give up essential road centers back on the shoulders of the penetration.

To complete this little strategic snapshot, Hitler had another big arrow pointed west, south of and parallel to Dietrich's: the Fifth Panzer Army. It was meant to protect Dietrich's flank, but when Dietrich bogged down, the Fifth Panzer was ordered to take over the main push westward. Its progress with its new mission was hampered, however, when it too snagged on two road centers: one, the town of St. Vith; and a bigger one, the town of Bastogne. It encircled Bastogne, and its commander sent General McAuliffe, U.S. defender, the famous order to surrender, to which McAuliffe responded more famously, "Nuts!"

Meal and conversation done in fifteen minutes, I thanked the General for lunch. He said, "It's your taxes, you're welcome." He bade me goodbye and was off. My driver and I resumed our search for the battalion CP, which, Gavin had told me, was in direct collision with arrowhead Peiper. It became tough going. A dingy day had turned white with a heavy snowfall. We caught up with a file of about twenty GI's trudging along what was visible of the road. They were seeking the same battalion CP to be assigned as replacements. At a grove of trees they left the road and went into the woods. I left the Jeep and followed. I got into conversation with a sergeant, who told me that Peiper was the author of the massacre of American soldiers. The GI's he was leading had lost all fright after hearing of the shootings, and now were in a bloody mood and anxious to get into the fight.

We came to the edge of this patch of woods and had to cross an open area to another patch. The sergeant warned that we were maybe two hundred yards from the Germans, so get to cover fast. About half-way across it happened: nasty little whines ending in ear-splitting crashes right on top of us. I went down face first in the deep snow and tried to wriggle my way to China. The whines and crashes melded together in a terrible racket. The Germans had this space zeroed in and were just waiting for game. How they could see anything in this curtain of snow was beyond understanding; they must have had observers very close. I was scared sick. It became clear to my addled brain that there was no safety in lying there and praying, so I got up and waddled through hip-deep snow to the next woods. The others were already there. The only casualty was one slightly wounded soldier.

The sergeant said to me that, if I wanted to help the war effort, I should go back. I was unequipped for combat, and he would be very pleased to have me on no part of his mind on a fluid front, where the foe one shot at might turn out to be a friend. I needed no prodding. I was supposed to write about it, not do it; I was not even allowed to carry a weapon. I trudged back, found the Jeep coated with snow and the driver warming his feet on the motor. It took two hours to get back through snow and traffic to Maastricht and a typewriter and a microphone.

Despite the long daily ride I kept in touch with the 82nd for the next few

days, which is all it took. One day I followed a unit that had just cut off a thrust
by Peiper. A string of five or six German vehicles were scrap. The lead tank had
a hole blown into its side by a bazooka. I looked through the hole. The driver's
body sat up erect, but it had no head. It had been sheared off neatly right at
the neck. The blood had settled, and it looked like one of those thick cables
that run under cities, cut off for repairs. Several corpses, blue in the cold, lay
in ditches. By the day before Christmas, Peiper was stopped well short of his
intermediate goal, the Meuse River. With no fuel, ammo, medicines or food he
put demolition charges in his tanks and led his remaining men back to Dietrich on foot. Of his force of 6,000 only 800 made it back. (At the end of the
war, Peiper was tried by a war crimes court, found guilty of a massacre of
American soldiers and Belgian civilians, imprisoned and then paroled. Peiper
sought to wipe out his past by moving to a village in France, where he lived under an assumed name. One morning he was found murdered. No one knows
by whom.) The day before Christmas the skies cleared, and Quesada's airplanes had a turkey shoot over roads jammed with German traffic. One German unit got to within sight of the Meuse, the halfway point to Antwerp, but
then ran out of gas. On January 3, American and British forces began the
counteroffensives that would seal off the Bulge. Ultimately, the Germans
never had the force or the fuel to retake Antwerp and would never have broken in at all but for a unique instance of an undermanned segment of front and
a terrible case of inattention.

One of the biggest German failures was the phantom mock Americans assigned to wreak havoc behind our lines. When Otto Skorzeny, the Führer's
daring-jobs man, combed the Wehrmacht for men able to speak American
English, he found only ten, all former merchant seamen. He found about a
hundred more with bookish English. Germans who spoke the enemy language
well were very valuable and had been grabbed by other services long ago.
Finding uniforms and Jeeps was just as hard. The chosen were sent into our
mass, four to a Jeep, sitting bolt upright like toy soldiers, easily discovered.
Eighteen were caught in roadblock interviews. I visited three of them in a
stockade. Their English was so poor we had to converse in their language. One
said he was a fan of American movies and thought he knew the manner well
enough to get by. Most of the others counted on that only friend of a soldier in
combat, dumb luck, and it let them down. I was back the next morning for the
execution. They were tied with backs to posts. A square of cardboard with a
big black circle on it was pinned just left to the center of their rib cages. One
of them managed to shout, *"Es lebe der Führer!"* just before the fusillade.
Each remained at stiff attention a split second after the shots struck, then
sagged in death. I wondered again, as I often had before, why Germans hon-

ored a leader who was as contemptuous of them as he was of us, and in the end would say his people were not worthy of him.

We had won. But you could not stifle amazement at the cleverness with which the Germans had prepared this blow, and the boldness and skill with which they carried it out. This, though later information reveals that the German commanders involved all thought it was hopeless. The explanation may lie in a story told me by an English soldier. Just after the war, the English occupiers in one town organized a rugby football match with a pick-up German team. The Germans won and exulted, "We beat you at your national game." The Englishman answered, "That's all right; we have just beaten you at yours."

CHAPTER THIRTY-FOUR

Movement at Last

When life depends daily or hourly on the close cooperation of your fellows, you tend to develop an emotional tie to the institution that holds you together. So it became with me and the Ninth Army. However, my basic feeling at this point was not pride but sympathy. When first put in line, the Ninth looked ahead to the highest missions: to race to take and cross the Rhine, to seize the Ruhr district and deprive Germany of its industrial base, to seize Berlin and cut off the monstrous head of Nazism that led to this bloody pass in human affairs. Instead the Ninth began its career on the Western front paralyzed by the action of dams in another army's zone. Then it was drained of its divisions by the unforgivable intelligence flaws to the south, and had to watch the Battle of the Bulge as an emaciated bystander. Now it was sundered from the rest of the U.S. Army and assigned to a British commander famous for his calculated efforts to prevent others from sharing credit. And in war, credit is not a matter of vanity; if you demand that men place their lives at risk, the purpose must seem to them to be important.

About a month after the German bulge in the lines was flattened out, the First Army at last took over the Roer dams, and on February 10 Montgomery ordered his whole Army Group (which included the Ninth U.S.) to advance. Unfortunately, the Germans had destroyed all the machinery of the dams with the cocks half-open, so we, ready to spring forward, watched the little river spread before us again. I slept the night in the cellar of a gutted house with a company of soldiers scheduled to be in the first wave. Or rather I did not sleep. I lay awake uncomfortably, studying hand grenades strung casually along clothes lines near the ceiling. At about three A.M. the lieutenant rousted us out. We forced some coffee and K-rations down, then filed out into the night of Fourth of July fireworks against a black sky. We walked in single file toward the river. About half-way there we were ordered to sit in a ditch and wait. The river went on expanding into a lake, and at about four A.M. General Simpson finally ordered our offensive called off. We would have felt guilty at thus endangering the advance of the British and Canadians north of us, but for the fact that they had worse and unrelated luck and weren't doing well regardless of us. It began pouring rain, and the low, soft Dutch soil turned into mud two feet deep. Then, the Roer overflowed into the larger Maas River and put much of the British front under water.

Thirteen days later, on February 23, the river had contracted enough, so we jumped off. I went down to the river but decided not to cross under fire in overloaded boats but to wait till a bridge already under construction was ready. A colleague and I took refuge from fire in a front line medical station on the riverbank. It was already filling with wounded. In half an hour it looked like an ill-run slaughterhouse, and we were told to get out; they needed all the floor space for wounded. I was glad to leave, for even my stable stomach was beginning to quiver at the sight of that much open flesh. The impression of disaster was wrong. Twenty wounded men in a small room look like a million. In fact it was a well-run hospital, and the wounded were being mended and moved to the rear rapidly.

Once past the mud of the Roer and onto the flat plains before the Rhine in dried weather, the Ninth ran wild. General Bradley later compared its operation to the breakthrough at St. Lô in Normandy. First, it turned north and secured the flank of the British; then it lit out east and was the first army to reach the Rhine, facing the great city of Düsseldorf. Along the thirty-four-mile section of the west bank the Ninth controlled, it found by reconnaissance a densely forested arc of the opposite bank unguarded by any nearby German force. Engineers and equipment were brought in to build a pontoon bridge. But when the plan was shown to General Montgomery, he said absolutely no. His plan called for spending two weeks gathering force, then having his British troops storm the river. He would not permit an unplanned tactical success to spoil the symmetry of it.

Four days later an unplanned tactical success occurred south of us, and it was one of the great coups of the western war. The First Army found an intact railroad bridge over the Rhine at Remagen. Before the old bridge collapsed a few days later, five divisions crossed it, and pontoon bridges had been built to replace it. Just before Montgomery was to cross in force, Patton, too, advanced across another intact bridge in the south. The Americans wanted to make a swift assault on the narrowing remainder of the Reich, but Eisenhower, wounded by too many fights with Montgomery and by the epic intelligence flub in the Ardennes, had promised that Monty would be the sole star of the Rhine crossing and would have by far the most supplies—fuel, in particular— and troops to support his role; so he restrained the American generals. Many called it Ike's worst mistake. I feel it was his second worst, for the worst was yet to come.

While the drama of the bridges was developing, two First Army divisions took on the great city of Cologne. The city was one of the few big ones located on our (western) side of the river, and therefore could be captured without crossing the great river barrier. I had always had a special fascination for Cologne, particularly for its enormous twin-spired red sandstone cathedral, the biggest Gothic church in northern Europe. Having already violated First Army press territory repeatedly to report on the Bulge, I decided to spend another day doing so, to witness the capture of the city and its majestic church.

The city was a field of rubble. It had been the primary target of the Allies' initial experiment in carpet bombing two years before, and had been bombed too hard too often since. It was thus all the more impressive to see in the midst of the ruins, visible ten miles away as you approached on a clear day, the great spires of the cathedral high and seemingly intact. By this day, the German defenders had been driven to the other side of the river, but they maintained a deadly artillery barrage against what remained of streets on our side. Deep inside the city we came upon a Jeep containing the chief of one of the two divisions assigned to take the city, a dark handsome man, General Maurice Rose, commander of the Third Armored Division. He recommended that we get out of our Jeep and make our way carefully on foot. If we could get there, the safest place was the cathedral itself. We had sent word to the defenders that we would not fire at it, or use it for artillery observation, if they did not. So far the agreement held. (Not many days later, General Rose, the son of a rabbi and the only Jewish division commander in the army, would be killed in action.)

We made our way down the margin of a street to the little central square. There, in the rubble of a café where I often used to sit and admire the great structure, I noted that the handsome medieval buildings near the river—the banqueting hall of merchants, the town hall—had been reduced to dust. I think it was the first time I forgot to think that all was justified to defeat the Nazis; I doubted that this utter demolition was necessary. Still, it made the two lacy gothic redstone steeples rising five hundred feet above us, apparently untouched, all the more amazing. We ran across the square and into the great central door and found that it was not untouched. Bombs had rearranged the structure for the worse and left a gaping hole in the roof. I insisted on doing what was not allowed, even in peace, and entered one of the towers and climbed the spiral stairs inside. Very high up the view became breathtaking and the staircase much narrower. At a point near the top the stones became unsteady, and a little shower of sand was released from the steps. I took one long last look at the sea of destruction below and around me, then consulted discretion and descended. By nightfall the city was quiet and ours. I was not there but was told that people came out of the cellars and waved and cheered, joyful that it was over for them.

We had long since outrun the Maastricht press camp and abandoned it. We now spent nights wherever there was a roof with horizontal surfaces inside to lie on, and ate with whatever unit's mess was near. At length, Barney Old-field came up with a big gray mansion near München-Gladbach. In a large ballroom, cots were set up at intervals around the walls, making the room look like a square cogwheel, of which the cots were the teeth.

I returned to camp one night late after a reconnaissance of the bank of the Rhine (our next mission) and found, lying in the cot next to mine and apparently sleeping, a very long man I had never seen before. One eye opened underneath his arm and he spoke my name. Then he swung to sitting and began slowly to unfold upward, until he stood towering before me. "I'm Eric Seva-reid," he said, "I've come from London to work with you on the crossing." Thus began a friendship lasting a lifetime and a professional cooperation lasting nearly as long. I found it fascinating just to watch this tall, handsome, lantern-jawed Scandinavian, until I got used to him. He did everything slowly, deliberately, a little like the movements of John Wayne in the movies, but even more deliberately, so slowly he seemed sometimes to find each movement painful. His voice was good and clear but was also used with deliberation. And it had a strange feature. It was as though the volume of his speech was a windup. As he spoke, his voice wound down till the volume became so low you could barely hear him. He seemed to have a few more foibles than most people. He was a writer, and microphones intimidated him. He had to have a glass of warm water next to him, from which he sipped in the belief that it relaxed his vocal chords. Still he remained very tense in broadcasts; and when he moved to television, his discomfort was visible. He said, "I was never at ease with radio till I tried television. I guess I won't feel at ease with it till they invent something worse." However he managed to do all right. He was a fine writer. His broadcasts read as handsomely as they sounded and have appeared in collections in books from time to time.

The next morning the Allies crossed the Rhine on a broad front. But I think the men of the Ninth Army were as ready to fight their army group commander, Field Marshal Montgomery, as they were to hit the Germans. He had taken a third of the Ninth's strength away and put it under the command of a British general. The remaining two-thirds, under General Simpson, were moved out of the front line and placed in reserve. An angry American outburst forced Monty to put the remnant of the Ninth back in the front, but he reduced its role by allowing it to use pontoon bridges over the Rhine only five hours a day, while the British had them nineteen hours a day. As a result it took a week to get all of the Ninth on the other side. Hitler was closer to being right than he knew about tensions between the two English-speaking Allies, though the cause of the tension was not the British but one small, vain human peacock.

Once across the Rhine, the Ninth sped through the dense towns on the northern edge of the Ruhr in a true Blitzkrieg. We joined hands with the First Army coming up from the south, locking the most important industrial area in Europe in a steel circle. At this point we were removed from Monty's command and restored to the U.S. Army Group. Eighteen American divisions were assigned to reduce the encircled Germans. It proved easier than expected. With the Russians near, the Germans began surrendering to us in droves. We sped on and encircled another German force in the Harz Mountains. From there we looked ahead, and all we could see was one river and, beyond it, Berlin. To me it seemed as though a century had passed since, in a lecture hall in Heidelberg, I first felt that this threat must be met.

CHAPTER THIRTY-FIVE

The Bowels of Hell

Moving with a conquering army at forced speed left one with only snapshots of an Evil being dismembered, some being pictures of innermost secrets, laid open to us day by awful day. One was a pithead in rolling mine country, an outsized elevator descending down, down, down, deeper into the earth than I had ever been, opening out at the bottom onto a room vaster than any I had ever seen, perhaps fifty feet high and three hundred long, brightly lighted with lights giving off uncountable tiny sparkles from salt crystals that made up every surface—walls, ceiling, floor. It was a hollow salt dome, shaved into box shape, a storeroom for thousands of crated paintings and statues looted by Göring from France, and a treasury for gold bullion stolen from every conquered country. There was even space set aside for paintings from the Hermitage in Leningrad. It was never to be occupied.

The Villa Hügel, home of the family of Krupp, arms maker to generations of Teutons, was a huge, dark pile said to consist of eight hundred rooms—we did not tarry to count—in Essen in the great Ruhr industrial region. Outsized, intimidating portraits of the three Wilhelmine Emperors of the Second Reich were conspicuous. That of the lone emperor of the Third Reich had been hastily removed. When we entered with a company of GI's, I observed a case containing medals and decorations received by family members over the lives of the Second and Third Reichs. When we left, the case was empty. War is hell plus looting.

A day in the hot, stinking bowels of hell. German civilians told me there was a concentration camp off on a spur in the town of Langenstein. At a field hospital on our way a doctor, hearing of our mission, asked to come along. In all the years I had lived with and studied Nazis, I had assumed that concentration camps were prisons—a level or two worse than others, but still just prisons. It would have been hard for me to believe the reality had I not walked into it. The guards were gone; they had put on civilian clothes and melded into the population. The gates were open; but the ghostly inmates, live skeletons, barely clothed in skin, with staring eyes, had not gone outside. None had the strength to leave, or to cut down two corpses left hanging at a gallows, clearly beginning to rot. Several fell at our feet babbling. We pulled them up, tried to assure them that they were free and that help would come soon. Inside long huts many lay side by side in long bunks, some nestling, trying to get warm, against neighbors who had quietly died. Outside, recently dug pits were half-filled with corpses covered with a layer of lime. Everywhere pervaded the odor of rotten reeking death. The doctor, who had brought an ambulance, stayed and summoned help. We left, rather ashamed at our feeling of relief at departing from hell and returning to mere war.

April 12, 1945, a day that will live in melancholy. But it began with a pleasant enough thought. A couple of us found a rare intact building in the Ruhr district, and bedding for us and a military censor (moving fast we carried our censor with us to legitimate our copy wherever we could find a place to broadcast) in a room belonging to an engineer, judging from his gear spread over tables. In his book case the absent owner displayed a set of the collected writings of Heinrich Heine. This was noteworthy because Heine's works were forbidden. Only his poem *"Die Lorelei"* had still been widely printed because it was a classic that every German cherished, but it was labeled at the bottom, *"Verfasser Unbekannt"* ("Author Unknown"). The set was new, which was even more noteworthy. Some publisher had taken his freedom in his hands by issuing a new set of Heine, the Jew. We went downstairs with breakfast on our mind, but our driver, who had been listening to the BBC, froze us in place. "Roosevelt's dead," he said. No one was able to comment. There was a hole in our picture of the world today. The great duelist for freedom in the twentieth century had fallen, while his opponent still lived. A good deal of the satisfaction of winning seemed for a moment to have drained out. I looked at my friend, "Bob, I didn't know you could cry. I never can," I told him. He said, "Then it must be raining, your cheek is wet." We got in our Jeep and went off and worked our way into a stream of trucks driving east. We passed a truckload of GI's, one of whom shouted, "War correspondents! Say it ain't so!" We could not think of anything to say.

The reasons for winning remained as urgent as ever. One more was added the next day near a place called Gardelegen: a big half-burnt-down barn, smoke still rising and with it the odor of burning flesh, so acrid one's lungs hurt. The barn's big door was flung open, and from it bulged the shape of bodies, burned black and fused together by the burning. They were prone and in layers. They were frozen in place with desperate expressions and grotesque gestures, mostly of black arms reaching out, as if grasping for freedom. What had happened? They were Russian POWs. Their captors had sought to keep them from being discovered by our advancing army by force-marching them eastward. Underfed men cannot march fast, and we were just hours away. The captors saw this barn. They filled it with hay and stacked hay around its outside walls. Precious gasoline was poured on the hay. The Russians in their hundreds were packed in, hesitaters were shot to persuade the rest. The door was shut and the hay set afire. Machine guns were stationed outside, facing the door, and when it was forced open, prisoners seeking to escape were mown down. The first wave fell on the ground, the second on top of them, then the third, and so on. Inside, several hundred corpses were fused into a big block of black forms. An American officer ordered the town population out to pass in line and see. Later they were ordered to dig graves and carry bodies, in part or in combination, to be buried.

The Harz Mountains. The high-water mark of ancient Rome's penetration of Germania. Here they were thrown back by Arminius, Herman the German. Of greater interest to our British allies, here was located the factory that built the V-2 rockets and bombs that terrorized England and Antwerp. U.S. engineers studied the factory before the Allies destroyed it, and the U.S. military hired the managers to go to Alabama and teach Americans how to make rockets. Some moral argument arose about that, but not much. The Pentagon really wanted those rockets. Here now, from a height, you could see tanks down on the plain laid out before us as if on a sand table. The Wehrmacht hoped to make a last stand there to keep us from the River Elbe. General Simpson was not having it; he encircled them, and left them to fester in loneliness, as he charged right on to the Elbe, first touching it at Hamelin, where legend said the Pied Piper once led the town's children to a watery grave.

Outside Magdeburg, the biggest city on the Elbe, Barney Oldfield set up a camp for us in a kind of German plantation home, approachable between rows of oak trees. We hoped to meet the Russians there, but the first Russians reached the river farther south in First Army territory at the town of Torgau.

General Simpson rapidly threw two bridges over the Elbe, and began to funnel a few troops over as a token of his plan to jump off to Berlin. We were equidistant with the Russians from the Reich Chancellery, but the Germans facing us preferred to surrender to us before the Russians could get to them. One day we hopped in an outboard motorboat and went up the Elbe. From over a ridge on the east bank, German soldiers began running toward us, dozens and scores, their hands up, begging to surrender. Some of our divisions were accumulating more prisoners than could be handled. An order came down from SHAEF that we should refuse further prisoners; tell them to go east and surrender to the Russians. One day we got the report that Richard Hottelet, who had been with me at UP in Berlin and now was with me at CBS, had ridden a Jeep all the way into Berlin without resistance and come back to broadcast the story.

We chafed during trips between the Elbe bridges and our plantation camp. Why didn't we go now? What was holding things up? Our briefing officer thought we could make it into Berlin in twenty-four hours.

Then General Simpson, the man who knew the answers to all the questions, paid us the ardently awaited visit. We sat in a large drawing room, as if in a classroom, and he sat in a chair facing us. He took off the helmet casing with three stars he usually wore. The old good-natured smile was on his face, but it seemed to have a nuance. Later, when I knew all, I decided it was the look of a man making peace with disappointment. "Gentlemen," he said, "we are *not* going to Berlin." We gave a roar of disapproval that shook him. "It is there for our taking," was my contribution to a man who knew a lot more about that than I did. "Well," he said, "these are my orders. We are going to obey them in as good a spirit as we can." We roared some more. "There is nothing more I can tell you," he said, "I felt I should come here and tell you personally. Maybe I shouldn't have done it. At least that makes it final." He put on his helmet, and with the old smile back on his face he bade us goodbye.

When he had left, our briefing officer told us more. The day previous, General Omar Bradley, commander of our group of armies, called Simpson to Army Group HQ in Wiesbaden, Germany. Simpson went in high spirits, carrying along his detailed plans for taking Berlin, which was what he assumed

Bradley wanted to talk about. Within a few hours, he would say, he could have two divisions barreling up the autobahn highway to the German capital. When Simpson stepped out of the plane, Bradley was there to meet him.

As soon as Simpson opened the subject of the time it would take him to move, Bradley stopped him. "You have to stop right where you are," he said, "you can't go any farther. You must pull back across the Elbe."

Simpson was dumbfounded. "Where the hell did this come from?" he said, "I could be in Berlin in twenty-four hours."

"I just got it from Ike," said Bradley. Simpson argued, but quickly realized he was blowing air. He had been called there to listen, not to discuss.

Rarely had Ike made a decision so final that he refused even to hear comment on it. Berlin would be left to the Russians to take. Rarely had he made a decision that was so totally his own, without counsel or advice, and even against the wishes of some wise heads who usually supported him. Patton, like Simpson, had been for our taking Berlin. The British chiefs of services all opposed Ike's sudden blunt decision to leave it to the Russians. Churchill sent off pointed telegrams to Ike and to Truman, protesting the decision. Ike sent notice of his plan to leave Berlin to the Russians directly to Stalin in violation of the rule that all such communications must go through the combined chiefs of staff. Ike told, he did not ask, his own commander-in-chief, and Truman accepted it favorably; by now Eisenhower was the apple of America's eye and had lost the human ability to be wrong.

The Eisenhower reasoning was that, with so much of Germany gone, Berlin had become a place on the map with no strategic value. It was not worth American casualties and the risk of colliding with the Russians on the streets of the city. Instead, he directed the American armies due eastward toward Leipzig and points south of there. The Russians were suspicious of us, Ike's case went on; what better way to demonstrate our good intentions than to leave the honor of taking the capital to them? He did not say it, but he was also probably influenced by false reports that Hitler had built a National Redoubt in the southern mountains, which the Americans would have to invade and overrun. The reports were so much blue smoke.

My own comment is biased by a newsman's wish to be in on the main story, but for what it was worth, I thought and still think the decision was abominable. Berlin was no longer of strategic value, but it never had been. Its strategic status was the same now as it was when Ike announced earlier that our ultimate military goal was Berlin. As a military man he might have asked himself why so much American blood in our Civil War was spilled near and around Washington. The holding or loss of these great symbols has powerful effect on human behavior for future benefit or disadvantage. With the politics of a postwar world already percolating in Eastern Europe, it was of great importance to establish a claim of conquest, in Churchill's words, as far east as possible. In later years, the Soviets tried at least twice to force us out of Berlin altogether, and their propaganda ploy always included the argument that, after all, they, not we, took the city from the Nazis. Again and again they told the story that, just as we failed to keep our promise to invade Europe in 1942 and 1943, leaving the Russians to bleed, so in the great final test at Berlin we quailed, and it was left to the brave Red Army soldier to root out the enemy of mankind.

With nothing but minor cleanup operations to report, I hung around Magdeburg for a few days, hoping that some angel of circumstance would change many-starred minds, permitting us to resume progress and allowing me to return to the city I had fled four years before. There was such an angel, but he was not flitting around the Elbe. He was waiting for me in Paris.

CHAPTER THIRTY-SIX

First Plane to Berlin

I still have the telegram. It begins, "Howard Smith U.S. Ninth Army Congratulations you have become a father . . ." signed by Collingwood. Usually transportation for reporters was limited to Jeeps. With this telegram in hand I got a ride to Paris on an airplane. Lots of Americans newly in uniform were having babies, but not within an hour's plane ride of the front.

The mother was never so radiant. Or so relieved; getting rid of that ever heavier, more demanding parasite is like being born again, I am told. It was a blessing that he was a happy baby, always smiling and chuckling. There was no trouble about a name. My favorite was my old nickname, Jack. I liked Howard as a family name, but somehow couldn't stand it as a given one. I would have liked being called Jack Howard. But we were stuck with Smith, so with my brother's name in the middle, we dubbed him Jack Prescott Smith. We strolled with him on the Champs and in the Bois de Boulogne, feeling crisp as figures in the Seurat painting. I am ashamed to admit that I accepted the privilege of a returned soldier and slept on when Bennie got up in the nights to answer Jack's infant calls.

I stayed with Bennie at the Verdant Nest but kept a room at the Scribe in case I was called to work in an emergency. The supreme emergency soon happened. Charles was called away on an unmentionable mission, and I was asked to be on hand in Paris to broadcast. In hours, it was announced. The Germans had surrendered at Ike's HQ in Reims. CBS had been alerted, and Murrow, ever generous with assignments, had sent Collingwood. Paris went wild. I had to stay at the Scribe near a microphone, but Bennie was out there on the Place de la Concorde in the mob with her baby in her arms.

That angel of circumstance was flitting around the Scribe Hotel looking for some place to land. Drew Middleton spied me in the lobby. "Don't ever forget that I was the one who did it for you," he said. I had no idea what he was talking about. He went on, "There were the initials of three networks in a hat. I picked out the one with a B in the middle and got it for CBS." I was gratified that it hadn't been NBC or MBS, but what was CBS picked out for? Before I could ask, Collingwood walked over and interrupted, "Congratulations. You are going to Berlin. First plane back."

The Germans had surrendered in Eisenhower's headquarters. The Russians saw the germ of a myth like the stab-in-the-back myth of WW I: A future generation of German military figures might declare that they had surrendered only to the Western powers, not to the Russians. So the Russians demanded that the whole surrender ceremony be replicated in Russian Marshal Zhukov's headquarters in a Berlin suburb. Zhukov asked that Eisenhower or a representative be present. The Western delegation agreed to take along three journalists, chosen by lot, to serve as pool reporters for all—one for the wire services, one for the newspapers, one for the radio networks. CBS won for the nets, and Murrow chose me for CBS.

I kissed my family goodbye again and slept that night in the Scribe. Early the next morning we assembled and took off in a plane escorted by two American fighters—there was still a lot of freelance shooting going on all over Germany. Our delegation was led by Ike's deputy, British Air Chief Marshal Arthur Tedder, a gentle pipe-smoker with the face of a little English schoolboy. America was represented by General Carl Spaatz, head of the Army Air Force, a choleric-looking towhead who appeared as bellicose as Tedder did not. The French delegate was General de Lattre de Tassigny, less well known now than he was to become in the future as the officer who lost Indochina for France. There were a couple of freeloaders, allowed to go along because Ike liked them. One was Harry Butcher, in civilian life a CBS executive but now a naval officer and highly capable Man Friday for Eisenhower; and a slim, beautiful young English (actually Irish) rose who looked more like a fashion model than Ike's driver, Kay Summersby, she of the romantic rumors.

At the Elbe, the two U.S. planes broke away and were replaced by a pair of Soviet fighter escorts. We landed at Tempelhof Airport in Berlin to the sound of a Russian military band and what may have been the last blow of the battle for Berlin: an undiscovered mine went off, blowing up the tower of the airport. We were driven around the south rim of the city avoiding the worst ruins. Two things impressed: all traffic-directing Russian military police seemed to be hefty and female, equal to dealing with a drunken soldier or two; and I, accustomed to motor transportation, was amazed that Red Army troop and supply transportation was mostly mule-, horse- or ox-drawn.

The headquarters was at Karlshorst, Berlin's race track where, earlier in the war, I whiled away an occasional Sunday afternoon losing marks on non-Aryan horses. Attached to the track was an army engineering school, and there Marshal Zhukov made his office. I think he expected a small formal delegation. When his office door opened, and we all came flooding through, he looked undone, as though an overlooked pocket of German footsoldiers had suddenly launched an attack. We supernumeraries were soon separated out from the principals and set up in a classroom to wait. I asked a Russian officer in charge of us if we might borrow a car and go look at some of the city. He said there were last-ditch, never-say-die snipers all over the city, and we could not move about the ruins freely. We would go later, with Red Army units making sure our way was clear. Also, unaccompanied, we would get lost; there were no street signs left, and in some areas no recognizable streets. I told him I knew the city well and would like to try. "You will find," he said, "that is not the city you knew. It is not the city anyone knew."

The high Western officers were lodged in a villa where food and drink were laid out. Wandering around hunting for it and them, a couple of us ran into the French General de Lattre, who recounted a small embarrassment. The Russians had not expected a French delegate. When they saw him descend from our airplane, they scurried about hunting for a French flag to hang alongside those of the other allies. There was none to be found in crushed Berlin, so some Russian girls set about creating one. They cut up an old Nazi flag to get the red and white bars, and some old clothing to get the blue one. They proudly displayed their handiwork to de Lattre. He told them, "It is beautiful. They will love it in Amsterdam. It is quite the handsomest Dutch flag I have ever seen." The girls went away to reverse the red and blue bars, and a proper French flag hung with the others over the ceremonial room that night.

The ceremonies, planned for two P.M, did not take place till near midnight. The delay was caused by some finagling with the language of the documents to be signed, and by a question of rank. The Russians had hoped Eisenhower would come. He did not. An aide in the Western delegation said that it was a matter of rank. Ike was commander of all the Western armies; Zhukov was merely commander of an Army Group. That sounded nonsensical to me. The truth was, Eisenhower had become, with success, a national treasure and was advised not to attend a history-making ceremony he did not control; no one knew what changes in surrender terms, Russian tricks, or delays to strain his short patience the Russians might insist on. Anyhow, the Russians wanted only Zhukov and Ike's representative, Tedder of Britain, to sign. Spaatz objected that a surrender not signed by an American was unthinkable. De Lattre said, "If there is not a French signature, General de Gaulle will have me shot when I get back to Paris." So the Soviets' super-lawyer, Andrei Vyshinsky (who as chief prosecutor had helped send hundreds of Soviet citizens to their deaths in purge trials), was flown in to settle it: Zhukov and Tedder would sign as the Soviets wished; Spaatz and de Lattre would sign as they wished, but on a lower line. This is the way the war ends, not with a bang but a lawyer's trick.

Finally, near midnight, we were ushered into a large hall, called the Engineer Officers' Casino, a kind of ballroom. It was so heavily decorated with flags and the streamers of Red Army units that had fought their way across Europe from the Caucasus that it looked like the interior of a great war monument. There was a central gallery in the balcony hidden by a curtain of gauze. Behind it an invisible band played folk tunes and patriotic music. It was opaque from our side; but the bandleader on the other side obviously could see well, for all Zhukov had to do to bring it to silence in midchord, to permit an announcement or a toast, was to glance up at it sternly.

Zhukov looked like a figure on the exterior of a great monument. Big, strong and heavy-set, he nonetheless moved with masculine grace. He appeared to be the kind of man who had zero tolerance for nonsense and mistakes and failure, a man in whose presence underlings trembled, the kind of man who could lead armies from the savagery of Stalingrad to the savagery of Berlin, fighting all the way.

While we, Russian and American bystanders, stood and watched, Zhukov led the Allied leaders to places behind a long table at an end of the hall. Documents of surrender were laid before him for final examination. He passed them around to his guests for their perusal. Then a side door opened, and in came Field Marshal Wilhelm Keitel, tall, starched, upright, carrying his field marshal's baton, looking rather more like a victor than the defeated, followed by an admiral and an air force general. With Nazi leaders on a suicide binge in these last days of the war, we were lucky to have Keitel still alive for symbolic effect in these surrender ceremonies. Though his actual role had been simply to keep Hitler's table of military organization in working order, he was nominally the Third Reich's number one soldier. Hitler had reorganized the leadership of the armed forces under a new body called *Das Oberkommando der Wehrmacht,* the OKW, famous because its name was repeated every day as announcer of military communiqués. Keitel was appointed chief of this new power. It was an intense joy to me to see this figure I had seen so often representing the invincible Wehrmacht in its glory years, now required to affirm its final destruction and defeat. The papers were laid before him and his two subordinates. Keitel studied the documents through a monocle, made a minor objection and was told to forget it and to sign, which he did. The three Germans betrayed no emotion save grimness, but an adjutant, standing behind Keitel, wept, tears rolling down an expressionless face. The three Germans signed nine times, three documents each for each of three allies, Russia, Britain and the U.S. Inexplicably, de Lattre was given no copies. Also inexplicably, he was cropped out of the official photo. "I am beginning to feel unwanted," he told us later. After the signing—the last official act of WW II in Europe—the three German signatories were ushered out. The naval officer, Admiral von Friedeburg, committed suicide a few days later. I next saw Keitel at the Nuremberg trials, where the prosecution introduced documents he had signed ordering the most brutal acts of torture and murder. He was found guilty and hanged.

After the formal ceremony that night (or early morning in Berlin) a couple of companies of Red Army soldiers rushed into the big room and in ten minutes cleared it, brought in tables, laid them end to end till the room was filled, put cloths over them and began to pile wonderful edibles along their middles. I moved to sit with my two journalist colleagues, but the way was blocked, and all places save one were rapidly taken. I saw that I was being forced to sit between two particular Soviet officers. I have not yet recorded that when the Ninth Army crossed the Roer I spent several days without shaving. When we were settled enough to deal with ablutions, I decided to let it go; I grew a beard, which was quite impressive by the time of the surrender. I surmised that it also made me an object of suspicion. In the 1920s the American conception of a Bolshevik revolutionary was a thin man with a wild beard. Now in the 1940s the conservative U.S.S.R. probably saw an anti-Bolshevik revolutionary as a thin man with a wild beard. I enjoyed the meal. It was too luscious and lavish, too often lubricated with fingers of vodka, to be spoiled by isolation between two Soviet agents, but I would have liked it more next to someone I could talk to.

Zhukov appeared really to enjoy that victory banquet. He began by toasting the Western armed forces, after which he left his place and went along the table and embraced each of his visitors in turn. Tedder then toasted the great Soviet Red Army. Tedder was not the hearty type to go around embracing men, but Zhukov stood and opened his arms wide, and Tedder had no choice but to go and let them close around him. Stalin, Roosevelt, Churchill and de Gaulle were toasted. Zhukov toasted the artillery, which he said was the secret of the Red Army's success. The brave warriors of Stalingrad, El Alamein and

Midway were toasted. General Spaatz, who didn't much like Communists even when they were allies, decided to use the occasion to lay it on the line. As if it were the first volley in a combat with Communist Russia, he raised his glass to "those nations who trust their own people enough to let them vote and enjoy free institutions." He turned to Zhukov expecting to face down an angry adversary. But his volley missed by a mile. Zhukov was on his feet, a look of joy all over his face. He went to Spaatz, and not only embraced but gave him a big smacking kiss on the cheek. I felt I could almost hear him affirm to the American that we free nations must stick together.

The party continued until after four in the morning. Then, with dawn breaking, we were supplied with a motorcade of cars and went off in the brightening light of morning to see Berlin. The Russian officer had it right. It was a city I had never seen before. In whole areas there were not even jagged walls standing, just rolling fields of brick dust and brick. Truly, in Churchill's words, "we bombed till the rubble bounced." Roaming Germany in my student days I was impressed with how indelibly Hitler had stamped his mark on the country in a few years. There were unerasable swastikas everywhere, cast in brass doors and doorknobs, inlaid in marble and granite floors and walls. I had often wondered how a successor would ever get rid of them if he wished to. The Allies' solution to the problem was extreme, but clearly it worked: there was not a swastika to be seen. In the middle of the city I could recognize nothing, until on a post in a clearing I saw a crude sign put up by the Russians, and made out its cyrillic letters: Aleksander Platz, the location of the prison where Dick Hottelet had been locked up.

Unter den Linden was easier to descry because of its breadth, and miraculously the Brandenburg Gate, though badly pocked, was still standing. The Wilhelmstrasse, the government street, might have been any bombed street in Germany till we came upon the distinctive remnants of the Chancellery, Hitler's government home. We got out and went inside. It is no wonder the Führer and his staff stayed in the bunker even when not under attack; there was not a serviceable room with an intact ceiling anywhere in the badly crushed building. In the littered yard we were shown a darkened spot where, we were told, the incinerated bodies of Goebbels and his family were found. About Hitler the Russians were coy, even suggesting he might have escaped alive. They would not let us go down into the bunker, saying it was unsafe and might collapse at any moment.

There were ironies. Amid the ruins, Göring's Air Ministry, the place where the awful precedent of terror bombing of cities was initiated, stood nearly innocent of damage. And American and British bombers left intact the embassies of Hitler's Axis partners, Japan and Italy, while they utterly crushed the U.S. and British embassies.

Our leaders were sleepy and hung over and wanted to return to Tempelhof, but I squeezed one more trip into their schedule—through the Tiergarten Park, where not one tree was left in a moonscape field, to Wittenberg Platz and my home. My old apartment was a hole in the sky, its building nonexistent. We sped to Tempelhof. As we climbed aboard our plane, each of us was given a package of Russian brown bread, a piece of sausage and a small bottle of vodka. We were not aloft ten minutes before everyone but the pilot and me was fast asleep. I had to organize what I was going to say to the networks.

Any network in our pool could order a broadcast exclusive to it at any time. Altogether I made seventeen broadcasts from the Scribe in the next ten hours. At number eighteen I feel asleep over my typewriter, and CBS persuaded its competitors to lay off. I took the Metro out to Neuilly and the *Nid de Verdure*, where Bennie and I made a meal out of the Russian package and talked about what had happened. She felt about the same as I did about the Nazis, or perhaps a little more strongly, having seen her friendly little country invaded and occupied by the jackboots. She said to me: "No matter what terrible things happen in the future, we must remember this: *We won*. We might not have. They might have won. Think what the world would have been like if they had won. *Nothing* can ever be as terrible as that."

CHAPTER THIRTY-SEVEN

Home and Back

I had by now been away from America eight years. I had never been to the city of New York, where my paychecks were made out. I did not know whether I still had a job, now that peace had come, or still had one but might be kept in New York to report city news or might be transferred to the Pacific War theater. All of which argued for a clarifying trip to New York at the nearest opportunity. Bennie, as a Danish citizen, could travel freely; but we had to arrange for the baby to stay with a French nurse for a few weeks; had we taken him to the U.S., we would not have been able to bring this American baby with us back to what was still a war zone. While I still had military accreditation I could get space on army planes home, so I decided to go immediately. Bennie arranged passage on a Dutch freighter full of British war brides and would arrive later.

Travel on army planes was an adventure. We took off from Prestwick, next to the birthplace of one of my favorite poets, Robert Burns, whose native cottage I visited for a brief moment of worship. I was bumped by superior rank in Iceland and spent two days discovering why the island did not have a flourishing tourist trade. I finally got a bucket seat to Presque Isle, Maine, which is not isolated from all civilization; it only seems to be. From there on a clear day you can see nothing, but it was fogbound throughout my two days' stay. At length I got a place on a flight to New York.

I was awed by the most obvious sight: the tall buildings. "Some airplane's going to run into one of those one of these days," I warned a cop on a corner. He paid me no mind, and two mornings later a disarmed bomber flew smack into the Empire State Building. I was intimidated by the crowds of extremely good-looking, well-clothed, well-shod people (I realized I hadn't seen a high heel in six years), all looking very self-confident and uninterested in anyone else, all trying to get somewhere else very fast.

I entered 485 Madison Avenue trembling. On the seventeenth floor I asked for Mr. Paul White and was told to go to the corner office, past a couple of glassed-in radio studios and a newsroom of desks and rattling wire-service machines. White looked the way I had imagined him, tough, broken-nosed (well, it wasn't broken; it merely looked pugilistic), hair parted in the middle making a broad head with a broad jaw attached appear even broader. I thought I might apologize for interrupting whatever he was doing, but he figured me out first. "Howard K.?" he said. I admitted it and the gates of general acceptance opened. He put his arm around me and told his deputy entering the room to shake my hand. Soon some of the writers came in and I was the center of a welcome party.

It was not quite the cocktail hour, but White insisted we go out and have a small drink. Small became large, and one became many. I decided that getting drunk with the boss at a first meeting was a legitimate ritual. But the next afternoon he again suggested we go out for a small drink, and we ended up soused. When it happened the third night I realized that newness of the relationship had nothing to do with it; my boss was an inordinately heavy drinker whatever the occasion.

I guess there are office politics in all big offices—I was too insignificant at the *New Orleans Item* to be involved or aware. I now discovered that the CBS office was deeply riven into clear-cut camps: Paul White, the creator of really big news on radio, versus Edward R. Murrow, the genius who made CBS's entry in the competition sparkle; the hard-bitten, lifelong newspaperman versus the handsome young man who chanced into the craft and quickly dominated it. The White men on the staff formed the "Murrow Ain't God" club. The club suffered a mortal blow when Murrow one day walked into a bar, where the members were seated like sparrows on a telephone wire, and said he wanted to join. The question arose as to which side I was on. White had hired me and sustained me in my Berlin crisis and in years of uncertain employment in Switzerland, and he had negotiated the contract to publish my book in America. But my relationship with Murrow was warm from the first meeting, and our interests were nearly identical: he wrote and spoke magnificently, and I aspired to that more than anything except pleasing my bride. I straddled till after the war, when the conflict was decided and Murrow was made chief of all CBS News. At the inauguration of a big, expensive, new program to be anchored by Bob Trout, Murrow asked News Director Paul White to deliver an on-air introduction. Paul entered the studio so drunk he babbled like a child. He left the seventeenth floor and never came back. After his death in 1952, the Radio and Television News Directors of America instituted the "Paul White Memorial Award." I was proud to be the first working newsman to receive it.

Anyhow, Paul and Ed reached agreement that I should go back to Europe and once again be CBS's Berlin correspondent. Murrow himself had half-decided to go cover the war in Asia. "I have these nightmares," he said, "getting shot down over the Pacific and swimming around in shark-infested waters. I used up all my good luck in Europe." Instead, Paley persuaded him to stay home and be boss.

Bennie had now joined me in New York, and we took a train down to New Orleans to see my father and my brother, who lived in the same city but rarely met. Both were doing well. Dad had his new wife and a good pension, after being rehired by the railroad for the duration. Prescott was married to a Honduran beauty and had five good-looking children. He had inherited Dr. Vignes' whole practice and was very well-to-do. It was cruel of me to take my still-new wife to meet her American relatives for the first time in New Orleans' suffocating August heat. There was no such thing as home air conditioning then and she suffered. Much later we learned that what made her miserable was not just the heat; she was suffering from incipient tuberculosis. Her misery was only one factor in our deciding to cut the stay short. Prescott had taken up with some country club friends who made dirty jokes about Eleanor Roosevelt. I could see Bennie's eyes narrowing and knew she was sizing up one jokester's mouth for a knuckle sandwich. I thought that inappropriate; a kick in the testicles would have been more suitable. We said farewell to my brother uptown and went downtown to say goodbye to my father. Then we returned to Europe on the *Mauritania* on its first voyage in years carrying paying passengers instead of troops.

In Paris we picked up Jack, grown six weeks more lovable; then he and Bennie flew to Denmark to stay with her parents. I got army transportation to Berlin. While in New York we had made a deal with the new tabloid newspaper *PM* that Bennie would string for them in Berlin. The Army, ever dubious about wives in the war zone, held up her accreditation. So I took up quarters alone in Berlin, in the Zehlendorf suburb in the American sector, and hoped for the day normality would be declared and I could have my wife and son back. News from Berlin was skimpy, but New York liked the dateline, so I was on most nights. For the first time, I carried a gun, a .38. Walking from my quarters to the broadcasting studio through the most desolate ruins every night was a scary experience.

My score for being right on public issues is fair. I was absolutely right long before most on the subject of the German Nazis. However, in the immediate postwar period my attitude toward Russia was wrong—good-hearted but, to use a phrase the Russians like, not in accord with the facts.

I felt a Utopian tug. If the two great nations left in the world after the war could maintain their alliance in peace, there could be no wars or large conflicts. Their combined influence could eliminate, or at least soften, economic crises like the Great Depression. I still believed socialism—public ownership of the basic mines and mills—was a workable system. Indeed, the world believed it; the postwar period was swept by a mighty tide toward centralized decision-making for national economies, led by the new Labour government in Britain and accepted enthusiastically by every liberated piece of the prewar colonial empires in Africa and Asia. The socialist tide did not abate till the 1980s, when nations discovered that central decision and control were inefficient and stunted growth. But then was then, and I felt joint action by American capitalism and Russian socialism would make for a robust world economy.

Ike's decision to leave the conquest of Berlin to the Russians was, I thought, a bad one, but his motive was good. The Russians felt they lived in a world of enemies. If we could show them we were friendly, this new era of cooperation for the world's good would be effective. I hoped that the tyranny of Communism might soften and disappear in a friendlier world atmosphere.

As I sought to create a mental frame in which to see world events—the news from now on—I was affected by plain sympathy. Our losses in deaths in the war were around 350,000. Russia's were 20 million. Our cities and farms were intact, indeed, better off than before; Russia's were in ruins. Russia had lived behind a *cordon sanitaire* of lesser nations bitterly hostile to her. Some of them had joined Germany in pillaging and killing. Now, victorious Russia was simply not going to allow the cordon of hate to be rebuilt; the Soviets would insist on a change in attitude on their borders. That this would be achieved by Russia's enslaving Eastern Europe was not clear immediately after the war.

I feared that the early hostile statements by Western leaders—Churchill's "Iron Curtain" speech in Fulton, Missouri, and Truman's statement of his doctrine—would cause the Soviets to draw back into their shell and seal it up, just when it might be possible to persuade them to try normal relationships. My thought was, give the shattered country a moment to bury its dead, recover, rebuild and get used to a world made up of friendly peoples, and the Iron Curtain might not descend.

It did not take long for events to make it clear that my view was untenable. Stalin was building an empire on foundations very like Hitler's, with Hitler's cruel methods on very nearly Hitler's scale. Some of us had been so preoccupied for years with stopping Hitler that we had overlooked the parallel. The Soviets had to be opposed, and only one nation had the strength left to do it effectively.

The men who constructed policies to achieve this in the Truman administration were to prove second only to the founding fathers in creativity. They broke forever with our isolationist tradition, took over the unwanted job of leading a free world in trouble, worked out ingenious solutions to previously unheard-of problems and initiated the rebuilding of Europe and Asia. And they achieved all this in a remarkably short time. Probably their greatest individual triumphs were the transformation of the two hopeless incorrigibles, Germany and Japan, into prosperous, genuine democracies and influences for peace in the world. My assignment was to witness and report the fumbling beginnings of the European part of that transformation.

CHAPTER THIRTY-EIGHT

Berlin and Nuremberg

I once read in the papers a story about a teenage boy who fell beneath the ice in Lake Michigan, was retrieved with no pulse or breath, to all appearances dead, but who after massage and ministrations of warmth began to twitch and slowly return to life. That was my impression of Berlin. So frenetically alive when I lived there for two years, so cold and corpselike when I came back for the surrender, the city now began to twitch and breathe. In return for allotments of food, women formed lines uphill on rubble eighty feet high in some places. They began picking bricks out of the ruins and passing them down in a human chain to others who chipped away much of the encrustation of mortar, then on to yet others who stacked them neatly by the side of the street. Thus, bit by bit, the rubble was cleared and materials for rebuilding made ready. The work was done by women because there were few able-bodied males left around.

As they appeared in the clearing rubble, paths became streets and the streets came alive with people. All at once, 10 million Germans were expelled from Poland and Czechoslovakia, where they had been Hitler's excuse for aggression and misery. I stood beside a road on the eastern edge of Berlin and watched the river of people—at least a million came that way in a month—walking individually or in family groups, pulling carts with belongings, all the male constituents very old or very young, many clearly ill. Their belongings were meager, because Russian soldiers all along the way had examined them and taken anything of use. The Russians and their devastated homeland were no better off than these miserable Germans. How this new population, said to double the city's numbers in a few months, made do I could not discover. Only a fifth of the city's normal population could find roofs. There were as yet no institutions set up to advise or help the newcomers. Any extra help the Allies could mobilize went to some of the millions of non-German victims of the Germans, wandering the roads of Europe that winter.

Amazingly to me, the utilities, the vascular system that ties a city together, were restored quickly—trams and subways running on many routes, electricity and telephone services functioning widely. Those who could compare said the phones worked better in ruined Berlin at that time than in Paris. This was the work of a surprisingly effective government. The city, deep inside Russian-occupied territory, was divided into four sectors, one per ally, all governed by a council called the Kommandatura. Our one quarter of the city was held by the 82nd Airborne Division, and our man on the Kommandatura was Major General James M. Gavin. The Kommandatura received information from and passed orders down to an appointed city council, which in turn transmitted detailed orders to twenty appointed borough councils. This structure rationed out pretty fairly a small allotment of food and forty pounds of coal per household of four.

It was not enough. In Berlin 13,000 people died in the month of September alone, eight times the normal rate, and it was not yet cold. There were 200 suicides; 60 percent of inhabitants were adjudged to be badly malnourished. Field Marshal Montgomery came to town to hold a news conference and tell us of his preparations to deal with troubles, possibly food and fuel riots, in the misery of the first winter. The British Army of the Rhine had detailed plans to guard essential facilities. Contrary to an early taboo, German police were being equipped with side arms. Montgomery, a resolutely frumpy dresser, appeared before us in magnificent full dress, wearing nine lines of ribbons on his breast (two more than Patton!). He was dressed for a party he was giving for Marshal Zhukov. We were informed that Scottish highlanders danced for the party, and Zhukov was astonished; he had never seen men in skirts before. As for Monty's civic concern, the winter passed without serious turbulence. The German people were all fought out.

Happy for any event that lent interest to my scripts, I broadcast the story of an American lady named Marlene Seiber. American civilians were not allowed to come, but the army flew her in as an act of gratitude for wartime services. She came to be present for the birthday of her mother, who owned a small jewelry shop. Her mother died just before she arrived. She stayed to arrange the funeral and to lay plans for her own burial to take place in the same plot, whenever. Her visit was not publicized until she flew out and back to the U.S. Her public name was Marlene Dietrich.

She later appeared in a film called *A Foreign Affair,* which celebrated the institution that probably did most to speed up recovery, the night spot. The demand for entertainment and recreation was great, and Allied soldiers had the resources to pay. An entrepreneurial spirit needed only a man who could play the accordion, a girl who owned a slinky dress and could sing fairly close to the music, a couple of cellars patched together and access to some home brew and bathtub *Steinhäger;* with these ingredients he had a thriving business. The dollar bills, cigarettes and nylons U.S. soldiers paid out became in time the seed capital that created the German economic miracle. There were laws against American soldiers "fraternizing," but there might as well have been laws requiring the moon to rise up square. Frequent raids by military police simply served to advertise a place. The cellars prospered, a thousand points of light in the Berlin darkness.

Allied cooperation in governing Berlin did not have a future. The Russians began distinguishing themselves from us immediately. They had no rules against fraternizing. They seemed to want to integrate Germany within their empire at once. In the middle of a main road soon to be renamed *"Stalinallee"* were large signs bearing Stalin's portrait and a quotation from him to the effect that the German people did not make war, only the Nazis and the Imperialists—we—did. They installed German Communists who had been exiles in Russia during the Hitler period as the native government of their sectors and zones. They took over the Nazi press that had printed the *Völkischer Beobachter* and began printing their own paper, *Neues Deutschland,* in identical print and format. The daily output of junk gave the impression that the war had been between the Russians on one side and the Nazis, Americans and British on the other. But their effort to win friends in Germany was fouled by their actions. With skills they learned while moving their own industries to the Urals, they now unbolted all the machinery in eastern Germany and moved it to the U.S.S.R. This violated an agreement with us, but it was hard to argue against the justice of their seizing the very machinery that had worked to devastate theirs.

Bill Shirer returned to the city where he had made his great reputation and stayed a week with me. I took him on a tour of the ruins. We had a good interview with General Lucius Clay, who was to become the American benevolent dictator and later the savior of the city in its deepest distress. I found that my friend from Tass, Ivan Filipov, had become a high bureaucrat helping manage Berlin, and we went to see him. He was about 25 percent glad to see us, but about 75 percent scared of being thought friendly to Americans, so it was an awkward meeting. We got an appointment with the Soviet-appointed head of the native government, old Wilhelm Pieck. Clearly senile, he did not follow our questions about reconstruction very well and began to reproach us, saying, "The American comrades cannot seem to find the correct path." Shirer said to me, "The old bastard thinks we are a delegation of American Communists."

Nothing especially newsworthy was going to happen in Berlin that first winter, but all history was about to break out in Nuremberg. A trial of the foremost Nazi leaders still alive was to begin. In November 1945, I closed my quarters in Berlin and moved to the southern city. I installed myself, with the rest of the world press, in a huge gray Victorian-medieval pile called the Faber castle, six miles outside Nuremberg. Unless you are near my age you are unlikely to know that lead pencils used by American schoolchildren, now stamped "Mikado," were stamped "Faber" before WW II. In the 1840s Lothar von Faber set up the factory that made them in Nuremberg and built himself a villa in the factory compound. By 1906, he was prospering, having won much of the American market, and he turned the villa into this big structure called the Schloss. The organizers of the trial expelled the descendent Fabers and made the Schloss into probably the biggest press center up to that time. It was chosen because it was spacious and was one of only about a dozen intact structures in the ruined city. One abandoned privacy on entering there. There were no private rooms. Cots and beds were placed at close intervals along the walls of very large rooms, with a chair next to each on which to place all one's property. My .38 pistol was stolen the first day. There were only two usable bathrooms, which caused a great human traffic jam every morning. Buses moved reporters to and from the courthouse in the middle of town.

In this great city of ruins and hungry, ill-clothed people, two social centers brimmed with food, strong drink and gaiety: the Grand Hotel, patched up in the middle of the city; and the Faber castle on the outskirts. I never had time to get to the hotel but attended two events worth remembering in the castle where I resided. An army band and choir spent an evening playing and singing for us all the music of the still-new Broadway show called *Oklahoma!* In the bleakness of Nuremberg, it seemed a revelation that somewhere on the planet people were doing carefree, joyful things. The other occasion was Robert Burns' birthday on January 12. The Scottish journalists among us decided to demolish their tribal reputation for thrift by throwing a great banquet for all journalists from less privileged nations. It featured the parading of the haggis, brought in all the way from Scotland (on tasting which one wondered why they had gone to all that trouble); a wonderfully witty speech by the head British prosecutor, Sir David Maxwell-Fyfe (married to Rex Harrison's sister; and later to be Lord Kilmuir and Lord Chancellor of the realm), and gallons of the famous native dew.

I was not very socially involved because, of the several hundred journalists present, I became incomparably the busiest. CBS had planned to send Murrow and Shirer and one additional reporter from New York, and I began to fear that my story would cease to be mine, shared as it would be with this contingent. As it turned out, Murrow stayed in New York to become head of CBS News, and Shirer came but caught the flu the day he arrived and was out for a couple of weeks. No one else showed up. So, to fill all assignments, I was up before seven every morning to get to the courthouse on time, and stayed there doing sometimes five broadcasts in a day until well after midnight, too late to eat or wash afterward. By nine P.M. each evening the big court complex belonged to the twenty Nazi prisoners, a lot of GI guards, and me.

The trial was too big for me to cover alone. The daily proceedings in the courtroom were obviously the main event. But behind-the-scenes activities of interest were going on inside the four national teams and among the German defense attorneys. I was able to keep up tolerably well by forming an informal syndicate with two reporters from noncompeting media, *Stars and Stripes'* Harold Burson (who later co-founded the Burson-Marsteller ad agency) and Alan Dreyfus of Reuters. When I came out of an arid morning in the courtroom facing a noon broadcast, one of them usually had an item I could build a piece around, and I performed a like service for them.

One morning my overwork produced a miniature crisis at the wash basin, one of only two serving more than a hundred masculine faces. (A special arrangement was made for the female minority; I never had time to ask what it was.) The queues were very long, and I had to break off waiting and depart unwashed, for two whole days, to make my many deadlines. The third day I was resolved to head off my gathering odor at the pass. When my time at the basin came, I not only washed and shaved my face, but gave the rest of myself a fast mini-bath. It was not fast enough. The alarm of the waiting males, looking, with towels draped around middle-aged paunches, like ancient Roman senators lined up for a whack at Caesar, turned from a rumble to shouts of protest in several languages. I got one foot washed, then gave up lest I become the first war criminal to be so designated, found guilty and executed at Nuremberg.

Frantic though my personal experience was, I held, and still hold, that the trial was a further step upward from darkness, a marked advance by the species. When we achieve some form of comity of nations, assuming we do not destroy ourselves before then, the war crimes trials at Nuremberg will be seen as one rung, or a couple of them, up the ladder by which we got there.

CHAPTER THIRTY-NINE

The Trial

The physical task alone of arranging a trial of this magnitude was enormous. It required a building to contain a courtroom with prison attached, plus offices for unusually large legal staffs from four nations and German defense attorneys, offices to translate and duplicate and store a library of documents, and a spacious workroom for the press of the world. Add a large cafeteria and a staff of cooks, cleaners, plumbers and carpenters to maintain plant and take care of all these people—how to find a building complex with roofs to cover all this in a country of smashed cities?

Berlin was the preferred site, but no such accommodations existed there or could be constructed in less than several years. Also it was surrounded by Russians, suspicious and bureaucracy-ridden, which made reliable supply a problem. Munich was the second choice, but it was rejected for lack of the necessary covered space. Finally it was found that, with some swift construction, the Palace of Justice in Nuremberg could be made to fit. Another advantage of Nuremberg was its location in the U.S. zone of Germany, as America alone at that time had the necessary supplies and means of delivery.

Creating a valid legal foundation for such an unprecedented trial was, this nonlegal person thought, brilliantly achieved. The basic objection to proceeding with such a trial was that it would have to rely on ex post facto law, that is, calling actions criminal that were not criminal when they happened, charging the Nazi leaders with breaking laws that did not exist when the Nazis did what they did. No, the Nuremberg jurists said, the crimes for which the Nazi leaders were to be tried were known to be abhorrent to law—international law and their own domestic, national law—before they were committed.

For example, aggressive war was outlawed by the Kellogg-Briand Pact of 1928, to which Germany and sixty-one other nations were signatories. The Nazis always boasted that they had come to power in Germany legally; thus they were bound by the pacts of previous German governments. Hitler had also signed nonaggression pacts with his neighbors, and then violated them.

Mistreatment or murder of civilians and prisoners of war was forbidden by the Geneva Conventions and by Hitler's own military law. The paybook every German soldier carried with him told him that he must not carry out orders from superiors commanding him to commit unlawful acts.

It was true, as critics said, that the trial was taking place only because the Allies were the victors. Yes, said the creators, but victory should not disqualify one from doing right just because defeat would. What was right was a public trial, in which the defendants would have the same access to evidence as the prosecutors, and the same right as the prosecution to call witnesses, to cross-examine, to question, to object and to argue their case in addition to having skilled advocates of their own choice to represent them.

The evidence in the trial was breathtaking in its depth and breadth. The German leaders had written down with exquisite care and thoroughness just about all they did and made sure to sign it, then carefully saved it. Documents were found in attics of government offices, in salt mines, in cellars and in bricked-up walls of ancient castles. It came to the collection centers in truckloads, 250 *tons* of signed and stamped official paper in one particular haul.

The individual who did by far the most to bring about the trial was an Associate Justice of the U.S. Supreme Court, Robert Houghwout Jackson, a brilliant and spectacular courtroom figure who was the last person I ever saw wearing spats. Equally out of fashion, he was a rare lawyer who was admitted into the profession not via law school but by studying under lawyers in a law firm. He was born in Pennsylvania and built his practice in New York State. FDR appointed him Solicitor General, then Attorney General and in 1941 U.S. Supreme Court Justice. Offered by President Truman the mission of leading an American team of prosecutors after the European war, Jackson enthusiastically took over shaping and organizing the whole trial, which had been an amorphous set of notions till he did so. He bullied and bulldozed opposition to get his way.

Appropriately, Jackson made the opening statement for the prosecution. It was thirty-eight pages long and was in fact a history of Nazism. The Nazi defendants listened to it, transfixed. I took a copy of it back to Shirer, in bed at the Castle, and he read it, fascinated. I am inclined to think it was the germ of his superb book, *The Rise and Fall of the Third Reich,* published fourteen years later, which became the all-time, best-selling work ever chosen by the Book–of–the–Month Club. At his request I began bringing back to him each evening all the documents presented in evidence that day. Later, when he was leaving to return to New York, he asked me to bundle up each week's documents and ship them to him in America. This proved to be too much for me—a week's documents could be a stack a foot high—so we persuaded the news center at the courthouse to do it. Thus was begun the collecting of raw materials for one of the outstanding histories of our time.

I do not think Justice Jackson realized that, when he left the rostrum after reading his landmark document, he also surrendered control of the trial he had done so much to create. In any event, control was quietly assumed by a figure who appeared to come out of an illustration of Dickens; indeed he might have been Mr. Pickwick himself. Sir Geoffrey Lawrence held the office Lord Justice of Appeal, a post not counted in the front rank of British judges, called the Law Lords. But he took over the Presidency of the International Tribunal as though specially made for it. Using the butt of his fountain pen instead of a gavel, he put the trial on the path of fairness and yanked it back on track with each beginning of a deviation. When sloppy prosecutors began to pile in documents, he said, "I believe those documents are cumulative [i.e., redundant support for a point already substantiated]. Would it not be to the purpose to pass to a fresh point?" When it was objected that Göring was answering questions with speeches, the plea was made to require the defendant to answer yes or no. Sir Geoffrey refused, saying, "We wish to hear what he has to say." Thus what many feared would be a circus was made to seem dignified and just.

Jackson's other competitor for starring role was Prisoner Number One, Reichsmarshall Hermann Göring, described by a good observer as "Lord High Everything" except Führer in Nazi Germany. His appearance had been vastly improved by captivity: he lost forty pounds in weight from eating wholesome, if dull, American military food. He was weaned off his drug pills by a physician. He looked sharp and relaxed and altogether pleased as a peacock at having all eyes watching him throughout the trial.

The first case taken up was that of Prisoner Number Two, Rudolf Hess, the hollow-eyed party deputy to Hitler who had fled to Britain to try to get British support for the attack on Russia. He appeared to be unbalanced as the trial began, and there was some question whether he was sane enough to be tried at all. After a week he asked to be allowed to make a statement. He was, and asserted that his manner had been a pose, and that he was able and willing to stand trial. In my broadcast that day I attributed Hess's change to his being impressed by the unexpected dignity and fairness of the trial, but I may have read more into his haggard countenance than was there.

After a fine opening week, proceedings became dull, a fact that may be unimportant to history but was vital to a reporter trying to hold the interest of a milkman in Peoria. Most of the team of American prosecutors—prominent among them, I am afraid, Thomas Dodd, later U.S. Senator from Connecticut and a friend of this writer—simply displayed no sense of the historic drama of the occasion, and read their prosaic remarks as though reading a telephone book. Still, a few individual presentations later on, like that by Telford Taylor, later chief of the prosecuting staff, were very good.

Fortunately the raw materials, the documents, were the stuff of great drama. Quoting from those I was able to make the proceedings sound exciting. Allan Jackson, one of CBS's finer voices later told me, "We were sorry to inundate you with requests for spots, but everybody who had two minutes of air time to fill had to have a piece from Nuremberg to liven up his broadcast." One who feared himself a drudge felt better with a little lather like that.

Except for Göring, few of the defendants were a reporter's helpers in sustaining listener interest. "How on earth could such a sorry bunch of mediocrities run a country, not to mention how could they conquer half the Western world?" Burson asked. Hess read cheap novels through much of the early weeks. Foreign Minister von Ribbentrop proved to be as dumb as his reputation. He wrote a letter seeking mercy addressed to "Mr. Vincent Churchill." I tried to identify him with the sharp, uniformed figure I watched in klieg lights announcing the attack on Russia. But without his uniform or his pride this sad little form, slumped on the bench, looked more like a wet little cat. Kaltenbrunner was a substitute for a substitute, and seemed to feel it. Himmler and his little-known successor, Müller, were dead; Heydrich had been assassinated; Eichmann had disappeared; so this inconspicuous desk administrator of the concentration-camp complex represented the Gestapo. Keitel, nominal head of the armed forces and signer of the surrender, at least maintained the dignity of silence, principally because now, as throughout his life, he had nothing to say. Julius Streicher, Gauleiter of Nuremberg, editor of the obscenely racist weekly *Der Stürmer*, was interesting the way something slimy found under a rock is interesting. He had been in this prison complex before, to apply the lash to two boy criminals because it gave him a sexual thrill. When the story was told in a document, he seemed undisturbed and unashamed. Hjalmar Schacht, whose middle names were Horace Greeley, was interesting as the original financial wizard who made the achievement of Nazi designs possible.

But as we had to take him from a prison where Hitler had put him, in order to put him in our prison, it seemed pointless to try him.

There were moments of high tension. Madame Vaillant Couturier, a pretty French girl who had suffered in Ravensbruck concentration camp, testified vividly of life and death in that hellhole. When she left, she had to pass the corner of the defendants' box, not two feet from Göring. Still heated from memories just revived, she paused a moment; her eyes seemed to flame and she appeared on the verge of going for his eyeballs with her fingernails. An American guard moved between them, and she passed on. Quite the opposite, when the pale remnant of Field Marshal von Paulus, defeated at Stalingrad, had testified and passed that way, it appeared that Göring was about to attack him. Otto Ohlendorf, a high Nazi officer, testified calmly and clinically how he personally had presided over the murder of 90,000 humans in the Ukraine. As coolly as a manager of a factory plant, he discussed comparative efficiencies of different ways of putting large numbers of people to death. Horror films of prison camps were shown. None affected judges, public and defendants so strongly as a grainy length of home movies shot by a soldier in Warsaw of guards expelling victims, mostly naked middle-aged women from a ghetto slum, some dragged out by their hair, others beaten with gun butts as they ran out the door. Through all the showings the defendants watched with more or less shock, except Streicher, who was unmoved, and Schacht, who looked away facing the other end of the room, never the screen.

After a month supped full with horrors, I asked the army to let me have a Jeep to Copenhagen for the Christmas break. Other journalists asked if they might go along; Copenhagen had the reputation of being very near to heaven in gray, wrecked Europe. In the end, two limousines took eight of us. My love came to get me as I waited at the Hotel d'Angleterre, and we went to the little town of Store Heddinge, where she and Jack lived with her family in a solid old eighteenth-century house located behind a thirteenth-century church so perfectly maintained that images of it appear on porcelain objects in Copenhagen shops. For the first time I met Jens Traberg—a big, elderly, masculine edition of his lovely strong-willed, red-haired young daughter, my wife. And his sweet, loving wife, Grete, who played the piano and painted still lifes and thought my little son was quite the finest creature since Jesus. The master of the house insisted that all seven of my colleagues be brought from Copenhagen for an epic luncheon that denied war had ever existed. Speeches were made by Jens and His Honor, the Mayor of Store Heddinge. None of the Americans forgot it for the rest of their lives.

Through the long winter the transcript of the proceedings in Nuremberg grew until it was a stack five times the height of a tall man. At last the prosecution's case was completed, and the defense's turn came. The population of Faber castle, which had gradually thinned over the months, now swelled again. I had come into lone possession of the story on radio as the other networks lost interest. Now I faced competition once more. The *juridical* climax of the trial would be the final judging and sentencing of the defendants, yet to come. But the *dramatic* climax came now. The number one defendant was to be cross-examined by the number one prosecutor. The occasion was foreseen to be a clash of titans. Göring was to be led to the gallows by his own words as elicited from him by Robert Jackson.

The gallery was filled to see Jackson and Göring face off for the first time. The American opened with words suited to a great occasion: "You are perhaps aware that you are the only man living who can expound to us the true purposes of the Nazi Party and the inner workings of its leadership?" The fat man answered briefly but suitably for a great confrontation, "I am perfectly aware of that."

Alas, after that lofty take-off the quality of the encounter fell away immediately. Jackson's questions were wordy and seemed to lack fine point. Göring responded even more lengthily but, at least, to the point. Jackson appealed to Justice Lawrence to require the defendant to answer with brevity. Lawrence refused. Jackson was irritated and let it show. Göring, feeling licensed by the Court, expanded his answers into speeches. Jackson became furious and lost his poise, leaving Göring to gloat while the prosecutor argued with the judges in open court.

A ridiculous mistake unmanned Jackson. He introduced a document to prove that Göring had planned the military takeover of the Rhineland in 1936. The document, dated 1935 and signed by Göring, was said to order the liberation of the Rhineland. Göring looked at the document and informed Jackson that he was the victim of a mistranslation. It was an order to clean up the Rhine River, to remove obstacles to shipping. I have the impression that Jackson never recovered. His face never lost an expression of irritated frustration. When he accused Göring of engaging in secret plans for war, the defendant noted that he had not heard that the U.S. ever prepublished its own military plans. Jackson had lost control; Göring had acquired it.

I do not think there is yet a consensus on what happened to the foremost prosecutor. Of course, Göring entered the lists with two advantages: one, having initiated the crimes, he was master of the material and knew where small loopholes could be used to subvert greater meanings; two, he knew he was going to die and was therefore invulnerable to words. It is possible that Jackson was simply not gifted in the endlessly detailed work of preparing verbal traps. In any case, the Nazi was the uncontested winner of the duel.

For Justice Jackson and his admirers, of whom I had become one, it was a sad interlude. For a while a feeling akin to that of "all is lost" prevailed at Faber. But for the ultimate outcome of the trial and the judgment of history it was of no account. Reporters and novelists look for drama in courtrooms. Justice looks to the weight of hard evidence. The case constructed against Göring and his associates by their own signed orders was so gargantuan that it could not be diminished by a stumble on the other side.

I was able to see only the beginning of Jackson's misfortune, and the rescue of the situation managed by the Scotsman, David Maxwell-Fyfe. For a sudden, radical change in my life usurped my whole attention.

1946-1957

CHAPTER FORTY

Elevation

The winter in the ruins was bleak and seemed endless. To give his overworked reporter a free evening, White agreed to break with his tradition that all newscasts had to be live, letting me record my evening report early for later replay. That day the sun came out. When the court session ended at about three, it was still there, and I decided to walk the eight miles back to the castle. Along a street of residential ruins I was brought up short by a tiny spectacle. On a window sill in a flower box, two pink pansies stared impudently down on me and the dreary gray scene. The effect was rather like my wartime entry into Switzerland. There was color left in the world somewhere, and dot by little dot it would return to Germany. I felt a mighty urge for a change of scene and the presence of my girl.

At the message desk at the castle, I found a cable from Ed Murrow to come see him in London. I cabled Bennie and asked her to meet me there and we would have a few days together. Murrow had taken the big job in New York and, a colleague informed me, wanted to say goodbye to his staffers individually. I landed in London just after noon on Sunday and, as he had instructed me, went right to his office. He was dictating his Sunday commentary, to be delivered that evening. Dictating done, and the script in his pocket, he took me to his apartment. We sat down and over a couple of drinks became so involved in chatter that the impermissible happened. A phone call from New York told him that he had forgotten the time and missed his broadcast, something I felt I might be capable of but not the world's heavyweight champion news broadcaster. "They said I was never better but that I sounded strangely like fifteen minutes of beautiful organ music," he said. He uttered a string of heavyweight champion oaths, then excused himself and Janet, his wife. They were engaged in a series of farewell dinners with prominent English friends; we would meet the next afternoon.

Bennie was not yet there, so I accepted an invitation to lunch the next day with John Osborne, a senior editor of *Life* magazine. He asked about my plans for a postwar career. I told him I had been too busy at Nuremberg to lay plans, but I had listened to myself enough to know that my future lay in print. Anyhow, CBS was probably cutting staff abroad now. I expected that Murrow had called me to London to tell me something like that. John then said the nice words—*Life* would like to take me on as a roving correspondent. I was elated and promised an early answer.

Then I returned to Murrow's office. I figured he might be pleased to know that I was one wartime acquisition he need not feel guilty about firing. Often deep and dark, and sometimes a little menacing with his beetled brow, Murrow now became more so. With a growl he said, "Henry Luce is crazy if he thinks he can get away with raiding my staff. You are not going to work for him, Howard. I am going to New York to be the unhappiest executive in CBS and run the news department. And you are coming to London to take my place as Chief European Correspondent." He opened his desk drawer and drew out a contract and laid it before me. "You can sign it now, or read it first and then sign it, but you are going to sign it. I make out the numbers on these things, and I will make you an offer you cannot refuse."

I was stunned. I genuinely felt that I was unsuited for broadcasting. My voice was not as bad as Shirer's—in fact it was all right—but it did not approach the baritone quality I felt necessary for lesser figures in the profession. The previous year en route to Berlin by Jeep I had stopped off at an Armed Forces Network studio, seeking shelter for the night. Word spread around the building that CBS's Berlin Correspondent was there. The voices began to gather around me, the big announcers of America's future, then still in uniform. I felt inadequate just chatting with them. They began to compete in depth with one another, each succeeding voice a shade browner than the previous one. Soon it was a cannonade of voices going back and forth over me, a competition so intense that I was able to sneak out from under it and go to bed, convinced that I had heard the Norman Brokenshires and Edwin C. Hills of tomorrow, and that I was not among them.

Now, here was Ed Murrow offering me what was about the most desirable job in broadcast news. (His answer to my objection: Radio has changed since before the war. It calls not only for a voice, but a trained brain, that and a knack for news. In fact the brain comes first, before the voice. My opinion: It calls for personality before either, someone the Peoria milkman can like and trust. I was not sure of my quality in that respect either.) With misgiving bells ringing in my ears I signed and went to the airport to meet Bennie. That night we celebrated the joyous prospect of reuniting our small family. The next day she moved with speed and precision to make it a fact. She persuaded Janet Murrow to let us take over their apartment. She surveyed the rooms and sized up our problem. We would not qualify for buying furniture in Britain's sternly rationed market for months. So she returned to Denmark to purchase what was needed there and arrange shipping to London. Meanwhile I hung about to listen to the master dictating his final broadcast from Britain. It was, as I mentioned earlier, a sparkler, and this time we got him to the studio on time.

For a farewell present I found Murrow a first edition about another famous London figure, Boswell's *Life of Johnson,* then returned to Nuremberg to pack my gear. It was the last time in my life that I could pack all my earthly possessions in one small bag.

My last night at the Faber castle, an agreeable friend working for UP took me aside and told me he was interested in switching to broadcasting; did I have any tips? I was not very helpful, having sleepwalked into it myself. He soon found out for himself, and once there, not besieged by my kind of self-doubts, Walter Cronkite never looked back.

Bennie got back to London shortly after I did, soon followed by handsome new suites of modern Danish furniture outfitting our entire apartment. Furniture was not more easily available in Denmark. It was simply that she knew how to make the Danish rules work for her. Soon she would learn the rules in England and would get whatever we needed there. At times I felt truly guilty about hogging this natural executive all for myself, when she would have worked wonders for any commercial firm or for a government. But, as it is said, question not a happy gift when life offers so many unhappy ones, or words to that effect.

However pleasant it was to be promoted, it was a jolt for me, very young, to be moving from the trenches to the command post in one step, in a news organization I barely knew from one short visit to New York. I was not prepared for instant prominence. I was less prepared for the ordeal of trying to substitute in the eyes of the consequential people of London for the admired and lionized Edward R. Murrow.

For a time I made an effort to replace Murrow. He much enjoyed English club life and offered to put me up for the Saville Club. I took a good look, and decided that if I had extra time I would prefer to spend it with my girl and my kid. I spent a few lunches with some of his friends, Lord Camrose, owner of the conservative *Daily Telegraph*; Brendan Bracken, Churchill's Minister for Information and now editor of the *Financial Times*; Lord Robert Vansittart, dismissed from the Foreign Office in the Munich years for his noble opposition to appeasement; and ultimately the colossus himself, Winston Churchill. The meetings were amiable, and those with Churchill thrilling. But no close liaisons with these figures were likely. Reporters inevitably gravitate to people in power; and after a very long time, these Tory magnates were not.

Murrow much improved my satisfaction with my new post when he informed me that I would inherit his weekly news analysis, fifteen minutes to run around in all by myself. It involved a wholly new form of writing for me and took some getting used to. Worried about being thought to "bloviate," as President Harding had described the making of sonorous speeches with little content, I erred on the side of saying too much too boldly. At that time the engagement of Princess Elizabeth, the future queen, to Philip Mountbatten, related to the Greek royal family, was announced. In my very first commentary I suggested that the royal liaison might make the ugly British sponsorship of the Greek fascist government easier to swallow. That did it; that really did it. The remark remained engraved on the minds of the royal secretariat, and bedeviled my relations with the Establishment forever after. I regretted it for that reason, but more because Philip turned out to be a nearly perfect consort, and the relation proved to be romantic with no political implications at all.

After a few weeks my weekly analysis—a word CBS preferred to commentary—became surer, gaining momentum and a following. It won the Overseas Press Club award for foreign reporting and comment four times. By the time of its death after thirteen years, it was the longest-running regular commentary on radio. It died, I believe, nobly, accused of taking sides in the revolution of civil rights in America in the 1960s, of which it was undeniably guilty.

CHAPTER FORTY-ONE

London

My two years at Oxford were intensely lived. But, aside from London, where I had several short impatient stays, England was to me just a large populated space surrounding the dock from which to get to or arrive from the attractions of continental Europe as quickly as possible. Now I was to spend eleven years experiencing England as a tax-paying, full-fledged participant in the life and problems of English folk almost as if I were a temporary subject of the King (and later the Queen).

Likes and dislikes crystallized rapidly. I had already developed in Oxford an altogether un-American liking for uncooled (warm it never was), flat English beer, finding it rich in flavor, strong in effects and, lacking carbonation, easy to drink in quantity without bloating. Now in London, with no Oxford proctors around, I let never a day pass without a session in a cozy pub with a pint or two. I never cottoned on to English tea—it looked too much like muddy water from my native river—which cut me off from a vital segment of society, the civil service, which really governs the country and seems to subsist mainly on milky tea. The joke was told of a father and son visiting India: *Son:*

Father, what are all those things that look like penguins ravaging the tea fields?
Father: Those are civil servants; it's cheaper sending them here than transporting all that tea to London.

I liked not the substance but delighted in the occasion of tea time in English homes. The unsurpassed native art of conversation was never exercised so winningly as at tea time over jam and toast and crumpets and watercress sandwiches. The famous epigram, England and America are separated by a common language, never applied to me. Chief of all London delights was hearing it in the theater. Theaters were plentiful; tickets were amazingly available, at prices that left one with legs and arms intact; and the fare and the quality of the actors were not to be matched. The Old Vic national theater produced over several years the entire canon of Shakespeare's plays. We saw them all except the three parts of *Henry VI* and bloody *Titus Andronicus.* The first were too dull, rewritten by another's pen; and the second involved the magnificent Vivien Leigh waving bloody stumps at the audience, which I felt I could forgo.

Theater folk being of interest to everyone, I relate two encounters with two of the foremost. We were invited to a post–opening night reception at the home of the actor John Mills. It was a handsome Georgian house, once the home of Sir Joshua Reynolds, with a garden that sloped down to the Thames. Inside I spotted young Laurence Olivier and dared to make conversation. He had shaved his head to get rid of the peroxide blond he had sported in the film version of *Hamlet,* and his hair had now grown back to crew-cut length. I asked him, "The first words spoken in your film were not by Shakespeare. They were 'Hamlet, the story of a man who could not make up his mind.' Who wrote them?" He said, "I did." I said, "How did you have the boldness to take liberties with the master's play?" He said, "I knew he wouldn't mind; we have grown close." At an apartment cocktail party given by the editor of the *News-Chronicle* newspaper, I found myself in a corner with a slight, bald man who, a commentator said, looked like nothing much. At one point I said, "I am afraid I did not get your name." He said "Guinness." I said, "Guinness, as in the beer?" He said, "Yes, Alec, as in the ragtime band." I forgave myself for my ignorance, for up to that time he had played a secondary role in only one film, *Great Expectations.* In a few years, however, Alec Guinness's films would be Britain's third most profitable export to the U.S., after scotch whiskey and Harris tweed.

No American survey of Britain can avoid mention of plumbing. In the scholars' community of Oxford I expected austerity. As a tax-paying citizen I was sad to discover that cold, unheated bathrooms were the rule, though some had heated pipes to warm towels. At 84 Hallam Street we considered putting an electric space heater in ours but were warned against electrocution, particularly in a household containing a small boy who did not consider a bath complete till he had splashed a wall-to-wall inch of water around the room. Of commodes, I had always thought that the name "crapper" given to them was a student whimsy. In fact, I now learned, the name was respectably legitimate. The firm of Thomas Crapper and Sons manufactured the early article, and the family name appeared in the bottom of each. Their performance was interesting. As a major from Kansas City wrote his wife from London during the war, "You pull the chain and nothing happens. You let it go and all hell breaks loose."

On the affirmative side, we early developed a strong liking for two particular London pleasures: bookshops and auction houses. It came about in this way. As a child of the Depression I was extremely cautious about spending money—was a tightwad, to put it bluntly—though I was now earning well. I was saving up to be ready for the next Depression. There was no limit put on Jack's beginning education or anything Bennie wished for herself, especially clothing, for I loved seeing her well got up. But I disliked acquiring possessions that would hamper movement in WW III, because I was also a child of war. One day after long hinting to no effect, Bennie laid it down flat: We arrived here with a substantial nest egg from sales of *Last Train,* taxes already paid on it. We are earning a not inconsiderable salary. You have *got* to spend some money. Isn't there something you have always wanted? I allowed as how I had always wanted a library. Together we drew up a list of classics of literature and began to spend my one day off each week walking around London or driving to other towns (autos were hard to come by for years after the war, but a departing *Time* reporter sold us his La Salle) seeking handsome leather-bound books on our list. In the course of this hunt, we attended a book auction at famous Sotheby's in Bond Street. In a separate room they were preparing displays for an auction of antiquities. We returned on the appointed day and began several years of collecting fragments of Egyptian, Greek and Roman figures, intensely pleasing to my history-minded disposition. In later years my salary could not have reached the prices for these desirables. But in those early postwar years, British aristocrats were selling off portions of their estates cheaply to pay taxes, and American dollars could fetch several times the booty now attainable.

One day in 1951 William Randolph Hearst died. In addition to owning San Simeon, the model for *Citizen Kane* had kept a medieval castle in Wales, named St. Donats. Once a ruin, it was now restored; and Hearst had stables and cottages brought, stone by stone, from other medieval ruins in the United Kingdom to be added to the complex, and then he furnished it with fine ancient furniture. Upon the death of the owner, the Hearst magazines in London handed it to the editor of *Connoisseur* magazine and an antiques dealer to dissolve, in order to turn the structure into a school for girls. He knew my ever well-connected wife and told her we might spend a night at the castle and choose some objects, and he would give us a good price before putting the rest up to auction. We spent a fascinating day roaming the wonderland, saw Hearst's personal bed, a very high oak-canopied piece painted red and bearing a gilded shield announcing that King Charles I had slept in it some time before Cromwell handed him his head. Across a corridor was a lovely room with an unmistakable feminine touch and a fine eighteenth-century cloth-canopied bed for Marion Davies. At one point in our roaming we asked the butler if we might see "Marion Davies' room" once more. With a bare soupçon of refined embarrassment he said, "If you don't mind, sir, we prefer to call it the Green Room." And so it was thereafter called by us. Anyhow, we bought an oak-canopied bed dated 1625 in which we still sleep and another dated 1594 for our guest room. I once met William Randolph Hearst, Jr., and told him I slept with a woman who slept in his father's bed. It was the mark of a genuine man of the world that he did not bat an eye.

Because I lived in Britain so long and have supported points in articles and broadcasts by referring to my English experience, many friends have thought me to be an Anglophile. Well, I was never Anglophobic, but I was blocked from having the kind of love affair Murrow had with the place by a conspicuous feature with deep clinging roots. It was snobbery, contempt for the middle and lower orders—never hatred, since it was not taken that seriously—sometimes even blindness to their existence and concerns, all symptoms of a manner and attitude that repelled me, as hatred of race did in my own country.

The source of the illness, I believed, was the educational structure. The uppermost 5 percent of British males went (and probably still do; I no longer feel as responsible for the world as H. K. Smith in his twenties did) to exclusive private preparatory schools from ages 7 to 13. Then from 13 through 18 they moved on to still more exclusive private secondary schools (called, in the English way, "public" schools). Then to Oxford or Cambridge for completion. After university they went into politics, or government, or business, or the armed services, where they would stay for the rest of their lives, mixing only with the same people with whom they had shared their exclusive education. Anthony Sampson quotes the headmaster of Eton, the most famous of these gardens where young aristocrats were grown, as saying, "We must not let public schools become too far out of alignment with the social developments of the country." Which I read to say, we are far out of alignment but must take care not to get too far out, wherever that is.

The other 95 percent of youth of both sexes attended schools that were really public, and there to my mind the real atrocity occurred (and despite improvements, still does). At age 11, they took an examination that determined the minority who might go on to college, and the big majority who might not.

I was hypersensitive about this because of serious doubts that I could have made it, were I British. At age 10 I was scoring A's and B's in the small-town coziness of Monroe. At age 12 I was in New Orleans, failing in all subjects available for failure. At age 17, moved by fear, I was making the highest grades. Britain had 1,815 college students per 1 million people, when in America there were 16,670 per million. I would surely have been ruled out in the British system.

The Britain I knew from my years at Oxford was in social stasis, governed by Conservatives for a long generation. On my return to Britain I was thrilled to witness a breaking up of the ice and the most serious movement since the Liberal Revolution of 1911.

CHAPTER FORTY-TWO

The Updating of Britain

When war in Europe ended, Churchill asked Labour members of his coalition cabinet to keep the coalition alive until the war in the Pacific ended too. The Labour leaders said no—they wanted an election immediately. So Churchill reluctantly dissolved the House and called for a vote.

Just before the election, Murrow had six or seven of his staffers, including me, in London for a conference. The British magazine *Picture Post* did a layout on forecasts by "Murrow's boys." Murrow said the Tories would win but with a reduced majority. The others gave variations of the same answer. My political prophecies are not right so often that I can neglect to point up occasions when they were. I said that Labour, my old party, would win, probably with a good majority.

The results, announced July 26, 1945, three months after the end of the war, were stunning. Churchill's Conservatives lost 181 seats in the House of Commons. Labour won a majority of 148 over all other parties combined. Churchill, a Labour MP friend of mine said, was great in war, "but we can't keep having wars to make him great. We want a new deal at home."

The new Parliament met to elect its speaker on August 1. Severely damaged by bombs, the chamber was being reconstructed according to Churchill's two prescriptions. First, unlike the semicircular designs of most congresses and parliaments, it must continue to be rectangular with an aisle separating rows of benches. If a member was going to "rat" and jump parties, Churchill explained, he must be seen to cross the floor, no sliding imperceptibly around a little to the left or a little to the right. He was an expert, having crossed the floor twice, from Tory to Liberal and later back to Tory—whence his boast, "Anyone can rat, but it takes character to re-rat." His second prescription: the chamber must be too small to seat all its 700 members. Most days few are present, so a large chamber would disappoint onlookers. On important days, when all are present, it looks suitably impressive to have members overflowing the benches and the room.

On August 15, 1945, the day the Japanese surrendered, the formal opening of Parliament took place. The King appeared, crown and all, and read the "King's Speech," which was written by the government of the day. The leftist professor, Harold Laski, once wrote that the monarchy would stand in the way of socialism's ever being adopted in Britain. In the event, here was the most royal Briton commending socialism to his subjects in words prepared by socialists.

Next, the first reading of the "Outlawries Bill" was moved and voted. This was a bill that did not exist. In the 1600s a bill of that title was introduced. King Charles II was offended and sent word that Parliament had no power to deal with the subject. So then, and every year since, the Outlawries Bill has been introduced to make it clear who is boss. (There were, I found, many provisions in the Houses of Parliament to accommodate things that did not exist. A cloakroom is equipped with straps on which to hang one's sword. When a member speaks, he must be sure to stand behind a line on the floor that keeps him two swords' lengths from such a line on the other side, to prevent sword fights that do not exist. There is a peg in the cloakroom of the House of Lords for the Queen's husband to hang his hat on, which he never does. I myself, after acquiring seniority, came into possession of a document that does not exist, a lobby pass allowing me to go into the room next to chamber to chat with MPs. When I asked for it, I was told there was no such document; the policeman at the door would simply know I possessed it, which was all that was necessary. I promptly sought to exercise my privilege, and sure enough the guard said nothing, and I entered without hindrance. Puzzled I went outside and found a fellow (but less senior) American reporter and asked him to try. He did, and the policeman stopped him, saying "I am sorry, sir, but only holders of Lobby passes may come in." I never discovered how he knew I was one of the select.)

There followed a flood of legislation far more interventionist in social life than the New Deal in the U.S. had been. Taken into government ownership were the Bank of England and most basic industries, including coal and steel. All the rest were tightly regulated. In the fullness of time most of these measures were amended or repealed to create motives for economic growth. But in a time of postwar scarcity when demand was infinite and supply skin-tight, they were essential. Labour's foremost social measure, the creation of the National Health Service, was immensely beneficial. Traveling in the Midlands, I was impressed that children seemed of a different race from their parents— bigger, stronger, more vigorous—thanks to a health care program the parents had never had.

The Lenin of Britain's social revolution physically resembled the Lenin of Russia's, from his bald pate and slightly Oriental cast of eyes to his brush mustache; only the build was slighter. But in temperament and values Clement Richard Attlee was wholly Western democratic, as different from the Russian as the House of Commons was from the Supreme Soviet. His temperament was undynamic. He was a hard interview, answering almost every question with a "yes" or an "I think not" or an "I daresay." He was solidly middle class, a graduate of Oxford who came by his leadership of Labour—and therefore the Prime Ministry—as a compromise between dynamic subordinates. Before the war Churchill called Attlee "a modest little man with much to be modest about." But in the darkest days of the war, when the Labourite consented to serve as Churchill's Deputy Prime Minister, the Conservative regretted the slur and discovered that the modest little man was a tower of strength of character.

At the beginning of the next election campaign, in 1950, I stood in a small clump of reporters across the street from the Prime Minister's residence at Number Ten Downing Street to watch Attlee commence his campaign for re-election. A garage mechanic drove Clem's little car up and parked it at the door. Clem came out to check petrol and water and take a peek under the hood. He reminded me of Mr. Pritchard kicking the tires of his well-kept little Durant preparatory to an outing in Monroe. He went back in the residence and soon came out again with his lone bodyguard carrying suitcases to place in the trunk. He disappeared for a few moments again, then came out with Vi (his nice-looking wife, Violet), who promptly took the wheel. Clem sat next to her, and the bodyguard settled in the back seat; and with his hand raised in a thrifty half-wave to us, the chief executive of the great world empire got lost in the traffic of London en route north for a luncheon with the Labour ladies of Luton. He led his party to a second victory for Labour.

The strongest of Attlee's lieutenants was Ernest Bevin, the boss of the biggest union in the world, called the Transport and General Workers. He had served as Minister for Labour in the wartime cabinet, and now became what seemed an odd choice to be Foreign Minister. He appeared almost as broad as he was tall and had a great leonine head with a steel gray mane. When he approached, you tended to move aside, lest he crush you like a steamroller. He spoke not the King's English but that of the H-dropping dockworkers he led, and he spoke it with wit and strength. "You mayn't credit it," he said in a speech, "but I went to Eton and 'Arrow just like these Conservative chaps. I 'ad lunch at Eton and made a speech at 'Arrow."

Bevin did not sit for interviews. But with the help of his private secretary, who had been a member of my Labour club at Oxford, I got a half-hour with him. Seated before a gigantic portrait of King George III he told me his appointment was the work of King George VI. The King was discussing with Attlee the composition of his first postwar cabinet, and asked whom the Prime Minister had in mind for the Foreign Office. Attlee named Hugh Dalton, a college professor. In a rare—nearly unheard-of—intrusion, the King asked whether Bevin, who had kept peace at the workplace as Minister for Labour, would not be a stronger choice to keep peace in the world as Foreign Minister. Attlee returned to his office, thought it over, called Bevin in and asked him to take over the nation's foreign affairs. It was an inspired choice. Labour's back-benchers were a little drunk with their victory at the polls and sought to propel policy toward Russia not America. Bevin distrusted ideology and had a clear knowledge of the contrasting fates of unions in the U.S. and the U.S.S.R. His mighty personality ensured level-headedness and continuity in foreign policy.

The most *interesting* figure in the new government was a Welshman named Aneurin Bevan, a former coal miner, an always rebel who had been expelled from the Labour Party for many years, but now was charged, as Minister of Health, with the toughest job in the cabinet: creating the National Health Service with unwilling doctors. Had there been a prize for political oratory in Britain at that time, it is not settled whether Churchill or Bevan would have won it. But the prize for using it savagely would have been all Bevan's. In the Munich period he described Prime Minister Chamberlain: "He has the lucidity which is the by-product of a fundamentally sterile mind . . . he does not have to struggle as Churchill has, for example, with the crowded pulsations of a fecund imagination. On the contrary he is almost devoid of imagination . . . listening to a speech [by Chamberlain] is like paying a visit to Woolworth's, everything in its place and nothing above sixpence." His view of Anthony Eden, Churchill's foreign minister and designated successor, was equally scalding. He was the "juvenile lead," and "he is more pathetic than sinister. He is utterly outmatched by his international opponents. Beneath the sophistication of his appearance and manner he has all the unplumbable stupidities and unawareness of his class and type." In a period of scarcities, he said, "This island is built upon coal and surrounded by fish. To have a shortage of both at the same time requires genius." Of Churchill he said, he mistook "verbal felicities for mental inspirations . . . he always refers to a defeat as a disaster, as though it came from God, but to a victory as though it came from himself." He did not think highly of British journalists; when there was talk during the war of limiting press freedom, Bevan opposed it, saying, "Why muzzle sheep?" American journalists, including me, he befriended.

When the Labour leadership decided that the Health Service had to take a step back from wholly free treatment and to charge token fees for prescriptions, Bevan resigned in protest. It was the high-water mark in Bevan's career and in that of the Labour revolution. He never regained stride in his aim to be Prime Minister. Labour had succeeded in bringing about a fairer distribution of wealth and rewards, but it had nothing special to offer in the next stage, when the mission would be to grow, to increase the amount of wealth to be distributed.

John Strachey, the guru who educated the generation of the thirties in his understanding of socialism, was Minister for Colonies in the Labour government. In the course of my reporting in London we became good friends. Once after dinner, I took a dog-eared copy of *The Coming Struggle for Power*, left over from my period of working for George Coad on the *New Orleans Item*, down from my library shelf and asked him to inscribe it. He drew back as if a sharp knife had been thrust at him. "I have written better books, I would prefer to put my name in one of those," he said. He admitted upon being pressed that his analysis of the times was flawed despite its widespread influence. It was nevertheless a bit of history and I wanted his name in it. Reluctantly he complied. I felt that the 1930s were at last well and truly over.

CHAPTER FORTY-THREE

Cold War Begins

It was routine just after the war to state that Britain was no longer the great power it had been for centuries past, but no one really grasped the extent to which this fact was true and important. Stalin spoke of British decline, yet he saw Britain, not the U.S., as the great power that would thwart his ambitions, and sought a deal on spheres of influence with Churchill, not Roosevelt or Truman. Americans said Britain was finished, yet they pulled out of Europe on the assumption that Britain would play its traditional powerful role and establish peace. Nine million American soldiers were released from service the first year. "It was not a demobilization," said General George Marshall, "it was a rout." Said General Wedemeyer, "America fought the war like a football game after which the winner leaves the field and celebrates." Family pressures forced it, said President Truman. Oxbridge Professor Denis Brogan responded, "How odd that only American boys have mothers." But the British, Churchill in the lead, took it for granted that Britain would resume its accustomed place. In his victory broadcast in May of 1945, Churchill said, "The British Commonwealth and Empire stands more united and more effectively powerful than at any time in its long romantic history." The new Labour government at first followed through, facing down troubles from Germany to Greece to India. It was a prime assumption of world order that Britain was as great a power as ever.

That assumption ran into the hard rock of reality in the winter of 1946–1947, my first winter back in England. It grew extraordinarily cold. In January, dark clouds opened and poured three to twenty feet of snow on the island in the worst blizzard of the century. I sent everyone home and worked from our apartment near the BBC radio studios. Midland villages had to be supplied by airdrop. Miners could not get to mines, coal ships were frozen in harbors. Without fuel, the economy shut down. Britain could not begin to pay its enormous bills much less sustain current standards of living. "Britain's lifeline," said a newspaper, "is no longer the 10,000 miles through Suez to Asia; it is the few hundred miles from the coal mines to the factories."

In the first months of 1947, the Labour government stopped pretending and began a huge divestiture. Foreign Minister Bevin announced Britain was giving up on Palestine and handing the place and the problem to the United Nations. Attlee offered Burma independence and then thrust independence on India. That announcement, I said in a broadcast, "initiated the stormiest session of the House in years. Attlee didn't have time to retake his seat before Mr. Churchill—pale, angry, twice his normal bulk in a thick black overcoat [there was no heat in Parliament]—rose and hurled questions across the floor at the Prime Minister. Attlee, weary from overwork, his nerves frazzled . . . stubbornly refused to answer. The chamber was alive with shouting for twenty minutes, until finally the Prime Minister got up and stalked angrily out, with Churchill fuming at his elbow all the way."

On February 24, the British ambassador in America gave the State Department a note that marked a turning point for everybody. Britain could no longer defend Greece and Turkey from rising Communist pressures and intended to abandon those two commitments in a month.

This—not Pearl Harbor, not victory in Europe or Asia, not the later Marshall Plan—was the true watershed at which America had to decide to give up self-sufficiency forever and assume worldwide responsibilities with no retreat. Unless U.S. power replaced that of Britain, then the Middle East, the ever-troubled nexus of three continents, would be laid open to Soviet penetration.

While President Truman was agonizing over this, a conference took place in Moscow. The Allies had agreed that, in the years after the war, their policies would be coordinated, and the world effectually run, by regular meetings of what was called the Council of Foreign Ministers—of Britain, France, the U.S. and the U.S.S.R. Such a meeting was held in Moscow late in the winter of Britain's discontent, the early spring of 1947. I made my small effort to breathe life into the wartime alliance in my first report:

> This is Moscow. And this is, I think, the first completely uncensored news analysis ever broadcast from Soviet Russia to the United States. [It was.] Put a ring around the day on the calendar. I personally would classify the lifting of the censorship here as one of the happiest international events since victory, certainly one of the most intelligent steps taken by Russia toward understanding among nations. . . . I wish I could adequately convey to my Soviet friends the enthusiasm that reporters feel about the move, and the hope that it will not be an isolated act but only the beginning of a removal of all the barriers of misunderstanding that divide us.

Those were probably the last nice words said about the conference by anybody. The next day I had my first impression of the savior of freedom and new Secretary of State, "General Marshall came down out of the plane alone . . . His attitude was forthright and almost too sober. He barely smiled during the whole reception ceremony." Molotov, his Soviet counterpart, was as congenial as a boulder.

On the third day of the talks, President Truman in Washington announced his decision, to replace the British as protectors of Greece and Turkey and any other nation deemed to be threatened—he made a doctrine of it. The Moscow talks, stagnating early in discord over how to govern defeated Germany, got nowhere. After a month, this colloquy occurred:

> BEVIN: "Where are we?"
> BIDAULT (of France): "God knows."
> BEVIN: "I didn't know He was here."

Apparently he wasn't. Soon after, defeat was acknowledged and the conference ended. There was one further meeting of the foreign ministers, in London in December of that same year. My broadcast described its end:

The most important event in the world this week was ten seconds of silence in the council chamber of Lancaster House, here in London. The Big Four had just agreed to adjourn. Mr. Bevin, in the chair, then asked, "Are there any suggestions as to time and place of our next meeting?" He looked from one of his colleagues to another. None of them looked up from the table. Finally, Bevin shrugged his heavy shoulders, waved at the door—leading to a bar—and said, "Then come and share some British austerity with me."

Those were the last recorded words of the Foreign Ministers' Conference. The absence of response to Bevin's proposal for another meeting seemed to be the razor's edge that cut off the past from the future. As the four men filed silently out of the room, a phase of postwar history left with them. The agreed instrument for peace-making, the Foreign Ministers' Council, has failed after two and a half years. As somebody remarked, it left a vacuum in world relations big as the hollow feeling of fear in your stomach.

On both sides of what Churchill denominated the Iron Curtain, forces arose that would take nearly half a century to still. A month after the Truman Doctrine was announced, the financier Bernard Baruch made a speech in Columbia, South Carolina, about the world condition. Baruch's friend, the journalist Herbert Bayard Swope, wrote the speech for him. Swope created the phrase, and Baruch named the strange new conflict, "the Cold War."

CHAPTER FORTY-FOUR

Virtual Armageddon

I became in effect a war correspondent again, CBS's chief Cold War correspondent, almost wholly absorbed by that conflict, pursuing its crises from country to country. "Cold War" was a good name but short on expressing proportions. It was really World War III, in which the main powers were constrained from fighting one another outright by the abominable invention of the fissionable atom. It involved more nations and more of the planet than either of the hot world wars, and cost more than either. It claimed nearly as many

American lives (in Korea and Vietnam) as did WW I, and it cost 7 million other lives in proxy wars over the globe. Its duration, nearly half a century, would bring changes in life at least as great as the two previous wars had.

The Moscow conference disaster in the winter of 1947 was the first great breakup. Splittings and crackings followed all over the continent. That spring, when Bennie and I were driving a new Chevrolet across industrial northern France to Paris, small crowds gathered on roadsides and threw stones at our car, crying, *"Impérialistes!"* This in towns where two years earlier American Jeeps and tanks had been garlanded with flowers.

This fury was caused by a breakup in Paris. For two postwar years, France had been governed by a coalition including the Communist Party. But the Communists proved too unreliable as partners. With 95 percent control of French unions they called an unending series of strikes, making recovery, or just governing, impossible. They sought to make the point that peace and progress could be achieved only when they were given all power. Finally, the non-Communist parties dissolved the cabinet and formed a new government leaving the Communists out. It was a week later that our imperialist Chevrolet was stoned in northern industrial towns.

From paralyzed Paris we drove to Italy, which was in worse shape. The Allies were still treating the country as a defeated enemy, and penury was deep and wide. One walked a gauntlet of motherly beggars outside restaurants. Communists were leading landless peasants in seizing unworked lands. When Italy's small residual army was ordered out against the seizures, it mutinied. The Italian coalition government then followed the French example and excluded the Communist Party. This was chancier in Italy, where enormous popular sympathy existed for it and for the desperate people it represented. The Italian Communists could hope to accomplish what no Communist Party had yet done: win a majority in coming national elections.

Crossing France and Italy was a prelude to a unique venture. I had secured Paul White's agreement that I tour eastern European countries and broadcast from the capital of each. They were rapidly being Communized, and I thought it might be smart to get a foot in the door and set precedents for future use. We went by auto because railroads were not fully rebuilt, and air travel was still limited to military personnel and civil officials. We packed the car with everything we might need for emergencies. We foresaw that our obviously American car would be stopped frequently for inspection by eager, eighteen-year-old Communist cops, so Bennie did all the driving. When they saw her Danish passport, they let us move on without the harassment my American passport might have caused.

We entered Yugoslavia at Trieste and drove through the mountains of Bosnia to Belgrade. This was partisan territory with few and broken roads. We had to repair six punctured tires before reaching the city. There I met Tito in his suburban mansion. As we conversed in German he smoked a cigarette held upright in a miniature pipe and poured us tiny glasses of plum brandy liqueur. The lean face of wartime photos was acquiring flesh, and in a few years he would look like the long-lost twin of Hermann Göring.

After spending a week in each of a half-dozen capitals and broadcasting from each, we ended our tour in Czechoslovakia. There I visited Foreign Minister Jan Masaryk in his top-story suite in the Foreign Office in Prague. He was the son of the founder of the Republic, Thomas Masaryk. He was wholly Western-oriented but said, "If forced to choose I would have to go east. Only Russia stood by us in the Munich crisis, and at the end it was Russia who liberated us." (He neglected to say that Patton was willing to do so and was on the way, but Eisenhower called him back.) "I would go east," he said, "but it would kill me."

My main conclusion from the tour was worrisome. Eastern Europe was coming out of the war with one big advantage over Western Europe: somebody was in charge (too much so) and was making plans for the future. In the Western nations no one seemed in charge, and the nations were planless, uncertain, getting desperate.

Toward the end of our tour, in June 1947, the political bombshell that changed the world was dropped: the Marshall Plan was announced. It was offered to the Communist East as well as to the free West. It was not, as it was often called, just a foreign aid plan. It was more complex and shrewd: the recipient nations must come together and make lists of what each could supply to the rest for recovery. What was left over at the bottom of the list would be supplied free by the U.S. It was the first push toward integrating and uniting Europe.

The effect was electric. Bevin of Britain called for a meeting of all in Paris to accept and lay plans almost before Marshall's voice died down. In France and Italy, American prestige soared. Even the French and Italian Communist leaders, Thorez and Togliatti, came out for the plan. Masaryk of Czechoslovakia declared enthusiastically for accepting.

On the other side of the continent, Stalin said no. American money financing the integration of Europe would be the solvent of Communism. Masaryk, Thorez and Togliatti were summoned to Moscow and required to change their minds. The Cominform—the Communist Information Bureau—was created to organize a world-wide propaganda campaign against the "Imperialist Master Plan." Stalin moved to consolidate his wartime gains.

He moved first against Czechoslovakia, the one country within his reach that still had civil freedoms and that was still governed by a coalition including native Communists. Elections were coming. Due to their rejection of the popular Marshall Plan, the Czech Communists were certain to lose heavily. In the dead of winter, the Communist Police Minister moved to prevent that outcome by arresting non-Communist politicians on vague charges of treason. The country erupted in anti-Communist demonstrations. I took the first plane to Prague.

I checked in at the UP office to get bearings, then went out on the street. Wenceslaus Square, the center for all demonstrations, was packed with students protesting the arrests. Police appeared and began firing. I ran with everybody else for the shelter of doorways. There were no casualties, so it was clear that the police had fired over people's heads to clear the square. That done, the square was filled with Communist demonstrators bused in from industrial areas. They brought out signs calling for death to imperialist traitors and the formation of a new "patriotic" government. Except for going to a studio to do one broadcast, I stayed on the square all night. The Communists held onto it in disciplined shifts. For four days, Communist groups wearing red arm bands, reinforced by a suddenly born "workers militia," took over all public offices. Then the new "patriotic government" was announced.

But the climax had really occurred that first night on the square. I knew a prominent Czech Communist journalist named Otto Katz, who wrote under the name of André Simon. We now met in a restaurant overlooking the square and spent an afternoon listening to speakers haranguing the crowd. In a remarkably unguarded moment he told me, "Only that first night mattered. The police were ordered to fire over the heads of the crowd. If the students had not left, the second order would have been to fire *into* them. That was the crucial moment. I believe the police would have refused to shoot the students. That would have meant that the Communists had lost control of the police. You would have seen the borders come alive with whole divisions of Russian troops flooding into the country."

A caustic purge began, throughout eastern Europe. Thousands of devout Communists—any who had ever had a Western connection—were imprisoned and many executed. In Prague one morning Jan Masaryk's broken body was found on the pavement below his high apartment in the Foreign Office. Officially it was a suicide. Masaryk's fiancée, an American, sought me out in London to insist he was murdered. In June President Beneš, dispirited by witnessing the second foreign rape of his country in a decade, resigned his office. In September he died. A year later, on notification by a friend, I tuned in Radio Prague and heard a recording of my friend Katz pleading guilty to treason in a show trial. He was shot.

A few months after the Czechoslovak coup, in April 1948, came Stalin's last best chance in the West, the Italian elections. The strong possibility of a Communist victory created a mighty alliance. Cardinal Schuster of Milan threatened to deny absolution to any who voted for the Communists. Big Italian money, cowed into keeping a low profile because of its support for fascism, came out in support of the main democratic party, the Christian Democrats. America mobilized aid and movie stars for the fray. It was odd hearing Gary Cooper commending democracy on Italian language radio.

I applied to meet the dominant figures in the contest. Both lived within the confines of Rome, and to my surprise, both came through for the same day—the Catholic Pope at 10 A.M., the Red Pope at noon. I had never known anything like the grandeur I encountered in the Vatican. Over a period of a half-hour I was led by whispering priests from one grand, overawing chamber to another and left to wait alone in each for a few minutes. When Pius XII appeared, with a secretary at his side, I was unnerved, ready to return to the bosom of the Church or something equally extreme. The Pope was the former Eugenio Pacelli. He was considered a "modern" Pope because he was the first to use the telephone and the typewriter. He shepherded more Catholics than any Pope before him and he excommunicated more—all who supported Communism. He gave me a whispered sermon in English about his gratitude for America's support in this world crisis, gave me a holy medal and silently glided from the room.

The Communist Party building was appropriately red, sandstone. Somewhere deep within I met Palmiro Togliatti, a pleasant-looking, smiling man with horn-rimmed glasses. A lone picture hung on the wall behind him. It was the original portrait of him that had been reproduced as a cover of *Time*. Neither he nor his holy opponent seemed the kind of man who would stoop to the brawl now in progress.

Under intense pressure, the tide turned. Late in the campaign, the U.S. donated thirty wartime merchant ships to Italy to carry forthcoming Marshall aid. That whipped the Communists. On election day, they won 182 seats in the national parliament to the anti-Communists' 307. One imagined hearing the sound of a high wind out of the West, a humongous sigh of relief.

To cover the Italian elections, CBS had deployed a considerable force, Murrow himself talking charge. One night just before election day he sat with us in a restaurant in Rome, looking with cigarette and dark expression like a handsomer Humphrey Bogart in *Casablanca*. His message was as grim as his demeanor. "I saw General Bradley just before I took off," he said. "It is now no longer a matter of *whether* there will be war but *when*." Supreme among Murrow's talents was his ability to adopt an utterly convincing tone of authority: if he said it, it was so. Bennie burst into tears. Afterward I sought to comfort her by saying that Murrow was happy only when spreading gloom, and that this was not to be taken seriously. In fact, I knew that it approximated the real situation. He was talking not about Italy but about events in Germany going on at the same time. Stalin attempted a buttoning up in Berlin that, in another time, would surely have led to war.

The month of the Italian elections, Stalin began a blockade around Berlin, deep in Russian-occupied territory, to stop ground transportation and starve the Allies out. General Lucius Clay, our leader on the spot, wanted to send a column of tanks up the autobahn into Berlin. If the Russians stopped it there would be war. While worrying it out, President Truman ordered the Air Force to fly in supplies—a hopeless recourse, like filling a horse trough with an eye dropper.

Meanwhile we had to face the decision Stalin was trying to forestall: If the Marshall Plan was to work, the German Ruhr, the most productive industrial complex in Europe, had to be brought back to life as the motor for all. Reviving the Ruhr, motivating its people to work and to cooperate with all its neighbors, meant changing our whole attitude. It would be the end of Germany as defeated enemy and the beginning of Germany as reformed friend. It meant allowing the Germans to choose an independent government and, soon, re-arming that new Germany as part of the NATO alliance!

I rode the Berlin milk-run and shared the prevailing gloom about the folly of trying to supply Berlin by air and the peril of rearming a nation we had just spent several million lives disarming. I applied to the mayor of Berlin for an interview. He agreed. He was Ernst Reuter, pre-Nazi socialist deputy in the Reichstag, later described in Dean Acheson's memoirs as "a truly impressive man of immense courage." In the course of our talk, I mentioned the universal fear of a revived Germany, and Reuter said, "At some point you Americans have got to commit an act of faith in your judgment in putting us on the right track, and in the resolve of people like me to keep us there. If you had done that in 1918 . . ." I felt a good deal easier about reviving Germany after that. A few years later, we repeated the interview on television, in the form of his taking me on a dramatic guided tour of the ruined Reichstag building.

Berlin's 2 million people needed 4,500 tons of supplies a day. The daily planeloads rose till, miraculously, they met the target and passed it. There followed a long and tense winter, but in the spring came victory. The Russians gave up and ended the blockade in May 1949. The Cold War in Europe settled down to years of glowering and menacing. On the scale of danger, the Berlin blockade ranks among the most serious of postwar crises, along with the war in Korea in 1950. Both were tests, at the two extremities of the Communist world, of America's will to stop the surge and protect its friends. At considerable cost, both tests were passed.

✿   ✿   ✿

ABOVE RIGHT   My mother, Minnie Agnes Cates, at twenty years of age

BELOW LEFT   Irritated by the news that the Senate has rejected the League of Nations, 1919

BELOW RIGHT   Two Howard K. Smiths—Jr. is the smaller one—Ferriday, Louisiana, 1915

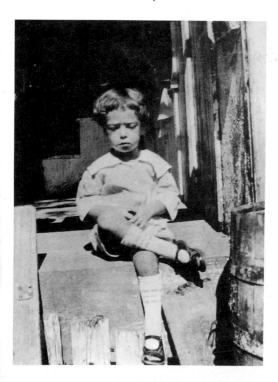

ABOVE Captain of the track
team at Tulane, 1936

RIGHT An editorial cartoon I
drew in 1939 for the Labor
Club periodical at Oxford, por-
traying Neville Chamberlain, in
the service of the Nazis, as executioner of the Spanish
Republic

THE EXECUTIONER.

TOP Newly engaged, in Berlin's Tiergarten Park, 1941

ABOVE LEFT AND RIGHT The newlyweds in Berne, 1942. Pictures taken by Peter Jellinek, the only surviving witness to our wedding

ABOVE 1944. Questioning Gestapo jailers, made to kneel before me by the French Resistance

RIGHT 1944. War correspondent

TOP At 9th Army Press Camp: Marlene Dietrich's escort at dinner, 1944. We drew lots, and I won

ABOVE The British Exposition some time in the 1950s and my first assignment before a camera

BELOW RIGHT The Smith family in 1951 when Bennie was recovering from tuberculosis in Davos

BELOW LEFT 1952. With Murrow just after he shot me down in my first and last (simulated) bombing run over New York

BOTTOM Murrow and his "boys" in New York, preparing for the 1954 year-end roundup. *Clockwise from left:* Edward R. Murrow, Larry LeSeuer, Bill Costello, Winston Burdett, David Schoenbrun, Bill Downs, Eric Sevareid, and Smith

TOP In the burned-out Reichstag with Mayor Ernst Reuter of Berlin during the Berlin Crisis

ABOVE LEFT The inscription reads: "This gesture pleases you because it suits the world of men. The civilian cannot do it. No diplomat dares do it. Your loyal and grateful listener A. Einstein. 53" BETTMANN ARCHIVE

ABOVE RIGHT Sometime in the 1950s, with Don Hewitt (later, creator of *60 Minutes*), writing my year-end roundup. Like other old newspaper men, I cannot write without a hat

ABOVE A little known fact: During the filming of a 1955 documentary on the Egyptian situation, Bennie served as the model for the Sphinx

RIGHT With Catherine and Jack in 1956

ABOVE AND LEFT Moderating the famous 1960 Kennedy-Nixon debate

BELOW Forecasting the 1960 presidential election with the help of an IBM computer

1. 1950. Gamal Abdel Nasser

2. 1950. Clement Attlee

3. 1956. Anthony Eden

4. c.1960. Carl Sandburg at Gettysburg

5. 1961. Walter Lippmann's first time on television (filmed in my house). Fred Friendly stands in the background

6. 1960. Senator John F. Kennedy before the steroid injections filled him out

7. 1963. Robert Kennedy

8. 1964. Lady Bird Johnson
ROBERT L. KNUDSEN

9. 1964. Arnold Toynbee
DAVE HILL

10. 1965. Brigitte Bardot and producer Tom Wolf WAGNER INTERNATIONAL PHOTOS

11. c.1968. Teddy Kennedy and ABC correspondent Bob Clark

12. 1968. Hubert Humphrey

13. 1976. Barry Goldwater

14. c. 1970 Nelson Rockefeller

TOP 1966. An Khe, Vietnam, interviewing my son, Jack, after he was wounded

ABOVE And in 1972, interviewing Lyndon Johnson

LEFT ABC's 1968 year-end wrap-up, "Dinner at Howard K. Smith's," in my drawing room

BELOW My oval study

TOP The first one-on-one television interview with a sitting president, Richard Nixon, in 1969

ABOVE LEFT In the early 1970s, *(from left)* Janet Murrow, John Chancellor, Bennie, and me

ABOVE RIGHT 1976. Co-anchor with Harry Reasoner

TOP Flag Day, 1976. The only newsman ever to address Congress

ABOVE At the 1978 Friars Club award banquet with Walter Cronkite and David Brinkley. Mayor Ed Koch made us honorary citizens of New York and personally offered to collect the first year's taxes

LEFT AND BELOW Anchorman

My sweat-warped old passport had long since run out of space for visas allowing border crossings. In some forgotten emergency, a consulate somewhere had clamped in it an accordion-like folder of additional pages. By the time I re-entered Britain from Germany, it too was filled with ink stamped tokens of perpetual motion. As I wearily folded it back into place at the customs house in Folkstone, the thought occurred to me that America and Russia might survive the Cold War but I was not sure I would.

CHAPTER FORTY-FIVE

Associates

In the early years of my stewardship, the CBS European staff changed considerably. To replace me in Germany I hired Edward P. Morgan of the *Chicago Daily News*. He distrusted the spoken medium, as I had, and soon left us to take a writing job with *Collier's* magazine. His error was quickly made plain: *Collier's* folded, and he made his way back to radio, where he soon became famous for his daily fifteen-minute newscast sponsored by the AFL-CIO union organization.

Morgan was replaced in Germany by old Murrow man Bill Downs, a red-haired Missourian with a mighty personality and a bad temper. He reminded me of the weather on Lake Pontchartrain in New Orleans, given to brief, violent squalls that died down as quickly as they arose, with everyone forgetting why they happened at all. Bill covered the whole blockade in Berlin, then was hijacked to Korea when war broke out there. Murrow told that, when he went to Korea on an assignment, he saw Downs running out on the tarmac and alongside his taxiing plane shouting, "Go back, it's not your kind of war!"

Downs was replaced in Germany by Daniel Schorr, a man with a plan. After the war Schorr wanted to be a foreign correspondent, and he struck on an idea: he chose an area neglected by most organizations—Belgium, Netherlands and Luxembourg—and he became the resident expert there. When any event of note took place in the Low countries, every outfit that needed a story asked Schorr to provide it. On one spectacular occasion, I think it was a massive breach of the Dutch dikes in a North Sea storm, he demanded a permanent staff post as his price. There was considerable competition to get him, and CBS won. I strongly recommended hiring him. One of my duties as chief correspondent was to be a utility reporter. When a noteworthy event occurred in a place where we had no correspondent, I was sent. After three trips to Schorr's shores—the last one to cover the referendum on keeping the monarchy in Belgium (the monarchy won the required two-thirds vote and was retained)—I saw him not only as an asset but as a relief for me.

When a friend, Alexander Kendrick, lost his job with the *Chicago Sun-Times,* I suggested that he follow Schorr's example and become too valuable to go unhired. Specifically I proposed that he set up in Vienna, a news-neglected city that could become a kind of listening post for news from behind the Iron Curtain. We would keep him in pin money on a string basis. As I expected, he soon became so expensive on a per-broadcast basis that CBS hired him to be a staff correspondent.

In Paris we acquired a particular prize. David Schoenbrun had taught French at CCNY and had been an American liaison officer with the French Army during the war. After the war he tried his luck with the Jewish (later the Overseas) News Agency. He worked with me during a small emergency in Paris, and I was much taken with his command of the Paris news scene. I recommended, and Murrow agreed, that he be taken on permanently. His contacts were legendary. He knew succeeding premiers of France by their first names. The great Jean Monnet, founding father of the European unity movement, called in Schoenbrun for advice in drafting communiqués. One night I phoned him from London that I was coming to Paris on business the next day. He asked, was there anyone in particular I would like to have dinner with? As a joke I said, Martine Carole, naming the reigning sex kitten in French movies. Lo, the next night I dined in Paris with the Schoenbruns and the beautiful Martine Carole (and her husband).

For a while the only holdover from the original Murrow staff, aside from Downs and me, was Winston Burdett in Rome. Burdett was a quiet young man with a dramatic past. A *magna cum laude* graduate of Harvard, he came to Europe during the war with a company called Transradio Press. He married a pretty Italian girl and took her on assignment with him to Iran. She was murdered in circumstances I have not been able to clarify. It turned out that Burdett had become a Communist, and she was an active Italian anti-Fascist. He was sure she was murdered by Fascist agents, and claimed to know precisely who did the hit, but was unable to bring the perpetrator to justice during the war; by war's end, the killer had disappeared. Paul White offered Burdett a job broadcasting from Turkey, discovered he had a beautifully modulated voice and took him on staff for good. Burdett stayed in Rome, where he married another beautiful Italian girl. After the war he returned to the U.S., but after a run-in with the House Un-American Activities Committee because of his short career as a Communist, he asked to be stationed permanently in Rome.

He was slight in figure, which suited a manner that could be described as spiritual. If conversation lapsed a moment, he would seem to drift off into a dream. When conversation resumed, he would take a moment to adjust to reality. He moved about as if only partly conscious. Once when I had him join me to cover a British election, he walked about the office with a gigantic limp, as though one leg were shorter than the other. He was assigned to do a noon broadcast, so I walked him to the studio, and the exaggerated limp became annoying. I asked what was the matter. He pointed to his shoe: the sole of one shoe had come loose, and at every stride he had to rise on the other foot to keep it from flapping. I suggested that he tear the flapping sole off, and have it fixed later. He did and was immensely relieved.

The most interesting new staffer was George Polk, a man with an even more dramatic past. His assignment was the troubled Middle East, scene of everything from the Greek civil war to the prebirth pains of the new state of Israel and the frictions between Britain and Egypt athwart the Empire's fraying lifeline at Suez.

George Washington Polk was a tall, blond, good-looking Texan. He had been a Navy air pilot on Gaudalcanal, had shot down eleven Japanese planes, was severely wounded himself and suffered nightmares about battle for the rest of his life. After the war he became a print reporter in the Middle East until Murrow hired him for CBS. He married a Greek girl, and focused his reporting on the government of her country and its civil war with Communist guerrillas.

The government of Greece in 1946 and 1947, under the reactionary Prime Minister Constantine Tsaldaris, was, as I described it in a broadcast from Athens, "the worst I have seen anywhere in Europe." Most of its budget went to the military and the police and pensions for members of its bloated and incompetent civil sevice, with only a tiny allotment for reconstructing the badly crushed economy. Government expenditures were three times higher than receipts. The rich paid no taxes. Money was printed to make up the difference, with the result that the drachma went from 140 to a dollar to 6,000 to a dollar. Order was kept by encouraging armed gangs, independent but generally rightist, to raid and pillage villages and murder anyone suspected of leftism. The Communist guerrillas in the mountains were not better, only more disciplined; and they did not rob, they requisitioned.

While the British sustained Greece, American officials freely criticized the Greek government. But when the Truman Doctrine was proclaimed, and America took over command, American officials suddenly felt it unpatriotic to criticize, and frowned on those who did. Polk thought the government was terrible. He had said so in some detail in his broadcasts before the doctrine, and he continued to think and do so after it. The fact that American officials began to frown may have indirectly helped bring about the climax.

Harried by nightmares of war and weary of eternal friction in this political environment, George asked to be brought home to America, and CBS agreed. Before leaving he undertook two actions. First, he sought a private appointment with Prime Minister Tsaldaris, saying he had important information to divulge. When he was alone with the Prime Minister, he told him that he had irrefutable evidence that Tsaldaris was taking a percentage of funds America put into Greece and was depositing it in a personal account in New York. There is no information about Tsaldaris's reaction, but one can imagine it.

Second, shortly thereafter George took his last shot at a story he had been working on for months. He went north to Salonika to try to get to the guerrillas in the mountains and see what they were made of. One night he was seen leaving his hotel. He had a seafood dinner with no one knows whom and then disappeared. Several days later his body was fished out of Salonika Bay. The picture of it lying face up is horrifying. This very handsome figure was waterlogged and bloated. His hair stood on end as if an electric shock had blown each separate hair outwards. His hands were tied in front of him, and there was a bullet hole in the back of his head.

I asked to go to Athens to find out what I might. I was told not to go; instead, Burdett was sent from Rome and told to stay with the story. I was told that CBS had to have my Sunday broadcasts, which I would have had to suspend if I had taken over the case. I later discovered that CBS feared I might come to a similar end ("There's room for another corpse in Salonika Bay," an executive had commented), for I had been broadcasting criticism along the same lines as Polk's.

The Greeks claimed they were investigating. When no progress was reported, the U.S. government pressed for answers; thereupon the Greek government produced a suspect and a trial. The suspect, a mild-mannered Greek journalist, was found guilty along with a leader of the Communists, who was unreachable in the mountains.

An unconvincing case was made worse by the behavior of an eminent American, General William ("Wild Bill") Donovan, head of the wartime OSS intelligence office and spiritual father of the CIA. A group of American newsmen, led by Walter Lippmann, formed an organization to ensure that the investigation would be thorough, and they commissioned Donovan to do it. During the long investigation he prodded the Greeks to make an arrest to allay the mistrust then growing in the U.S., but he gave the impression that any arrest would do. When one of Donovan's on-the-scene investigators, U.S. Army Colonel James Kellis, began to find trails leading away from the Communists and toward agents of the Greek government, Donovan removed him from the case. When the trial was over, Donovan and Lippmann accepted the Greek government case and verdict as legitimate.

The lone defendant, long since pardoned, has denied complicity and shown scars indicating that his incriminating testimony was forced by torture. Circumstantial evidence points to an agent of the Greek government of the time as the murderer. But as with the Reichstag fire and the death of Jan Masaryk, that last piece of hard evidence that might settle guilt has not been found. The first Western journalistic casualty of the Cold War is honored each year in the giving of the George Polk Memorial Awards for reporting excellence.

Ed Murrow's executive career was short. He did not like it. The confrontation with Paul White caused him lasting pain. Finally came his break with his first colleague, Bill Shirer. Shirer's sponsor dropped him, as happens often in the business; and Murrow provided another commentator, Joseph C. Harsch, for the sponsor. Shirer asserted that his being dropped was politically motivated; among other things he had sharply criticized the Truman Doctrine. Liberals picketed CBS in support of Shirer. Murrow and Shirer worked things out, but then Paley intervened and said Shirer was fired and that was that. Shirer was bitter that Murrow did not come to his support. He remained unforgiving to the end. I was far away and not closely informed, but what I know of the circumstances moves me to Murrow's side. Shirer seemed to have lost interest in his commentary, and it was rather flat. I did it for him a few times and had no trouble improving on his standards. I was at least as liberal as Shirer, as was his replacement, Joe Harsch.

Anyhow, the long-term results were altogether good. Murrow quit managing and became a journalist again, which proved good for everyone including the nation. Shirer resorted to writing books which, after a hungry period, led to wealth and glory beyond his dreams. Murrow brought us, the foreign staff, back home repeatedly to take part in year-end discussion programs and to make appearances on his new program in the new medium, television. The frequent visits back enabled me, so long absent from the U.S., to establish some valuable contacts, one of them with Professor Einstein.

During one visit I was invited to Los Angeles to lecture on the state of the world. The fee was $1,000, a high fee at that time. I had not wanted to accept, because it meant too much traveling. But my wife had fallen in love with an ancient tallboy chest, the price of which was $1,000, so off I went. A first visit to southern California is always breathtaking. For a denizen of London in January it was that and much more. In 1950, before the air became a visible fume, merely to sit outside and take a breath of the air was to sample a life-enhancing tonic. With bright-eyed people all about in bright attire, it seemed very near to heaven. I was put into a cottage belonging to the Beverly Hills Hotel and wrote Bennie how wonderful it was to see ripe oranges on trees just outside my window and wake up each morning to a garden in which they changed the flowers every night.

The following year I was invited again. The occasion was memorable less for my lecture than for an instance of unrequited adoration. My friend, Robert Ardrey, who made so much money writing screenplays for films like *Khartoum* and *Madame Bovary* that he was eventually able to return to his beloved anthropology and to author *African Genesis* and several successor volumes, took me to see a film studio in action. It was a huge barn. A far corner had been done up to resemble a river bank, and a film crew was reshooting some scenes for *River of No Return,* starring Marilyn Monroe. Ardrey left me at the threshold of the barn and went over to greet the star and ask her if she would be gracious enough to go over and say hello to Mr. Smith who had come all the way from London. The lovely creature skipped the length of the studio, shook hands daintily with a man standing near me, and skipped all the way back.

However, at least I was into lecturing forever. For me it was a new journalistic medium which I came to enjoy immensely. Thereafter I included in every network contract a clause giving me two weeks unpaid leave each year to run around the U.S. lecturing, answering questions, meeting new people, seeing new places and rediscovering my own country.

CHAPTER FORTY-SIX

Pictures

The new art and trouble of television became a fact of my life, by way of Murrow, on November 18, 1951. He appeared on the picture medium for the first time in a weekly program called *See It Now.* He was seated in the control room with screens behind him. As Murrow called for them, the director, Don Hewitt, put up on one screen a live picture of the Pacific Ocean at the Golden Gate Bridge, in San Francisco, then on another, shown at the same time, the Atlantic Ocean live from the proximity of the Statue of Liberty in New York. It was a trick that signaled a new era in journalism—the future—and I was not sure I was going to like it.

The ego-prod that got Murrow into the pictures was a bull-like giant named Fred W. Friendly. In addition to having a sure eye for the kind of spectacle that suits the small screen—like the eloquent faces of individuals—Friendly's foremost asset was a talent for bullying people while making them think he was wooing them. After my return to America I developed a friendship with Walter Lippmann, the famous newspaper columnist. I tried to persuade Lippmann to appear on television, interviewed by me. At one time I felt I had him on the verge of consenting, only to see him draw back. I phoned Friendly in New York and asked him to come down to Washington and help me put the case. Fred joined me in Lippmann's study and, barely pausing for an introduction, began what appeared to be a verbal caress but was in fact a half-nelson on Lippmann's will. In a few minutes we were agreeing on a date and place for the interview.

The Murrow-Friendly combination, abetted by Don Hewitt (who would soon establish a journalistic tradition of his own), became a huge success. They tied up four of the best camera teams in the business. One cameraman, Charley Mack, was spectacular, 6 feet 4 inches tall with a wavy silvery mane and a profile more commanding than Lionel Barrymore's. When he was sent to film a world tour by Senator Margaret Chase Smith, foreign journalists who did not know which was which repeatedly addressed Charley as Senator Smith, and he repeatedly had to tell them that the demure little lady, not the towering picture-taker, was the star.

The program's small domestic news staff performed wonders. The first *See It Now*s were about things at home and are still, decades later, considered TV classics and shown over and over again. Soon the hunt for subjects spread abroad, and we on the foreign staff were conscripted; Friendly assured us that we would like it, or (more effectively) that Murrow would like us to do it, which settled it.

My premiere was painless. One terrible week, the North Sea flooded low-lying parts of the English coast. We went out to the flooded margins and stood on levees of sandbags, where I interviewed distressed and frightened citizens. The fact that a camera was there recording it did not make it different from what I would have done purely for radio. As we began to tackle more complex themes, the task of searching out picture locations related to topics became a new art for word-reporters to learn—one that often took more time and sweat to manage than did composing words.

Once we were doing a report on unemployment in Britain, and chose the Yorkshire Wolds textile country as our example. On a tip from locals, we walked far and high into the trackless moors to find a ruined deserted stone house. It had the name of "Withins" and was the place that inspired Emily Brontë (who with her sisters lived in Haworth far below) to write *Wuthering Heights*. We decided we had to have it on film. Conscripting Bennie as a fourth bearer after the camerman Bill McClure, his sound man and me, we spent weary hours carrying heavy camera equipment up the roadless heath, and more hours carrying it back down. But when we saw our developed picture of this bleak ruin on a blasted heath, scrub brush around it trembling in the wind, we thought it worth every aching limb.

In South Africa we combed the veldt of Kruger National Park to shoot footage of animals. We got most of the usual beasts, but the giraffes, looking like a moving forest of stiff tree trunks above the bush, always ran away before we could get close. I took it upon myself to go alone into the bush to circle around and chase a herd into the camera. When the trick was done and I had started walking back through wild country, I came to a clearing where fresh paw prints of lions were all too visible. Nearby I heard a bone-shaking roar. The ranger had told us never to run lest we attract what we sought to escape, so I walked with petrified deliberateness a more horrified half-mile than any I walked at the front in the war. The last hundred yards I threw prudence to the winds and *ran!*

Colleague Ned Calmer told of shooting film in a Sicilian cemetery. When the cameraman later looked at rushes, he found that a small dog had wandered into the picture and sat on a tombstone. To make the scene work, he had Calmer go back into the town and spend three days hunting for the mangy animal, then another day coaxing the little beast to sit on the tombstone again. Calmer, author of novels, interrupted weary promptings of the dog to look up at the camera and wail, "I spent three years getting a Ph.D. in Literature—to do *this*."

Then came interviews. Since the English speak a (mostly) comprehensible dialect of American, I had to do a great many interviews with a great many celebrities. I enjoyed—Friendly was right—chats with Bertrand Russell, Dame Rebecca West, Claire Bloom, Aneurin Bevan, Arnold Toynbee and a considerable fraction of the remaining well-known Britons.

But for a long time many public figures in Britain feared what the little box might do to their images and refused to appear. I once approached Laurence Olivier (as yet neither Sir nor Lord) to take part in a tribute to Winston Churchill (not yet Sir). He agreed with an enthusiasm that surprised me. "When may I see the script?" he asked. I told him there would be no script; I would just put a few puffball questions. "Oh no," he said, "Television? Without a script? I would never think of it!" Churchill himself would not appear—with good reason, I thought. The world remembered him as a vigorous sexagenarian, not as an old man near eighty. Let it stay that way.

The greatest problem was posed by the people I dealt with most, politicians. Bevan agreed to brave the camera for reasons of friendship, but most others would not appear. "A politician walks a field of mines every day," said Herbert Morrison, the Deputy Prime Minister, to me. "Why should he willingly add one more, probably more dangerous, opportunity to blow himself up?" Friendly was prevailed on to bring Murrow and a half-dozen past programs over to exhibit. I arranged an evening for Labour Members of Parliament, then an evening for Conservatives. We thought the ploy softened them up a bit.

More influential was a plum that fell in my lap. Anthony Eden, who was to become Prime Minister one day, returned from a visit to America, where he had appeared on the new talk program *Meet the Press* and asserted that he had enjoyed it. Very well, said the BBC to him, you appeared and answered questions for them, now do it for us. He consented, provided he might choose the interviewer. It was agreed, and he chose me to do the interviewing. Although I was not yet at ease before the camera, I was practically lounging around in relaxation compared to this world statesman. He developed a severe headache just before the program, took aspirins, and wondered out loud whether he shouldn't just chuck it. In the course of the interview he was so taut I thought he would snap.

A couple of weeks later came a request from the Conservative Central Office. Would I and Malcolm Muggeridge, then a just-returned Washington correspondent for the London *Daily Telegraph* (and a regular on *Meet the Press* when in the U.S.), give an audience of Tory MPs a little lecture on how to appear on television? We both readily agreed. To an audience of eager Tory faces we delivered little speeches that were mostly malarkey. I had not yet come to terms with the picture medium and had no idea how to behave properly in front of a camera. I would have been ashamed of myself, but I thought Malcolm did no better. Shortly after our twin outrages, the Tories won the election and we were suddenly esteemed as gurus. We each were rewarded with three volumes of Churchill's war speeches, autographed by him. I was invited by the BBC to do a series of programs titled *An American Looks at Britain*, and Malcolm's reputation as a regular on British TV, both wise and entertaining, took off.

Television had an expansive effect on work in every way, although the adjective might just as well have been "expensive." Symbolically, the *$64 Question,* a game show on radio, became the *$64,000 Question* on TV. I went to Berlin and interviewed Mayor Ernst Reuter while we walked around the ruins of the Reichstag. I had done the same thing on radio, and it had taken perhaps an hour. For television it required a considerable support staff, and it took several days of moving equipment to light and soundproof the successive scenes.

On the other hand, impact was magnified. A sizable minority of journalists, including me, had dared to criticize the ignoble Senator Joe McCarthy in print and on radio. But when Murrow did it on television, it became a blow from which the malevolent Senator never recovered. As impact grew, so did the sensitivity of our executives to what we said and reported. Their stake became gigantic, and in time I would find that they were not of a mind to let one of their news employees endanger it.

Television expanded my reportorial beat greatly. Before, my movements had been limited to Europe, which seemed to me to be spacious at the time; now my beat became the world, which seemed to grow magically small. In an age when foreign correspondents tended to be assigned to single countries, I was ever in airplanes going everywhere with camera crews: to cover the first "liberation" of an African colony in Ghana, doing an essay on the "population explosion" in India, shooting a film on the coming water shortage in the ruins of Babylon. I even flew in a Flying Fortress from Ireland to New York City assigned to bomb Manhattan to rubble, simulated of course. The program sought to assess America's air defenses at the height of the Cold War. To make the attack more realistic, our bomb bay doors opened to a dramatic view of Central Park straight down. Murrow flew against us in a fighter plane. It satisfied both the realities of our superior defenses and the need for Murrow to be the winner that he saved the city by shooting us down—also simulated, thank God.

One memorable assignment, for Saint Patrick's Day, was to seek out the westernmost family in Ireland—the one nearest to America—and spend a week depicting its life. We hunted around and finally settled on a remote farm family in a bleakly picturesque corner of Galway. It was a primitive situation, and the family never quite comprehended what we were up to. At the end of our week I sat on a stump with the farmer and tried to explain what television was: it was radio, with pictures. He nodded without losing his puzzled expression. After a while he said, "What is radio?"

CHAPTER FORTY-SEVEN

Clouds

In the years immediately after the war I led a life of high privilege. I was pretty much left free by CBS to go anywhere and do anything I wished so long as I provided one long broadcast and occasional short ones each week. I spent about half my time in London and half traveling, generally with my wife at my side. It was as near to heavenly as a reporter's life gets. Still, there were a few clouds.

One of these covered Bennie. She had lately resumed the higher education she had interrupted in Copenhagen during the war, enrolling at the London School of Economics along with an engaging crew of fellows. One was a 6-foot–6-inch New Yorker who would in time be known as the largest leprechaun in the world and as a U.S. Senator, Daniel Patrick Moynihan. Others were Paul Niven and Sander Vanocur, both of whom I later hired; they were among the student friends who came often to our house. Another was the fiancée of Roger Bannister, whom we met at a dramatic time in the history of sports: he was preparing for a shot at the four-minute mile while completing his education in medicine.

Then just before final exams came one of Bennie's mysterious, recurring periods of exhaustion. An annual examination given to students solved the mystery. She had tuberculosis, had probably contracted it during the war in Berlin, and had somehow been suffering bouts of it for years. The onset this time was deep and bad. We sought out Sir Geoffrey Marshall, the King's doctor, and she was put into Guy's Hospital at the other end of London Bridge for treatment. Let me hasten through this unhappiness. She spent two summers resting at home, and two winters in Davos in Switzerland as a sanatorium outpatient; then the doctor pronounced her sufficiently healthy to go back to the university or to have a baby. She could not do both, however, or the deadly bug would return. She chose the baby, and in the spring of 1953, Catherine Hamilton Smith was born, a beautiful child who was to grow into a beautiful girl.

The ailment that struck me was an epidemic in America. Like the Dutch boy plugging holes in the dike, we were running all over the world stopping surges of Communism. Its seductive power was mysterious. Along came Senator Joe McCarthy with an explanation: its success was really due to treason by Americans; we were being eaten alive by secret Communists. The panic struck hard at my profession. Some former FBI agents created something called

"American Business Consultants," which published a thin periodical titled *Counterattack; the Newsletter of Facts on Communism*. In the early fifties, they published a paperback volume called *Red Channels: The Report on Communist Influence in Radio and Television*, which listed 151 people who worked in the media and were allegedly tied to Communist organizations. Among them, in hard black-and-white, there it was: Howard K. Smith. My student politics, my vociferous anti-Nazi speeches, and my having headed the Oxford Labour Club had apparently caught up with me. The guardians of patriotism even invented a new class of malefactor: "premature anti-Nazis." I guessed that was my sin. Also on the list were Leonard Bernstein, Lee J. Cobb, Aaron Copland, Orson Welles and a dozen others one would be proud to be associated with. The only other CBS man on it was Alexander Kendrick, our new correspondent in Vienna.

Kendrick was guilty of having written a couple of book reviews for the *New Masses,* a now-defunct Communist literary magazine. He was purged of taint in a remarkable way. Murrow was advised that the FBI had a file on Kendrick containing "raw" or unevaluated information—unsupported hearsay—hostile to him. Murrow asked Kendrick to write his own evaluation of himself, a kind of political autobiography. It was inserted into the same file as raw information friendly to Alex. The two balanced, and Kendrick was home free! I do not know who Murrow's high informant was, but I suspect it was Allen Dulles, head of the CIA.

One other colleague, Winston Burdett, might have been listed but for his having been summoned to testify by the House Un-American Activities Committee, before which he revealed all he knew and much he did not know. As earlier recounted, Burdett removed to Rome after the experience.

I waited for my listing in the bad book to bring me harm, but nothing happened. Then a consequential action by CBS renewed my worry. Everybody's favorite vice president at CBS, Joe Ream, decided to dispose of the charges of Communism by taking preemptive action. He produced a loyalty oath that every employee of the network must sign or be fired. He did it reluctantly, and Paley and Dr. Stanton, the network president, agreed to it reluctantly. Dissenters asked Murrow to lead a movement within CBS to refuse to sign on grounds that CBS had no right to ask questions about political affiliation. But Ed was too deep in controversies on his crusading TV program. "I have too many other fights on my hands, and I'll weaken my position on them if I fail to sign," he said. No one could honestly argue with that. It was one month before he sped an arrow to the heart of the issue by attacking Joe McCarthy on TV.

I had to confront the damned oath for myself. It read, "Are you now or have you ever been a member of the Communist Party USA, or any Communist organization?" On the back of the sheet was a list of allegedly Communist organizations, the so-called Attorney General's list. I went to see Joe Ream and asked him, what was the point of printing the list along with the oath? He said that the organizations on the list were those meant by the phrase "or any Communist organization." I had no problem answering truthfully, but I went to see Murrow about the ethics of signing at all. He said, "Go ahead and sign it. I have. Everybody has. It's not that important." I signed but was not happy about it.

Now Senator McCarthy began his investigation of the U.S. Army, on charges that it harbored sympathizers with Communism! The Murrow team went to work, piecing McCarthy's own words together as a rope to hang him. The story of this feverish act of creation deserves reading in the many books about Murrow. I had no role to play except, in response to a request from Friendly, to try to induce Winston Churchill to say something nice about Murrow to protect him against McCarthy. I phoned, and a secretary phoned back the answer: Mr. Murrow has not, to Mr. Churchill's knowledge, been accused of anything by anybody. If he is, Mr. C. will reconsider.

The week after the Murrow treatment of McCarthy, and before the Senator was to be given time by CBS to respond, I devoted my Sunday commentary to the true story of an Englishman named Titus Oates who lived three centuries earlier. England at the time was an approximate parliamentary democracy. It was Protestant and lived in fear of the spreading power of despotic France—Catholic, aggressive, blessed by the supranational Vatican and served by the resolute and secretive Jesuits. There were clear parallels. I said in my broadcast:

> Into this potentially emotional situation walked one of the strangest scoundrels that ever appeared on the stage of history. Titus Oates manufactured out of imagination and hate what came to be known as the Popish Plot. He claimed to possess the names of hundreds of Catholic traitors in all branches of English life.

For seven years Oates terrorized England with his stories of plans by Englishmen to overthrow their government, burn down London and deliver the country to France. At length a few dared denounce Oates. "Bravery and intelligence begat bravery and intelligence." Eventually Oates was captured, tried and found guilty of massive perjury and was punished in ways terrible even for his time.

At the end I indulged in an editorial comment: "The blemish Oates left is in the nature of a scar from a successful inoculation. There is hope here that England can compare operations with America—soon."

CHAPTER FORTY-EIGHT

The Greatest Man

As 1951 began, *Time* magazine, which began each year by choosing for its cover the "Man of the Year," decided to choose a man of the half-century. Einstein, who deprived our physical world of satisfying absoluteness and objectivity and showed all things to be unhappily relative, was considered. So was Lenin, the most upsetting figure. But in the end the honor fell upon a citizen of the nation where I then resided, Winston Leonard Spencer Churchill. I had a few small dealings, very small but mightily savored, with this great man.

I first saw him in a most suitable and majestic setting: Westminster Hall, onto which the Houses of Parliament are pasted. It is a vast cavern, very nearly as big as a football field (240 feet as opposed to 300 feet) and is older than the English language. Worn brass plaques imbedded in the floor tell of all the great events, like the trial of the first governor general of India, Warren Hastings, that happened there. Henry VIII's tennis balls were once found in the rafters, indicating a mighty swing but poor aim. Oliver Cromwell's head—his real head of flesh and bone—adorned the peak of the structure on a pike for a quarter-century, measuring the world record extreme to which political hatred can go. Cromwell's reputation is balanced by a fine portrait statue of him standing beside the great hall outside.

When the reconstruction of the House of Commons (smashed by Hitler's bombs during the war) was completed, the Labour government filled Westminster Hall with dignitaries and reporters to celebrate the occasion. A damaged arch was left damaged to remind future MPs of what had happened, and it was designated the "Churchill Arch." Churchill was summoned to a stage to be honored by his political opponents. Prime Minister Attlee delivered a fine encomium, then unveiled Parliament's gift to Churchill and left the lectern to the great one for his response.

It was a privilege to be present on possibly the only occasion on which the great orator was at a loss for words. The gift was a portrait of him by the noted modern artist Graham Sutherland. It did not make the subject appear handsome or forceful; he looked rather as though in need of getting to the bathroom. Churchill did not like it. He said nice words about Parliament and Attlee and the British people, saying it was the people who won the war; he was only privileged to be the lion's roar. Then he coldly thanked his colleagues for "this, uh, this, uh, this example of modern art." The painting was wrapped in brown paper and slid under a rarely used bed in Churchill's London home. The rumor was, it was later destroyed.

Shortly afterward, there was an election. We stalked the old man through the campaign, but he remained dead set against being interviewed on the little record box we carried about with its tiny plastic microphone. At that time Paul Niven was my associate. One day, we were in the front row at a Tory rally, watching Churchill and Mrs. Churchill sitting on the platform, when Paul had an idea. I was acquainted with the MP sitting next to Mrs. C., so Paul asked me to call the man off the platform for a chat in order to vacate the seat next to her. I did so, and as the MP left, Paul moved onto the platform and took his place. My Conservative friend and I stood to the side and watched what followed with fascination. Paul enlisted Mrs. Clemmie Churchill in his stratagem and she, ever sweet and clever, agreed. She took the tiny mike in her hand, held it close to her famous spouse, and as Paul uttered questions, she turned to Winston and repeated them, and he responded. After awhile, the questions seemed to Churchill to be altogether too stilted and he said, "What the blazes is going on here?" Then he found the microphone and said, "Get that thing away from me." A wave of laughter moved down the row, and after a grimace, the great one smiled too.

I had two private sessions with the man of the half-century, after each of which I thought of seriously changing my name to Malaprop. The first was on the occasion of the annual Al Smith banquet in New York. Churchill had agreed to be the main speaker, but by radio, not in person. He was coming to a climacteric (to use one of his favored words) in the writing of his memoirs and did not want to leave the country. CBS agreed to carry the speech, and I went out to Chartwell Manor, his country home in Kent, for the evening to make sure all went well. Walter Graebner of *Time*, assigned by Henry Luce to keep tabs on how the old man was progressing with books Luce had paid for in advance, drove us in his car.

We were seated in his study. He appeared in a blue "siren suit," a kind of overall or jumpsuit worn by the best-dressed air raid wardens. He was perky and in very good humor. The striking feature of the room was a breast-high slanting ledge nailed to the wall, along which pages of his manuscript were spread. He liked to work standing at the ledge, which was about ten feet long and afforded plenty of space for many pages. He went to the ledge and took off several pages that constituted the text of the speech he was about to deliver. "Look over this to see if I misuse any Americanisms," he said. We did; he had not. At the proper time we went downstairs to a dining room where, at a table, he delivered his talk into a microphone on signal.

The speech done, he invited us back to the study where he poured us glasses of cognac, and we sat about and chatted, or rather, as is the case with great men, we listened to him and offered occasional brief remarks to cheer him on. At one point he left the room for some purpose, and Graebner opined, "He has taken amazingly well to you." Possibly that encouragement made me overconfident enough to perpetrate my first gaucherie. Discussing his relations with the ruling Labour government, he paused in his criticism and, to reassure an American presumably skeptical of Socialists, said, "Actually, they are not all bad chaps." I responded promptly. "Oh, I know that, I know many of them and like them very much." That came a little too quickly, and the approbation was a little too strong. He looked at me as if to say, now, they are not *that* good. My remark put a damper on the conversation. He slumped. I hastened to offer some other observation. I forget what, but it revived him, and the lively soliloquy soon regained speed.

Then I committed the unforgivable. His talk arrived at the Labour government's recent withdrawal from India, an act that disturbed him deeply. I have described earlier how angrily he reacted to the announcement of the event by Attlee in the House of Commons. Now he said, "Ah, Mr. Smith, in two hundred years of British rule not a hundred natives have died in religious quarrels. Now, in a month of so-called independence, tens of thousands have died in that unhappy land." This was the Churchill who had proudly rebuked the anti-imperialist Roosevelt by saying that he had not become the King's first minister in order to preside over the dissolution of the British Empire. It must have been Satan himself who came up and stood at my ear and made me say, "Yes, but, Mr. Churchill, they have not been unhappy enough to ask you to come back." That tore it. It was a sword plunged into the belly of conversation, which fell dead on the spot. I made a new sally to revive talk. It was of no use. He was through. After a few words more Graebner suggested that it was late. Our host did not gainsay the observation. With a limp handshake I followed Walter out of the room to the car and home and moral destitution.

In the third postwar election, Labour was at last defeated and the Conservatives were returned to power, with Winston Churchill as Prime Minister. He ceased to be the charging lion of the war. I remember a meeting on the island of Bermuda of the Prime Minister and President Eisenhower. At the airport the P.M., as host, stood at the bottom of the ramp. I was not three yards away. The President rapidly descended from his plane and grasped Churchill's hand in both of his saying, "My old friend!" Then Eisenhower turned to a British honor guard and moved to review the waiting troops. Churchill tried very hard to keep up with the spry guest, but his hobble was not up to the strong stride of the President-General. In the large open space between the airplane and the serried ranks of soldiers, he nearly stumbled and fell in his effort to catch up. He stayed there, immobile and crestfallen at the physical evidence of his greatest fear—that his enemy, time, had rendered him unequal to the task of wielding the power he loved. I felt I could weep.

Murrow and staff in New York, with some aid from us in London, produced a lavish radio memorial for Churchill's eightieth birthday. It was sent to me, and I phoned Number Ten to ask whether the Prime Minister would like to hear it. He would. So I arranged for two engineers to set up equipment in a parlor of the residence. After dinner on the agreed-upon night I went there and sat in the parlor looking with disapproval at the fireplace. In it was a log-shaped cylinder of clear plastic spattered with red and brown paint, with an electric light inside, so that, revolving, it bore a faint resemblance to a fire. This, in Number Ten Downing Street!

At length, the Prime Minister entered, accompanied by Lady Churchill (for he had now at last consented to the Queen's repeated wish to honor him with a knighthood and had taken on the title Sir Winston, which allowed him to remain in the House of Commons). She looked very grand in a floor-length gown, with a kind of red shawl over her shoulders that was fastened at her bosom with a handsome gold broach. He wore a siren suit again, apparently his standard informal evening-at-home wear, but this time it was not blue but a shocking red. For a man of eighty he looked bright, relaxed and in good condition, his skin a healthy pink, his eyes clear. On his feet was a pair of new red velvet slippers with the initials WSC embroidered in gold on them. Apparently they were too new; half-way through the evening he eased them off and a butler, without being told, knelt and replaced them with an old black pair.

He listened to Murrow's voice opening the program with interest, but when his own voice was heard, in a speech made in 1909, he looked slightly surprised. As the excerpts continued into his war years, his eyes grew watery. When he heard himself proclaiming "their finest hour," he openly wept.

Lady C. had warned us that he might not remain for the whole of the hour replay. But he did and seemed captivated. At the end he seemed to feel a need to summarize. After a moment of silence he looked at me and said, "One does not ask to live. But when one is alive, one tries to take an interest in the things that make up life. That is what I have done."

At the end he wiped his cheeks and gave me a cigar from a box. I did not smoke cigars but put it in my pocket just because it was Churchill's cigar. He said, "You will thank Ed?" I said I would but pointed out that the purpose of the program was to thank him. Then I produced the first volume of his memoirs and asked him to autograph it. He said he would write my name in the inscription. I expressed gratitude. He said, "That will make it sound as though I have given it to you?" I said I could live with the deception. I made to tell him my name, but he stopped me, saying he knew it. I clasped the book to my side, thanked him and his gracious lady and left. Only when I reached home and was inside my door did I open the cover and look at the inscription. It said, "To Harold Smith. Winston S. Churchill."

A few days later he announced his retirement from politics. That day in the mail I received from Ten Downing Street a volume titled *My Early Life* by Winston Churchill. It is the book that ends, ". . . September 1908 when I married and lived happily ever after." It bore his autograph.

CHAPTER FORTY-NINE

Tribalism Reborn

When the twentieth century began there were forty nations in the world, though some were great empires containing many peoples. As I write now toward the end of the century there are more than 190 nations in the world, nearly five times as many. At midcentury, in the early age of the frightful atom, attention was too focused on Cold War ideology to pay much attention to the worldwide unleashing of Tribalism, a phenomenon that may eventually have consequences as great.

The single largest source of new nations was the great empire of Britain, not quite as spacious as Stalin's, but far more populous and so distributed that some part of it was always in sunlight. In spite of Churchill's wartime resolve it did disintegrate, rapidly, month by month and year by year. Much of my time assigned to London I traveled from one cracking part to another trying to get a mental grip on this ongoing colossal wreck and to divine what it might mean. West to Ireland, now free and slowing its progress into the future by requiring citizens to learn Gaelic and searching the luggage of arriving visitors for immoral or upsetting books. Down to southernmost Africa, where White Afrikaners were reversing the outcome of the Boer War and building a racially divided state with themselves in total control. Up to Ghana, the renamed Gold Coast, once the dispatching place for many America-bound slaves from West Africa. Over to Uganda, then peaceful and beautiful but soon to fall under a Black Hitler named Idi Amin, and to the Sudan, ancient Nubia. From there to all of England's Arab creations and to its unruly client of the time, Persia, called Iran; and eventually to India and Pakistan.

Each stop was an adventure. Ghana was the first Black African possession to be deliberately relinquished by a colonial power. I was sent with a camera crew to cover the ceremonies. I first met Vice President Richard Nixon as he descended from his airplane, and I introduced myself. The next day I met Dr. Martin Luther King strolling the campus at the new university in Accra. "You know the Vice President?" I asked him. "No," he said, "I have asked for an appointment in Washington, but it has not come through." So I led him and his small coterie to the other side of a dormitory where I had last seen Nixon. There, like a Henry Stanley revealing two Dr. Livingstones to one another, I did the honors. It began a friendship between the two that flourished before reaching an abrupt end in 1960, to be related. The two stole some of the show from Kwame Nkrumah, the American-educated Ghanaian George Washington. Nkrumah restored his self-esteem by placing a double-life-size statue of himself, made in Italy, on the main square, labeled, "The Redeemer." It and he would be rudely displaced after a decade of misrule of a hitherto prosperous country.

In Sudan's dusty capital, Khartoum, I sat on a bench on the main square looking at one of the most entertaining monuments I have ever seen. It was a statue of General Charles "Chinese" Gordon, the British Governor who died there in 1885. His bronze figure sat high atop the hump of a bronze camel upon an elaborate saddle whose tassels hung down to the animal's knees. An Englishman about to depart told me the story of a fellow civil servant whose little son insisted on a visit to the square every weekend to sit and admire the statue of Gordon. Came orders to return home to England. The Englishman took his son to the square for the last time. Said the boy, "Father, the statue of Gordon is my favorite statue in the world, but there is something about it that has always puzzled me." "What is it?" asked the father. And the boy said, "Who is that fellow sitting on top of Gordon?" Whichever of the two beasts in the bronze pile one held to be Gordon, both were being disassembled and removed, along with British power and, alas, civil order.

Down the Nile, which runs confusingly upward on the world map, Egypt was at the beginning of a most emotional parting in the great imperial dissolution. It took a while, so I made many trips and was always happy to do so, for Egypt is a wonderland to anyone fascinated with the human record—5,000 years of it preserved intact, even its human remains, in the dry heat of the desert. Where else can you note with sadness that GI's have scratched their names on ancient temple columns, which is aggravating till you look closer and see that it was Julius Caesar's GI's not Bernard Montgomery's. To the ghosts of the builders of Karnak it wouldn't matter which, since both would count as recent. Such continuity: The people in the bas reliefs look like the people on the street, and none more so than picture-handsome Gamal Abdel Nasser.

Most of the dissolution of Empire was admirably peaceable, but the

Egyptian chapter was explosive; Nasser was the author of it, and humiliation was his spur. Gamal Abdel Nasser Hussein Khalil Sultan was the most active of a remarkably well-educated corps of young Egyptian army officers whose chief emotion was impatience with subservience to Britain. Impatience was brought to a head by a new incitement: the birth of the Jewish nation of Israel in flat-out Arab land. In 1948 the surrounding Arab armies led by Egypt, moved in to crush the baby in its cradle and had the hell beaten out of them. Ashamed and angry at corrupt contractors who supplied guns that jammed in combat, Nasser set off riots that burned down the English social citadel, Shepherd's Hotel, and overthrew the fat, England-compliant King Faruk. The British resisted the rioters until the new Foreign Minister, soon to be Prime Minister, Anthony Eden, saw the folly of it. Holding on to Suez had ceased to be important now that the terminus of imperial lifelines, the Indian subcontinent, was independent. And the tens of thousands of sturdy soldiers doing the holding on were needed in the labor force at home. So Eden negotiated for the British to get out. Unfortunately that was not the end of it. It made Nasser such a hero that Eden reconsidered, as will be told.

Egypt was at all times the tone-setter to all Araby. Egyptian newspapers were read from the Atlantic to the Indian Ocean. If you could drive fast enough you could drive from Casablanca 2,000 miles to Baghdad and hear the voice of Umm Kulthun singing from every house on the way over Cairo Radio. Cairo was second to Hollywood at turning out movies, a hundred a year, pot-boilers roiling with sentimentality but loved wherever any dialect of the language was understood. Nasser's success encouraged revolt along the whole Mediterranean coast and deep into the desert. Just as tinted pictures of the Virgin Mary could be bought in little shops on the north shore of that sea, so on the south shore every bazaar offered gaudily improved portraits of Nasser, his eyes asparkle. One day, people were sure, his ever-improving army would erase the insult of Israel by force.

I witnessed Nasser's effect first in Jordan, the artificial nation created by the British to provide a friendly sheikh with something to rule. When Israel was born, Jordan was flooded with angry Palestinian refugees. The place was governable only due to the best little army in the Arab world, the Arab Legion, organized by a borrowed English commander, John Bagot Glubb, called Glubb Pasha. As I arrived with a camera crew, Nasser had just proposed that King Hussein of Jordan divest himself of British influence. There were riots and attacks on Britons in the capital, Amman. Whenever our camera appeared on the streets we were pelted with stones, so most of our street scenes were shot from overlooking windows. Glubb was forced to resign, and Jordan emerged from the British orbit. After awhile Britain's last Arab stronghold, Iraq, would be subject to a Nasser-inspired revolution and lost.

The last stop for the moment of this rapid tour of defections was the magnificent island of Cyprus, north of Egypt, south of Turkey, sixty miles from Israel. When Eden announced his plan to sign away Suez, Tory MPs in Parliament staged an angry revolt. He assuaged the rebels by promising to build Cyprus, Britain's last base in the troubled area of whipsawing interests, into a super base. Only the Cypriots didn't like it. They were tired of being someone else's base. The ruins of the castle built by Richard the Lion-hearted as his headquarters for the Third Crusade were there. Before that it had been a Roman base with Cicero (the orator) as Governor and Brutus (of the unkindest cut) as Inspector of Finances. Mark Antony made the gem a gift to his girl, Cleopatra. In the postwar world, the Cypriots seemed peaceable; but the Labour MP, Richard Crossman, who loved playing *enfant terrible,* made a lecture in Nicosia saying people were heeded only when they began throwing bombs. So the Cypriot Greeks began throwing bombs, and I had a new assignment: to make frequent visits to Cyprus to report on a fresh source of troubles for Britain.

To communicate in Greek we hired a good-looking young Cypriot with a beard, a college education and a happy disposition. I often wondered why our crew always heard of the night's bombing and reached the site first, and why, with all the fireworks, we were never hurt. When the troubles ended some years later, I discovered why. Our Boy Friday was no carefree youth hunting for a job, but a leader of the rebellion who found us a good cover and in return provided us with security.

Not all the consequences of the explosion of nations in the second half of the century are yet clear, but a few generalizations can be made. Their period of apprenticeship as colonies of Europeans was a blessing and a curse. After visiting trim new Ghana, a group of us moved on to Liberia, the African nation dominated by the descendants of freed slaves from America who returned to Africa. The longtime President of Liberia, William Shadrach Tubman, allowed us a press conference. "Ghana is clean and sparkling," said a questioner; "why does Liberia look the opposite, like a scene from the wrong side of the tracks in the Mississippi Delta?" Tubman answered, "We have not had the advantage of British rule." So it was.

But British rule, the British model of government, was probably not as strong a formative influence on the new nations as was exposure to British education. From all over Asia and Africa, wherever families could scrape together the funds, sons were sent to Europe, mainly England, to study. Some went home, often via prison, to become leaders of the new nations, like Nehru of India and Lee Kuan Yew of Singapore, both graduates of Cambridge. Almost all the numerous rest became civil servants, the governing class of their infant sovereignties. The London School of Economics, said Pat Moynihan, trained more hands that rocked the cradles of newborn nations than any other institution in the world.

The curse was a distorted philosophy of governance. They were educated in a nation where Conservative government was discredited by its inability to deal with a stark Depression. The dominant nostrum bred in student life was Socialism, triumphant in Britain as war ended. But that compassionate alternative did not travel well. Instead of translating into popular control of major economic institutions, it ended up in former colonies meaning simply government-owned or government-run enterprises and often led to rampant corruption. India was the scene of the story of a Western businessman seeking a contract with a government official in that socialist-inclined nation. When the Englishman rose to leave, he stooped and seemed to retrieve something from the floor. He said, "I think you must have dropped your wallet; let me give it to you." The Indian official studied the contents and then said, "No, it cannot be mine. This one contains a thousand rupees. Mine contained ten thousand." That philosophy badly hampered the development of new nations. At the time of liberation, Ghana had the same per capita income as South Korea. A generation—twenty years—later, South Korea, operating under the American system of, if not free, then rough-and-tumble, devil-take-the-hind most enterprise, had a per person income five times that of Ghana, with the disparity still rising. It would take awhile for the new nations to learn to combine the caring of socialism with the energy of capitalism, as indeed the Western nations are still learning.

The most worrisome aspect of the multitude of new nations was dominance of the tribal instinct: Our kind must fight and kill their kind before their kind fights and kills us. Within a quarter-century after World War II, seventy-five full-scale bloody wars had occurred in the so-called Third World.

The occasion for conflict most of the time was border disputes. When these peoples were absorbed into the British, French, Turkish, Belgian, Dutch, Portuguese and Russian empires, most of them were tribally organized with no clear frontiers. They emerged now as nations needing distinct borders, which proved difficult to draw. Separating the peoples of Yugoslavia into new nations in recent times, for example, has been like separating scotch and soda with a fork.

I began my occasional tours of crumbling empires in a mood of Wilsonian fulfillment. Peoples were freely determining their own sovereignties at last, no longer yoked to the will of aliens. Soon, however, as the ease of acquiring the fissionable atom became clear, I began to hear in the rise of hundreds of relentless nationalisms what Jefferson heard in the ripening issue of slavery in America—a firebell in the night.

CHAPTER FIFTY

The Twin Crises

The year 1956 witnessed the worst world crisis after the Communist invasion of Korea in the early 1950s and before the Cuban missile crisis of the early 1960s. It was actually several simultaneous and interconnected crises that followed the death of Joseph Stalin and the "thaw" introduced by his worried heirs. They lifted the lid a little on their sore-pressed satellites, but too much pressure had accumulated and the lid blew right off, resulting in a nasty reinvasion. At the same time, the British and French felt that, with Russia preoccupied elsewhere, they could divert some power to crushing their *bête noir,* Nasser. Russia threatened them with nuclear attack. U.S. Secretary of State John Foster Dulles said the threat was "the gravest political incident since World War II." The Swiss called a world conference to try to remove "the shadow of a third world war [which] hovers over mankind."

At the center of the crisis was a duel between two tall, handsome men— the exotic Nasser and the English aristocrat Anthony Eden. I happened to have good relations with both. I think Nasser felt that I was marginally sympathetic to Egypt's condition. I had just taken part in an elaborate two-part documentary program about the Arab–Israeli dispute, with Murrow filming in Israel and me in the Arab lands, after which we met in a UN-held neutral zone to discuss conclusions. I did show sympathy with this remarkable and ancient country, which consists largely of two thin fringes of green riverbank on which humans are living and breeding in numbers competitive with rabbits. Nasser was, as a colleague well described him, "courteous, smiling, soft-voiced, reasonable, untruthful, untrustworthy." After our first interview, he always agreed to further meetings and always received me cordially. (I note in passing that the last of my long series of talks with him never reached the tube. On the flight back to the U.S., the Pan Am pilot called me to the cockpit and said, "See if you can make sense of these broadcasts from the States we are hearing. They say President Kennedy has been shot.")

Sir Robert Anthony Eden, the other duelist, should have been ideally suited to deal with Nasser. He grew intimate with our bloody century early, serving from age eighteen all four years of the Great War. He then won first class honors at Oxford in Oriental languages. He acquired diplomatic star status as a skillful negotiator in the 1930s, and kept his record clean by resigning from Chamberlain's cabinet over the appeasement issue. When the Tories returned to power in the 1950s, he negotiated the Russians out of Austria—a signal triumph, for it was the only soil the Soviets gave up until the era of *perestroika*. He also made a broad-minded deal with Egypt to remove British troops. He took over from Churchill as Prime Minister, led his party through elections to a landslide victory, and was looking forward to a brilliant term.

But Eden turned untrue to himself. There were a number of elements in his personal crisis. Many of Eden's Tories did not like him, and that worried him. Politically, they thought him too liberal in acceding to the demands of colonials within the Empire. He divorced his wife, which they disapproved of. "Do any bloody thing you fancy with the girls," one Tory said to me at a dinner, "but don't divorce the buggers. That's really bad form." Eden always felt some pressure to justify himself to this Neanderthal branch of his party. He had two further problems. One, he had a gall bladder operation involving the insertion of a plastic tube that deteriorated when he was under stress. During the coming period of stress he suffered painful illnesses and frequent hospitalizations that must have affected his judgment badly. Two, he had married Churchill's niece, who shared her uncle's obsession with Empire. She became a source of constant domestic pressure on him to stand firm when he shouldn't have.

Eden and Nasser met but once, when Eden was passing through Cairo on his way to somewhere else. One who was present said they chilled the warm Nilotic air with instant mutual dislike. Eden had promised his objecting troglodytes that his agreement to pull out of Egypt would make Nasser friendly. Instead, Cairo Radio launched a barrage of attacks on Britain and on Arabs friendly to Britain.

Ironically, the sequence of events that led to explosion was started by America. Secretary of State Dulles, weary of the Egyptian dictator's tactic of playing Russia off against the U.S., announced that America would not finance the building of the great dam at Aswan that was the heart of all Nasser's plans to feed his nation. Nasser reacted angrily by "nationalizing" the Suez Canal. This did not involve any military action; Britain had already handed over physical control. It simply meant that he disowned British and French shareholders, and promised to compensate them later.

Eden's prior generosity to Nasser was now seen by his critics as weakness, and he was furious. He joined France and Israel in a secret plan to overthrow Nasser: Israel would attack Egypt, revealing abundant evidence that Nasser was planning to attack first. Britain and France would then send bombers and troops into Egypt to "protect" the canal from the war. Nasser would be discredited by defeat and overthrown.

If Eden thought other nations would appreciate his blow against a leader considered a universal scoundrel, his disillusion was immediate. America and most of the British Commonwealth nations condemned the action as aggressive and, worse, as folly; after all, Nasser was doing only what Britain had done: nationalizing a resource. In Britain itself, the Labour opposition was outraged by the secrecy of the plan and demanded Eden's resignation in tumultuous sessions. My friend Denis Healey, now an MP, took the floor to ask Eden whether he had exchanged congratulations with the Communist leaders over their mutual atrocities. For Port Said on the Suez Canal had fallen to British troops the same day Budapest succumbed to a reinvasion of Hungary by the Soviet Red Army.

In badly exploited eastern Europe, 1956 was a year of bad crops, of low incomes squeezed lower by inflation and of a new incentive to raise some hell. Khrushchev made his book-length secret speech to Soviet Communists—the text secured by the Israelis and passed on to the Americans, who published it for the world to read—revealing that the late Joseph Stalin was not as bad as we thought but much, much worse. Bold citizens interpreted it as a sign of new freedom and they spoke out. Demonstrations occurred in Hungary and Poland, the boldest in the Polish city of Poznan in July. This action became a strike and then a rebellion that was put down with 48 killed and 270 injured. Khrushchev flew to Warsaw and warned Polish comrades to get things back under control. The London *Times* mocked the old *Communist Manifesto:* "A spectre is haunting Europe. It is the spectre of freedom."

I had to decide which of several crisis venues to cover: Egypt, Hungary or Poland—or whether to stay in London where debate had split a furious Parliament and nation. I chose Poland. Russia had to control Poland, the historical invasion route from the West into Russia. Whatever others might do, I knew the Poles *would fight* if attacked. I first flew to Zurich and bought a wallet full of Zlotys and another full of five-dollar bills. On arriving in Warsaw, I went to the apartment of Sidney Gruson and his wife, Flora Lewis (he to become managing editor, she to be foremost foreign correspondent of *The New York Times*), and begged a briefing.

It is said that a good reporter always manages to be in the right place at the right time. By that standard I failed. The Polish comrades had got old Communist Wladislaw Gomulka out of Stalin's prison and made him head man. Gomulka made it clear he would fight. "Our cup is full," he said in a speech. "It cannot be overfilled with impunity. You cannot escape the truth. The loss of the confidence of the working masses means the loss of the right to govern." Khrushchev thought it over. At least Poland was still in the hands of a Communist. Fighting him would be too expensive for Russia, especially as Hungary was beginning to riot out of control. Khrushchev decided to leave Poland alone.

I hung around a day or two, expecting Khrushchev might change his mind.

He had pulled his tanks out of Hungary, only to blast back in a day later and bathe the capital in blood. He might do the same here. I went out to Warsaw's primitive TV facility and borrowed a cameraman and filmed a report on the city; I could add the sound narration back in London. I found an old friend who was an architect, and he took me to the Architects' Club for tea. The architects were more contemptuous of Russia than others because of Stalin's special "gift" to the city, the thirty-story Palace of Science and Culture, which was the subject of a standard joke: "Q.: Where does one get the best view of Warsaw? A.: From the Palace of Science and Culture. Q.: Why is that view best? A.: Because it is the only place in Warsaw where you cannot see the Palace of Science and Culture." My friend and all his colleagues were buoyant. "I cannot tell you how proud I am," he said. "We Poles have always been the reckless heroes, tearing the enemy's cannon apart with our bare hands—and getting beaten. This time we were not only courageous but wise. We have gone far enough to win and not too far to risk losing."

On a tip I went out to the airport. Occasional planes from Budapest arrived to fetch shipments of plasma and medicine. The planes bore the design of the flag of Hungary but with hammer and sickle in the middle whitewashed out. The pilots were red-eyed and paused in a reception room only to gulp down a cup of hot tea or soup.

I sent a telegram to New York suggesting that I get a lift on one of those planes and fly to Budapest. It crossed a telegram from New York ordering me to fly to the U.S. immediately. CBS was putting together a special documentary on the twin crises and wanted me to anchor it. I had done my first hosting of such a report about black Africa the previous year, and one about Cyprus this year. As it appeared that my future, if any, would be with TV, I was pleased to be invited for another shot at the new art, and I took the next plane out.

I spent little more than 24 hours in New York writing and appearing in the program, before flying back to London. By then the reconquest of Budapest was complete. Russian tanks had attacked and killed some 3,000 resisting Hungarians and had destroyed an estimated 4,000 buildings in the city. Thousands were fleeing across the border to Austria. The Russian puppet, János Kádár, was installed in power.

In the House of Commons, debate raged on for days over Eden's invasion of Egypt. At one point the Speaker had to order a half-hour recess to restore order. In the UN, the Commonwealth front was broken as Canada, India and South Africa voted against the mother country on the issue. The U.S. State Department sent harsh messages to the three conspirators, Britain, France and Israel, demanding that they withdraw from Egypt. The Suez Canal, open before the attack, was now blocked with 51 sunken vessels. The value of the British pound plummeted as holders all over the world tried to exchange them for other currencies, deepening an already long-term economic crisis.

A curious little incident now occurred. The imperial-minded "Suez Group" of Tory MPs invited four American reporters, of whom I was one, to cocktails in an apartment. One of them made us a little speech based on the unflattering assumption that we did not understand the situation and that, once we did and reported it properly, America would turn around and support the British government's position. It was too much. I counterexplained that we understood perfectly. They had made a gross mistake, which we were reporting fully and accurately. Later one of the Tories asked me what could be done to restore good relations; how about sending Harold Macmillan (Eden's Chancellor of the Exchequer, thought to have good relations with the U.S. through his family's publishing firm) to talk with Eisenhower? I said, "Not that antique caricature! No one in America knows who he is." Later I asked someone who my questioner was, and he said it was Maurice Macmillan, son of Harold. My standing was not enhanced when weeks later Harold became Prime Minister.

On the last day of the debate, the final speech for the Labour opposition was made by Aneurin Bevan. With mock sympathy he said, "They are not bad men. They are synthetic villains who do not even understand the language of villainy." Then he leaned forward and in a kind of confidential whisper said to the Tories, "You will now vote confidence in your government. But in your heart of hearts you will know that it does not deserve your confidence." More than a few on the opposite benches nodded their heads.

Bevan was right. Eden won a sizable vote of confidence. The Tory rebels had been called in one by one and told that, if the vote went the other way, the party would fall from power and not return for a generation. The pound would collapse and Britain would never recover. They swallowed hard and decided to behave. Labour cooperated, not wanting to inherit Eden's wreck and be identified with years of austerity. Labour MPs were told to take a holiday when the vote was called.

So the deep-down cause of the crisis was hollow. Eden's fear of the Tory rebels and their crude definition of manhood was baseless. For them he had abandoned his singular skills as negotiator, as a creator of consensus, as a leader with a broad-minded approach to colonies wanting out. For them he had sought to give the Egyptian dictator a solid punch in the nose. Yet all the time they were hollow men—in a crunch, conformists.

Toward the end of the debate I took a good look at Eden. So did another writer, a reporter for the London *Observer*, and his unsigned description of the man was better than mine: "The Prime Minister sprawled on the front bench, head thrown back and mouth agape. His eyes, inflamed with sleeplessness, stared into vacancies beyond the roof except when they switched with meaningless intensity to the clock, probed it for a few seconds, then rose again in vacancy. His hands twitched . . . mopped themselves in a handkerchief, and were never still. The face was grey except where black-ringed caverns surrounded the dying embers of his eyes."

British troops were recalled from Egypt. Eden was diagnosed as being on the edge of a nervous breakdown and was ordered to Jamaica for a complete rest. Eventually he was prevailed on to resign and let Harold Macmillan succeed him as Prime Minister. At last it was clear that Britain had become the emperor without clothes.

CHAPTER FIFTY-ONE

Roots Seeking Soil

Breathes there the man, with soul so dead,
Who never to himself hath said,
This is my own, my native land!

I often scoffed at Sir Walter Scott's observation about attachment to home earth. It became ritual when driving back from track meets in Texas or Mississippi that I would, as we crossed the state line, say to a teammate, "Did you feel a jolt?" He or they would answer, "No. Why?" "Then," said I, "you like me shall die 'unwept, unhonour'd, and unsung.' It is so decreed by Sir Walter Scott." But now I began to notice that the poet's words were coming back to me again and again like some haunting refrain and were taking on a more compelling tone. It was getting on toward twenty years since I packed up, left depressed America and went to Europe to live. Most of the people I dealt with and lunched or dined with were English or (previous to that) German or Swiss. I had a wife who carried a Danish passport and two children who spoke with English accents but were somehow quite aware that they were outsiders; my son's classmates in London even called him "Yank," though he had only a movie conception of what that meant. Yet, they and I felt we did not belong in America either. We simply did not belong anywhere. If you woke up in the middle of the night and said that to yourself, it was slightly terrifying. I began to feel a gnawing need to establish some roots in the land of my fathers.

I had paid many short visits back over the years. Murrow had appointed me chief in Europe and Sevareid chief in Washington, assuming that we would want to trade places with one another after a while. But Eric didn't. Once I persuaded him to switch for a summer, and I was able to see why he didn't. Washington was a reporter's candy shop, a many-ring circus with free season passes, a wide-open town where one wondered why the Russians paid spies when they could have obtained all the information worth having free of charge.

Now, Suez opened my eyes, and the world's, to Britain's transparent suit of clothes. London was a wonderful city to live in. But it was no longer, and had not been for quite a while, "a story." Largely through habit CBS and NBC continued to schedule a London spot on the daily broadcast roundups. But in fact nothing of moment was happening. Once I looked over a past year's scripts and found I was mostly reporting what Britain thought of what was decided in Washington the day before.

I had casually asked my bosses, Sig Mickelson, vice president for news, and John Day, news director, to think up a use for me in America. Now I asked urgently. Happily a relevant idea was a-borning; something that had been crystallizing now crystallized. The network's premier daily television news program was *Douglas Edwards and the News,* a fifteen-minute roundup every weekday evening. Edwards had about the finest voice on radio, and the program was the nation's best. But the executives felt it was a two-dimensional headline service, and needed some depth. What they wanted was a short news analysis. The idea was casually broached to Murrow. He dismissed it, saying it would have to be too short and was unlikely to work. Sig asked if I would like to try.

In the earliest years of television it took about thirty-six hours for film shot in Europe to get back to the U.S. and be developed and edited to go on the air. I was asked to do something, anything, before a camera that would hold up for thirty-six hours. So I had begun doing very brief standup commentaries in recognizable locations—a bad cliché today, but at that time it was considered to establish a foreign correspondent's authority if he was shown coming to you from outside the Houses of Parliament, or the Kremlin, or the Quai d'Orsay. Lately a piece by me, filmed as I stood outside the home of Benjamin Disraeli before a bust of the Prime Minister who had bought control of the lately fought-over Suez Canal, had been used so often on air by CBS that jokes about it were coursing the nation. So, said Mickelson, how about doing one of those on-camera commentaries in Washington, every day on the Edwards show?

It was quite a literary challenge—writing one minute of copy, a rhymeless sonnet, relevant, every bloody day, and having the courage to sit in front of a camera and say it to the critical world. And I would be expected to provide my weekly fifteen-minute Sunday commentary on radio in addition. I pondered hard and long, perhaps a minute or two, before deciding that I would like to take a shot at it.

Selling the switch to my bride took a little doing. She loved London and our circumstances. After eight years in Murrow's small wartime hand-me-down apartment, she had scouted around and found our expanded family an elegant Regency-period townhouse overlooking Regent's Park, the biggest, lushest area of green in the far-flung town. My overflowing library and our antique furniture fitted nicely in its high-ceilinged spaces. It also nicely accommodated dinner parties and was the basis for a pleasant social life. My residual Bible-Belt Puritanism, allied to my Depression upbringing, caused me occasional concern about enjoying myself, but CBS executives assured me that such was expected of their European Director, as my title sometimes was. When Bennie and I were not traveling abroad, we had wonderful busman's holidays on Mondays (my only day off), spending the night in country inns in Broadway or near Stratford or at medieval Bailiff's Court on the south coast. Bennie could think of no comparable delights in America.

I think she was also concerned about adjusting to Washington and America—a continent too big to be a proper nation like those orderly ones in Europe she was accustomed to. Moreover, it was populated by organisms with outsized elbows they seemed to use excessively. Once at dinner with a friend, we met the columnist Joseph Alsop, who was visiting England. At table, he bullied an English guest mercilessly about some aspect of Britain and behaved as if Bennie and I were not present. She did not know we were witnessing an extreme on the scale of Washington journalists, and that most others would be as polite as Europeans—who only offend one another in wars. I am sure Bennie wept out of sight about my wish, which was stated with such enthusiasm that she could tell it was a decision. After a while she did the heroic thing and blessed the enterprise.

Once the decision was made I wanted it to begin yesterday. Charles Collingwood arrived to replace me. I organized a reception to introduce him to a few people and to say goodbye. I made a final broadcast, saying, "There may be a time, perhaps fifty years hence, when Europe will unite and thereby become a great power with the strength to make big decisions again. But for now, at least for the next generation, the fate of the way of life it has taken so long to build up is going to be determined by the wisdom or the folly of the United States. There the decisions are going to have to be taken and there, in Washington, I hope this broadcast will originate next week." My behavior at the end was of a kind to justify militant feminism. I packed a small bag, and left the mere detail of packing and moving our accumulations to my wife. And what a detail it was. We had arrived in London with my possessions in a duffel bag and hers in a single suitcase. Bennie would depart in charge of a boxcar-sized container.

1957-1961

CHAPTER FIFTY-TWO

Bad Days at Little Rock

I landed in New York, went to the office to punch the clock, so to speak, and then took the train to Washington the same day. John Day had given me four weeks without assignment to get my feet steadied in the New World. But on my fourth day he phoned and told me the school trouble in Little Rock was flashing ugly: a mob was rioting around Central High School and was at that moment beating up people to prevent desegregation as ordered by the federal courts. He was sorry to interfere with my leisurely adjustment, but CBS was sending a big TV unit to Little Rock, and he wanted me to do the on-camera reporting. I took the first plane and arrived there in the late afternoon. The rioting was over for the day. In the gloaming, clumps of shirt-sleeved men and boys were standing and talking on street corners around the school, and a few policemen were walking in twos on the sidewalks. It was hard to match that scene with reports heard on the radio hours earlier about the mob beating up four Black and two White reporters working for *Life* magazine, and generally raising hell while the police watched. Quiet now, but tomorrow when the nine Black youngsters tried again to enter the school?

I felt I was on distantly familiar ground. For a short period, my father had been assigned by the Missouri Pacific Railroad to work out of McGehee, Arkansas, and we had taken up brief residence there. After college and before the *Item* I had traveled to Little Rock on my father's pass, for lack of anything else to do. It was a quiet, neighborly, orderly, well, ordinary, little Southern city, more famous for its fictional celebrities—Lorelei Lee (of *Gentlemen Prefer Blondes*) and Nellie Forbush (of *South Pacific*)—than for its real ones, little Willie Clinton of Hope, Arkansas, being only eleven at the time. The city had no previous record of racial troubles or of civic violence. The University of Arkansas admitted a Black student in 1948 and was the first in the South to do so. The 1954 decision by the Supreme Court ordering desegregation of schools throughout the South had been met by whites in Little Rock with regret, but with compliance. All of the city's public colleges were desegregated promptly, as were eight public grade schools. In the fall of 1957, a federal district court judge ordered the desegregation of Little Rock's Central High School; nine Negro youths were to be registered along with the school's 2,000 white students.

The Governor of Arkansas at that time was Orval Faubus. He had a mildly liberal record. His son was enrolled in one of the schools that had been quietly desegregated. But—and this was the source of the trouble—Faubus knew that in another year he would be running for a third two-year term in office, and he was sensitive to the urges of the most easily worked up and therefore most ardent of the voters. When the court order came down, he claimed to see trouble ahead and called out his state's National Guard to prevent violence, an act that was a clarion call for rednecks from counties around to gather. Faubus used the Guard not to carry out the court's order, but to violate it by blocking the Negro youths from entering the school. He was then called to a conference with President Eisenhower, who told him to stop violating the law. A conciliatory statement was hammered out for the two to sign. But the praise being heaped on Faubus by segregationists had gone to his head. He had now become a national figure and was asked to sign autographs on a trip out of the state. He attended a football game, and such was his intoxication with his new fame that, every time the crowd cheered a play on the field, Orval stood, took off his hat and bowed all around. He issued the agreed-upon statement, but changed the words around to make it seem that the President favored resistance to desegregation. The federal district judge promptly reminded Faubus of the order he had issued, declared Faubus in contempt of court and repeated the order to let the Black students into Central High immediately. The morning the students were to enter, Faubus withdrew the Guard without warning, the mob took over and the riot that ended my apprenticeship in Washington took place.

That was on Monday. On Tuesday, my first morning there, the mob was seething, but there was no violence, as the Black youths did not appear. The Mayor of Little Rock said his police could not handle the situation; he needed federal help. Our TV unit was organizing itself. I did a number of radio broadcasts from outside the school. Eisenhower was no supporter of civil rights; his brief argument was "You can't legislate morality." But he said that, by using troops to violate the law, the Governor had created "the worst constitutional crisis since the Civil War." The President ordered that the best riot-trained soldiers in the U.S. Army be sent to Little Rock to enforce the law. Within eight hours of his order, a thousand troops of a battle group of the 101st Airborne Division were on the ground in the troubled city. It was a pleasure to watch them deploy through the late evening and into the dark. They came in trucks and soon filled much of the school's grounds. Communications lines were strung all around the neighborhood. Vehicles were parked, and tents were set up on a sports field behind the school. By dawn the next morning, Wednesday, they manned streets and set up roadblocks a block out from Central High in every direction. The operation was smooth and very impressive.

Just after dawn I went to the Governor's mansion expecting to meet a camera crew and then to try to get some words from Faubus. I rang the doorbell and asked a young aide who appeared whether my crew had arrived. He said, "Maybe they are in the back," and invited me to follow him. I did, right through the lobby, the parlor and a hall, and into the breakfast room where Faubus sat alone eating his Wheaties. He looked up with astonishment that equaled my own. The aide beckoned me not to tarry, so without a word I went on through the kitchen to the back door. No camera crew. The aide suggested they might be out front by now, so I followed him back. This time I felt it only polite to stop in the breakfast room and introduce myself. Faubus wound up quickly. "I hope you are telling the truth," he said—this is recollected, since I took no notes—"Arkansas is like German-occupied France. There is a precedent for this, but not in America. I've got a constitutional lawyer who says the precedent is Nazi Germany and Communist Russia." I told him I wanted to get my crew and come back and put his words on sound film. I went out the front door. Still no crew. There had been a misunderstanding, and all crews were sensibly setting up at Central High where the action was about to take place. I sped back to the school as fast as a rented car would take me.

I got past a roadblock by showing my CBS credentials; then I found Major Jim Meyers, who was in command, and told him I was going to follow him. He said, "Just don't get in the way." The mob had begun to form at one roadblock, and before the number reached fifty, Meyers took a bullhorn and ordered them to disperse, go home, or he would be obliged to make them do so. Sullenly they moved away. At another roadblock, the crowd was bigger and its surly members stood their ground against Meyers' commands. He ordered the soldiers to form a movable wall with their bayonets pointed outward, and to clear the street. A sergeant shouted to the crowd, audible without bullhorn, "We are moving, boys. If you stand still you are going to get in the way of these bayonets and they ain't gonna stop." Some of the crowd ran away onto front porches, but the soldiers went right after them. One man stood his ground and, sure enough, the bayonets did not stop. He posed for our camera with blood streaming down his face. "It's like the Russians in Hungary," he said. "There ain't no freedom left."

That was the last violence in the Little Rock crisis. By 8:45 A.M., when the school bell rang, an army station wagon, with jeeps fore and aft, unloaded the nine dark-skinned youngsters, and they went into the school with no resistance. President Eisenhower had by now federalized the National Guard, removing them from Faubus' command and putting them under his. General Edwin Walker was placed in overall command of paratroopers and National Guard. The students were called together, and General Walker read them a statement: "You have nothing to fear from my soldiers, and no one will interfere with your coming, going, or your peaceful pursuit of your studies. They

are here because they have been ordered to be here . . . they are as determined as I to carry out their orders."

(General Walker was the hero of the occasion, but not of much beyond it.
He soon resigned from the Army and became a strange crusader for segrega-
tion. He also became the target of a still stranger citizen's fanaticism. One
night a bullet was fired through the window of Walker's home in Dallas. It was
intended to assassinate him but missed. The would-be assassin had better luck,
to pervert a word, with his next target. The man who fired the shot was Lee
Harvey Oswald.)

I was on television making four-minute reports outside the school eleven
times that day. That night we organized a half-hour documentary, with
Cronkite anchoring from New York, Sevareid commenting from Washington
and me reporting and interviewing in Little Rock.

At the time, many commentators called Little Rock the turning point in
the Civil Rights Revolution. The Black young people got into Central High.
Disobedience to federal law was broken, and anarchy dispersed. They thought
an example and a precedent had been created to discourage resistance elsewhere. Alas, it was not to be so. Locally Faubus had made himself a hero and
martyr. "I was removed like General MacArthur," he said, "even though I was
elected by the people." Faubus not only won his third term, but a fourth and a
fifth and a sixth. Little Rock's moderate Congressman, Brooks Hayes, whom I
interviewed at some length on our program, was defeated in his next election
by an enthusiastic segregationist. Hayes told me that his identification with me
and with TV, the ultimate outside troublemaker, did him in. I knew while I was
still in Little Rock that our side had lost points in that crisis when I received a
telegram from my beloved Cajun relatives in Pointe Coupée Parish, Louisiana,
who had kept their TV on all day to be sure to see me. It said, "We love you
anyhow."

Applying a longer perspective, though, our side may in fact have won. In
1967 Faubus was succeeded in the Governor's mansion by a civil rights supporter, Winthrop Rockefeller, and he by a succession of figures who insisted on
equal rights: Dale Bumpers, David Pryor, Bill Clinton. But the road to success
in making Tom Jefferson honest about all men being equal was paved with victims. I had no way of guessing that one of them would be me.

CHAPTER FIFTY-THREE

The Moscow Traveler

There were no heroes out of Little Rock. It was an awful reminder of a huge problem that must one day be faced; but not now, please God, never now. Even Senator J. W. Fulbright, the foremost of all Arkansans—broadest-minded, archetypical Rhodes Scholar, creator of the famous Fulbright scholarships—refused to comment one way or another or in between; he just wouldn't talk about it and left company when the subject came up. Many people wanted to forget it in the worst way.

The worst way occurred within a week of the crisis. Radio hacks wondered briefly on October 4, 1957, whence a repeated "beep-beep" sound was coming. Then the Russians announced that they had rocketed a satellite up into space and put it into orbit around the Earth, a little moon they had created and positioned for themselves, and that "beep-beep" was its impudent little voice. It was called Sputnik, which meant traveling partner or fellow traveler. Asked about the school crisis, a Congressman said, "Little Rock is now just a place Sputnik flies over."

If anything was sure in the world of the mid-twentieth century, it was that America had an uncatchable lead in science and technology. Suddenly certainty was blotched with doubt. In wars, even cold ones, a first principle is to get the high ground. The Russians had got it and we had not. It took no great leap of imagination to see hydrogen bombs topping the missiles and orbiting around the Earth till they found just the right spot to descend and blow the place up—or till they just threatened to do so, unless we obeyed some command from Moscow.

There were many rings of action in Washington, but the central one was Eisenhower's press conferences, which were conducted almost weekly. Even with weeks off for illness or travel, Eisenhower held a total of 193 of them, surely the all-time record. One mounted the high granite steps of the Executive Office Building, an enormous pile next to the White House. It had been built to house three executive departments—State, War and Navy—but the expanding White House staff soon engulfed it and flooded them out. Its architecture was much criticized, but I loved its cool, high ceilings and wide halls. Eisenhower appeared standing at a desk in what was called the Indian Treaty Room, with his Press Chief Jim Hagerty sitting to his left, intimidatingly alert to missteps by the President or trick questions from us.

The reporters who assembled before the President in October were alarmed. Comments from the Hill a couple of miles away sounded unmistakably alarmed, as did some already in from abroad. But Ike was calm, almost phlegmatic. Pressed on the dramatic shift in the balance of power, he simply denied there had been any. Sputnik, he said, did not raise his apprehensions about the nation's security "one iota." You could almost hear the sucking in of breath across the Treaty Room. Later in the day a member of the President's Cabinet referred to the Russian earth satellite as a "silly bauble." Secretary of State John Foster Dulles derided concern about what he called an outer-space basketball match.

For the first time since before he vetoed our taking of Berlin, I was in agreement with Eisenhower on something. It would turn out with the perspective of years that Ike was much closer to the truth than the alarmists were. He knew that we were not so far behind the Russians in the satellite craft that we need be alarmed. And he knew that a lot of skill and time would be needed before an atomic bomb could be attached to a satellite, and that the U.S. was far better at that than the Russians were. But this was a situation in which perception was more important than fact. Before Sputnik there was an abiding fear that the U.S. had become rather complacent after successfully cutting off the Russians at the pass in Berlin in Europe and in Korea in Asia. Now this spectacular Russian achievement highlighted every flaw in American society, including some that did not exist, and let loose an avalanche of self-criticism. Edwin Diamond noted later that the Edsel car died its terrible death in auto showrooms, not due to any faults in itself, but because Sputnik triggered a reaction against the showy "tinniness" of America's fin-tailed motor cars, and Edsel had a little more chrome showing than did the rest. Sputnik, or reaction to it, may have caused Vice President Nixon to lose the 1960 Presidential election by creating in people's minds the myth of a "missile gap" that in fact did not exist.

The perception of U.S. inferiority filled my commentaries, daily and weekly, for the season to come. The perception was amplified by the dismal failure of the first U.S. effort to duplicate the Russian success. A pencil-thin Navy missile called Vanguard sought to carry a three-pound object into orbit, but it simply cracked in half and died in its own smoke on the launchpad. Meanwhile the Russians sent up Sputnik II, carrying a dog into orbit, to secure their reputation for superiority. The U.S. could have forfended all this by choosing not the Navy Vanguard missile, but the Army Jupiter missile, to do the job it was more than ready to do. The trouble was, Jupiter was made by the expert ex-German staff under Wernher von Braun, who had made Hitler's missiles before surrendering to U.S. troops at the end of the war. It would not be good propaganda to reveal that America's success depended on ex-Nazis.

But in despair the Pentagon finally let the Germans do it. In January 1959, a Jupiter rocket put a satellite into orbit with no difficulty.

But that awful perception of a "missile gap" rode like a tidal wave over the world. A Ghanaian diplomat, speaking for many in the Third World, said at the UN, "If Russia is so oppressed, how can it accomplish this highly creative act?" A meeting of European politicians, discussing the prospect of unifying their nations in Strasbourg, put the question, could the U.S. any longer be considered capable of defending them? The British clothed their concern in humor. On the floor of the House of Commons a Tory MP, recently critical of the U.S. for opposing the British at Suez, suggested reconciliation on grounds that "we second-rate nations must stick together." Sarah Churchill, Winston's prodigal daughter, arrested for drunkenness in Hollywood, said to police, "There'll always be an England, but I am not so sure about America."

And the Russians, elated after a decade of setbacks in the Cold War, hastened to exploit their advantage. Khrushchev told W. R. Hearst and staff that the arms race was over and Russia had won. To underscore this point he ordered his diplomats to walk out of a disarmament conference at the UN. He sent letters to all nations that hosted U.S. military bases urging them to reconsider the danger they put themselves in. In one of his cocktail party boasts, Khrushchev said Russia would make "cemeteries" of them. In one of the Hearst team interviews, Marshal Malinovsky, the Soviet Defense Minister, said the Soviet submarine force had become strong enough to sink the whole U.S. Navy at the outbreak of a war. Exploiting the breast-beating going on in America, he said American soldiers had no stomach for war and would not resist very long in a conflict.

The breast-beating was probably the best consequence of Sputnik. There *was* a lot wrong in the U.S. There generally is. Much earlier, the Rockefeller brothers had put together a large team of knowing Americans and provided the funds for a study and a report on all the things that were wrong. The results appeared at the height of the nation's worry: several huge volumes of print. Dave Garroway, host of a popular morning TV program, displayed the voluminous report and offered to send copies to concerned viewers. He expected a few, at most a couple of hundred requests. Instead he received 200,000! And the panel had ordered only 10,000 copies printed.

Other knowledgeable Americans had studied the nation's defense structure and decided it was badly flawed. This report was secret, but parts of it leaked out as soon as Sputnik raised sensitivity. Dr. Frank Stanton, president of CBS, had been a member of the Gaither Commission, which authored the report, and he decided that CBS News should go public with its own study and report on the American state of things. Cronkite and I were chosen to anchor the presentation—a ninety-minute report on the missile industry, the war between branches of the armed services inside the Pentagon and the condition of American education—all under the program title "Where We Stand." Cronkite introduced the program and appeared in part of it during the first thirty minutes; then he disappeared, and I took it over for the remaining hour. I questioned the odd format, but the producers explained that Cronkite was mostly busy with his excellent new weekly program, *The Twentieth Century*, while I was there working and doing the interviewing and the writing, so it was easier for them to shove everything to me. The program ended with CBS's first and only corporate editorial. I wrote a first draft and handed it to an editorial board made up of producers and executives headed by Stanton himself. They added and subtracted some from my draft, then allowed me to rewrite it in my own idiom or style. I said that Americans were "over-complacent, over-addicted to comfort and indifferent to good government," and that "We must be prepared to make sacrifices and pay higher taxes and face controls if necessary to achieve our goals." Not original commentary, but the public was now receptive to it. The CBS effort was widely praised in the press.

The crisis was worth all the anguish just for the attention it focused on American education. For the first time since enacting the GI Bill, which provided the country with its best-educated generation after World War II, the federal government put money into higher education and into scientific projects that could not have been undertaken without government help. It supplied the President of the United States with a Science Adviser always at his elbow. It helped persuade American soldiers that the contest that mattered was between the U.S. and the U.S.S.R., not between different arms of the U.S. armed services, as often seemed the case.

When at last we had launched a dozen satellites to circumnavigate the Earth, the Pentagon, as a public relations trick, asked each of the three TV networks to compose a message that one satellite could relay out into space. I was chosen to compose and deliver CBS's message to whatever intelligent life was out there. The Pentagon officer said, remember, it has to be short. I told him I would make it very short—one word, to be exact. He asked what it was and I said, "Help!" He and CBS rejected that as impertinent and made me write one of my patented rhymeless sonnets, which I did. It was not as good as my short impertinent one.

I had some kind of relationship with each subsequent President who served while I worked in Washington, but none at all with Eisenhower. Before attending his press conferences, I had met him but once, when he returned to Paris after the war to take over command of NATO forces in the Cold War. I nursed relations with his PR man, the famous combat soldier General Charles "Buck" Lanham (model for the hero in Hemingway's novel *Across the River and into the Trees*), and eventually got an interview with Eisenhower. I was conveyed to one of a small village of prefabs outside Paris; Ike came out from behind a desk and greeted me. He was wild about golf. As we talked, he took out a putter from an umbrella stand and began to play pretend golf, gently nudging a pretend ball into an imagined hole. It was a time when he had just about agreed to the importuning by Republicans that he run for President, but he had not yet announced it, so I dared ask him nonmilitary questions like what to do about offshore oil. At each question, he would fix his eyes on that imaginary hole, swing gently with the putter and say, "I think we can handle that," then register satisfaction at seeing the unseen ball roll into its unseen refuge. Our fascinating but insubstantial interview ended when an aide came in and announced that another group of Senators from Washington was there to see him.

As President he ran a tightly buttoned-up crew from whom it was hard to get much information. When I arrived from Europe, he was only a year into his second term, but they seemed a depressed crew. The President was tired and had suffered a third hospitalization. An editorial cartoonist depicted him in a dark cell called the White House and marking off the days on the wall. His foremost Cabinet officer, Secretary of State Dulles, was also tired and unwell. Ike's listless response to Sputnik was the nadir. People became worried about his leadership. To try to reassure them, Ike and Dulles appeared together on TV to discuss the world. The two tired old men made a calamitous impression. "They made it sound worse than it was," said James Reston of *The New York Times*. Something had to be done, and it was. Magically, Ike came alive. He made a TV speech defending a foreign aid bill, and rescued it from death with an electrifying performance. Dulles appeared at the National Press Club to speak. I was one of a small delegation appointed to receive him in a room apart. He was restless in the manner of an athlete before a contest he welcomed. He had a dab of makeup on a spot on his nose to look his best before cameras, something he rarely gave a damn about. The speech was good, almost rousing. The Administration's temper was on the mend.

The magician who wrought the rescue was the de facto Assistant President, Jim Hagerty, the White House Press Secretary, about the most remarkable single figure in the Eisenhower Administration. I did not know Hagerty well in those years but we later became close friends. He was not really a newsman. He was truly a professional Presidential Press Secretary. He left reporting to serve Wendell Willkie, the Republican Presidential candidate in 1940. Then he did the same for New York Governor Tom Dewey, who ran twice for President. Ike inherited him from Dewey, and immediately saw that Hagerty was the most useful figure near him, a genius at providing advice on what to say and when to say it. When Eisenhower suffered his first illness, and chaos threatened, someone came to the President's bed to inform him Hagerty was on the way back from a trip to New York. Ike relaxed immediately and said, "Good! Tell Jim to take over."

The New York Times's brilliant political voyeur, Scotty Reston, again said it best. The Eisenhower government lived on "Faith, Hope and Hagerty." Jim was a master image-maker. When Ike took a few days off to play golf and just goof off, Hagerty stayed at the White House with a batch of handouts saved up for such times and distributed them several hours apart, giving the impression the President was continuously working. When Ike was in the hospital, Hagerty arranged schedules for Cabinet members to come and visit, and often handed the arriving officer a little script of what he was to say to the press, upon emerging, about how well Ike looked. It was Hagerty who insisted that the President hold frequent press conferences. With no standing in Congress, the only accountability a President can display is to the press. When a President appears infrequently, as Nixon was later to demonstrate, the saved-up and stored-up curiosity of questioners often turns to animus with sharp, testy exchanges. By having meetings so often as frequently to be dull, Hagerty spared Ike the nasty confrontations that occasionally occurred with other Presidents.

Hagerty paid for his expertise and skill with seven-day weeks, eighteen-hour days and ulcers. It was with relief that he retired from managing politicians and accepted a job managing reporters, of whom I was to become one.

CHAPTER FIFTY-FOUR

Regent's Park upon Potomac

I have often wondered—silently so she would not hear me—what would have happened had the trend of wives working outside the home taken place a couple of decades earlier and affected Bennie. It is certain that she would have been a mighty executive and made her firms successful. She knew instinctively how to make things happen. At one sorry time in my life I acquired a television agent to represent me, and I was very unhappy with him. To alleviate my irritation I persuaded Bennie, who had long been my agent for books and lectures, to take over from him and negotiate my TV contracts, too. My salary doubled in the ensuing year. When we began to be concerned about approaching age, she drew on her background in economics and learned investment. We had the unusual experience of investment consultants phoning her for advice. Whatever misfortunes beset me, I have always felt that I was overcompensated by having as lover and bedmate a sweetheart who could have made a success of the aforementioned Edsel. Now what she missed most was her London home on Regent's Park, and what she wanted most was a replacement for it. She got it.

She arrived in America two months after I did; the kids followed, transshipped via grandparents in Denmark, two months after that. We found a temporary place on N Street. It happened to be located just across the street from the Georgetown home of young Senator John F. Kennedy, whom I met casually. (I am breathtaken now at remembering how casually.) One day a week Bennie and I went house-hunting together; six days a week she went alone. When we were about to bid on a Georgetown house we could not afford and did not really want, we were led to another, just outside D.C. in Maryland. It was an old house on a bluff overlooking the Potomac, built a century before as a summer home for Mr. Stilson Hutchins. He was a high roller who had founded *The Washington Post* and speculated in real estate. His name may be seen at the base of statues of Ben Franklin and Daniel Webster on Pennsylvania Avenue, where the inscriptions read, "Gift of Stilson Hutchins." On some wooded acres of the many he owned in the area, he built this plain three-story clapboard house. It was stuccoed over in the 1930s by a new owner. In WW II most of the neighboring farmland was taken over by the Army to build a plant to produce maps for all our armies everywhere. The five acres around the house were left undeveloped, being too irregular and steep to build on. Now it was offered cheap and we bought it.

The place was not a wreck but was getting there: listing to one side, with a leaking basement and all badly in need of repair. The grounds were mostly jungle and weeds, with ropes of poison ivy predominating. Benn had the downside jacked up and had steel beams put in place, and found a man immune to poison ivy to dig out the roots. About half of the acreage was seeded with grass, but the dense rim of jungle was kept; nobody knew the house was there, and we found that an advantage. Then, from a folder she had brought, out came the Regency blueprints of the home she loved in London. Over years, building only in recessions when labor and materials were cheap, going out herself in a station wagon to recruit heavy lifting labor, hiring trucks to visit demolition sites to salvage old brick for a patio, discovering a rural miller in a crossroads called Paris, Virginia, who did detail work on churches and getting him to mill the paneling and moldings for her house—in a few years, there it was, her home from Regent's Park, London, now overlooking the scenic Potomac River near Washington, a country house in the city, as she still likes to define it.

The attachment of the Regency addition to the old house was done so cleverly by Shirley Kennard, our architect, that from the inside it all looked like one unit. The high-ceilinged drawing room was nothing short of magnificent. Walter Lippmann walked in one night before dinner, looked around and exclaimed, "This is the most beautiful room in Washington!" A few years later, Charles Colson, President Nixon's White House lawyer who was later sentenced to a term in prison for his role in Watergate, walked in and exclaimed the same thing. A television producer took a look at it and begged to produce a program in it. Reluctantly, Bennie agreed. Some furniture was moved out, our long dining-room table was moved in, twelve reporters were placed around it and a year-end discussion program was done live. So successful was it that a year later we had another like it. (Apropos of nothing, I recall that one of the reporters who participated was Louis Rukeyser, looking very uncomfortable with the format. Later, Lou found a format he liked and launched the hugely successful *Wall Street Week* on public television.)

At the end of the drawing room a study for me was created with huge sliding doors to shut it off and soundproof it when I wished. I felt far beneath my surroundings, but after a while I managed to adjust. My English desk is coeval with the American Constitution, made in 1789. I came to enjoy working at it and looking out occasionally at the riverine source of the Constitution: At a conference about where in the Potomac to draw the border between Virginia and Maryland, delegates decided to call a second conference of all the states to meet in Philadelphia and talk over the larger issues of confederation.

I am not sure what life would have been like had my lover chosen a career of her own. But I am sure that I would not have been able to take on the work load I assumed. I prepared a daily TV commentary and a weekly, longer radio one. I did special programs like the aforementioned "Where We Stand." As a result of its success, CBS arranged a series of discussion programs entitled *The Great Challenge,* with eminent cognoscenti like Reinhold Niebuhr and Arnold Toynbee; strategic thinkers like the new bright light, Henry Kissinger; brand-new politicos like the freshly elected governor of New York, Nelson Rockefeller, and provocative economists like Robert Heilbroner. I was moderator of all of these programs, and had to do a great deal of preparatory work to be able to steer and discipline the conversations. I appeared frequently on CBS's Sunday interview program, *Face the Nation.* Soon a new series of in-depth documentary programs was initiated under the title of *CBS Reports,* done mainly by Murrow and me. On top of these, there were occasional spur-of-the-moment special programs like one pulled together overnight to celebrate the addition of Alaska and Hawaii as states of the Union. In retrospect I am mystified both by how I managed all this and by why CBS saw fit to assign a virtual newcomer in television to all this exposure.

Newspapers that occasionally commented on various branches of this output generally gave me passing marks. One decidedly did not. In *The New York Herald Tribune*, literary critic Diana Trilling gave me a lecture that made my head spin. Of my style of moderating, or chairing, discussions she said I was an accomplished "avoider or smoother-over of differences. . . . Let one of the discussants so much as intimate a fresh idea or engage another of the panelists in controversy and there is Mr. Smith, quick on the switch, shunting the discussion into more neutral territory. The result of Mr. Smith's tactful control is that no one on his program ever manages to say anything that will lead . . . the audience to considerations other than those already established. . . ." I wrote Ms. Trilling a note saying I was new in the picture medium and still learning, and would truly be much obliged if she could cite me specifics; but I received no answer. I make a point of this because the problem that began to emerge in my new career in TV was diametrically the opposite. I got notices from upstairs that I was engaging in too much controversy and had better watch my words.

The sheer quantity of my appearances had the effect of throwing me into brief, unpremeditated and unsought competition with a rising star of the network, my fellow UP alumnus, Walter Cronkite. A career in the electronic media was not for Walter, as it was for many of the rest of us, accidental. He charged into broadcasting by his own decision and with will and purpose, loving it as I feared it. Though a prototypical news reporter, he willingly did anything that would give him time on the air. His first large role was in a fictional program called *You Are There*, a drama of historical events like the death of Socrates, in which Walter appeared as a reporter explaining such things as the workings of hemlock. For years, CBS tried to produce a morning show to compete with NBC's famous *Today* show. Jack Paar, Dick Van Dyke and Will Rogers, Jr., were all tried, and each failed before going on to success in other pursuits. At one point, Walter gave it a whirl. As his producer remarked, a funny thing happened to Walter on the way to being funny. Actually he possessed the traits needed, in theory, for the role of host—the charm of a good fellow and a rare sense of humor. But there was a curse on the idea, and he was turned back toward news.

In our factual realm he was a natural, preferring the freedom of ad-libbing to reading his remarks from a teleprompter (Murrow hated teleprompters too and memorized his lines, never being as good at ad-libbing as Walter was). But freely talking uses more time than reading from a text, so his practice threw the timing of news programs out of step, and he had to surrender to the instrument known as the idiot machine. Either way he had a cornball delivery, swinging his emphasis up, down and around like a ride on a roller coaster.

That, however, seemed to add to the effect of his outgoing personality and make him, as the saying went, comfortable as an old shoe to the public. He loved to do television, his co-workers liked to work with him, viewers were at ease with him, he did not cause executives any worry and—most marvelous of traits—sponsors liked to sponsor him.

I had an amusing encounter with Cronkite while covering the 1958 off-year elections in a barnlike studio. I was assigned to the Southern state boards. Walter phoned in and told Sig Mickelson, the boss, that his throat was sore and he might not make it. Mickelson called me off the Southern boards and told me to sit in the anchor chair and get accustomed to the visual displays. Then he phoned Cronkite and told him it was all right, and I would do the anchoring. Within fifteen minutes Walter was in the studio sucking on cough drops and sending me back to the Southern boards. Murrow told me that as author of his recovery I should send him a doctor's bill.

CHAPTER FIFTY-FIVE

Decline and Rise

Ever since Paul White took the medium away from announcers and entrusted it to reporters, CBS bestrode the narrow world of electronic news like a colossus, and Murrow bestrode CBS. As the 1950s turned into the 1960s, the fortunes of both CBS News and Murrow suffered partial eclipses.

Murrow was tired and dispirited. He read his nightly radio news broadcast listlessly, rarely doing any writing for it himself. He was secretly less than proud of his weekly TV program, *Person to Person,* in which he interviewed celebrities—Marilyn Monroe, Nat King Cole, Senator Kennedy and his pretty wife, anybody famous—in their homes while he sat in the studio. He was not good at the small talk it required, and the Puritan who lodged in the back of his cranium scolded him for its triviality, high ratings and immense profitability. His own fulfilling effort, the weekly TV documentary, *See It Now,* created a small army of acerbic enemies led by the columnists Westbrook Pegler and Jack O'Brian, whose constant sniping at the man they called Egbert Roscoe Murrow took its toll on nerves. His controversies caused aches of head, heart and stomach up and down CBS's executive table of organization, as well as in

Murrow himself. One day he incautiously admitted to Paley that he felt unbearable pressure. His remark coincided with the sponsor's dropping financial support for *See It Now*. Bill Paley used the occasion to justify killing the troublemaking program for good. An angered Murrow then made a bitter speech, harshly critical of the rulers of the medium, at a convention of the Radio and Television News Directors. With tension near the breaking point, Ed wisely asked for and was given a sabbatical year to travel and sort himself out. Then, unwisely, he began to fracture his sabbatical to do TV programs from a distance with Fred Friendly. He ended the fragmented sabbatical two months early and returned to the grind in New York, his spirit unrested.

Murrow's problem, soon to become more devastating to me than to him, was his illusion that CBS was like *The New York Times* or any other newspaper; that it was mainly a medium for informing the public. In reality, CBS was an entertainment business, operated primarily to make and expand a profit. To achieve that end, it needed to appeal not only to the right-minded people Murrow pleased but also to wrong-minded people; they all bought things advertised on CBS. Murrow saw Paley as a good friend who would sacrifice in favor of the true and the good. Actually, Paley was a pretty typical big businessman who would allow Murrow a little extra leeway but would not let any newsman damage his business for any purpose whatever.

The series of high-budget documentaries was resumed after an interval, and Fred Friendly was the producer as before. But they were titled *CBS Reports* to indicate they were an all-CBS product and not exclusively Murrow's. Of the reporters assigned to share them with Ed, I did most.

Meanwhile, competition was coming at CBS from without. The story is told, true or not, that David Sarnoff, the legendary founder and ruler of NBC was invited to an Overseas Press Club awards banquet. With rising embarassment, he watched a parade of CBS reporters to the microphone to receive the bulk of the awards. He is said to have called in William MacAndrew of his News Department the next day and told him, in effect, you provide what it takes to beat the bastards; I will provide the money.

In one of many tries to match CBS and Murrow, NBC hired as its anchorman handsome, well-spoken Chet Huntley, a West Coast broadcaster who cultivated the Murrow manner but lacked the Murrow effect. It seemed another failure, until the network happened upon a remarkable exercise in chemistry. NBC's Washington office had hired a young print reporter named David Brinkley (from UP, where else?) to write news for others to read on the air. Brinkley proved approximately perfect at writing for radio, in short and perfectly shaped sentences that came out with a kind of pop, like an expert hammer driving a nail into a soft pine board just right in a single blow. Applied with a rare sense of humor, his artistry was something really new, a big deviation from the all-knowing oracular delivery that was standard in American electronic journalism. When this new creature was eventually allowed to appear on TV, he was noted for a unique twinkle in his eye that made the day brighter.

At the political conventions of 1956, Brinkley was placed at the anchor desk with Huntley, and magic occurred. TV critics noted it first, Jack Gould of *The New York Times* writing, "A quiet southerner with a dry wit and a heaven-sent appreciation of brevity has stolen the television limelight." Critics converted the public. Harry Flannery, once my boss in Berlin, told me, "I felt I was downright disloyal switching to NBC, but I had to see what I was missing." He didn't switch back to CBS.

The Huntley-Brinkley team was then assigned to NBC's daily news program and after a while shoved CBS out of top place in that prestigious slot. The annual flood of awards that used to go almost automatically to CBS found a new course to NBC. A joke circulated at CBS that Paley was prepared to offer a fortune to Brinkley to come over to CBS, just so Paley could have the pleasure of firing him. Several years passed before CBS, with Cronkite replacing Douglas Edwards, again rose to the top.

I recall feeling somewhat guilty that, while my mentor and my network were struggling through a time of troubles, I was enjoying my work for both immensely. I had made the transition to television with an ease that wholly surprised me. Rich assignments flowed my way. The very best involved escorting Carl Sandburg over the battlefield at Gettysburg for a week with cameras and microphones recording our movements and words, and Friendly directing. Like many lesser humans Carl liked to be admired, and admiration for him oozed from all my pores. I showed him the first volume of his biography of Lincoln that I had long ago had bound in beautiful morocco leather with gold toolings and bade him inscribe it. He declared it was the finest raiment his work had ever been clothed in. After that he was putty in my hands. Friendly fashioned the result into a highly successful, often-rebroadcast documentary. Later we did the same with Lincoln's prairie years—Carl and me walking and talking all over Lincoln country in Illinois.

I was assigned to do deathbed interviews with Dr. Tom Dooley, a young physician who worked among back-jungle peasants of Southeast Asia until he developed cancer and was brought home too late for hopeful treatment. It was harrowing having to watch this young figure shrink and decay before my eyes. When asked to do the same with Dr. Leo Szilard, I was filled with dread. Szilard was the Hungarian physicist who induced Einstein to send the famous letter to FDR that led to the creation of the atomic bomb. Though dying of cancer in a New York hospital, he was eloquent before our cameras. A few weeks later we had a second talk and he appeared stronger and was more eloquent. Weeks later at our third meeting he walked in the corridors in his robe. The fourth time I met him was in my home in Washington, where he, hale and hearty, was our dinner guest.

It was a joy getting Walter Lippmann in front of cameras for his first time. He would not go to a studio, so the interview was done in our home. It was so successful that he agreed to make it an annual event. I was even more thrilled to sit down with the brilliant Robert Oppenheimer, father of the dreadful bomb, in his office at the Advanced Studies Institute in Princeton, but the experience nearly destroyed me. He was still suffering from the controversy that led to the removal of his security clearance on false suspicion of disloyalty. This thin nervous figure with large expressive eyes gave answers even to questions about ordinary things that were poetic. It was no effort; he could express himself no other way. Afterward, back in the cutting room in New York, inserting the talk into the "Where We Stand" documentary, I received a call from Mickelson telling me that he had orders not to let the interview be aired. I feared that the quitting issue that had long worried me had arrived. I told the boss I did not think I could accept the decision. Cronkite, who shared the anchoring of the program, called and said he wanted to be identified with any decision I made, which was courageous beyond call. The tension was broken by a call from Oppenheimer in Princeton. He had heard about the dispute and had reconsidered. He said I was no longer in charge, and neither were the bosses at CBS; he was ordering that the interview not be used and would take legal action if he was not obeyed. I was not happy about it, but could not insist on using an interview to which both CBS and the interviewee were opposed.

Another interview had the possibility of being controversial but turned out instead to be hilarious and a considerable popular success. The subject was my namesake, Congressman Howard W. Smith of Virginia, Chairman of the House Rules Committee, executioner of every Civil Rights bill submitted to Congress. He was eighty-two years of age, proud of representing the district that had produced five Presidents, tall, thin, humorous, and moved one gangling part at a time, like a long puppet linked together by strings. To my surprise he agreed to a long, thorough interview in his office in front of cameras. His face was gaunt, his eyes peered owlishly over glasses, and he smoked a big black cigar throughout. He made me think of a figure in Disney's cartoon film of *Alice in Wonderland*—the caterpillar seated on a mushroom, puffing billows of smoke from a hookah. He insisted on calling me "Cousin Howard" and on my addressing him as "Judge Smith." His views were outrageous and about to be outdated, but he defused rage by being flat outright frank about it. I quoted to him from a newspaper saying Congressman Howard Smith of Virginia was "the most negative and destructive obstacle to Civil Rights in the nation." He took a long draw on his cigar, thought a moment, exhaled a cloud of smoke toward the ceiling, then looked at me and said, "That's about right." And so it went. I titled the hour "The Keeper of the Rules." Among the many reactions to the program was a telegram from a conservative Virginian saying, "What this country needs is more Howard W. Smiths and fewer Howard K. Smiths." We framed it and sent it to him. But demographics were transforming his constituency from a rural district into the suburbs of Washington. When Lyndon Johnson got Negroes the vote, the old Judge was dismissed by an electorate that before long would elect its first Black Governor.

Documentaries were rich experiences in those days. But for a newsman nothing competes with the busy-ness of doing today's news today—with, as the saying goes, writing a rough first draft of history. And of all breaking stories, none compares with an election campaign. In 1948 I was allowed to come home from London to spend several weeks covering the Democratic and Republican conventions, both in Philadelphia, preludes to the biggest upset ever, by Truman over Dewey. Likewise I was back to cover the campaigns of Eisenhower and Stevenson in 1952. In 1956 I was busy with the twin crises abroad, but that was a dull campaign year anyhow. Now I was settled in America for the 1960 campaign.

Early in the year it threatened to be a dud: Vice President Nixon against whomever of the six leading Democrat prospects got the party's nomination. The commonest view was that "they looked like a lot of Vice Presidents with not a President among them." In fact, three of them (Kennedy, Johnson and Nixon) would become President and a fourth (Hubert Humphrey) would come within a hair of it. All of the three who made it would prove unusually gifted, but all were tragic, interrupted figures.

After a knock-down, drag-out, partly bought-up primary season, young John Kennedy went to the new Forum in Los Angeles with far and away the most delegate votes. There he made short shrift of a challenge from the Senate majority leader and until then number one Democrat in the nation, Lyndon Johnson of Texas. Kennedy then took the one step without which he could not have been elected: he induced Johnson to run as his Vice Presidential candidate. Two weeks later in Chicago Richard Nixon was coronated by the Republicans.

Broadcasting from Los Angeles, I said of the Democrat: "Whatever Mr. Kennedy's numerous virtues, he makes the impression of being a hard and cold young man." Broadcasting from Chicago I said of the Republican:

Some commentators have made something of the point that Nixon displayed a humility before the world's greatest office which Kennedy did not. While the young Democrat announced with cocksureness to his convention not that he would *try* to, but that he simply *would,* be worthy of their trust, Mr. Nixon expressed a conventional awe and uncertainty at the prospect of taking up the lease on the White House. The impression is deceptive. It is an acquired mannerism from observing the habits of the leading humility-displayer of all time, President Eisenhower. As one privileged to watch the Vice President from close up many times, I am serenely doubtless in the view that Mr. Nixon approaches the Presidency as Mr. Kennedy does—with a sense that the job was made for him, and that he knows what to do with it, and is eager to begin doing it as soon as possible, and that he will be a howling success at it.

In the ardent contest that followed, the networks offered their services, and the two young champions agreed to a debate, the first ever between Presidential candidates. CBS was the first of three networks to be host, Chicago the place, and I was chosen by CBS to be moderator.

Coming down in the hotel elevator that morning, I met Pierre Salinger, Kennedy's Press Chief. He said to me, "Are you ready for tonight's bout?" I said, "I don't matter; what matters is, is your man ready?" "Ready?" he said. "He's been up shadow-boxing since daybreak."

And so it seemed, an hour before the debate, when the two came into the studio. It was apparent to Nixon that he had made a mistake. He should not have agreed to debate. He was the famous Vice President who had bested Khrushchev in debate in Moscow, had been decorated by heads of state, had starred in many documentaries including some I had done. Kennedy at that time was less well known. In this one encounter Nixon would elevate Kennedy to his level of prominence. Nixon had been in the hospital and was pale. I offered a makeup expert, but he refused and allowed an aide merely to dust a little powder on his face, which made him paler. He was downcast; he knew it was a mistake.

Kennedy was the opposite. He entered the studio looking like a young athlete come to receive his wreath of laurel. Addison's disease made him look bronzed. He was no longer the skinny boyish figure in photos taken of him with me when we had a talk in his office earlier that year. Steroids, taken for back pain, had caused him to fill out to an attractive manliness.

Having the two appear live, side by side, answering the same questions, was a welcome innovation. But it was not much of a debate. Because the reporters on the panel were not allowed to pose follow-up questions, both candidates shamelessly slid by questions rather than answering them. I, sitting modestly and as inconspicuously as possible between them, thought Nixon was marginally better. But when I saw a replay later, it was clear that the handsome, confident Kennedy was victor. He later told me he won the election that night.

In the first year of the Kennedy Administration, my career at CBS reached a peak. I was appointed Chief Washington Correspondent, and thus was the first (and so far, only) reporter to have served in both of the network's two highest reporting positions: chief abroad, and chief of main office at home. I assumed the title with misgivings. Just on the other side of peaks are declivities, and there were some indications that this one could be precipitous.

CHAPTER FIFTY-SIX

The Flight of the Yo-yo

Most of my assignments ranged from satisfying to outright joyous. But problems began to arise early on over the principal one, the one I had been brought home to do. A daily commentary for television was something entirely new to the medium and proved very difficult to write. Saying something fresh and of interest to an audience every day, and doing it within a single minute, taxed my ingenuity, skill and imagination as well as my store of information. For the first year, the script editors in Washington were tolerant of my efforts. But then they began to carve up my little essays in what seemed to be an arbitrary way and were impatient of my arguments. One day they left a script so mangled that it could not be used, and I blew my top. Then they confessed that they had been put under severe pressure by New York to be harder on me. They were told that they were letting me "get away with murder" in violation of the company's policy of objectivity.

The pressure was coming from Richard Salant, a corporate vice president who had become Dr. Stanton's troubleshooter and, in that capacity, the overseer of my scripts. Salant was a thin young man with a face that appeared to have been carved by the artist who made Charlie McCarthy. He was a lawyer who did not seem to like law nearly as much as he did the news business he had stumbled into. We engaged in endless conversations and arguments over the nature of commentary and news analysis, yet never, even after the end, lost friendship. When in time he became president of CBS News, I was proud to have given him, in the course of our interminable debates, most of the instruction he had in the craft.

He said that I was uttering personal and partisan opinions on issues. I said that, indeed, I was making judgments on issues; one couldn't write one's name without making a judgment, and judging is by definition personal. My assignment, I said, was to provide a gloss on current events, give a little depth, another dimension to some news story that was necessarily two-dimensional. My purpose, I said, was to make the viewer say, "That's interesting," or "I hadn't thought of it that way." To get that reaction, I said, I had to make a point, come to a conclusion, if I was to interest a preoccupied and indifferent TV audience at dinnertime; no Swiss editorial conclusions like "time will tell" or "this will bear watching" will capture or hold their attention. I said that I was making a special effort not to inflame, but I had to arrive at some kind of conclusion to achieve my purpose. CBS's mail from listeners indicated I was succeeding.

I told Salant the story of the Emperor of Japan, who was trained to avoid personal judgments. General MacArthur sought to get him into conversation, but it was heavy going. At one point the General motioned to the window and said, "It's a nice day." The Emperor looked at the window, thought a moment, then said, "It's a day." That, I suggested to Salant, is what my commentaries would sound like if you enforce your complaints.

The argument against me was not always strictly honest. Once Salant phoned from New York and told me the Federal Communications Commission was furious at my breaches of objectivity. He said the FCC was inundated with complaints about me. He did not know that the FCC's new Commissioner, Newton Minow, and its Chief Legal Counsel, Ash Bryant, were friends of mine. I called Bryant, who said they received routine complaints about everything on the air but no particular ones about me. Minow told me he was surprised at Salant's complaint; Minow had thought it a good idea to have a staff commentator and wondered why the other nets did not copy (they did after awhile). I phoned Salant about my conversations with officials, and he hit the roof. He told me I was unauthorized to deal with officials who regulated our business; that was strictly the province of executives. It reflected his ignorance of journalism. I also think he was embarrassed by being caught in a fib.

In this endless argument I knew one thing that Salant had not yet begun to comprehend. It was the same thing Murrow had trouble with. Our dispute was due to the basic, unbudging fact that CBS was not primarily a medium for informing the public but an entertainment business hostile to anything that endangered its profitability. Before me, CBS newsmen H. V. Kaltenborn, Elmer Davis and now E. R. Murrow had run up against this contradiction. I was not as big as they and thus had to face the fact that our argument was beyond resolution if I remained in the commenting business. Later Don Hewitt would invent the program *60 Minutes* and restore strong judgment to news on CBS, principally by exposing individual misdeeds victimizing individuals, which everyone could agree were abominable. But for now I had to deal with those giant, nation-splitting matters that were sure to make half the audience mad.

After about a year and a half, Mickelson, still head of news, came down to Washington for a chat. He said the complaints about me upstairs were piling up. I took the initiative and suggested to him that maybe I had better end this experiment in commentary. He was relieved; he said that was in fact what he had come to say to me. So I disappeared from the evening news program. A couple of newspapermen assigned to be TV critics phoned to ask what had happened. I made light of it and remarked only that my type of contribution had no suitable place on a fifteen-minute TV report.

In years to come, CBS contended that our breach was due not to CBS and its standards of objectivity, but to me and the confrontational way I chose to write comments. Much later, Eric Sevareid was induced to take up the daily news comment on what had become the Cronkite evening news program, and it worked.

In a book written still later, a respected author helped CBS make the point. David Halberstam in *The Powers That Be* wrote:

> Both Howard Smith and Eric Sevareid had already by the late fifties run into similar problems of translating their talents and styles [to TV]. Both of them were superstars, and they were not just reporters, they were commentators, and their commentary was fine for a time, particularly when it came from foreign countries, but as they came home, the negative pressures had increased. Sevareid angered the brass by his regular criticism of [John Foster Dulles], but for a long time he was overseas [a factual error: Sevareid had remained in Washington; it was I who had remained overseas], so there was not a great problem. But Smith had been in constant troubles, there was a lot of blue-penciling of his copy when he had come back to Washington, and the problems he caused [because I, on TV, reached ten times the audience Sevareid did on radio] were far greater than those caused by Sevareid. Part of it, friends thought, was the difference in style. Sevareid was a more subtle writer, perhaps more deft, and he learned to make fierce points without seeming to be fierce, whereas Smith was a more forceful writer, using more sharp, straight, declarative setences, and very direct, and there was never any mistake about what he was saying or how he was saying it.

I will grant Halberstam only one thing. Eric was a fine writer, probably better than I. But a fair comparison must note that the evening news program was lengthened from fifteen minutes to thirty, so he was allowed more than twice the time slot I had. That permits somewhat more graceful writing and the softening of judgments with nuances. And because CBS had been criticized for terminating me, CBS's editors were allowed to go rather easier on their censoring of Eric. And finally Eric, having been put in the crisis seat before and faced with extinction by Paley, worked diligently to temper his messages. The name Eric Everyside was applied by critics. When he finished a commentary, it was often hard to tell where the issue had been left. In my commentaries there was no doubt. But what he had said was said beautifully, which covered a little sinning against CBS's notion of objectivity.

The inherent flaw of the CBS policy became clearer in the fate of the documentary programs of the time. As the policy was clamped down, the documentaries became less pointed and less interesting, and audiences fell away. Soon they were nearly extinct on network television and were rescued only when public television took over the genre and injected life into it. One of the last CBS documentaries to make a strong point was one done by Murrow and me, to be described in the next chapter.

I retained my Sunday radio commentary and still worked on documentaries and moderated panel programs. But I felt diminished, almost idled, by the termination of my daily stresspoint. Soon a generous step was taken to elevate my sunken spirits—the "yo-yo effect," someone called it. It was a sign that CBS wanted to keep me, but wanted me to lay off controversy, that I was appointed Chief Washington Correspondent when Sevareid moved to Europe. But something new was added: I also had to be Washington Bureau Manager. I think it may have been a hint to me to move out of reporting and seek a future on the managing side. Whatever the underlying purpose, it died soon after in a crunch too big to allow our dispute to be contained.

CHAPTER FIFTY-SEVEN

The Beginning of the End

John Kennedy became President of a country that was near the climax of one of the two or three most formative crises of its history. The Civil Rights Revolution, sparked by a Supreme Court ruling, and fanned by an Alabama preacher, was aflame. Resistance to the Court's ruling was rising all over the South. Lucky the Northern states, which were rescued from revealing their own bigotry by the South's fierce resolve to hold onto center stage. No place was quite as stubborn as the industrial metropolis of Birmingham, Alabama. *The New York Times's* Harrison Salisbury, winner of the Pulitzer and most other reporting prizes, came out of the city and wrote a series of articles saying Birmingham was a home of White terror. He wrote, "Every inch of middle ground has been fragmented by the emotional dynamite of racism, enforced by the whip, the razor, the gun, the bomb, the torch, the club, the mob, the police and many branches of the state's apparatus." White leaders of the city protested that his report was false. The *Birmingham News* wrote, "There is little race hatred here. . . . This Birmingham of ours is a lovely place. It is a city in which fear does not abide. What Harrison Salisbury reported, we all should know, is in substance wrong." Ed Murrow and a producer and a couple of camera crews went down to see who was right and to do a documentary program to be titled "Who Speaks for Birmingham?"

Meanwhile, at CBS Sig Mickelson and his News Director John Day were fired. Sig had begun at ground zero and built a very good worldwide television news organization. He had not yet been able to get Cronkite named anchorman of the evening news in place of Douglas Edwards, which would begin a new day at CBS, but he would later be credited as "the man who invented Walter Cronkite." His sin was that CBS News lost its lead to NBC on his watch. Salant was appointed to replace him.

Salant appointed Blair Clark, a CBS reporter of good repute, to be his news director. Clark had been a classmate of Kennedy's at Harvard and a friend of mine from his days as Paris correspondent for CBS. One day in his new position Clark visited me in Washington, and we sat in my tiny office chatting. The phone rang. It was the White House; the new President wanted to talk to Blair. I handed him the phone and left the room. Two other versions of this encounter have been printed since then, but this is what Clark said to me after the call: Kennedy was down to three names in his hunt for Director of the

U.S. Information Agency: the recent president of NBC, Pat Weaver; the fellow who moderated his election-winning debate (namely, me); and Murrow. Clark said, "I hope you are not offended; I recommended Murrow." I agreed that Murrow was far and away the best choice.

Later that day Murrow phoned me from Birmingham and arranged for us to meet in Washington the next day. He told me that Kennedy had offered him the post and he was inclined to accept. I had long felt that Murrow was terminally sick of CBS and needed to start a new and different life somewhere. This was as good a new beginning as any, and I said so. Moreover his assignment in Birmingham, I said, was likely to end up in another of those stomach-aching brawls he didn't want. He had only one doubt. "If I take the job, I will have to eat an awful lot of words I have spoken," he said, referring to his irrational expressions of dislike of "that boy in the White House," as he had put it. I told him he had spoken those words only in private, notably to Lippmann and me at a lunch. I added, "Eating one's words is a regular diet here in Washington. You develop a taste for them." I recited for him the Politician's Prayer: "Oh, Lord, make my words sweet and crunchy, 'cause I'll probably have to eat them after the election." He went on to New York and conferred with Paley, then phoned me and said, "I am going to do it. But you have to go to Birmingham and do that documentary. Remember, you recommended this."

I knew Birmingham pretty well from track meets at Legion Field. It fit the famous formula as a place "of Northern charm and Southern efficiency." It grew up after the Civil War as a mining and steelmaking city, lacking the lavender-and-lace charm of antebellum traditions. More than Louisiana and its oil industry, Birmingham and steel suffered from absentee ownership. Promising young executives from Pittsburgh or New York were sent down to make a mark running the mills, then brought back north when they had done so. A civic-minded upper-middle class was late in growing, and when it did emerge, it lived in the lovely suburbs to keep its distance from the city of Black and White labor. In a mining city there was considerable trained skill at using dynamite, and it was often used when a Black sought to move into a house in a better, White neighborhood. Long before the Civil Rights Revolution, it was known as the "most segregated city in the South" and occasionally nicknamed "Bombingham."

The producer assigned to the job was one of the very best, David Lowe, who had produced and done much of the writing for Murrow's famous "Harvest of Shame" documentary about the plight of migrant workers. We had worked together a year or so earlier, in the ruins of Babylon in Iraq, on a program about the world water shortage. Lowe now summed up our mission, "You know how this report is going to turn out. However balanced we try to keep it, the Establishment is going to look awful because its position is awful.

So we have got to work harder than ever to give it a form of balance." And he outlined a series of ten or fifteen interviews with local notables who believed the city had been maligned, and a like number who disagreed, knowing full well that the latter would make the stronger impression no matter what he did.

And so it turned out. The number one champion of rights, the Black minister Fred Shuttlesworth, by himself, outshone the whole array of city defenders. Shuttlesworth was born in rural Alabama and worked at heavy labor until, as a wiry, high-spirited youth, he discovered he had the gift of eloquence and a special, private command from the Lord Himself to serve his people. He used to go from one small town to another, preaching sometimes five times a day, until he got his own church in Selma. When the Civil Rights movement became serious, Governor John Patterson passed laws—unconstitutional as all hell—virtually dissolving the National Association for the Advancement of Colored People in the state. Shuttlesworth, having now become pastor of the Bethel Baptist Church in Birmingham, announced that he was going to form his own rights organization just for the city of Birmingham. A worried fellow preacher told Fred that he had received a visitation from the Lord telling him to call off the founding meeting of the new organization. Fred said, "When did the Lord start sending messages through you? The Lord has told me to call it on." And on it went. His home and church were bombed. He was beaten up on the street. Alas for our mission to establish a phony balance, there was film of both incidents, which made his case better than words.

The interview I most wanted but could not get was with the city's Police Commissioner, Eugene Connor, nicknamed "Bull" because of his sizable voice. A former radio announcer of baseball games, Connor was the mighty heart of resistance to racial equality. His job was the dominant one in city government, embracing not only the police but the fire department, the health department and the public library, plus several other functions. When I approached him he had just been reelected to a sixth term as the municipal official Whites could count on to keep Blacks in their place. He was smart enough to know that nothing would damage his cause more than a personal appearance on national TV. He turned me down flat and even refused to let me into his office to chat off-camera.

One day when we had nearly finished our filming and were having lunch in a restaurant, I was called away to a phone. The caller was a leader of the local Ku Klux Klan chapter who wanted to tell me he had decided to refuse my request for an interview, but also to tell me that if I wanted to see some action I should be at the Greyhound Bus Terminal the next day. I remembered that the next day, Mother's Day, the first Freedom Riders were scheduled to come into Birmingham by bus. The Supreme Court had issued a ruling desegregating facilities—restaurants, toilets, waiting rooms—in bus stations; but the ruling was ignored in the South, so a small corps of Blacks and Whites was formed to take a bus ride through the South to use those facilities and bring attention to the violations. Birmingham was the next stop.

Next day we were at the Greyhound station early. We kept our camera equipment near but packed in the station wagon lest the gathering crowd should decide to harm the expensive stuff. By noon we estimated that a hundred young Whites were loitering in and around the station—a few scrawny ones, but most composed of fat-cushioned beef. As the expected arrival time came and went, I engaged a couple of them in conversation. I got a clear impression that this was a highly planned operation by Klansmen without sheets, with the full cooperation of Bull Connor, whose City Hall Police Headquarters stood just across the street.

All at once, in midafternoon, policemen began moving from the street into the basement of the Police HQ—individuals and men in twos, and police cars. Within five minutes there were no police to be seen anywhere. Then came a shout from a man in the street relayed into the station: the bus was arriving not here but at the Trailways bus station four blocks away. I called to David to mobilize his slightly strayed crew and follow in the station wagon, and I ran down the street, not as fast as I had run in the Legion stadium but as close to it as a middle-aged scrivener could approximate.

The scene at the Trailways station was horrifying. The riders were being dragged from the bus into the station. In a corridor I entered they were being beaten with bicycle chains and blackjacks and steel knucks. When they fell they were kicked mercilessly, the scrotum being the favored target, and pounded with baseball bats. One man made his way to the waiting room still vertical, but his head was a red mass of blood. Another was on all fours and could not get up. I helped the bloody one outside to the curb and tried to hail a taxi to get him to a hospital, but the only taxi that slowed down sped away after the driver saw the injured man's bloody countenance. I ran up the street a ways to get David and his car. But when I returned to the curb, a Black taxi driver had picked up the victim and driven him away. I went back to the waiting room, but a local reporter who had been roughed up told me they were out to "get the CBS guy." So I went outside. At that point I saw a kind of gang foreman look at his watch and go inside the station shouting that time was up. A string of empty cars had been parked outside. The Klansmen jumped into them, and all took off. Not a minute later policemen appeared and began questioning bystanders. The Klan had obviously by prior arrangement been given fifteen minutes to have the streets and the riders to itself. At the end of that time not a violator was to be found.

Three Black youths, bleeding and uncared for, remained outside the station. We piled them into our station wagon and took them to our motel for on-camera interviews. They entered unseen through a side door. While lights and cameras were being set up in David's room I went to my room, phoned CBS Radio in New York and offered to report. I broadcast then and every hour thereafter for the rest of the afternoon. *The New York Times* published the text of one of my broadcasts on the front page as an eyewitness account; I was the only national reporter present. When the riders' interviews were done, they were taken to Fred Shuttlesworth's home; all had been given his address as a haven. I then went to the studio of CBS's Birmingham affiliate to do a spot on the Edwards TV news program. It had been set up by phone that afternoon. But when time came to broadcast, the local station was mysteriously unable to patch me through to the network. I went outside and, with the station wall as a backdrop, related to our own film camera all that had happened, in order to have a filmed record made while my impressions were fresh.

We had a busy evening. Two FBI men came to question me. David received many phoned threats to my person. I received a telegram from an angry mayor of my old hometown, Monroe, Louisiana. It said, "When are you going to do something we can be proud of?" We phoned Clark to ask that I be allowed to return to Washington. Our documentary work was pretty well done, and I could not get any broadcasts through from Birmingham. Clark was strangely cool to the request and told me to stay, the first sign I had that I might be in trouble at home as much as in Birmingham. So David found a private detective bureau and hired an armed bodyguard for me. We stayed on for a couple of days, shooting some establishing shots of places, none needing my presence. I composed a conclusion to the program, and we shot it on a hill overlooking the city. It included a famous quotation from a speech by Edmund Burke: "The only thing necessary for the triumph of evil is for good men to do nothing." At last Clark yielded to my request to return to Washington in time to do my Sunday radio commentary from there.

CHAPTER FIFTY-EIGHT

The End

Witnessing the savage beatings in Birmingham was my worst experience since the opening of the concentration camps at the end of WW II. But as a reporter

I must confess that I was rather pleased by my professional performance. I had not been on top of a big breaking story since Little Rock. Now I had given CBS a national scoop on radio and a "tell" scoop on the TV evening news, and had packed a lot of exclusive stuff onto film to make our forthcoming documentary impressive. It was the kind of achievement that would have elicited a note of congratulations from the editor on another medium. But I returned to Washington to a silence from my bosses that felt very cold. I began to realize that, far from approving, they were offended. I proceeded to write my Sunday commentary, knowing that they would become more offended.

The script almost wrote itself. I had the strange, disembodied sense of being forced by conscience to write what I knew would be unacceptable. I tried to comfort myself by recalling Martin Luther, "Here I stand. I cannot do otherwise," but the thought only deepened my sense of loneliness. Like the Civil Rights troubles inside the U.S., the Cold War across the globe was rising to one of its most threatening crises over Berlin. I opened by linking the two:

> It is a fair, if rough, rule of thumb that the great conflicts at turning points in history are generally won by the side that *deserves* to win them. This week an American of proven patriotism said to me—"When I see events like those going on in Alabama, I begin to wonder, in spite of myself, whether *we* really deserve to win the Cold War."
>
> The answer to my friend is—we *do* deserve to win the Cold War. The Attorney General, Mr. Robert Kennedy, seems about to provide evidence that the rule of barbarism in Alabama is going to be made a temporary exception to the general rule of law and order—and Justice—in America.
>
> However, it is no wonder that sensible people can have doubts. For what has been going on in Alabama is not just one more instance of racial friction. The riots have not been spontaneous outbursts of anger, but carefully planned and susceptible to having been easily prevented or stopped, had there been a wish to do so. The people involved are identifiable and well known.

And then I proceeded to the best part of the broadcast: a naming of names and a revealing of the co-planning by Connor and the Klan.

But toward the end, my commentary became flammably editorial again: "If the conclusion in the Southern mind [about whether the Supreme Court rulings are the law of the land] is genuine and not willful, then the laws of the land and the purposes of the nation need a restatement, perhaps by the one American assured of intent mass hearing at any time, the President."

I do not have a record of my conversations with my bosses, but I recall Clark phoning me the next day and saying something to the effect that "You know you are violating company policy, don't you?" and my saying, "I know, but I do not know any other way to comment on this matter," and his giving me notice that my future at the network was under reappraisal.

Meanwhile I went to New York and worked with producers Friendly and Lowe putting our documentary together. We were well apart from the CBS offices, in a workshop rented for editing and viewing film on Ninth Avenue. A *New Yorker* writer was present, preparing a profile on Fred Friendly, but he was not allowed to be present for the crucial two hours.

We had just about finished it, and a battery of lawyers and company vice presidents came to see it. At the end of the showing, as the lights went up, one of the lawyers opened the premature autopsy by saying, "Smith's quotation from Burke is straight editorial; it's out." It was too quick for me to argue, but it made me angry, and from then on I fought their every objection, justifiable or not, without letup for a long bitter hour. I came out with two spiritual medals I needed. Lowe said to me, "You were superb." And one vice president told me soon after, "You sure know how to make a case." Even with the cuts forced by the brass, we had a respectable documentary, effective enough for our Birmingham affiliate to disaffiliate from CBS, and for the City Commission of Birmingham to sue CBS for a large amount. I note that in the end they lost the suit, as was inevitable. Also, in the next year, I heard CBS correspondents reporting on events in the Civil Rights Revolution, using my quotation from Burke with no trouble from the executives. It apparently grew to become a fair comment. I remembered the old adage that it is smart to be right, but it is stupid to be right at the wrong time.

My lack of notes on this hectic, short period will not allow me to quote, but I was told by Salant that I would be given a chance to argue my case. Write it down and send it to him, and he would study it with Paley. I did so over several days and sent it. At some point after that, Clark phoned to tell me that CBS had decided to suspend me for the time being. I was to give up all assignments and not appear in the office. I accepted the order, but then, thinking it over, called him and told him that office work would pile up; might I not go into the office after hours and spend an hour fulfilling the day's managerial duties? He agreed, and I spent the next week going to work after nine P.M. and managing the office by dictaphone. I was ordered not to contact any members of the staff.

One day, Friendly phoned and in an alarming tone told me, "Don't come to New York. No matter who calls you or for whatever reason, do not come." I tried to get the reasons behind this message, but he would say no more. It was clear to me that my dispute was at the terminal stage. Salant did call and told me I was to have lunch with him and Paley and Stanton and Clark the next day.

That was an order one could not possibly disobey. As often as possible I took Bennie with me traveling. This time I was sure her presence near me would be essential, so she came and waited in the hotel room while I went to the office.

I could not help wondering at how odd and sad a climax this was to long, good relationships. I had met Paley during the war, and after it he came often on visits to London. Though I did not move anywhere near his stratospheric social circle, we met and talked from time to time. When the foreign reporters came to America for year-end meetings, he always had a lunch for us. With Stanton, relations were even more cordial. Salant was a friend, and Clark a close friend.

We five sat down to lunch in Paley's office. A casual observer witnessing the conversation over drinks and hors d'oeuvres would have assumed it was a comfortable gathering of old friends. But tension was tangible. Cordiality in small talk was somewhat excessive all around. When the plates were cleared for the entrée, Paley reached into an inside pocket and drew out my brief. He narrowed his eyes as he looked at me. Then he threw the document across the table to me. "I have heard all this junk before," he said. "If that is what you believe, you had better go somewhere else." I did not know what to say. I was tired of the subject of objective reporting, now chewed to bits in months of argument with Salant. The document was a distillation of all I had to say; there was nothing left. I had emptied my quiver.

In the personal earthquake of that day, the document was lost, but its essential point was that giving equal weight to Bull Connor and to Earl Warren and leaving it at that was equivalent to saying that truth is to be found somewhere between right and wrong, equidistant between good and evil. In the clear simplicity given to the matter by the actions of Faubus and Connor, the Civil Rights issue was not one over which reasonable minds might differ. One side was clearly constitutional, the other clearly not. I stopped short of stating the basic problem, that CBS was a business; in a crunch it needed bigoted and fair-minded listeners alike, and did not want to alienate either. At the lunch Stanton seemed taken aback when I muttered, "I can't think of anything to say that isn't in the document. I think I had better go." And I got up, pushed my chair back and left.

Theodore White, who left the Luce organization to seek a living on his own, once said to me, "They said there are disadvantages to working for a big corporation, but I don't know what they are. There is much to be said for the sheltered life, warm and cozy, while people up at the top worry about where the money is coming from." I remembered Paley's comment when Murrow got testy once, something to the effect that "while you boys are attending awards ceremonies for your latest bold thrust, it is left to me to look after the source of your livelihood, to massage the offended Southern station owners who threaten a mass disaffiliation. You give me a stomachache." Walking back to the hotel on New York streets suddenly grown cold, I could think of many things to be said for CBS and not much for me. Principle has to be its own reward, but at times like that it doesn't seem quite enough.

1961-1965

CHAPTER FIFTY-NINE

Transition

I think I feared unemployment—functionlessness—more than anything in life, more than death in war or physical pain. It was the equivalent of being useless, supernumerary, irrelevant to society, unneeded and unwanted. I knew the feeling from coming of age in a Depression and from watching a nearly functionless father. I considered it the basic cause of some social ills, for example the decay of Black American families. Jobless fathers fled from women and offspring they were unable to provide for. I left 485 Madison fearing the worst. But now, in retrospect, with the saving knowledge that there was a job in my future, I remember my spasm of unemployment as an uncommonly eventful period.

I first informed Bennie. Then, feeling that I was in over my head negotiating severance and seeking a job, I for the first time hired a professional agent to advise and represent me. It proved a big mistake. He was not very effective. Though I was at the beginning of a five-year "unbreakable" contract, was the only CBS staffer to have been Chief Foreign Correspondent and Chief Washington Correspondent and had just passed the twenty-year mark on the CBS staff, my agent was unable to get me any severance pay. It was, as Murrow described it, a shabby deal by CBS. I was given just enough notice to finish three long documentaries begun with me on camera and, therefore, needing me for completion. Incidentally, the traditional gold watch for a generation's service had been promised to me, but some underling, overeager to please the boss, canceled the order. Years later my incensed wife mentioned it to Dick Salant, and a week later—seventeen years after severance—the watch, engraved with CBS's gratitude, arrived!

The day after the break we returned to Washington, and I went to see Murrow at his awesome new address, 1776 Pennsylvania Avenue. He said, "You had one of those 'unbreakable' contracts, didn't you?" I said I had. He said, "Sue 'em. I'll swear to anything you say." As I had agreed to the breach, I had to let that one pass.

Now I had to have a job. I wondered if this might be the time to go back to my origins, newspapering. I went to see Al Friendly, editor of *The Washington Post*. He didn't think so. "I know a lot of reporters who have moved from papers to TV, but none who have come the other way. Remember that old WW I song, "How you gonna keep 'em down on the farm once they've seen Paree?"

We could find something for you. But you wouldn't be happy. Neither would we." I tried writing a column, but it paid little. Most columnists eke things out by getting on TV panel programs and by lecturing. Also, at that time columns were distributed by slow mail, so you had to soften them up in order to be sure to retain relevance for a few days. I was hopelessly spoiled writing today's news today.

For a moment, it seemed I might go right back into network reporting. My agent put my name up to NBC's news chief, Bill McAndrew. He was interested, so I paid him a visit. Afterward I got a phone call from Chet Huntley. He had heard NBC wanted to deal, and he said, "Don't let pride stand in the way of working for what used to be your opposition. We want you on NBC." I was much encouraged. But soon after, my agent stunned me with the news that McAndrew had phoned him to say the deal was off, forget about it. I phoned McAndrew to ask why. He hemmed and hawed but made one thing clear: he had been ordered from upstairs to stop negotiating with me or my representative. In those days, the networks did not hire from one another. I could not stifle the suspicion that an angry Paley had found ways to communicate with his counterpart at NBC: if you let this guy get away with flouting us, we will never have control over our staffs again.

There was one fascinating interlude. Stanley Kramer, producer and director of outstanding films (*High Noon, The Defiant Ones, None but the Brave*) had a big winner ready to go—*Judgment at Nuremberg*. He decided to have the premiere in Berlin and thought it would be appropriate to have someone produce and appear in a short documentary about the event. And who more appropriate than a reporter who had left Berlin on the last train and gone back on the first plane, and who had broadcast the Nuremberg trial on radio—and who, by happy chance, was unemployed at the moment and needed the money?

I was given money, tickets for Bennie and me to and from Berlin, a camera crew and full access to the stars. My foremost impression was how they, unarmed with a script, were terrified of the camera. Montgomery Clift squirmed in his chair throughout, ending up sitting on his neck. Judy Garland's lower lip trembled, and she continually looked about the room as if hunting for someone to protect her from my questions, which were puffballs. I sympathized with her; she was on the way back from a bad trip with alcohol. Kramer had given her a straight acting role, which she filled beautifully, thereby regaining confidence—until my camera and I came along. When Kramer came into the room, she threw her arms around him in a long grateful hug. Spencer Tracy refused to sit for an interview, but allowed me to come and chat with him privately to prove that it was not I but the camera he found objectionable. I think that getting old had saddled him with inhibitions. He held his hand near or over his mouth for much of our talk as if hiding unbecoming uppers. Anyhow, whether my effort was useful or not, *Judgment* was a great success and won several Oscars.

A prospect of going into government arose. George Ball, Deputy Secretary of State, called me in and told me Kennedy was preparing a world economic conference aiming to reduce tariffs all around and bring about a surge in world trade—the so-called Kennedy Round of talks. The State Department would be in charge, and he wanted a spokesman. He offered me the post of Assistant Secretary of State for Public Affairs to perform the role. I was powerfully tempted. I went to see Murrow and he told me "Do it. I need an ally in this fudge factory." For balance I went to see Walter Lippmann, who said, "Don't get near it. If you think corporate limitations were hard, wait till you see what they do to you in the State Department." Finally I went to the Justice Department to seek Bobby Kennedy's advice. He asked for a weekend to think it over, then told me, "Forget it. No matter what you decide to do, you will do it better on television." So, with a tinge of regret that has survived, I told Ball no.

In my second month of idleness my old friend Associate Justice William O. Douglas invited me to lunch privately with him at the Supreme Court. He gave me the flattering news that a good many people were missing my presence on TV, and he wanted to know what it would take to get me back on the air. I think I could deal with hostility, but I was at a loss how to take unalloyed kindness. I told him it would take too much to get me on national television, and I wouldn't encourage such a private effort. I thanked him, but said I would have to make it by the requirements of commercial television or give up TV.

I went to New York to see William Benton in his majestic suite, next to General MacArthur's, in the Waldorf Towers. He was a founder of the successful Benton & Bowles advertising firm, and a former U.S. Senator from Connecticut. Recently he had offered me the job of chief editor of the *Encyclopedia Britannica*. I had turned it down. He informed me that it was too late now. Harry Ashmore, editor of the *Arkansas Gazette* during the Little Rock crisis, had filled the post.

I became seriously worried about my future. Bennie came to the rescue. "You haven't been answering the phones," she said. "I have, and there have been about thirty-five calls from a lot of interested people, about a dozen from local TV stations." We sorted the nibbles out. None offered me the chance to resume where I had left off and to keep the considerable momentum I had acquired as a national television journalist. But I had to choose something and go after it.

I had been three months out in the cold and was about to pursue something I did not really want to do, when, as my friend Raymond Swing put it, a giant hand reached out and arrested my fall. It was the hand of Murray Lincoln, president of the Nationwide Insurance Company. Lincoln was a one-time farm agent, one of the unintending revolutionaries whose improvements reduced farmers from 30 percent of the population to under 2 percent. In the course of helping farmers with auto insurance, he created Nationwide, and nurtured it into a major national insurance firm.

Out of the blue, his public relations chief, Calvin Kytle, phoned me and invited me to meet Mr. Lincoln at Nationwide's advertising agency in New York a few days hence. I appeared and took a place at a conference table with several Nationwide officials and agency executives. After a while, Mr. Lincoln stormed in, shook hands and asked me what sort of news program I could offer as a vehicle for Nationwide to go on national TV. His balding head and arched eyebrows behind eyeglasses made him look like a large owl perched in a tall tree.

I was a fair hand at sketching and showed him my rough sketches of a dummy weekly program, aiming to comment on and illuminate the week's foremost news event. I displayed the graphics that could be used for a first program comparing the U.S. and the U.S.S.R. In 1961, the Cold War was at a new peak. The Berlin Wall had just been built. Khrushchev was threatening. He was testing some giant H-bombs and regaling diplomats at cocktail parties with tales of his having assigned six bombs to wipe out Britain and nine to do the same to France. In America, the atomic shelter industry was booming with, it was estimated, one out of every five American families buying one for their backyard. The nation was pervaded by an atmosphere of dread and of defeatism. Typically, a letter to a news editor of that time said the Russians would not attack us because "they don't have to. They're winning anyway." My program would compare us on many different levels and conclude that we were vastly superior to the Russians in every respect, demonstrating that there were no objective grounds for this epidemic feeling of inferiority.

Lincoln immediately liked the general idea, and the specific one for a starting program. "Work it out with Calvin, and start as soon as you can," he said, before storming out. I was dazed at the suddenness of my rescue from the pit. I would have expected that an ad campaign on always costly television required more and longer negotiation. But I was not prepared to suggest this. Now I had to face the fact that I had invented a vessel but did not have a network to float it on or a crew to sail it.

CHAPTER SIXTY

A Lean Enterprise

The American market had economic room at that time for two and three-quarters national TV networks. The two networks were now shut to me, so I took my planned news program to the three-fourths one, which was the American Broadcasting Company, headquartered on West 66th Street in Manhattan. ABC unblushingly put business first and concentrated on making money. It did so with programs exploiting the two sure themes of sex and violence. Interoffice memos, leaked to the embarrassment of executives, described some of them. One memo, about the gangster series *The Untouchables,* said, "We are killing too many people per episode." The producer described another episode, "Not as much action as some, but sufficient to keep the average bloodthirsty viewer fairly happy." Another memo, dealing with a series called *Bus Stop,* noted that a recent episode had featured a nymphomaniac and a teen-age alcoholic/murderer, and that twenty-five stations had refused to carry it. Compared to programs the other two networks carried decades later, when they too were feeling economic pinches, ABC's were tame; but at that time they stood out, and they did make money. Leonard Goldenson, the chief, with whom I later developed a friendship, decided to devote some of the proceeds to making a bolder initiative in news, and hired Eisenhower's ex-Press Chief, Jim Hagerty, to do it. I went to see Hagerty with my idea and my sponsor. He leapt at it, as well he might: it laid an unsolicited million dollars on ABC's doorstep without requiring any creative effort by the network. Soon after, Jim appeared before a Senate committee dealing with TV and boasted that, while the other two nets were laggard, he had increased news time on ABC by 37 percent. He did not say that most of that increase was my contribution.

Hagerty was a great presidential press agent and probably a good newsman, but he was wholly innocent of knowledge about TV news. He informed me grandly that of the huge sum Nationwide was paying for the program, I would be allowed $14,000 a week to put on my show. At that time, NBC had launched a comparable weekly program at a cost of $75,000 a week. That was a public figure; in fact, however, that program used NBC studio and camera facilities at nominal cost, so each week its real cost probably exceeded $100,000. ABC had no film cameras available for me to share, so I had to rent camera teams from outside at high cost. I also had to pay the full rate for using studios and the thirty or forty union people needed to put my program on the air. Rehearsals alone ate up nearly half my budget. I asked Hagerty for a bigger budget. I pointed out to him that, at the other networks, news-type programs let out commercials to sponsors at below the going rate. Nationwide was being charged the full commercial freight for an underfinanced program. I don't think he understood a word I said. He said he would take my request under advisement, but I am sure he felt I was a spoiled TV person habitually pushing for more. To him, $14,000 was, if anything, too generous.

Thackeray's classic, *Vanity Fair,* includes a chapter in which a spendthrift couple learn "How to Live on Nothing a Year." I thought of them as I set about producing a prime-time TV program on nearly nothing a week. ABC had no space for me, so, while an office was being created out of a prop room, the whole team worked out of our home. I hired a producer who looked at my plan and my budget and flatly told me it could not be done. I did about five programs with him, but his conviction that the mission was impossible stood so firm that he became an additional burden rather than the manager I needed, so I sacked him and, with great luck, lured a friend from CBS, Bill Kobin, to take over. After a little harassing, Bill got a few dollars added to the budget, but it was not much.

We developed a routine. Bill hired the minimum staff he had to have in New York, and I hired two researchers to work with me in Washington. The routine was basically that I wrote a script in Washington, where the experts and the information were to be found, and Bill worked from my script to produce visuals, propose changes and ready all for airing in New York, where the production facilities and the studios were. My researchers, very bright young college graduates, leapfrogged subjects, one working with me to assemble information for use in this week's program while the other worked on an issue we guessed might be timely next week. We often guessed wrong and had to drop everything and do crash research on some late-breaking story. Let us say the topic was a just-issued FBI report that violent crime had increased greatly. On *Day One* and *Day Two* the researcher would go to the library and dig up for me the best books or recent articles he could find on the causes of crime. (There was no computer research then.) He would also go to the headquarters of the International Chiefs of Police or other sources to set up interviews for me. I did parallel research. By morning of *Day Three* we had a list of people, all to be interviewed before camera in one day to get as much out of the hired camera crew as possible for one day's rental (all we could afford). By the night of *Day Three,* I began using his material and mine to write an extended commentary on the subject. By midday of *Day Four,* I had finished the script, and it was flown up and hand-delivered (there was no fax then) to Kobin in New York. Kobin meshed words and pictures. I went up to New York on *Day Five* and found that some of the visuals I had proposed—old library footage of famous cops and criminals of the past, or charts on the subject—were not available, or that they had found different visuals or had different ideas. I considered it all, and the morning of *Day Six,* air day, rewrote the whole script in Kobin's office. Late that afternoon we took everything to the studio, put the whole jigsaw puzzle together and rehearsed it with Jack Sameth, a truly outstanding director, in charge. Then, an hour before air time, we put the program on tape. We stayed throughout the actual airing of the show for me to be ready to go out in front of the cameras and make late changes live on air. *Day Seven* I was back in Washington, conferring with the alternate researcher about the next week's subject. A day off was unthinkable. From long experience both before and after, I can say that never in TV news was so much done so fast by so few with so little.

The series began on February 14, 1962, with this opening (it should be recalled that at this time TV news consisted of daily straight news programs and documentaries and interview panel shows; there were no news-related talk shows or programs of comment except what I had done on the *CBS Evening News*):

> Good Evening. My name is Howard K. Smith. And this is going to be an experiment in television journalism. In the golden age of radio—which was only a few years ago—the time around an hour on either side of supper time used to be a kind of an American forum of the air. You could choose among a dozen or more well-informed commentaries on the meaning of the events of the day to listen to. I believe that institution helped us make the quick transition from being an isolationist nation indifferent to the outside world to being a responsible world leader learning to think about and act upon some very difficult problems.
>
> This weekly report is going to be an attempt to put that kind of commentary back on television. News commentary on television, as distinct from documentary reports, has been tried before. But nobody has ever succeeded at it yet. However, we feel that since then we have learned a little more about how to use television. ABC News wants to try. Our sponsor, the Nationwide Insurance Company, wants to try. And so do I. So here goes.

In the ensuing two years, the Cold War—growing tense anew as Khrushchev threatened to push us out of Berlin—filled a plurality of programs. One opened with a complaint by President Kennedy about the contrariness of his allies. Plaintively he noted that Napoleon won most of his battles because he always fought against allies. The program closed with my comment:

Early in this program you heard President Kennedy complain that Napoleon won most of his battles because he always fought against allies. What the President did not go on to say was—Napoleon lost the war; the bumbling, difficult, quarreling allies won.

Next to the Cold War, the most frequent subject of programs was the progress of the Kennedy Administration, one of which concluded, "In short and in sum, if you will pardon the combining of metaphors, here at home the New Frontier is running like a dry creek."

Many programs analyzed the nation's economy and worried about rises every year in the price of basic steel, no matter what happened to demand. "Adam Smith said an invisible hand would regulate prices. But in fact at the other end of the invisible hand has been Mr. Roger Blough [CEO of U.S. Steel]."

One was devoted to de Gaulle of France, then in the news:

De Gaulle worships the people. But he dislikes people. In his books he has rarely referred to them as *"le peuple."* He prefers calling them *"le Commun"* and occasionally *"la Foule."* . . . When France was just liberated, and he visited a city and met the ragged French partisans who were in charge, he asked offendedly why the constituted authorities were not there to meet him? The head of the partisans answered meekly, "They are in jail, *mon général.*"

Some of the interviews were fascinating. Brigitte Bardot, the prototypical "sex kitten," made her first visit to America and consented to be interviewed only by my network. My bosses thought it would be an interesting pairing if I would do it, and I did. I was surprised at how petite she was. Remembering the film in which she displayed the length of her pins to Jean Gabin, I assumed her to be taller and somewhat more substantial than a wisp. More surprising was her economy of language. A typical exchange: *"Q:* What was the most interesting day of your life? *A:* It wasn't a day; it was a night. *Q:* Tell me about it? *A:* No." I sat down to a half-hour chat with about thirty questions in mind. I had exhausted them in ten minutes. The network made a special program of it, so it was not included in my regular series.

With some difficulty I arranged an interview with Malcolm X, the only Black leader who came close to matching Martin Luther King's power to command audiences. I arrived with a camera crew at an agreed place on Lenox Avenue in New York. We were met by six handsome, muscular, impeccably dressed men who conveyed us to what appeared to be a restaurant but was labeled a Muslim Temple. The room was empty but for tables and a lone figure puzzling over a small camera. He said he wanted to take a picture of us together as a memento, but couldn't figure the box out. Our cameraman, master of such boxes, fixed it and took our picture. Malcolm X was tall, slim, very handsome, light-colored, red-haired, impressively articulate and friendly. The views he expressed and the demands he put sounded radical then, but they have almost all been achieved now, though he did not live to see it happen. He was killed by an unknown assassin shortly after.

It was almost as difficult lining up Jimmy Hoffa. With half an agreement from his office for a talk, we went to a hotel in Detroit at the agreed time. After a while, in he walked, with large men who appeared to be bodyguards on either side. It was the kind of entrance made by Edward G. Robinson in *Little Caesar.* He stopped, stared at me a moment, then said, "I've seen you. I think you are all right," and he sat down and was interviewed. He invited me to attend a cocktail reception hosted by his union to be held in Washington. Bennie and I went. We knew not a soul in the room. One distinguished-looking fellow smiled a welcome, so I shook his hand. "I didn't know you knew the head-waiter," Bennie whispered. Hoffa never showed up. I never saw him again.

I was unable to get Muhammad Ali, a.k.a. Cassius Clay, to sit for a non-sports interview. But over breakfast in San Diego he did share a story with me. He was there to address an all-White audience, and he said that all he was going to say was a joke, to see how they would react. I asked to hear the joke, and this is what he said, "I'm going to ask them, what did Abraham Lincoln say when he woke up from a three-day drunk? Since Abraham Lincoln never drank, they are not going to know. When they give up, I'll tell them, when Abraham Lincoln came to after a three-day drunk, he said, 'I freed *who*???'" I told the same joke the next morning in my commencement speech at San Diego State. As James Reston has said, if you banned plagiarism, the Washington press corps would fall into a deep silence.

One of the programs in my series dealt with the medium I was using:

One false charge against television is that it has killed conversation. On the contrary, nothing has brightened and enlivened conversation so much. Frank Lloyd Wright called it "chewing gum for the eyes." Marguerite Higgins said it is a case of "the bland leading the bland." Someone else said, "Television is all for the eyes, not for the brain. The next generation will have eyeballs big as cantaloupes, and no brain at all."

Television is one of the most remarkable, and frightening, features of a remarkable time. Today 90 percent of American homes have TV sets. That is more homes than have plumbing or telephones, and the average television set is on and being watched more than five hours a day. When you consider that we only have about sixteen waking hours of life each

day, the American people are devoting nearly a third of active life to looking at this box. Put another way, in the next ten years, the average American will devote two complete years plus to nothing but staring at the
screen.

Amid grim news, our wish to find light interludes was resolute: "The best
story from Washington this week is said to be true. A Senator made a speech.
A lady came up and said with admiration, 'Senator, your speech was superfluous, simply superfluous.' The Senator answered, tongue in cheek, 'Thank you.
I intend to have it published, posthumously.' The lady said, 'What a good idea.
I hope it will be soon.'" A year later, Adlai Stevenson told me he had made up
my true story.

To fill one installment of the show I induced the giants of WW II radio commentary to sit and talk with me, Ed Murrow, H. V. Kaltenborn (also famous for
President Truman's mimicking of him as he predicted Dewey's victory on election night 1948) and Raymond Swing. It was a dark, rainy night, and Murrow
arrived at the studio late. He looked ill and sipped from a bottle of codeine-
laced cough syrup throughout. I learned later that he had been unable to find
a taxi and had walked ten blocks through the rain to keep the date. And a little
later still I was shocked to learn that it was not a sore throat that was troubling
him; it was cancer. I reproved myself for not having inquired and canceled his
obligation to me.

After a first operation to limit the spread of the cancer, he and Janet, his
wife, came to see us at our home. He left the car to Janet halfway up our long
drive and got out and walked the rest of the way with Bennie who had been
out gardening. As he walked, he tilted to the right. Near us the tilt had his upper body nearly horizontal, and I started out to help him. Janet told me to stay
and let him make it on his own. The operation had damaged his inner ear and
affected his balance. I nearly cried at the incongruous sight of this figure,
above all graceful, approaching us crudely bent sideways at a sharp angle.

I visited him in his apartment in New York one night when it was known
that he would not make it. He wore a turban around his operated head but
otherwise seemed normal. We had a drink which I knew was a farewell one.
He died a short time later.

After lectures I am often asked who was the most impressive figure I have
met in a lifetime of interviewing. I have never hesitated to name Murrow,
ahead of prime ministers and presidents. He not only excelled in the art of
communicating, above anyone before or in the increasing years since; he was
also a superior human being. The list of friends he rescued or protected from
the assaults of bigotry is very long, and I am sure I am on it. I do not know for

certain, but I believe that the reason nothing untoward befell me after my listing in *Red Channels* is that potential offenders knew that they would have to get past him to get at me. What I do know for certain is that it was Murrow who told Murray Lincoln that CBS had dealt with me disgracefully, and who prompted Lincoln to put me back on the air in a commentary program. I learned only very recently of this addition to my debt of gratitude.

I was an usher at his funeral. By chance it fell my turn to direct the next mourner to a place just as Bill Paley appeared at the door. I froze. He, eyes red from crying, gave me one cold glance, then bulldozed his way past. His wife, Babe, took my hand and said she was sorry, but did I know that I had offended him deeply? I thanked her and did not suggest giving thought to what he had done to me.

CHAPTER SIXTY-ONE

Troubles Endured

My contract with ABC and my sponsor gave me a wholly free hand to engage in controversy. It was the only TV contract of its kind and will probably never be repeated. I made use of it with great prudence. But twice in the life of the program I produced tremors that I thought might bring an end to this happy condition. Each time it steadied and held.

The first involved a report on Cuba. One day in 1962 Castro dropped all pretense of being a national revolutionary. He announced that he was a Marxist and had been all his adult life. It became evident that Cuba was now a full-fledged Soviet satellite and a conduit for Soviet force to Latin America. In the late summer of 1962, the docks of Cuba were host to forty or more Russian ships a month, mostly loaded with weapons. The quantities seemed far more than could be used by a Cuban army, suggesting that they were to be transshipped in the dark of night to the harbors of Central and South America to arm Communist bands there. And, indeed, the police of Venezuela interrupted a nighttime unloading and took possession of a huge shipment of Russian weapons from Cuba on its open shore.

My report detailed shipments and plans, obtained from an entirely trustworthy source, and the picture was alarming. My conclusion regarding what we needed to do stated flatly that military intervention might be necessary, if we intended the Monroe Doctrine to have meaning, and if we wished to prevent a mighty and hostile foreign power from setting up bases in the hemisphere while it was still preventable.

My sponsor, Murray Lincoln, was a famous liberal and was shocked at my conclusion. His vice president for public relations conveyed to me by phone after the program that my piece smacked of imperialism, and all at Nationwide were deeply displeased.

One night shortly afterward, Washington was diverted by strange visions. Every window in the Pentagon, then still the metropolitan area's biggest office structure, was lighted, a rare sight indeed. In downtown D.C., every window in the new State Department was likewise illuminated. And every window in the Army's map-making complex next to our home was brightly lighted all night long. Something very big was clearly going on. I remembered that the White House Press Office had not returned my calls that day. I put in a call to an official and was told that he could not speak to me by phone but that my earlier report on Cuba had been "right on target."

The following night, President Kennedy appeared on television to inform the American people and the world of the single most dangerous crisis in the series of crises making up the Cold War. Having saturated Cuba with conventional weapons, the Soviets suddenly and in utmost secret began shipping in nuclear weapons. Reconnaissance photos showed clearings in the woods to accommodate forty big nuclear-tipped rockets lying nearby. They were of intermediate range, able to strike American cities as far north as Houston, St. Louis and Washington, with far more accuracy and effectiveness than could any fired from the U.S.S.R. Photos showed other clearings and gear suited for longer-range missiles to come—weapons that would be able to hit all of the U.S.

In Europe at this time the Russians were renewing their threats to force the Western nations out of Berlin. It was foreseeable that, after the new missiles were emplaced, Khrushchev would demand that the U.S. get out of Berlin, and would then reveal his frightening new means of persuasion in Cuba to force us to obey. It was also foreseeable that Latin American nations, who were vigorously opposing their native Cuban-armed Communists, would be intimidated and would begin accommodating the revolutionaries. With this one action the Russians were seizing the initiative in the Cold War, where the U.S. had long held the advantage, and were shifting the balance of power drastically to their side. The U.S. had to act with speed and vigor.

President Kennedy did so. He said that any action with these weapons against any part of the hemisphere would be regarded as an attack on the U.S. and would be answered with all our force. He demanded that all the nuclear weapons now on Cuban soil be dismantled and removed. He announced a blockade by the U.S. Navy to intercept any further missiles en route to Cuba. He also offered concessions; he would remove outdated U.S. missiles from Turkey, near the U.S.S.R. A few tense days followed. Finally, Khrushchev broke and began removing the missiles.

These were most dramatic days, deserving the many volumes written about them. I had no further reportorial part in the story. It was not yet established whether I was a member of ABC's news staff or a temporary contract journalist. I had to stick to my one all-absorbing, agreed-upon mission, so, the morning before Kennedy's evening talk to the nation, I began frantic work on my next week's show. At least, Nationwide's criticism of me for being a militarist or imperialist went instantly limp. At my next meeting with Mr. Lincoln he remarked favorably that I seemed always to be "right on top of the news."

My other brush with disapproval was more serious; indeed, it almost blew me out of the water. Richard Nixon had run for Governor of California (he was resolved, Red Skelton said, to get to the White House even if he had to do it state by state) and lost to the likable incumbent, Governor Edmund "Pat" Brown. On his way out of his hotel the day after, Nixon spotted a number of reporters in a room off the lobby. Against the advice of Herb Klein, his press man, he went in and gave them a bitter little speech. He said he would never run for office again and, therefore, "you won't have Richard Nixon to kick around anymore."

My next show was to take place on Veterans' Day, so I researched and planned a piece comparing the performances of American fighting men in a succession of wars. Then the Nixon incident happened. I love to write about politics, and I do my best when writing under pressure of an early deadline. I could not resist the temptation to do both, so in midweek I switched my topic to "The Political Obituary of Richard Nixon." I drew up a list of people who had played significant roles in his career and interviewed them, taking care to keep them balanced—for example, Nixon's first campaign manager, Murray Chotiner, for, and Jerry Voorhis, the Democratic Congressman he defeated in that campaign, against. That week, Alger Hiss, whom young Congressman Nixon had seen imprisoned in a famous case, was released from prison. Hiss had already appeared on CBS, interviewed by Walter Cronkite. I made a phone call and asked him to let me interview him for my program. He refused. So I proceeded with the others. Then, the day before we were to air, Hiss phoned back and said he wanted to be interviewed for my program. I was busy writing in Washington, so I sent one of my colleagues in New York to question him. To balance Hiss, I went to Capitol Hill and asked Congressman Gerald Ford of Michigan, a particular friend of Nixon's (who a generation later would be chosen by Nixon to be his Vice President), to sit for an interview.

I made a big psychological mistake. An audience, told they would see a patriotic program, "The American Fighting Man," were told it would instead be "The Political Obituary of Richard Nixon," which was too readily assumed to mean I would be beating up on the man who had brought Alger Hiss to justice. In fact, Hiss's contribution was weak, and no kicks were delivered in the course of the program. But the word was out, and the protests began to pour in well before I had finished writing the program.

I had not written under such pressure before, and have not done so since. Jim Hagerty sat at my side and policed every paragraph as it came off my typewriter. Ex-President Eisenhower phoned from Gettysburg to warn Hagerty against kicking Nixon while he was down. Jim assured him the program would be a fair but penetrating analysis of Nixon's career, then sat beside me to make sure it would be so. During the writing I had to take the phone to hear from the executive vice president of Nationwide who wanted to know whether the company was in the clear. I told him that the piece was scrupulously fair, but there was going to be some heat to take. "If it's honest, we're with you," he said. Then came a call from interviewee Jerry Voorhis. The pressure was too hot; he wanted his interview excised. I told him that this late in the production schedule it was impossible to cut him out. Then a call from someone who said he was one of Nixon's lawyers. I told him to leave his address, and I would send him a copy of the script; what he was complaining about was not even written yet. When I finished the script, I went to work with Kobin to put the show together. Hagerty went to his office. An unending series of phone calls ensued, all protesting the beating up on Richard Nixon. Hagerty noticed something. The wording of the protests was the same in most cases. At one point he interrupted a woman caller. "Madame, may I ask you something? Are you *reading* what you are saying to me?" She was. Almost all of them were. It soon became clear that the ultra-right-wing John Birch Society had circulated a formula of protest for all to use. Bill Buckley's magazine, *National Review,* announced that its next issue would contain an investigative report revealing all my liberal past, titled "Who Is Howard K. Smith?" Altogether, someone counted more than 60,000 communications. Oddly, later I fared no better with the liberal left. Frank Mankiewicz, a Kennedy operative, was one of several who publicly accused me of rescuing Nixon's career by creating sympathy for him.

I think that I personally stood up to the pressure well. Here was the program's conclusion:

> The Great Republic—as Winston Churchill likes to call us—is an ungrateful master. He pays his servants ill, and like a Roman Caesar drops them without so much as a thank you at the first nod of public disapproval.
>
> But the Great Republic's economy, by way of compensation, is very

grateful. Mr. Nixon in defeat is condemned to work for a living in that economy as a private lawyer. With his ability he will probably in a few years be a very wealthy lawyer. He will have time for his family and for friends and for other things that make life worth living, which he has never had before.

So, the many people who phoned us not to criticize a man when his luck is down are not on strong ground. There are much harder fates than spending your youth in close pursuit of the Presidency—then, at life's prime, turning to this country's highly rewarding private life.

We therefore feel it is fair to be frank about a man who chose public assessment as a way of life. Mr. Nixon has been called a complex personality. But his career is not hard to analyze. He was a poor, unknown young man, hungry for distinction. Given a chance to run for Congress, he was fiercely determined to win.

America was alarmed, justly, about Communism, as it must continue to be. Mr. Nixon made that his catapult. He buried his first opponent, a good American, in insinuations that Mr. Voorhis never caught up with.

In 1952, Mr. Nixon carried that tactic into national politics. As Earl Mazo in his highly favorable portrait of Mr. Nixon recounts, he applied the word "traitor" to President Truman and Governor Stevenson and Secretary Acheson. He was vague as to what they were traitors to; but in that atmosphere, the word meant the worst to the public.

That kind of talk is not part of the normal rough and tumble of politics. It not only damages good men; it damages our national life.

There is no doubt that Mr. Nixon performed great services, in his investigation of Communism, and on his tours of the world for America. But his achievements have to be weighed against those tactics. I suspect that is what the voters did.

Good night.

Nixon's lawyers found nothing to sue about. I thought that would be the end of my relationship with Richard Nixon, but it was not. Our paths crossed and recrossed. He took the initiative in reviving our friendship before he returned to politics. As President, he granted me the first one-on-one interview with a President ever broadcast on TV. When the Watergate horror thickened, I was the only TV commentator to propose that he resign his office. To my surprise, our friendship revived even after that, as will be recounted.

CHAPTER SIXTY-TWO

What's in the Way of JFK?

For the mass of literature it inspired, the Kennedy era in America was very brief, less than three years long. Its advent wrought a change of atmosphere, of style, in Washington almost as marked as that of 1933, when Hoover, and his businessmen and lawyers, gave way to FDR, and his professors and lawyers. I think that not since the first Roosevelt in 1901 had the nation enjoyed a President and his beautiful young wife and his numerous and ever-bubbling extended family so much. Reading the papers in the morning amounted to getting one's daily fix in an ongoing addiction. What witty thing had he said in a toast to a foreign leader at a state dinner last night? (It could not top the one he spoke at his dinner for American Nobelists: "This is the most extraordinary collection of talent that has ever been gathered together at the White House—with the possible exception of when Thomas Jefferson dined alone.") At his side what gorgeous gown had that lovely living statue with the set jaw and the level gaze worn? (No one has ever carried raiment as she could.) The nation was like a famous photo taken when Princess Grace of Monaco visited the White House. In the picture the President looked straight ahead, but the beautiful Princess looked, as if stealing an illicit gaze out of the corner of her eyes, at him.

The arrival of style in the capital was to a high degree the work of Jacqueline. The interior of the White House, mainly just impressive before, became truly beautiful under her detailed direction. The great East Room heard less of Irving Berlin and more of Tchaikovsky and Casals. The governmental style was defined by Kennedy's ringing inaugural, "Let the word go forth from this time and place, to friend and foe alike, that the torch has been passed to a new generation of Americans, born in this century, tempered by war, disciplined by a hard and bitter peace. . . ." They were called "the best and the brightest," or "the OSS generation," for they typically had populated the intelligence organizations ("the last refuge of the well-connected") during the war. They included two-score Phi Beta Kappas, four Rhodes Scholars and one Nobelist. They sought to be written about with the adjectives "tough-minded," "cool," "able," "resilient," "can-do," "laconic" and "sardonic"; they were proud to be possessed of a "puncturing humor." Their permanent occupation was the "pursuit of excellence," with overwork the rule, speed-reading the rage, and landmark achievement the purpose of all exertions. The English commentator Henry Fairlie wrote that the Kennedys had the nation permanently standing on tip-toe with expectation.

From the start I was as ardent an admirer as any. After all, my generation was now installed in the high places from which Truman and Marshall and Acheson had saved the broken world after the greatest war. In the campaign I had watched the hero's physique grow from the skinny boy I met at Eden Roc and who was still the skinny boy in the photo of us together in Washington, into the robust, filled-out man of the debates, now more suited to fit a frame in a collection of portraits of Presidents.

During the campaign I was still at CBS doing nightly commentaries. When Martin Luther King was jailed in Georgia, I noted in my broadcast that King was favorable to Nixon and recounted the story of the two men meeting in Ghana. Within minutes, Harris Wofford, then a very young operative in the Kennedy camp, phoned me and said, "He may have been on Nixon's side then, but phone him and ask him about now." I phoned. Martin had not yet been re-leased, but his father took the phone and told me Kennedy had called his wife, and his brother Robert had called the Governor of Georgia to get Martin out. "We *were* for Nixon," Daddy King said, "but we are switching."

After moderating the debate, I was assigned to follow each candidate in turn on the campaign trail. On election night, 1960, my assignment was to monitor a room-sized computer—now a commonplace apparatus, but then an incredible mechanical Merlin—in the IBM building on Fifth Avenue in New York. From time to time I appeared on the screen next to the wonderful ma-chine and recounted what secrets it had uncovered. For hours its main revela-tion was that Mort Sahl was right. Neither candidate was winning, and it seemed that neither would. It was as close as skin. I insisted to the operator that he dare a result. He said Nixon would win by a hair. He was angry at me for forcing a commitment that in the end turned out to be wrong. But in fact his computer may have been right. After a long, long night and next morning, Kennedy came out on top, but his victory margin was so thin and was obtained under such dubious conditions in two states famous for creative vote counting that the opposite result may have been the true one.

Cold inauguration day was unique. Crisp, clear air was made bright by sunshine on new-fallen snow, bespeaking newness and freshness. I was as-signed to the warm indoors, standing in the Rotunda of the Capitol and watch-ing 535 members of Congress file slowly past on the way out to their places in the inaugural stands. From time to time I was called on to draw some Solon from the procession and to interview him. The only mildly memorable ex-change occurred when Rep. Howard Smith of Virginia appeared. My one-hour program with him was still recent, and it was assumed he would have something to say. "Judge Smith," I said, "what happens if this new young President sends you a civil rights bill?" Missing no beat, he said, "I'll put it on the mantel piece and look at it awhile. A long while. I won't let it get in harm's way. I won't let it get in anything's way."

There, not thirty yards from the podium, but separated from it by the walls of the building, I heard and watched on my little TV monitor the stirring speech of the new President. I was impressed by the "Let's" that sounded like commands from the Creator, "Let the word go forth. . . . Let every nation know. . . . Let all our neighbors know. . . ." I was a little put off by its neglect of our growing domestic problems in favor of the grander aspects of world affairs. Still, the speech resonated as no political oratory had in a long time. I was on tiptoe with expectation.

In the first year of the new administration I began the train of events that would switch me from doing 60-second comments for CBS to 30-minute ones for ABC. Deeper research and more time to do it may have contributed to my beginning to feel dissatisfied with the new administration. Little legislation was offered by the President; and the Congress, though Democratic, dug its heels in at that. My first dissonance was, as noted, that "the New Frontier is running like a dry creek." What happened to the urgent tone of the campaign? I devoted a program with Dr. George Gallup of the Gallup poll to seeking the answer.

It was said that Kennedy was holding back because the election showed he had thin popular support. I asked Gallup. He said, "The President's popular support is 79 percent, which is extraordinarily high. It's phenomenally high."

Well, I said, it is also said that he is hesitant because a conservative wave is sweeping the country. Gallup: "We have indications that this is not the case.. . . . In fact, the evidence is to the contrary."

Did Kennedy fear to take vigorous action lest Democrats lose the next off-year election? Gallup: "The Democrats are far ahead. As a matter of fact, the Democrats have a bigger lead than they've had for many, many years, 61 percent for the Democratic candidates and 39 percent for Republicans."

I asked how opinion stood on issues the President talked about—medical care for the elderly, the new foreign trade bill, federal aid for education, the plan to cut taxes to stimulate the economy? I quote my script of the time: "On all issues, the people supported the President's plans by high margins. The fact was, both in Congress and with the people, Kennedy enjoyed support. Something else was wrong."

I did several programs over time on the mystery of the President's paucity of result. One of the most penetrating responses came in an interview with the historian and author of *The American President*, Sydney Hyman:

There has been a kind of psychic split between the President on one side and his natural friends in Congress on the other. The natural friends have begun to use the word "they" when referring to the White House. . . . I think there has been a kind of a clublike attitude, or a fraternity attitude, to the White House entourage. When you talk about a Presidency, you are talking about some 200 men. What is distinctive about the 200 men that Mr. Kennedy brought in as his chief aides is that, as he himself said, they are all on his wavelength. There's a kind of inbred quality to them, I regret to say . . . enough to make those who haven't been tapped for Skull and Bones hesitate about approaching them. There's really no free and easy communication between the 200 men and the friends of the President in Congress.

In Kennedy's second year, *Time* called the Congressional session "the least productive ever." The President was not making an impression. I interviewed a number of high-powered analysts for a program I called "What's in the Way of JFK?" One was Professor Malcolm Moos, a Republican academic who wrote Eisenhower's famous farewell speech that warned the public against the power of the "military-industrial complex." I asked him to estimate Kennedy's progress. He said, "Well, it's my feeling that, if you took a yardstick and took the first two years of the Eisenhower Administration and put it alongside the Kennedy Administration, that the Kennedy Administration looks pretty thin so far."

Richard Hofstadter, one of the nation's leading political scientists, said, "The question that most of us raise, who, like myself, voted for him in his campaign . . . is where the President is going, and when this dynamism that seemed to be so characteristic of his campaign is likely to affect domestic affairs."

Sidney Hyman again: "I think one of the most significant things about the phrase 'New Frontier' is that I can't remember the President having used it since his acceptance speech. People talk about it, but he doesn't talk about it."

I also quoted James Reston that week in *The New York Times:* "There is something wrong with his leadership. Something is missing. He plays touch government and tackles nothing." And Walter Lippmann: "He's too cautious. I think that a public leader at times has got to get into struggles where somebody gets a bloody nose."

Senator Paul Douglas (D–Ill.) described an occasion when Senators pushed for a Kennedy measure without waiting for Kennedy, "When we were trying to curb the abuses in the expense accounts, we got no support from the Treasury, and I must say, we felt a little let down, that we had been left to die on the Berlin Wall, so to speak, and not even an ambulance had been sent out to rescue us."

Senator Jacob Javitz (R–N.Y.): "The way to get action is not to be afraid, after you've done all the things which cooperation and accommodation require, to take on a fight, if you have to. We have yet to see that from President Kennedy."

In Kennedy's third year the legislative process all but stopped. *Time* called the session "the longest, most tedious, least effective first session [after the midterm elections] in U.S. History." Walter Lippmann called it "a conspiracy to suspend representative government." Pierre Salinger, Kennedy's Press Secretary, wrote that government was "like a bus stalled against a brick wall." In an interview with me, the liberal Republican Senator Clifford Case of New Jersey, sympathetic to the Kennedy program, said of the session, "Little was asked, and even that was not granted."

I found Sidney Hyman, the presidential scholar, a liberal Democrat, the most articulate of the commentators. In a long talk he said on my program:

> There has become a kind of star quality, or element rather, in the Presidency, in that it becomes terribly important to be popular, as though government itself was devoted solely to keeping the President popular. My own feeling is that a President is elected not to be loved but to rule. . . . The Administration hurls up the white flag before it has any need to do so. It is not willing to go down fighting. It is willing to compromise before there is any need to compromise, and this is hardly the kind of policy that inspires fear in your adversary. Rather it encourages your adversary to believe that if only he will be tougher, the Administration will cave in.

Professor James MacGregor Burns of Williams College, another guest, had written an authorized biography of Kennedy prior to the election campaign. It displeased the Kennedy family, who insisted on some changes. But his concluding judgment remained and is still a good measuring rod for the man. To the duties of the President, Burns wrote, "Kennedy could bring bravery and wisdom; whether he would bring passion and power would depend on his making a commitment not only of mind, but of heart, that until now he has never been required to make."

I asked Burns how the measure stood after two years in the White House. He said, "He has not yet shown that commitment of heart." And so it was.

CHAPTER SIXTY-THREE

Brief Candle

When the Nationwide series ended after two seasons on the air, ABC had no idea what to do with me. The network had few news-related shows, and to the places on them Hagerty had fitted a few very good reporters very snugly, leaving no extra space. What was needed was more shows, more outlets, which in turn necessitated more and new producers and crews to create them. The task called for a news department head who understood that TV news was not a pictorial extension of newspapers, but something new and different. So, Hagerty was moved upstairs and made a corporate vice president, and a man who knew what to do was made head of news: Elmer Lower, who with Sig Mickelson had created a TV news organization from nothing at CBS, then worked at NBC.

Meanwhile I was idle, doing little beyond occasional appearances on the Sunday interview program, *Issues and Answers*. As I was returning from one such interview, with Gamal Abdel Nasser in Egypt, the earth split open and the universe shuddered, and amid catastrophe a new function for me presented itself.

Everyone remembers where he or she was when hearing the awful news. I was 35,000 feet above the endless, featureless Atlantic, sitting above two plastic boxes containing tapes of my interview. The captain sent a stewardess to ask me to come up to the cockpit where he had me listen on phones to broadcasts from the American mainland. The news hurt, it physically hurt. "Do you think I should tell the passengers?" the captain said. "I am in the Now Business," I told him, "my tendency is to tell everything you know to anybody who will listen." He said, "Will you do it?" I said, "It's your ship; I think it will sound right only from the captain."

When we landed at Idlewild, there was an unaccustomed compliment: a car and a chauffeur waiting with a message that I was badly needed in the studio on West 66th Street, as soon as possible. "I don't know all that has been reported, and have nothing much to say," I told Lower at the door to the studio. "Neither does Ron," he said, nodding to Ron Cochran, the former FBI agent with the fine voice who was the network's evening news anchor, "Get out there and help him say it." After a few hours, when we narrated the scene of the dead President's body arriving in Washington, I was pulled out of the studio and told to get to Washington. The story would be there for the next two days, and all broadcasts would originate there.

The assignment called less for announcer voices than for newsmen accustomed to handling breaking stories. Edward P. Morgan, a newspaper reporter I had once hired for CBS, but now doing a nightly 15-minute radio newscast on ABC sponsored by the AFL-CIO, was teamed with me to stay on the air with the story almost continuously for the next two days.

It was a unique and mournful pageant. Heads of state from half the world flew in, and immediately fear arose for the safety of the soaring figure of Charles de Gaulle, already the target of two assassination attempts in his own country. He brought ten French security guards with him, and the State Department assigned 200 American ones. Still, he walked long city blocks in the open for the ceremony, towering over tiny Emperor Haile Selassie of Ethiopia, without incident. John Kennedy's body was drawn up the hill to the Capitol in a coffin never to be opened, so badly was he disfigured. Senator Mike Mansfield, leader of the Democratic majority in the Senate, read a tribute over the catafalque in the Rotunda, but he sobbed so much that he had to repeat parts of his remarks several times. We switched to Dallas for a glimpse of the burial of the now-murdered assassin, Lee Harvey Oswald. Back in Washington crowds, guessed to number about a quarter-million, lined up to come in and pass by the coffin. The former heavyweight boxing champion, Jersey Joe Walcott, said he waited in line eight hours to reach it. The next day the coffin was carried back to the White House, then to the church on the caisson that had borne FDR's body nineteen years before.

Throughout, we switched to observing Jacqueline whenever possible. She was the mistress of the long melancholy celebration, had sent to the Library of Congress for books and pictures about Lincoln's funeral and ordered that her husband's follow a similar course. It was she who decided that he should be buried at a chosen spot overlooking Washington on the slopes of what once had been the plantation of Robert E. Lee and was now the Arlington National Cemetery. It was she who ordered that a blue flame be made to burn eternally over his grave.

I do not weep easily, much to my regret, for tears can bring surcease. I lasted out three days dry-eyed. Our coverage was praised by several TV critics as sensitive. When the Smithsonian Museum of American History created a television exhibit of the tragedy, parts of our coverage were chosen for inclusion. Cronkite saw it and demanded "equal time." At the end of three days, for no better reason than had existed before, I burst into tears at our dinner table at home. When the torrent was over, I did feel better.

✶   ✶   ✶

The change marked by the brief Kennedy era was more one of ambiance, of style, than of substance. It was an interlude, not the beginning of anything new or durable. There were some footprints in the sands of time—the skillful handling of a very mean missile crisis, the treaty banning nuclear tests, the broadening of world trade—but too few in a nation whose arrears in domestic development were growing monstrous. A Black population was refusing to continue three centuries of subordination in a country that asserted equality of all before the law. This richest nation on earth countenanced a mass of poverty greater than in any other Western nation. *Time* in November 1963 judged, "The rhetoric of his inaugural led to extravagant overpraise. . . . If a historical scorecard would not record many errors, it would list a few hits and fewer runs. . . . In the long view of History his Administration might be known less for the substance of its achievements than for its style." The style was certainly breathtaking, the surpassing grace of both the King and the Queen of the Republic. But the image was somewhat sullied when the King was revealed to be a practiced extra-connubial womanizer, and when the widowed Queen married an old man with no visible attraction but money.

Yet the impression of the Kennedy era as a special time with a special cast endures. In the series of documentaries on the American Presidency I did for Public Broadcasting many years later, we cited an opinion poll on what Americans thought of their Presidents. If our poll was right, U.S. citizens felt that John Kennedy was the greatest President, with Lincoln, Washington and Roosevelt lost in the crowd! A publisher of books said, "There are three subjects on which it is impossible to have too many books: the Civil War, WW II and the Kennedys." The explanations of this phenomenon probably include the tragic end of a figure of unusual charm; the first assassination visible to all on film; a corps of gifted image-makers; and above all a widow with a clear idea of what she wanted and a will of steel. Without previous notice, Jacqueline one evening summoned to her side one of the finest journalists in the world, my friend Theodore White. She told him that she wanted her husband's brief tenure remembered as Camelot of the Arthurian legend, as lately romanticized in a musical show of the same name. She literally coached him over his shoulder as he typed the image into words to be telephoned to *Life* magazine for immediate publication. It became a public relations triumph of unparalleled effect and durability. The legend received the certification of an important historian, Arthur M. Schlesinger, Jr. Sadly, many lesser propagandists burnished their hero by retouching history and uglifying others.

Among the legends created after his death was that Kennedy secretly planned to withdraw from Vietnam and spare the nation a trauma. That contradicted every insistent statement he himself made right up to the season of his death. In the official state papers of the time, which were released in 1992, no hint of such a move can be found. Another legend was that he did not offer Lyndon Johnson the Vice Presidential place on the ticket in 1960—Johnson grabbed it from him. In a later paragraph the historian of *A Thousand Days* avers that Johnson asked Kennedy for time to think it over; not even a good historian can make both versions true.

The attempt was made to re-create modern history with Kennedy's death as the seminal event. Oliver Stone's ridiculous film, *JFK*, was the most elaborate contribution to mythology, but by no means the only one. Had Kennedy lived and been reelected, one legend propounded, he would have dealt with all our outstanding problems, abandoned Vietnam, approached world peace, banished poverty, equalized the races and led us into bright uplands. But the evil interests on whose toes he was treading and the ambitious whose path to power he blocked would not allow it. There was a vague plot by nearly everybody—gangsters, Communists, Senators, Congressmen, LBJ, the FBI, the CIA, the Chief Justice, everybody but the White House janitors—to eradicate the threat of improvement. Kennedy died, and the course has been downward ever since, deeper into ruinous Vietnam, a lawless Republican Administration, irresponsible debt, decaying national morale, increasing divorces, more violent crime.

The legend is sustained by romantic faith and little else. The Speaker of the House at that time, Carl Albert, complained to me that Kennedy refused to take the initial step, to exert himself to get laws passed:

He would phone me and ask me to try to persuade three or four Congressmen to vote right. I would say, "Mr. President, why don't you phone them yourself? They would be so flattered that they would do it. I don't, nobody does, carry the wallop you carry." But he wouldn't do it. He would say to me, "I don't like to bother them."

Professor Burns missed Kennedy's commitment of heart because it probably was not there.

On the subject of Vietnam, two months before his death, Kennedy was asked by David Brinkley on NBC if he doubted the domino theory—the notion that, if South Vietnam became Communist, so would the rest of Southeast Asia. Kennedy responded:

No, I believe it. I believe it. I think that the struggle is close enough. China is so large, looms so high just beyond the frontiers, that if South Vietnam went, it would not only give them an improved geographic position for a guerrilla assault on Malaya but would also give the impression that the wave of the future in Southeast Asia was China and the Commu-

nists. . . . What I am concerned about is that America will get impatient
and say, because they don't like events in Southeast Asia, or they don't like
the government in Saigon, that we should withdraw. That only makes it
easy for the Communists. I think we should stay.

These are neither the words nor the spirit of one who plans to withdraw.

The truthful part of the legend is that the fortunes of the Republic did decline in subsequent years. But not immediately; first there were a couple of
years of brilliant performance by Lyndon Johnson in dealing with neglected
urgencies. The troubles that followed had, I believe, different and more complex causes than the tragic death of a charming young man.

CHAPTER SIXTY-FOUR

The LBJ Way

Kennedy's successor was like a negative of a political photograph of
Kennedy—his opposite in most important respects. Lyndon Johnson was all
substance and action, but with a style that was often crude. Whereas Senator
Kennedy had never been or sought to be a member of the "club," the Congress
was to Johnson what the briar patch was to Br'er Rabbit, his element. It told
much about him that the first committee he was assigned to chair in the Senate had a reputation for being contentious, yet all forty-six of its reports under
his management were unanimous. He became the youngest Senate Leader
ever chosen by the Democrats; and as such, in opposition in the Eisenhower
years, he was considered the number one Democrat in the nation. When he
became Vice President, commentators said that he was the only man who ever
stepped down to take that office. His charm resembled that of a buzz saw.

To a new Washington reporter, the first impression of the Majority Leader
of the Senate was bigness. His out-sized height and weight were magnified in
their effect by a torrential energy. When he could not persuade, he over-
whelmed. When he homed in on a target, it was easier to get out of his way
than to resist—which is what I did. I watched him from a safe distance in the
press gallery or at his occasional news conferences. Then came a kind of command attendance. Nancy Hanschman was a capable and handsome CBS staff

correspondent who was on good terms with Johnson. He asked her to bring a couple of her CBS colleagues to have lunch in his office, and specified that he wanted me to be one of them. The other was Raymond Swing, who at that time was writing commentaries for Ed Murrow's radio program. We sat around a large round table in his "throne room"—a palatial space in the Capitol with an elaborately painted ceiling. He had appropriated it from some ceremonial purpose to be his command post. I sat next to his wife, Lady Bird, a graceful woman, selfless and devoted to her husband. I commenced to address her but was cut right off by the host. This was to be a monologue, not a conversation. The Majority Leader discoursed at length on a range of topics, from his lack of any wish to run for President (despite what we reporters were saying) to how President Eisenhower continually blamed Congress for budget deficits (though he, Johnson, personally always reduced spending below what Eisenhower requested). He was repeatedly interrupted by secretaries handing him chits over his shoulder, but each time only briefly. He scanned each, whispered back a response and resumed talking without forgetting where the last predicate was leading him. Occasionally a Senator would come in—I identified Monroney of Oklahoma and Mansfield of Montana. He would walk each to a corner, settle whatever their business was in seconds and be back with us, still chewing. It all gave the impression of his being in charge, which he clearly was.

Occasional glances from the corners of his eyes made it clear that I was being subjected to a mild form of what was known as "the Treatment." It was not an unusual honor. Anyone who might be useful received it. I was, after all, at that time the first member of the Washington staff of the first TV network, with frequent access to the public eye and ear, and could recount just such experiences as I am recounting now. Over time I discovered that Johnson sought two sets of facts about those he might influence: what they wanted most, and what they feared most. With those items of information he had the leverage to exercise influence. What I and almost all reporters wanted most was access to information, which he was offering me. But what I feared most was becoming captive to a politician and losing the quality of objective judgment. At this time my fear was stronger than my want. A couple of weeks later I was invited to cocktails at their home by Senator and Mrs. Johnson, but my concern was such that I sent regrets. Still the Treatment was strong. At our original lunch hamburgers cut in the shape of the state of Texas were served. I was so fascinated by the performance that I never got past the Amarillo on that culinary map. "Corny," I commented in a whisper to Ray Swing on my other side. "You better get over your European illusions," Raymond whispered back. "You belong to a corny nation and he is just right."

When he became Vice President, his premier aide, Rev. Billy Don Moyers, to become a figure of moment himself one day, asked me to go and visit with Mr. Johnson, for he was lonely. It was the worst period of his life, I was told, being subject to the constraints of a position with awesome potential but the most vapid of actuals.

When he was catapulted to President that terrible day in Dallas, my respect for him soon moved way upward. All that roaring energy was released and was directed to purposes much larger than self-aggrandizement—purposes directly aligned with my own values. When I first returned from Europe, I devoted several of my Sunday radio commentaries to features of America in 1957 that struck an American who had left the country in 1937. Two features made strong impressions. One was the evidence that Negroes—possibly with the help of the GI bill—had nurtured a highly effective leadership class of ministers (led by Martin Luther King), lawyers (Thurgood Marshall) and compelling spokesmen (Malcolm X) that did not exist before. With the Constitution on their side, they were not going to stand any longer for Black subordination. The other conspicuous feature was poverty. Even with all the New Deal laws available to rescue FDR's one-third of the nation in want, too many remained in the mire. It was at least unseemly and at most immoral for the world's richest nation to permit a greater proportion of its citizens to languish in poverty than any other Western industrial nation.

The new President went to work on both matters, but only after performing an initial act to establish his authority. The Congressional session was ending. As there was no more business of moment, most members had left town. There were, however, enough Republicans left to defeat a minor bill on foreign aid that would have given the President a margin of freedom in dispensing it. It was of no great moment, until Johnson made it so. He sent the Speaker of the House, John McCormack, a note that he simultaneously made public:

> The countries of the Communist world are watching anxiously to determine whether the new President is so strong that they will have to come to terms with him, or so weak that they can start hacking away at the free world with impunity. It is not difficult to imagine the reaction of the rest of the world if the first disagreement between the Congress and the new President results in a restriction upon the powers of the President.

In other words, Khrushchev would think he faced a pushover. With that mighty argument made, he put his staff on the phone to dispersed Democratic legislators, and arranged to scour the land with airplanes to bring them back to Washington. One told me that he was signaled, while in a fishing boat in the Gulf of Mexico, to get to the nearest phone. There the message awaited directing him to the nearest airport where an Air Force jet would soon arrive to bring him back to Washington. Overnight there were enough votes back in town to get the legislation reconsidered and passed. The mission was completed on Christmas Eve, and Johnson sought to ease irritations by inviting all to the White House for eggnog and a party. The message to the world was that the new President was in control.

In a few weeks the next session began, and Johnson made his aims clear in his first State of the Union address. It opened with some astonishing sleight-of-hand magic on the federal budget. Kennedy had long been seeking to get Congress to reduce taxes in order to leave Americans more to spend, and thereby to give some life to a sluggish national economy. But government spending was rising; that year it would pass the magic figure of $100 billion for the first time ever. Senator Harry Byrd of Virginia and the Democratic conservatives he led rebelled. They felt it was sinful, as well as bad economics, to reduce taxes while increasing spending. Johnson consulted the budget director, Kermit Gordon, an Oxford classmate of mine. Gordon told me he showed the President the next budget, as proposed by Kennedy, which was to run past the terrible $100 billion limit, and assured Johnson, "There is still time to change it and make it your budget." The new President called in all his Cabinet Secretaries, and ordered them to work with Gordon to squeeze their departments' spending plans till the pain was unbearable. After several days, he sent Gordon to Senator Byrd's hotel to present him with the result, which was then announced to the public: the budget for the coming year would not only be below $100 billion; it would be even lower than the previous year's Kennedy budget at $97.9 billion. With that, Byrd and the conservatives yielded, and the tax cut was passed, providing Johnson with years of economic growth in which to work on his ambitious programs.

I was assigned to introduce the new President's appearances on ABC, and afterward to comment on his words. After his first State of the Union address to Congress, in early January 1964, less than two months after taking over the office on the death of his predecessor, I described the speech as breathtaking. It began:

> I will be brief, for our time is necessarily short, and our agenda is already long . . . Let this session of Congress be known as the session which did more for Civil Rights than the last hundred sessions combined; as the session which enacted the most far-reaching tax cut of our time; as the session which declared all-out war on human poverty and unemployment in these United States; as the session which finally recognized the health needs of all our older citizens; as the session which. . . .

And on it went, until at last it climaxed:

> All this and more can and must be done. It can be done by this summer, and it can be done without any increase in spending.

Among those I called onto the air for comment from the Capitol afterward was Senator Jacob Javits, Republican of New York. He said, "There is an enormous gap between what a Democratic President says and what a Democratic-controlled Congress does." I shared his skepticism. We were proved wrong. Before the leaves fell that year, and Johnson faced the 1964 elections, legislation achieving most of those ends was either passed or well on the way to passage.

A minor controversy arose about this remarkable record. It was said that Johnson owed his success to the death of his predecessor: Congress was overcome with remorse for having treated Kennedy negatively, so it passed whatever legislation Johnson asked for. Johnson himself averred this to be partly so. But the transformation of the most negative Congress into the most affirmative one since FDR's Hundred Days took more than sentiment. Moreover, it continued for years after the shock of Dallas. Without doubt, the driving force was Johnson's political genius applied intensively and without let—such acts as his calling every single doubting Congressman into the Oval Office for a drink and a talking-to that lasted as long into the night as it took; such things as stationing three Justice Department lawyers around the Senate floor to provide friendly legislators with rebuttals to arguments of opponents. The nation had a new President with a mighty vision of what had to be done and a mighty will to do it.

I shall return to an estimate of that legislation shortly. Now, as Johnson's first session ended and the politicians prepared to disperse for the campaign of 1964, the new President was so pleased that he threw a gigantic party of thanks to Congress. A stage was erected on the spacious south lawn of the White House. The chorus from a Broadway musical was brought down from New York to perform. Lady Bird's Girl Friday, Liz Carpenter, phoned and asked me to join Nancy Hanschman to master the ceremonies, which I did. After the show, the President and Mrs. J. mounted the stage and shook hands all around. To me, Johnson said, "If you want to see me for a talk, ask. It may take a week. It may take three weeks, but I promise, you'll see me." I picked up the offer and soon commenced a series of off-the-record interviews that gave me insights into the most active Presidency since the second Roosevelt's, and perhaps the saddest since Lincoln's.

CHAPTER SIXTY-FIVE

1964 Cakewalk

The Smith–Morgan team, put together for the funeral late in 1963, was sufficiently successful to be retained by ABC News for the election season of 1964. In every prior election I had served as a correspondent assigned to one aspect or another in election campaigns; this was my first experience at anchoring the whole effort. I found being at the top and in charge very pleasant.

The election itself was unique. Unlike most, it was about clear principles. Johnson was for hyperactive government solving the people's problems. His opponent was for inactive government, decimated in numbers and generally kept "off our backs." That opponent was Barry Goldwater, the ultra-conservative Republican senator from Arizona. He had the advantage of style over the President. He was as open and honest as the summer day is long, plus handsome, manly, warm and altogether likeable. In all other respects, he did not have a chance.

Goldwater seemed to carry a metaphoric gun around with him, always pointed at his foot, and had a tendency to pull the trigger frequently. His most conspicuous self-inflicted wound occurred in an encounter with me. The program was our Sunday interview program, *Issues and Answers,* and on this occasion I questioned him one-on-one. He criticized Johnson's handling of the war in Vietnam, particularly the failure to interdict Chinese supplies from the North. I asked how he would interdict them, hidden as the trails were in jungles. He said, "There have been several suggestions made. I don't think we would use any of them. But defoliation of the forests by low-yield atomic weapons could well be done. When you remove the foliage, you remove the cover." There are two things the prudent politician steers clear of in U.S. elections: Social Security (he proposed privatizing that, and thus handed over the senior citizen vote to LBJ) and The Bomb. True, he said we would not use it, but it sounded very like a recommendation. The next edition of the papers averred just that in big headlines. His denial, which I confirmed to reporters, did not help. The thought that he would be reckless with the bomb clung to him for the rest of the campaign, and the Democrats made sure it did. The standard Goldwater campaign ad was a picture of his square-jawed, honest face above the slogan, "In your hearts, you know he's right." The whisper went around that the words should have been, "In your hearts, you know he might."

The 1964 Republican Convention, held in the venerable Cow Palace out-

side San Francisco, did little to reduce fears. Goldwater's supporters, ultra-conservatives all, were bitter, vengeful people. When Nelson Rockefeller took the podium to speak, they screamed, stomped and demonstrated till the most famous of moderate Republicans had to give up. After Goldwater had secured the nomination and made his acceptance speech with its controversial theme that "extremism in the defense of liberty is no vice," they went for us, the TV horribles. The hall was small for such a large assembly, so the glassed-in TV anchor-booths were on high, thin stilts to leave floor space for seats. The rhetoric-drunk delegates took hold of the stilts and began to shake them. For a long five minutes it felt as though earthquake city were going to claim victims from a man-made tremor. Our floorboards creaked, and objects on our desks slid from side to side as on a ship in a storm. Only frequent appeals from the podium, and some forceful action by sergeants at arms, saved us.

Barry had one additional disadvantage. He didn't really want to be President. Campaigning kept getting in the way of his saying what he wanted to, which was quite often language unsuited to family listening audiences. Once, seated at the anchor desk with me, he let fly with a few hells and damns. My phone rang as soon as the camera was off us. Mrs. Peggy Goldwater wanted to speak to her husband. She did, and told him to mind his phraseology; nice folks in Phoenix were watching. He had a dilemma. When he stuck to his script, he was dull. When he let himself speak freely, he was interesting but lost votes.

That strange tribe, the Republicans, happened to possess that year in Rockefeller a figure who was strong in every place Barry was weak. He was a strong campaigner, powerful on issues that win elections, a proven vote-getter and a man who wanted very much to be President. Nelson Aldrich Rockefeller, grandson of the monumental John D., had been a fine public servant in the Eisenhower Administration, and in 1958 was elected Governor of the (then) most populous state, New York, and proved to be one of its best governors ever. Had he been able to beat Nixon out for the Republican Presidential nomination in 1960 he could—it was John Kennedy's view, too—have beaten Kennedy, won the election and become President. I met him when moderating a TV panel discussion in which he was a participant, and we became friends. He wore a deliberately rumpled overcoat and expressed gratitude by saying "thanks a thousand": a natural winner, but the right wing had a veto on their party's Presidential nomination. They preferred losing with pure Barry to winning with liberal-minded Nelson.

Goldwater's most winning occasion was star-studded. It was held out of doors at Knott's Berry Farm, one of the oldest of the nation's theme parks, in Orange County, south of Los Angeles. There was a big crowd, sensitized to the presence of the enemy. As my wife and I moved through it to benches up

front, the hiss of "Eastern liberal pressss!" followed us like a trail of snakes. Unrecognized, Theodore White, only *slightly* less loathsome than I, got through unmolested. We got press seats in the very first row, facing a small grandstand filled with important conservatives. Several movie stars were seated, including the tap dancer, George Murphy, who would surprise the world by getting himself elected Senator from California. The whole thing was organized by handsome Ronald Reagan, at that time a retired actor who now made a living in public relations, mainly by hosting a TV show for General Electric.

Barry was brought in to applause. After he had shaken hands all around, the real star appeared to wild applause: John Wayne, with a crew-cut hairpiece and looking generally terrific. Reagan delivered a little introductory speech, thanking Wayne for his rare willingness to appear and do politics in public. Then Wayne took over to introduce Barry. The professional hero's best passage was an attack on the nation's enemies led by—and he looked straight down at me as he snarled—"the Eastern Liberal Press!" Seen often on TV, the enemy was more identifiable than a writer of subversive books like Teddy White who sat beside me. I confused some members of the audience by joining in the wild cheering. I pointed out to Teddy that I am from Louisiana and not too enchanted with Easterners myself. Barry then made his speech. He spoke from a script, which made it dull. The affair was ended by a stem-winder from the organizer, Ronald Reagan, who finally supplied the red meat for the hungry audience. With a touch of extrasensory perception, Teddy suggested that Reagan had missed his profession; he should have been a politician.

Reagan's speech was, by the way, the dress rehearsal for a speaking tour of the nation he undertook to gather funds for the Goldwater campaign. It was the speech that induced conservatives everywhere to take an interested look at the actor as a possible political figure, and led moneyed people in California to induce him to run for Governor. It was also a speech that labeled me an enemy of the U.S. who was fouling the minds of the public with liberal comment on TV. Eventually I wrote Reagan a letter protesting that his facts were not in accord with my views. Back came a response, under the heading, "Ronald Reagan. Public Relations. Palisades, CA," expressing satisfaction that I did not accept the views attributed to me, and saying, "I too was once a liberal Democrat." I dropped the subject. Further exchanges with an *ingénu* too old for his craft seemed unprofitable.

Lyndon Johnson lived through the summer and fall that year in political heaven, with ambrosia for every meal, with nothing but good news in the papers and on the screen. He didn't have to campaign—his furious executive activity was keeping him in favorable headlines without it. When he did go out to campaign, his tours amounted to a series of triumphal appearances. His huge,

armored Lincoln Continental, big as and shaped like a boat, was unloaded from a second airplane at each stop just before the press landed. The long sleek whale of an airplane, bearing the words "United States of America," that seemed to go on forever, made his emergence from it look like a second coming. He worked the airport crowds, then got into his limousine and went into town, pausing at corners to take a bullhorn and speak. Johnson looked like a man who could and did win the biggest landslide election victory in Presidential history. Once he somehow got on the very top of a car and stood there, a gigantic figure way above the cheering crowds, bullhorn in hand. I had a premonition that I was looking at him at the peak of his life. It had never been so good before. It would not be nearly so good again. In fact, it would get downright miserable.

CHAPTER SIXTY-SIX

Making Jefferson Honest

Since the close of the Civil War, the U.S. has been hesitating between two worlds—"one dead, one powerless to be born." War brought an end to an old order . . . but proved unequal to founding a new one.
—ROBERT H. JACKSON, *Associate Justice, Supreme Court, quoting Matthew Arnold*

I count the passage and enforcement of the Civil Rights laws, alongside the overcoming of the Depression, the winning of the Second World War and the winning of the Cold War, as the United States' supreme achievements during my lifetime. I followed no act of government as closely as I did the Civil Rights laws of the 1960s, from the streets to the White House and through committee and floor debates in the two houses of Congress. As they preoccupied me and my broadcasts for years, it is essential to this story to revisit the milestones.

John Kennedy sought to achieve equal rights for Black Americans by taking individual executive actions as crises arose—for example, sending federal marshals to protect Black students enrolling in White Southern colleges. Past experience suggested it would be nearly impossible to accomplish the desired results in the most reasonable way—by passing a rights law through Congress.

There, committees, the iron gates to the floor, were dominated by Southerners, and the floor action was sterilized by an alliance of Southern Democrats with Conservative Republicans. But by 1963, the temper of the people who elected those representatives had changed. Television pictures of recurring horrors such as the attacks that bloodied the Freedom Riders—and incidentally unhorsed me—had become nightly fare. Even indifferent citizens were beginning to feel and to say, "Something must be done." Also, some Republicans in Congress were becoming alert to their party's Lincolnian past. So, in his third year in office, Kennedy determined to try to push a Civil Rights bill through Congress. It aimed essentially to achieve the goals of the Freedom Riders: to open all public accommodations, restaurants, hotels and terminals equally to all Americans, with the federal government taking over enforcement from the states.

In August 1963 came the March on Washington. A quarter-million people, Black and White, from all over the nation, congregated at the Lincoln Memorial to demand that after a century of neglect the President and Congress fulfill the requirement in the last sentences of the Fourteenth and Fifteenth Amendments—pass laws to enforce equal rights and put an end to the continuing horror shows on the streets. I was assigned by ABC as its sole reporter at the Memorial. At one point the network switched to me on the steps, and I described the scene, pointed out celebrities, quoted excerpts from a couple of unremarkable speeches and then switched back. I assumed there would be nothing more, so I left the podium area and the crowd and went around to the side of the Memorial to take a nap on cool marble. Then, from one of the loudspeakers near my prone head came that ringing voice that always commanded attention. It came like waves rising in the ocean, each cresting in a refrain, "I have a dream. . . ." In an instant I was as alert as ever I have been in my life. I scrambled up and back to the podium. The audience was beginning to respond to the refrain; Martin Luther King was commanding the waves. I grabbed our open phone to the control room in New York, "You have got to get this," I said. They answered, "We haven't missed a word. Stand by to introduce a replay the moment he finishes." I knew that I was hearing one of the great utterances of the nation's history.

Kennedy worked on his Civil Rights bill as he had not on any before it, organizing pressure from all sides on Congress. Coup of coups, he won over Charles Halleck, the Republican House minority leader. With that, he got the bill out of the Judiciary Committee and, on November 21, 1963, into Judge Smith's Rules Committee. The very next day, Kennedy was killed in Dallas. Some thought the ascent of Johnson would mean the end of the campaign. Said *The New York Times*, "Lyndon Johnson is regarded with suspicion by many of the Negro forces and their natural White allies. It will be difficult for many to conceive of him as a leader on that front." The *Times* had not been listening. As Vice President, with the Southern trammels cut away, Johnson had become fervent on the subject. In 1963, the Capital Press Club, formed by Black reporters years before, when they were excluded from the National Press Club, presented awards to Herblock (the great editorial cartoonist), to the Vice President and to me. In an emotional acceptance speech, Johnson said, "It seems to me that in the field of human rights we are well past the stage where half a loaf will do. Until Justice is blind to color, until education is unaware of race, until opportunity is unconcerned with the color of mens' skins, emancipation will be a proclamation but not a fact."

On Johnson's first night as President, an aide suggested that odds were three to one against passage of the Civil Rights bill, and that taking over the fight for it would jam the legislative process. The aide said, "You shouldn't lay the prestige of the Presidency on the line." Johnson replied, "What's it for if it's not to be laid on the line?"

With Republican help, the bill reached the floor of the House. There Southerners sought to amend it to death. I still see my owlish namesake, Judge Smith, standing to introduce a crippling amendment, saying, "This bill is so imperfect, what harm will a little old amendment do?" It was killed. Judge Smith then introduced a second amendment, saying, "I dare you to reject this one." The House dared, and it died. He introduced a third, to secure equality for women. It was meant half as a complication, half as a joke. It passed to cheers from a gallery of women. After the defeat of 100 amendments, the House passed the most far-reaching Civil Rights bill ever, 290 to 120. Opponents were consoled that the Senate would kill it, either in the Judiciary Committee, chaired by Senator James Eastland (D-Miss.), or by filibuster on the floor.

Pro-Administration Senators resorted to a maneuver called "Meeting the House bill at the Senate door." That enabled the bill to be brought directly to the Senate floor for a vote on whether it had to go to the Eastland mortuary or not. By simple majority it was voted ready for debate without the deathly interlude. But now Southern Senators prepared to filibuster it to death, for it took two-thirds of the Senate to close off a filibuster. *The New York Times* editorialized, "There are doubts that Mr. Johnson can surmount the filibuster without a compromise of a sort that might alienate Negro voters." Johnson himself stated, "So far as this Administration is concerned, its position is firm and we stand on the House Bill." A reporter asked, "Do you anticipate a filibuster? . . . Do you think, in order to pass it in the Senate, the Bill will have to be substantially trimmed?" Johnson said, "No, I do not think it will have to be substantially trimmed. And yes, I do expect a filibuster."

The spotlight now focused on a lone Senator, the Republican Leader, Everett Dirksen of Illinois. He was the most colorful figure in Congress for many generations, a large man with a foghorn voice, a wanton curl of hair that hung down over his forehead, and a face storm-tossed with crests and hollows of flesh. Spoke Senator Mike Mansfield the Democrat: "I appeal to the distinguished Minority Leader, whose patriotism has always taken precedence over his partisanship, to join with me. . . ." Countered Senator Richard Russell of Georgia, leader of the Southerners: "I cannot refrain, even if it does harm to the Senator from Illinois, from expressing to him my great admiration. . . ."

Dirksen, savoring his place at History's center stage, stated an elaborate noncommitment to my microphone in an interview:

> I trust that the time will never come in my public career when the waters of partisanship will flow so swift and so deep as to obscure my estimate of the national interest. I trust I can disenthrall myself from all bias, from all prejudice, from all irrelevancies, from all immaterial matters, and see clearly and cleanly what the issue is, and then render an independent judgment.

(Dirksen was so entertaining in several talks I had with him that ABC cleared time for us to do an hour-long program together. It took the form of his giving me a guided tour of the Capitol, with cameras following and microphones open.)

The thought of succeeding to the tradition of his state's greatest citizen began to move Dirksen. His negotiations with Democrats, all held in Dirksen's office beneath his pride and joy, the tinkling crystal chandelier that once belonged to Thomas Jefferson, started to sway him. As a Johnson aide put it. "We were creating a saintly niche for Ev; all he had to do was to step into it."

Senator Hubert Humphrey (D-Minn.), floor manager of the bill, felt confident enough to say of his opponents:

> This is no longer a battle of the heart for them. They simply have to die in the trenches; that's what they were sent here for. They are old, and they haven't any recruits. They know it. One of them said to me, "You simply have to overwhelm us." And so we have to beat them to a pulp. No one can make peace. They have to be destroyed.

Meanwhile, a new threat had been rising on the right. George Wallace, the diminutive Governor of Alabama, was running in all the 1964 primaries, trying to win the Democrats' nomination for President. People opposed to the Civil Rights Movement saw that Southern Senators could no longer protect them, so they turned to Wallace. He shook Civil Rights advocates by winning 34 percent of the Democrats' votes in Wisconsin and 29 percent in Indiana.

The term "White backlash" was created to describe the phenomenon. When Wallace won 43 percent in Maryland, Johnson acted to create a countervailing "frontlash."

The President went to Atlanta, where he could claim the widest attention in the South. Riding down Peachtree Street he halted repeatedly to harangue swelling crowds by bullhorn. In a speech to the Georgia legislature, he said, "Because the Constitution requires it, because justice demands it, we must protect the constitutional rights of all citizens, regardless of race, religion or the color of their skins. I would remind you that we are a very small minority living in a world of 3 billion people. We are outnumbered 17 to 1 and no one of us is fully free until all of us are fully free." His ovation was stormy. His success in canceling out Wallace became evident in the election results later that year. Johnson felt sure enough of the outcome to neglect Congress and begin a marathon of phone calls to Southern governors and police officers, inviting them to the White House to share in making plans to enforce the coming law.

In June, the issue of closing off the filibuster finally came to a vote. Senator Mansfield said, "The Senate now stands at the crossroads of History." Senator Humphrey said, "The Constitution of the United States is on trial." Senator Dirksen said, "The time has come for equality. . . . It will not be stayed or denied. It is here." By a vote of 71 to 29, the longest filibuster ever was broken. On July 2, 1964, the bill was passed, 73 to 27. Five hours later, the President signed it into law. I felt a little as I had when I watched Field Marshal Keitel sign the unconditional surrender at Karlshorst. It was a brilliant victory at the end of a long, dark tunnel.

In its main purpose the Civil Rights Act of 1964 was an immediate success. Johnson insisted on regular reports from all over the South to confirm that it was being enforced. Visiting old haunts in Louisiana, I found Blacks accommodated in hotels and being served along with Whites in restaurants, visions beyond imagining in my youth. In the town of Lafayette, Louisiana, where I once had the joy of setting a track record, I saw a notice in the papers apprising the populace of the phone number and address of the nearest U.S. Attorney, available for complaints about noncompliance.

The next year the capstone was placed on the edifice of legal rights. Southern officials had continued to apply tricks to prevent Black citizens from registering to vote. Reverend King led a movement to force the issue and ran into police violence in Selma, Alabama. Johnson called the two Houses of Congress together and presented a bill to settle it, to become the Voting Rights Act of 1965, by which the federal government would be authorized to enforce equal access to the ballot box when local registrars did not. I introduced the President's address on ABC and commented on it afterward. It was his finest hour.

At one point, he spoke of Mexican-American schoolchildren he had taught as a young man:

> Somehow you never forget what poverty and hatred can do, when you see its scars on the hopeful face of a young child. I never thought then, in 1928, that I would be standing here in 1965. It never even occurred to me in my fondest dreams that I might have the chance to help the sons and daughters of those students and to help them all over the country. But now I do have that chance—and I'll let you in on a secret—I mean to use it.

Majorities in Congress were organized with the same vigor as before. The bill became law. Its enforcement was closely monitored and strictly executed. This was the peak of the mountain after a climb of centuries. At the moment when I first put these words on paper, twenty-five years after the first Rights bill was enacted, America's first soldier, the Chairman of the Joint Chiefs, was a Black American; the Governor of the premier Southern state, Virginia, was too. So was the head of the biggest and oldest political party. Black Americans were mayors of twenty-six of our biggest cities. The entertainment world was well populated by Black artists, and the world of sports by Black athletes.

As in all extensions of liberty, residues of old ways and attitudes linger. They will hang on longer in respect to the only minority that did not immigrate of its free will and that was locked in subordination of one kind or another for centuries. The recent incursion of heavy drugs, afflicting the poorest most, slows assimilation. There will be conflicts, some for real reasons, some synthesized by demagogues, Black and White, for race prejudice has mysteriously deep, clinging roots in the dark recesses of the human psyche that will require time and effort to dig out. But whatever the shape of conflicts to come, in all that is durable, the decisive battle in the struggle against race discrimination was won in 1965.

Young Roger Wilkins, a Black youth working in the Johnson administration, tells that he once asked the President—all Texan, all Southerner, all political accommodator—how he become *the* Civil Rights President of all time. Johnson replied, "The answer is in words you may have heard somewhere before: 'Free at last, free at last, thank God A'mighty, I'm free at last.'"

CHAPTER SIXTY-SEVEN

Warring the Tubercle

Most of Johnson's legislative record consisted of assaults on race problems and on poverty. Later events have shown that the two are often interchangeable evils. His record on race is unchallenged. But his War on Poverty is widely publicized as a great failure. That indefatigable quipster, Ronald Reagan, always won snickers with his summation, delivered with a sly grin, "We had a War on Poverty and Poverty won." President Bush's last Attorney General said of the terrible Los Angeles riots of 1992, "We are dealing with the wreckage of the War on Poverty." I believe such judgments are at best shallow and at worst sufficiently wrong to damage efforts to deal with a problem that is a clinging, low-grade tuberculosis in our society.

In the 1950s glow of postwar prosperity, opinion makers generally assumed that poverty had disappeared from American life or was rapidly doing so. The poor were disguised in euphemisms—the "underprivileged" or the "disadvantaged." In his book *The Affluent Society* in 1958, so penetrating a commentator as John Kenneth Galbraith said that poverty was no longer "a massive affliction [but] more nearly an after-thought." In going over the dispersed, rather than collected, scripts of the less penetrating H. K. Smith, I found a statement that slums no longer existed in Washington, D.C. The truth seems to be that Eisenhower's antiseptic freeways, by which Americans moved from and to suburban homes without seeing the city, plus increased air travel enabling them to fly over it, made poverty invisible.

In 1962, two writers discovered and quantified the poor. Leon Keyserling, formerly President Truman's economic adviser, and then head of the private Committee for Economic Development, issued a study concluding that a fifth of Americans lived in abject want. Michael Harrington, a young Catholic Socialist writer, published a book titled *The Other America,* revealing the same but more compellingly. John Kennedy invited each in turn to the White House, and then ordered all relevant agencies to make studies and recommendations for programs to get at poverty. Nothing was ready when Kennedy died. His chief economic adviser, Walter Heller, went to try to persuade Johnson to follow up and was surprised to find the new President ahead of him. Johnson wanted plans ready to present to Congress in 1964.

The President declared his "unconditional War on Poverty" in his first State of the Union address in February, and a month later he sent Congress a special message launching ten separate programs to be coordinated by a new agency called the Office of Economic Opportunity, and to be headed by Kennedy's brother-in-law, Sargent Shriver.

Much of the subsequent criticism of the program seems to rest on the assumption that no special anti-poverty action is needed. If we simply get the economy roaring, it will absorb the poor: a rising tide lifts all ships. The retort must be: broken ships with holes in them do not rise with a tide. Having neither skills to produce supply nor incomes to engage in demand, the poor do not participate in the supply-and-demand economy. The New Deal enabled temporarily poor middle classes to recover, for they knew what to do with the jobs offered them. But like the really rich, the really poor are different. Provided with money, the truly poor are as likely to spend it on a diet of Pepsi-Cola and potato chips (and, later, crack) as they are to spend it on nutrition. Given jobs, they know less than others how to handle the work, are sick more often, miss work more often, make more mistakes, need more supervision, get into more fights and abandon the jobs more readily. Now, in more recent times the drug curse has entered the picture, and the transformation of too many impoverished youths into mindless, heartless, nonhuman zombies, harder than ever to deal with, has happened. Courtesy of the National Rifle Association, they acquire death-dealing weapons without difficulty. Courtesy of movie and television executives and producers, they learn the ease and attraction of shooting people to death, often for no reason but the fun of the blast. No: poverty is a special problem requiring special treatment. And it had waited too long for treatment to be tried. Johnson accepted the challenge.

It is said that he oversold his program with winging rhetoric that could bring only disappointment. Well, the title, War on Poverty (borrowed from David Lloyd George of Britain's landmark Liberal government of 1911) *was* winging rhetoric. But I look through LBJ's public pronouncements about it and find none without warnings. In first mentioning it in the State of the Union address: "It will not be a short or an easy struggle, no single weapon or strategy will suffice. . . ." In a TV interview with reporters from the three networks: "We realize it is a beginning, it is not an extremely comprehensive program." In his message to Congress asking for passage: "We still have a long way to go. . . . We are fully aware that this program will not eliminate all the poverty in America in a few months or a few years. Poverty is deeply rooted and its causes are many."

Other critics argue that he should have waited till sociologists had learned more about poverty. His answer was, "We were experimenting on the outer edge of understanding. . . . However, we could not wait until our understanding was complete and our procedures were perfected. We had to act. We had to begin." It did need longer study, but Johnson knew that there are tides in governmental affairs. He was riding one, and had no idea whether it would last more than a few months. If it was to be done, it had to be done now. Occasionally it is said that he asked for too small an appropriation for so big a job. He responded that it was experimental. Nobody had ever tried to eliminate poverty before. "We had to work by trial and error, and there *was* error." More often, though, the opposite criticism is made: it was the granddaddy of all big-spending programs, a bad example for future Presidents. The rebuttal lies in a remarkable fact that our later Presidents should have learned: In 1968, his year of highest spending on the war in Vietnam and on all the Great Society programs—including the War on Poverty—Johnson produced a balanced budget! And it was the last time in my lifetime that the nation saw a balanced federal budget.

The most conspicuous and consequential of the program's errors was the Community Action Program, whereby the poor were to form community groups to work up their own plans. Their proposals would then be studied, and those accepted would be financed with grants of money to be administered by local groups. This in response to the act's call for "maximum feasible participation" by the poor themselves in planning and operating the program. The phrase sounds harmless, but it was charged with the dynamite of contention between local elected officials and the leaders of new ad hoc organizations of the poor, many of whom promptly became militant opponents of elected officials.

This contentious and damaging clause was included for a good reason. The poor really were excluded from American life. Consider the case of the Bedford-Stuyvesant section of New York. It contained nearly half a million people, more than many whole cities. Yet in terms of civic life, it was as though it was not a part of America, with no representation or even recognition. It had but one high school, and 80 percent of its teenagers were dropouts. Infant mortality was twice the national average. Unemployment was probably between 30 and 50 percent. But in fifteen years of the urban renewal program it had received not one dollar of funds. It took a lawsuit in 1968 to give the area its first congressman of its own. This huge, deeply troubled piece of America was simply ignored by elected officers. It was to correct this that the "maximum participation" of the poor was required.

But the cost of the policy may have proved too high in the long run. The poor were, virtually by definition, not up to it. Charlatans moved in to take the lead; and in a little time such areas grew their own charlatans, who learned how to profit by being professional victims. Other minorities learned the lesson, and in time grew their own agitators to make their own uncompromising demands. Far from being a melting pot, America was growing into a congeries of minorities, of victims, making governance very hard.

Still, the War on Poverty produced both short-term and long-term successes of moment. In the short term it reduced the proportion of Americans living in poverty from 19 percent to 12 percent. Over the long term it produced the single best key to exit from poverty, which was and is improved education that sticks. In 1960, 22 percent of Black adults had high school diplomas. At the present time, in the 1990s, the figure is 67 percent. Much of this improvement was due to the Poverty War's Head Start program. Kids given special education from age four—or better, from age three—tend to fall in love with education, don't drop out, and, if followed up, go on through high school to jobs or college. One reason the inner-city ghettoes remain in bad condition is that the Head Start generations have made it and moved out to the suburbs, leaving the city tax base ever thinner. Thus the District of Columbia shrinks and suffers while neighboring Prince George's County grows and prospers with a predominantly Black population. Politicians all praise Head Start, but haven't, up till now, loved it enough to fund it adequately. Currently there are only enough resources to accommodate about one-third of eligible children.

Medicare and Medicaid have proved blessings to the elderly and the poor. There are bugs in these and all programs, but they are mostly the products of negligent later generations. It has been the pleasure of recent Congresses and Presidents simply to let them grow out of control. Complex programs such as these have to be maintained and brought up to date. The jobs program was widely criticized in its time. It was only when a giant of a Black youth from Houston won the heavyweight-class gold medal for boxing in the Olympics and ran around the ring waving a tiny American flag, that the nation discovered that it was a success. Interviewed then by everybody, George Foreman recalled that his life was headed toward permanent imprisonment or death on the streets, till he got into the Job Corps and was turned around 180 degrees. A little investigation showed more successes than failures. Johnson's War on Poverty is rich with lessons. If a future President decides to move effectively against the disease, he will have to go back to the Johnson effort and avoid its mistakes while building upon its successes.

I shall devote more space in this chronicle to the Johnson Presidency than to others, because more events worth studying occurred during those years. The Civil Rights Revolution made the period historic. The War on Poverty is rich with long-range lessons and controversy. Those were the good things. But bad historic things happened, too, and they darkened the nation's memory of the good ones.

At the end of his first full year in the White House, the President's record was excellent; his standing with the people, quantified in a landslide election, unmatched. The nation's economy had never been better, and the horizon was bright with promise. Then two small clouds appeared. They were at first not thought to be important. But they were to grow remarkably fast, until they filled all the sky.

Sixteen days after the triumphant passage of the great Civil Rights bill of 1964, in New York City's Harlem neighborhood, a Black youth lunged at a policeman. The policeman shot the boy dead. The streets of Harlem filled with angry Blacks. Buildings were set afire, shops were looted. It was an unusually violent reaction to a police encounter of a kind that had happened before. Still, it was at first seen as an isolated event. No one could guess that violent riots were to become regular horrors for the rest of the Johnson years, up and down the East Coast, then in Los Angeles, then in cities all over the nation. Those the President sought most to help were lashing out and destroying in rage.

Sixteen more days after the Civil Rights Act of 1964, in far off Southeast Asia, Communist Vietnamese torpedo boats attacked a U.S. destroyer in international waters, beginning another train of events that would transform luminous dreams of a greater age for our nation into an ugly nightmare.

1965-1974

CHAPTER SIXTY-EIGHT

Vietnam

One evening in the fall of 1965, a reporter in daily contact with his office in Vietnam phoned to tell me our son, Jack, serving in the Air Cavalry, had been wounded. I phoned the Pentagon for details, but no one who would know was there. The next morning while I was bathing before going to the Pentagon myself, the phone rang and Bennie answered. After a moment she shouted to me, "The President wants to talk to you." That office being common to the Press Club, ABC News and the P.T.A., I asked, "The President of what?" She answered, "The President of the United States." There is still the vague print of a wet foot where I bounded from bath to phone. President Johnson told me Jack had been wounded in a major battle in the central highlands of Vietnam, but had been helicoptered to the coast for repairs, then flown to an American hospital in Japan, where he would recover quickly.

I was reassured. But had he told me the whole story, I would not have been. Most of the fighting in Vietnam was with bands of guerrillas. But the battle Jack was in was a rare head-on collision of U.S. and North Vietnam regular troops in the Ia Drang Valley in the central highlands. Overall, the battle, the bloodiest of the whole war, was a major victory for American troops. But for Jack's company it was a disaster. He was part of Custer's old outfit, the Seventh Cavalry, and what happened to him was all too similar to what happened to Custer. Jack's company was ambushed and just about wiped out: 93 percent casualties; of these half were killed, half wounded, and most of the wounded would be crippled for life. Jack was wounded three separate times. Once, a North Vietnamese soldier used his body as a prop for a machine gun. Jack said later, "The only reason he didn't discover I was alive was that he was shaking more than I was." He was locked in a hell of fire, bleeding, hurting, terrified, seeing buddies maimed, killed, blown apart for twenty-four unrelenting hours. He said to me in a television interview, "There's no way you can think back and imagine how horrible it was; it was so horrible that, if the devil would stop the war for a second and ask you, would you sell your mother into slavery, and execute your father, you would do it in a second. Every once in a while when I think about it, I start getting chills, and feel I want to die just thinking about it." Long after, at home, when his body had recovered, the horror lay cocooned in his mind. We would hear Jack screaming in his sleep. When we woke him up, he would blink at us and say, "Something wrong? What's up?"

Jack's misadventure marks as clearly as any event the transition of the dirty little Vietnam War into a dirty big war. ABC decided to devote a half-hour program solely to it every week and I was assigned to write and anchor it. I was grateful that my friend Tom Wolf was made producer, for without his skill and humor I don't think I would have lasted long in intimacy with so depressing a topic. Normally we did all but the combat reports in the U.S., for production facilities did not exist in Vietnam. Also much of the drama of the issue was in the streets of the States and the halls of government. After Jack's ordeal we moved to Vietnam for a while and turned out a number of programs. I sat on the grass with Jack, who by then was somewhat repaired and back with the Air Cavalry at An Khe in the highlands, and we talked at length about the war. The program was titled, "A Father, a Son and a War" and it won praise from critics. Then once I simply sat on the parapet of a building in Saigon and told the camera my analysis of the war at some length. It won me my sixth Overseas Press Award—shared with Harrison Salisbury of *The New York Times* and his opposite viewpoint—for Best Interpretation of Foreign Affairs.

Assignment to the Vietnam issue became a unique and troubling professional experience. I watched a gap grow ever wider between me and the Washington punditocracy of which I had thought myself a tolerable member. My comments were frankly hawkish; I felt the Communists were on a roll in Southeast Asia: great China to the north; Indonesia, planning to join the Communist bloc, just below; and North Vietnam, amply supplied by Russia and China, on a rampage in between. Later, shortly before his death, the President of Indonesia, Sukarno, stated his design. As quoted in *The New York Times* on September 7, 1966, he said, "The strategy for defeating imperialism . . . is for Communist China to strike a blow against American troops in Vietnam from the north while Indonesia strikes from the south." My commentaries were dominated by a belief that a firm stand had to be made or there would be the devil to pay.

Also I felt that Johnson had inherited a mess there on Kennedy's death, was dealing with it as well as anyone could, and that many in the media were not reporting it fairly. The seminal event of the whole war, for example, was the Tonkin Gulf Resolution, reported by much of the press as an act of deception by the Johnson Administration to trick Congress into supporting the war. Quite the contrary: I saw it as an act of high wisdom. As Communist attacks against U.S. bases intensified and public opinion in America was registering 80 percent for hanging on, Johnson made a decision. He told his staff, "I'm not getting any deeper in this without Congress." A resolution of support was drawn up to be submitted to Congress when the next attack occurred. It would, it was expected, be an attack on a land base. In fact, it came at sea, in the Gulf of Tonkin. An American destroyer was patrolling the delta of North

Vietnam's Red River, which runs through Hanoi. The vessel's mission was the same as the one Russian vessels carried out against U.S. naval ports, and ours against theirs: to nose into territorial waters, set off alarms and acquire a record of the other side's responses, never yet a cause for fighting. This time, however, the Communists attacked. The incident at sea caught Johnson by surprise. But two nights later when a second U.S. destroyer reported a similar attack, he was ready—and also conscious of a political need to show firmness—and sent his resolution to Congress. Congress's enabling act of the Vietnam War passed unanimously in the House and 98 to 2 in the Senate.

I later asked Johnson why he did not seek a declaration of war. He said that we did not know what treaties Hanoi had with Russia or China; a formal state of war might have triggered something like a Chinese attack on U.S. forces, as happened in Korea.

In light of their later views, it is interesting to note that at that time most of the national press in America blessed the President's initiative. *The New York Times* said the Tonkin Resolution was proof of "our united determination to support the cause of freedom in Southeast Asia . . . against the mad adventure by the North Vietnamese Communists." In his book on Vietnam published a few months later, David Halberstam wrote that Vietnam "is a legitimate part of [America's] global commitment. A strategic country in a key area, it is perhaps one of only five or six nations in the world that is truly vital to U.S. interests."

Alas, there was a flaw in the initiative. The first Tonkin Gulf attack was in daylight with many witnesses. In the case of the second attack, on a stormy night, the American skipper warned that a new sonar man may have mistaken his sounds, and there may in fact have been no attack. Secretary of Defense McNamara said there were records of radio transmissions between North Vietnamese assault boats and the shore, proving that an attack occurred, so the Tonkin resolution was sent to the Congress. When the public humor changed, this uncertainty about the second attack was the opening through which charges of trickery and deviousness poured. A moment's thought should have told critics that the Tonkin incident was not essential. Had it not happened, Johnson would have simply sent Congress his bid later that year on the occasion of big attacks on Bien Hoa and the Brink Hotel billet, and Congress would have passed it then.

Another favorite subject for press outrage was peace talks allegedly agreed to by Hanoi but forestalled and prevented by Johnson. A case in point appeared on the front page of *The Washington Post* on February 3, 1967: Poland, it said, had arranged for talks to begin in Warsaw; but in time's nick, Johnson had ordered bombing attacks, and the Communists withdrew approval. The story was picked up by papers all over the world and recounted in a dozen books which researchers from now till doomsday will refer to. Nearly two years later, on December 5, 1968, the *Post* reported new evidence revealing that the original report was wrong; North Vietnam had never been interested in and had never agreed to any talks. The first story had appeared on the front page. The correction appeared among the ads on page 26. It might have occurred to the writers of wrong stories that, if Johnson was actually rejecting talks Hanoi wanted, Hanoi would have been the first to say so to exploit such outrageous hawkery. In fact, Hanoi never mentioned any instance of thwarted peace talks. Ho Chi Minh had no wish whatever to talk.

Examples of bad reporting proliferated. It was widely reported at one time that our UN Ambassador, Adlai Stevenson, had found a means of opening talks but Johnson turned him down. Stevenson, it was said, was disenchanted with the Administration and planned to resign, but died before he was able to do so. Little attention was paid Stevenson's own words. Three days before his death, he wrote a group of dissident intellectuals, "The purposes and directions [of American policy in Vietnam] are sound. I do not believe that the policy of retreat in Asia or anywhere else in the world would make any contribution whatever." Pulling out of Vietnam, he wrote, would "set us off on the old, old route whereby expansive powers push at more and more doors, believing they will open until, at the ultimate door, resistance is unavoidable and a major war breaks out. . . . This is the point of the conflict in Vietnam."

There was a feeding frenzy on, devouring a capable, if unpopular, leader who was moving the only way the real circumstances of the time allowed. Johnson's policy was well expressed by Peter Lisagor of the *Chicago Daily News*. To comprehend the point of his story one must know only the fact that at that time one of the leading department stores in Washington was named Garfinckel's. Lisagor said he was invited to cocktails by a few officials of the Soviet Embassy, probably the usual KGB operatives hoping to squeeze a morsel or two out of a well-connected reporter. Why, they asked Peter, does Johnson so resist talking peace with Hanoi? Lisagor said, "You people really have the wrong impression. The last time I talked with the President we discussed just that and he said, and I think he was telling the absolute truth, 'If Ho Chi Minh would agree to talk with me, I would kiss his ass in Garfinckel's window.'" Peter's story fell flat. There was an embarrassed silence as his hosts shifted from one foot to another and nervously puffed cigarettes held like tiny bazookas. Eventually, one of them sidled up to him and whispered, as if on the verge of acquiring deep intelligence, "Who is this Garfinckel?"

My commentaries, critical of the anti-Vietnam rioters and in favor of fighting on in Vietnam, ran head-on against the Liberal mainstream. I lost old friends as a bison loses hair, in large swatches. Lippmann was a most regrettable loss. Cronkite wrote me a sharp note saying I had challenged some view he had uttered on television. I did not recall any personal challenge, but as I was nearly alone in the positions I was taking, I may have done so without realizing it.

One loss was downright spectacular. The American Society of Newspaper Editors, in convention in Washington, asked me to debate Arkansas Senator J. William Fulbright on the whole subject of Vietnam. I was irritated by what I felt was the Senator's pose of liberalism though voting against every Civil Rights bill, so I agreed. Fulbright opened the encounter with his standard case against the Johnson Administration, as prepared by his staff. I dismantled his case in what I felt was surgical fashion. When I sat down, he leaned over and whispered to me, "A strong argument." I whispered back, "I have only begun." In response to questions from the floor I attacked him with an animus I did not know I was capable of. In my notes I have the wounding blow: "You have said our involvement in Vietnam is the most disgraceful action ever undertaken in America's name. You have neglected to mention that you were the floor manager in the Senate of the Tonkin Gulf Resolution, which made the disgrace possible, and that you were instrumental in its passing by a vote of 98 to 2. Now, you will want to put an end to that disgrace. The Tonkin Resolution can be revoked by a simple majority vote. I will yield the podium to allow you to announce that you will introduce a resolution in the Senate to revoke the Tonkin Resolution." I stood aside. Fulbright looked away. What I proposed would have been an act of political suicide for a Senator from the South. I won the argument, but I think I lost the audience in a surge of sympathy for the victim. I think they did not like the sight of the distinguished author of the Fulbright scholarships being beaten up on by a reporter, and a TV reporter at that.

In fact, I did not much like the sight myself. As I collided again and again with long-admired friends, I heard Cromwell's imperative as if directed across the ages specifically to me (though without the anatomical reference): "I beseech you, in the bowels of Christ, think it possible you may be mistaken." After two trying years of living with the subject, I resolved to seek out why honest and intelligent people could differ so drastically on the subject of Vietnam.

CHAPTER SIXTY-NINE

An Unfinished Book

I asked ABC for a year of unpaid leave to devote my time wholly to trying to plumb two mysteries. One was the complex President, who "lit more fires than any and never set people on fire," and of whom the perceptive columnists Evans and Novak said, "90 percent of what he does is right and 90 percent of how he does it is wrong." The other was his perverse war, in which the world's mightiest military power won every encounter against a native peasant army in a progress headed clearly to failure. This resolve of mine coincided with a recurrence of doubts about wanting to stay in television. Bennie and I went into conference with one another for a couple of weeks and came out with a decision to try to turn this year-off into a permanent departure. The plan was to make a living by writing books and lecturing, with my search for light on Johnson and Vietnam as initial subjects.

ABC News' new boss, Bill Sheehan, agreed to my request, on condition I make myself available to anchor all political events in the following election year, 1968. A publisher was interested in my plan and offered a comfortable advance on the book. As this became one of my worst professional failures, I ease the pain by hastening to the outcome. The more I delved, the more complex both topics became. When election time approached, I decided I needed more time and distance from Johnson and the war. With nearly half a manuscript done I returned the advance and went back to the tube.

But the experience was not wasted. About the war I developed themes that seem to have grown more valid with time. And the adventure of studying a tragic historic leader close up was infinitely fascinating.

I began work on the project by conducting two or three—sometimes more—interviews each day with political and intellectual critics, with Johnson's staff and most intensively with the subject himself. Mostly Johnson met me in the tiny hideaway cube of a room off the Oval Office. A recurrent theme was his anger with my profession:

> They [reporters] hate Texas. They hate Presidents. They said terrible things about Hoover. The Liberals said horrible things about Truman. Kennedy was called a do-nothing President, until he died and became a saint. They hate me. If I look good they'll say I'm living it up. If I look tired they'll say I've got syphilis.

He got a tremendous lift from the approval of his few peers. "You know what Harry Truman said to me?" he told me nose-to-nose one day. "Harry Truman said, 'Mr President, you can't do anything wrong in my eyes.' That's what Harry Truman said to me." Once he took me to a quick lunch alone upstairs in the family dining room. We had cheeseburgers; I had one, he had two. Lunching on that fare in the exquisite room with its hand-painted wallpaper depicting the victory at Yorktown was like finding a McDonald's in the Hall of Mirrors at Versailles. In midbite, he said, "Now I want to read you the kind of mail I like to get." And he took from an inside pocket and read aloud to me a letter from ex-President Eisenhower sympathizing with him and commending his actions in Vietnam.

There are two broad requisites for being President, being a doer and being an explainer. Johnson had problems explaining but as a doer he was matched only by that of the second Roosevelt. He was a remarkably accessible President, as easily available to businessfolk as to union men, to academics as to politicians, even to reporters. "We have to keep the White House doors oiled," an aide said to me, "he keeps inviting everybody in for a talk." He "machine-guns" visitors with questions, and "he really listens," one said and others confirmed. He paid special attention to dissenting views. His lone staff dissenter on Vietnam, George Ball, Deputy Secretary of State and later Ambassador to the UN, said, "He always insisted that I take as much time as I wanted. He would say to me, 'Don't cut corners,' and 'Be sure you say it all.'" Mrs. Johnson spent a long morning with me in the lovely little Lincoln sitting room, reading from her White House diary. With two and three meetings going on at once in different rooms, and Lyndon moving from one to another, she said, "Life in the White House is one big, never-ending seminar."

In past presidencies (and in later ones) the average member of Congress might hope to be invited to the White House once a year for a mass reception. Johnson had them all in, individually or in groups, several times a year, and he talked to them on the phone more often. Once when I was let into the cubicle, he was on the phone to someone on the Hill. He put his hand over the mouthpiece and said, "One out of three calls is to kiss somebody's ass." Once in summer he told me he had been through all of Congress twice and "now I'm bringing in their legislative assistants."

A measure of his devotion was told me by Larry O'Brien, the likable redhaired Irishman who was once Kennedy's campaign manager and was now Johnson's liaison officer with Congress (and would become more famous later as the target of the Watergate burglary). One morning at 2:30 A.M., a vote in Congress that O'Brien had promised the President he would win, fell apart. At seven A.M., O'Brien phoned Johnson to confess failure. "Why didn't you phone me when it happened?" Johnson said. "At 2:30 A.M.? I didn't want to wake you up," O'Brien answered. Johnson said, "Don't ever wait again. When you are bleeding I want to bleed."

Johnson's effectiveness, demonstrated by the remarkable number of landmark laws he maneuvered through Congress, may be even better measured by the action I mentioned earlier: in 1968, his last year, he left the nation its last balanced budget.

Consistent with my tendency to find myself out of the mainstream in this peculiar period, I developed a highly favorable view of Lyndon Johnson. He was an amalgam of qualities, most of them strong: fierce ambition to outcompete and excel; a genuine and deep compassion with the misfortunate; an x-ray mind that could see through faces into hearts, and could read motives, fears and prides with rare rapidity and clarity. Among his flaws were a personality that could be rough and coarse, and a tendency to hide his cards from public view; but James MacGregor Burns, who studied both, concluded he was not as devious as FDR.

His crippling flaw was an odd one. When he rose from Texas to national politics, there came rumbling up from his depths an irrational regional inferiority complex that dogged his performance. He found no humor in the grinning remark about his education by a Kennedy holdover, meant to amuse him, "The nation owes much to those finest of its institutions of learning, Harvard, Yale . . . the Southwest Texas State Teachers College." Fannie Flagg on *The Tonight Show* on TV impersonating Lady Bird with an exaggerated Texas accent amused Mrs. Johnson but offended LBJ. He was similarly displeased by the denomination of his family as the "Beverly Hillbillies in the White House." I found it hard to understand how a man who loved his region so dearly could feel embarrassment about it.

I think he was cowed by Camelot. His defensiveness had a marked effect on his performance. He was deferential in the extreme toward Kennedy men. Where Harry Truman, on assuming office, replaced FDR men with his own very early, Johnson clung to the end to those blessed with having been appointed by Kennedy. He was absolutely entranced by Robert McNamara, him of the steel-trap computer mind who always seemed right and could prove it with numbers. McNamara consented to an interview, but only I think because Johnson wanted him to. He was tense, prepared only to give answers that were the equivalent of name, rank and serial number, no more. Once in an interval he questioned me. "You were a Rhodes Scholar?" he asked. I said I had been. He asked, "Did you know Bruce Waybur?" I said I did. (He was a good friend, an ally in the Labour Club, as relaxed and genial as McNamara was taut.) With a smile that lacked warmth, McNamara said, "He beat me out for the Rhodes from California." Tension returned. He was clearly even then not comfortable with his own policies, which a quarter-century later he would actually denounce in a book. Had Johnson shed McNamara and replaced him with someone of his own choice early on, a new course might have been recommended earlier. The later Nixon policy of de-escalating, pulling American troops out in installments and forcing the South Vietnamese to fight their own ground war might, in Johnson's early term, have worked.

What of the war waged in the dim light of an interminable tunnel? Critical reporters have provided strong reasons for its failure in a half-dozen books of outstanding journalism. The suffocating overorganization of the U.S. support role; the flood of goods and dollars that fed native corruption and all but wiped out the native economy; the bombings and free-fire zones that made homeless refugees of 3 million peasants we had come to benefit; the failure effectively to embrace native South Vietnamese troops into American military units to make a fighting force of them, as was done in Korea. The patriotic John Wayne movie, *The Green Berets,* was unintentionally revealing. In its last scene, Wayne takes the hand of a small Vietnamese boy and tells him that our fighting for him is what the war was all about. The film closes with the two silhouettes against the seashore at sunset—the massive, hulking American leading the tiny, toothpick-limbed native boy away. It was too overwhelmingly America's war for the South Vietnamese to feel it was theirs.

There are other possible sources of failure. A military involvement based on unsuitable combat strategies is often asserted. But I incline toward two further major causes that are rarely mentioned by critics and that may have been decisive.

One was the total Communist control of the people of both Vietnams by an unconditional ruthlessness we could not match or break. The visible presence of American forces in the countryside was known to the peasants only by destructive armed sweeps lasting one day or a few. When the Americans moved back to their camps, the VC returned and ruled there for the balance of the year. I do not know if the figure of 300 individual political murders a week by the VC is correct, but from peasant testimonies, such terror acts were frequent and effective. One farmer told me about a local schoolteacher who was hung by his ankles, eviscerated and left with his entrails hanging for all the villagers to contemplate. After such a lesson, no peasant within range of hearsay would dare show any degree of compliance with anti-Communists. We made much of one horrifying American atrocity at My Lai, as we should have. But for the VC, atrocity was standard, a way of winning hearts and minds we could not match.

I do not think the Communists ever enjoyed wide popularity. In 1954 when they took over North Vietnam by treaty, about a million Vietnamese fled south. I cannot believe the argument that they were all Catholics obeying their priests. A mainly peasant people wedded to the soil, they pulled up roots and fled for the motive that makes most refugees flee: they were scared to death, and with reason. In a speech, the overall Communist commander, General Vo Nguyen Giap, said of their occupation of the North, "We tortured and killed too many," implying that they should have tortured and killed just enough. Of the VC who were left in the south in those years, Douglas Pike, a scholar of Southeast Asia, wrote in his book *Viet Cong:*

> Steadily, quietly, and with systematic ruthlessness, the NLF [the Communist Front organization, National Liberation Front] in six years wiped out an entire class of Vietnamese villagers. . . . This loss to South Vietnam is inestimable, and it will take a generation or more to repair the damage to society. By any definition, this NLF action against village leaders amounts to genocide.

In the great Tet offensive of 1968, the Communists counted on popular uprisings in their favor. None happened in any of the cities they attacked. After the final Communist victory in 1974, half a million Vietnamese filled rickety boats and rafts and sailed out into the South China Sea in the dismal hope that some passing ship would rescue them and take them somewhere else, anywhere else. Generally, the horrors inflicted by the Americans, such as bombings, alienated the people; the horrors inflicted by the Communists controlled them.

That, I believe, was one major reason Americans could get no grip. The other rarely mentioned source of failure was more important. It was only a hunch of mine when I sought to make it the theme of the book I undertook to write, but now it has became startlingly evident. In 1960, native Communists, supported by the giants China and Russia, could realistically expect to win the whole region and pose profound dangers to vital American interests. But while we fought there, the continent-wide surge lost force. The Cold War was in essence a competition between ways of life. Our way of economic life was quietly seducing all Vietnam's neighbors with no extra effort by us. The beneficent infection began when American companies formed joint companies in Japan in the early 1950s. The other Asian nations came in succession to discern the delightful fruits of capitalism and went after them with a gusto that made their peoples immune to the morose doctrines of eternal conflict offered by the Communists. Vietnam became marginal. Put succinctly, in 1960 there were strong geopolitical reasons for us to fight, but by the 1970s they had vanished. It is not an inexact metaphor to say that circumstance moved the goalposts on Johnson in the middle of the game.

The Communist decline in Asia began with American firms hustling investments in Japan just after the war. In 1953 alone, RCA, Westinghouse, Du Pont, Armco Steel and General Electric were just a few of the leading firms selling patents or helping start factories there. As Japanese costs rose—they would exceed America's by 1990—production spilled over into the nations that became the "Asian Tigers," with immense visible benefits. The negative effect of economics on Communism's chances was deepened by other events. In the archipelago nation of Indonesia, the seventh largest nation in the world, the huge Communist Party, which nearly owned the country, decided to take over completely. One night in 1965, in raids on their homes, six of seven army commanders were assassinated. But the seventh escaped, took command and set about destroying the Communist Party. In India, massive new investments in agriculture—forced by a President Johnson weary of supplying two shiploads of grain a day to India to forestall starvation—led to that land's becoming self-sufficient in grains and marked another lost opportunity for the Communists. Finally, by the 1970s great China, humbled by the disaster of her Cultural Revolution, was able to understand how little Taiwan could create a per capita income five times greater than its own, and began to liberalize its economy and soon would take the extended hand of President Nixon.

This evolution, not seen or fully appreciated while in progress, created a climate in which like-minded people could disagree. *The New York Times* could be throatily for intervention one moment and bitterly opposed the next. This is why the Senate could vote 98 to 2 for Tonkin in 1964 and vote to repeal it in 1970.

In a junglelike world, there was merit to the U.S. keeping a reputation for sticking to its guns. Dean Acheson defined "prestige" as the force that restrains you from shouting, "I can lick any man in this room," when you spot Joe Louis sitting in a corner. However, it was not enough to justify the death toll and the damaging of the American spirit.

CHAPTER SEVENTY

Annus Horribilis

If 1968 was not the most turbulent year since WW II, it was a gifted competitor. It opened with a blindside from a distant corner. The U.S. intelligence ship

Pueblo was attacked and seized by North Korean sailors and its crew imprisoned. The impression of the U.S. as a "helpless giant" was reinforced.

Seven days later, the war in Vietnam simply blew up. At the beginning of the Vietnamese New Year, called Tet, Communist forces attacked from within thirty-five cities and towns. In Saigon, they blasted their way into the U.S. Embassy compound. It proved a military failure for the Communists; they held onto only one town for a limited time, and their losses were catastrophic. But it was a psychological triumph. The vigor and scope of the Communist offensive shocked Americans and drained confidence in our government's leadership.

One political consequence was that, shortly after, in the Democratic Presidential primary elections in New Hampshire, Senator Eugene McCarthy of Minnesota, least political of politicians, more poet than politician, came within 231 votes of President Johnson's total. As agreed with ABC, I interrupted book writing to anchor the primary election night broadcast. In the course of it I did an on-air interview with the chief pollster of the University of Michigan, whom we had retained, and he revealed a startling new fact: the blow to the President came not just from Vietnam doves; hawks had now joined doves to express their lack of confidence in Johnson's ability to win the war.

Smelling blood, Robert Kennedy declared himself a candidate for the Democrats' nomination. A disheartened Johnson decided that he had become part of the problem. He appeared on television and shocked the nation by announcing that he would not seek reelection and would leave politics when his term was over.

In April, the sainted Martin Luther King was assassinated in Memphis by a professional gunman. Anger preempted sadness, and riots by Blacks broke out in many American cities, most conspicuously in Washington, where I watched buildings burning just blocks from the White House.

Then, the strangest phenomenon of a troubled time claimed the headlines: the student rebellion. Students began a hyperactive year by seizing the buildings of Columbia University in New York on one coast and of San Francisco State on the other. Simultaneously came a wave of strikes, among which a shutdown of the New York public school system by the teachers union was the most important.

Americans were left to ponder some stunning oddities of this turmoil. One was that each form of turbulence remained isolated from the others: the students never got mixed up in the racial outbursts, and vice versa; when Blacks rebelled, they made it clear they were separate from White students. And the labor strikers rarely interfaced with Blacks or youths in rebellion.

I think I stood with the great majority of Americans in being mystified by the students and what they wanted. Their massive exasperation with life and their country occurred at a time of highest prosperity ever, of record ease in getting a college education and the highest peak yet of minority progress towards full equality. Equally mystifying, it was not just an American phenomenon: student explosions were happening in, among other nations, South Korea, Egypt and (most violently of all) France. It was the biggest year for student rebellion since the revolutions of 1848.

Only Vietnam provided a clear motive. Young Americans were dead against the war with reason: they would have to fight it and they felt it was a wrong war. But equal or sometimes greater enthusiasm was lavished on other issues that were not clear. On one occasion I walked across the Illinois State campus to speak in an auditorium, and was besieged. I stopped and was submerged in a babel of complaint. To bring order, I singled out one student and asked what exactly was wrong. He said, "My courses are not relevant." I said, "Name one course." He said, "Child Psychology; it is a waste of my time." I asked, "Is it elective?" He said it was. I said "Drop it," and forced my way on to the auditorium.

It was, I came to feel, a mood thing, not well expressed in specifics. The mood was well shown in the generation's theme drama, the movie *The Graduate*. An altogether admirable Harvard honor graduate, Benjamin (Dustin Hoffman), comes home to the suburban Sodom of his upper-middle-class elders, is subjected to their ingrained corruptions and at last is tempted to carnal sin when a shameless, but mighty magnetic, Mrs. Robinson undresses in front of him, lingering with dexterity over the removal of her nylons. Young decency bends under the pressure. But like Dr. Faustus, Benjamin is saved by the love of a daughter, and flees the scene with, one is certain, a resolve never to trust anyone over thirty.

On another occasion I assembled all the specific complaints I could discern and sought to make a bonfire of them. Accepting an invitation from Roosevelt University in Chicago, I walked through student demonstrators to make a lecture. I was purposely provocative. I outlined the achievements of their parents' generation, from the defeat of Hitler to that of Bull Connor, including the inroads against poverty, which at that moment were impressive. Then I listed their complaints, which seemed insubstantial. At first the students hooted, but after a while they sank into sullen dismay. The *Chicago American* newspaper ran the whole of my talk on the whole of one page the next morning. I had been an occasional speaker at Roosevelt and the proud owner, along with Mrs. Eleanor Roosevelt and Averell Harriman, of one of its rare honorary degrees; but after this I was never invited back. I think the administrators felt they had enough rage on their hands without my fomenting more.

Asked on an occasion slightly later what I thought was wrong, I suggested this:

It is tenable that every new generation of adolescents is the equivalent of a barbarian invasion. The currently rising generation, the babies conceived in the big American rush home from war, is the biggest generation ever, and probably the most spoiled by the ease of getting what they want.

The times in which they come of age may play a part: Too rapid change and too rapid an increase in numbers are the father and mother of social turbulence, and in the last third of this century both parents have gone extremist.

As a measure of change I noted that "we live in an age when a citizen must, to earn a living, master technologies his father never dreamt of and his children will find obsolete." Of numbers I noted that there were 1,350,000 youths in college in America when I left to go abroad in 1939. And now in 1968 there were nearly 8 million.

The great mass of Americans stood by that year stunned by the incidence of riots, Black and White. Law and order for a while displaced the war in Vietnam as an election issue. Alienated by the limpness of the traditional parties, more of the public were attracted to George Wallace, now leading his own third party. One afternoon, I was called from my typewriter to the studio; they had arranged to nab Wallace, campaigning to record crowds in Maryland, for an hour and summoned me to record an interview for *Issues and Answers*. I complied, but in an hour found no new grounds for understanding the charisma of this small, ill-spoken, ultra-regional figure. However, as the election year drew on, it would become clear that he articulated the discontents of a whole stratum of Americans in an emotional year. Their fear of crime beyond control was soon fueled by a tragedy in the campaign itself.

To cover the Democratic primary in California, ABC sent a staff to do the legwork, and I remained in New York to anchor. Kennedy won a resounding victory. We carried his victory speech from the Ambassador Hotel in Los Angeles; then I signed off at about midnight. While the credits were running over my picture on the screen, I got an alarm call from the control room. Kennedy had been shot by an unknown assailant. They broke off credits, the lights came up and, receiving information by my earpiece, I began a marathon report on camera that lasted all night. I flew back to Washington at midmorning in deep depression about the state of my nation.

I considered Bobby Kennedy a friend, had interviewed him repeatedly— he never rejected a request—had lunched at his home and swum in his pool. I prized an autographed copy of one of his books he sent me. When I had to make a (for me) crucial decision as to whether to take a place in his brother's administration, I sought out, and abided by, Bobby's advice. But I could not be a part of the near-deification of him that followed. I somewhat resented his tendency to build himself up by tearing Johnson down. Glowing books and articles praised him for his attitude on poverty and rights for Blacks. Against his *attitude* stood the aggressive and landmark *activity* on both those subjects by Johnson. Many accounts have prophesied that, if elected President, Robert Kennedy would have rescued us from the tortures so evident in that year and would have changed the course of History for the better. I do not believe he could have been elected in that year of worried Americans trending toward Nixon, and even Wallace. Had he been elected, I think it likely that he would have faced a Congress in no degree ready to support further social engineering. But the fact that a mad and trivial assassin could prevent him from trying was infinitely depressing. We in our great nation were testing the levels of political life in a banana republic.

Later that summer, Johnson went to the ranch for some days for spiritual repairs, and I received from his new appointments secretary, Jim Jones, a summons to the presence. For a man who had become fortune's punching bag, he appeared to be in good shape, relieved rather than downcast. He informed me that a mutual friend, William Benton, the former U.S. Senator and owner of the *Encyclopedia Brittanica*, had persuaded him to write a book-length article for the *EB Yearbook*, to be called "Agenda for the Next President," and that he had chosen me over Professor James MacGregor Burns to draft it. As the man ridden out of town on a rail in Abraham Lincoln's story said, if it hadn't been for the honor of it, I had just as soon have been left out. My researches for my own stumbling book project had brought me too close to a figure far too rich for a journalist's blood. Also, Johnson was known to be very hard to write for, with exact notions of the effect he wanted to create, but niggardly in providing the patience and information to allow a writer to do it. However, it is hard to say no to a President. I was still in the indistinct margin between winding up my ill-fated book and working full-time for ABC News. So, festooned with misgivings, I agreed.

The immediate reward was a rare cozy supper at the ranch, with only the family and me present. I remember vividly two incidents. As Johnson listed things he wanted in the article, he said something about making voting compulsory. Mrs. Johnson said, "Now that's interesting, did you just think of that?" Looking almost wounded he said, "Well I do a lot of thinking. It may surprise you, but I think of things a lot." For a moment it was hard to see the creator of an avalanche of laws through the haze of a husband feeling unappreciated by his wife. At the end, the cook brought us each a plate of peach ice cream. LBJ looked at his plate as thought it were a personal insult. He called the cook back and said something that must have been Presidential. She took the plate away and a moment later brought him instead a large bowl of the delicacy. He lifted it to his chin and ladled the wonderful confection into his mouth like a fireman stoking a boiler.

I was given only a very short time to write, with nothing but his old speeches to draw ideas from. I knew he would demand a rewrite, so I delivered the manuscript to the White House in the dead of night, and Bennie and I immediately took off for a long-delayed vacation on a Caribbean island with nearly no communications. There, one day, as I sunned on the shore, I saw a dot on the horizon growing larger. As it neared it turned into a handsome motor craft with gilded trimming and a flag bearing a strange device. Ashore came a uniformed officer, inquiring after someone of my name. When I owned up, he saluted and said, "Compliments of the Governor of Puerto Rico and the President of the United States," and he handed me a bundle bearing the stamp of the White House. It was the manuscript with instructions for a rewrite. I was allowed only a week more. When the article appeared, it had acquired a new title, "The Choices We Face," and all distinctiveness had been erased by a dozen other hands. It was published with a Norman Rockwell portrait of Johnson, which pleased him. But his problem of not knowing how to get his message to the people existed in print as on television. Of the article he said, "We didn't lift our skirts too much." That, I thought to myself, was the trouble.

CHAPTER SEVENTY-ONE

Annus Horribilis (cont'd.)

I was fully back in corporate harness by the time the conventions rolled around in August. Sheehan pronounced a change in the way we would cover them that I thought was brilliant. Political conventions were mostly dull stuff, dominated by the Warhol privilege: every politician was allowed to be famous for fifteen minutes. That is to say, an endless succession of politicians mounted the rostrum to make bad speeches introducing other politicians to make bad speeches. ABC now decided to abandon the pretense of gavel-to-gavel coverage in favor of joining the proceedings for a couple of hours of prime time each night. I would provide a half-hour pictorial summary of events, then I would switch to the floor live for the rest. If floor events grew dull on our watch, we would turn cameras onto our odd couple of fascinating commentators: William Buckley, who with his magazine *National Review,* his TV program, his books and his newspaper column had almost single-handedly revived the modern conservative movement; and Gore Vidal, ultra-liberal Democrat and hyper-provocative author, who managed to be at once closely related to (in a complicated way: he was half brother to the stepsister of) Jacqueline Bouvier Kennedy and arch-critic of Kennedys.

The 1968 Republican Convention was distinguished mainly by its nominee. Richard Nixon, lately pronounced dead by the sage H. K. Smith (and, to be fair to me, by his own edict that he would never again run for office), enjoyed resurrection and coronation as his party's candidate for President. He had won appreciation by campaigning widely for Republican candidates in the off-year 1966 elections, in which the Republicans gained forty-seven seats in the House. The convention was held in an ideal location for a time when demonstrations and riots sought out politicians: Miami Beach, a deluxe sandbar accessible only by easily policed bridges, and with an ecology that induced reporters like this one to loll in the sun mornings and forgo the thrill of the chase.

Three weeks later, in Chicago, the Democratic Convention presented a contrasting, ugly, tangled, occasionally bloody mess to report our way through. It was a suitable climax to a terrible year, and we had no more trouble keeping an audience than your standard explicit horror movie. Tom Hayden, the student leader, called for 500,000 young revolutionaries to be present in order, his summons said, "to vomit on the politics of joy." His reference was to a speech made by Hubert Humphrey begging for a cessation of the politics of misery then in fashion. In the end between 10,000 and 20,000 resonated to Hayden's high purpose, but they proved to be enough.

Mayor Richard Daley feared that student rebels and Black resident rioters might at last conjoin in one bloody affray. He made the convention the best guarded since Lincoln's second nomination, in Baltimore in 1864. But Blacks determined to have nothing to do with the ceremonies of young White elitists. Still, Daley cordoned off the Amphitheater in the former stockyards with a 7-foot-high fence, surmounted with three rows of barbed wire; put 12,000 cops on duty; packed five schools and two parks with 7,000 National Guardsmen; and had federal troops elsewhere alerted for possible emergency duty. Manholes were tarred shut and streets leading to the hall blocked. Demonstrators at the airports appeared with signs saying, "Welcome to Prague." The reference was to the shocking Russian reinvasion of Czechoslovakia a week earlier.

Proceedings on the floor were bile-bitter, but the antagonists were too angry to see that their differences were in mood rather than substance. Long hours and much blood pressure were devoted to debating a Vietnam plank for the platform. Even the reporters became overheated. *Time* magazine called the rebel-offered plank an "unequivocal" demand for U.S. withdrawal. So fine a journalist as Teddy White wrote that it demanded "a forthright renunciation of America's commitment." In fact, the proposed plank was altogether equivocal, calling not for American withdrawal but for a "mutual withdrawal," and for negotiating "a political reconciliation," which everyone wanted. Had the debaters not been so mad at one another, they would have had no difficulty composing a plank satisfactory to all.

Likewise barren of substance was the rebels' attempt to paint the majority candidate, Hubert Humphrey, as an Establishmentarian forced on the convention by manipulative bosses. There was no more liberal Democrat than Humphrey, father of Civil Rights, the Peace Corps, Medicare, and much else. His opponent, "Clean Gene" McCarthy was clean the way something little used is clean. Though a charming man, his record in the Senate was not impressive.

But what really rotted the party was the scene on the streets the night of Humphrey's nomination. I was locked onto my anchor desk at the stockyards hall but had to spend most of the night calling in reporters and cameras moving all over the riotous streets of the downtown city. The youths marched on the Hilton Hotel, headquarters of the party and of Humphrey and McCarthy. Then they sought to march on the convention. The police blocked them, then attacked without mercy. Reporters, cameramen and photographers were among the casualties: twenty were injured, three hospitalized. Scenes from the streets appearing on TV screens caused uproar in the convention. Stewards and police floored or arrested TV reporters in the hall. The behavior of the police could not be justified. But it could be explained, and I sought to do so. I pointed out that in a time of assassinations it was a duty to forcibly prevent a mob from getting too near the potential candidates, and the cops were dealt some awful provocations: golf balls spiked with nails were thrown at them, and from the windows of the hotel bottles and plastic bags of excrement dropped on them. Injuries removed 152 policemen. My being "soft on the brutes" did not sit well with some of my colleagues.

Our own two special commentators captured the spirit of the general dissension all too well. One assault by police occurred after some crazies had captured a flagpole in Grant Park and pulled down the American flag, then run up a Vietcong flag. I have no record of the dialogue about the incident in our studio save my own notes: Vidal said there was no justification for police behavior. I said, "You must admit, it is provocative to pull down an American flag and run up a Vietcong flag." Vidal, "Why should it be provocative? We are not at war with them." I said, "Well, consider the parallel: We were not at war with the Nazis the first two years of WW II. But if anyone had pulled down an American flag in a public place and run up the Nazi flag, would you not have felt that to be an unacceptable provocation?" Vidal: "Well there are no Nazis here, except perhaps Bill Buckley, a crypto-Nazi." Buckley's face turned beet red and he said, "Listen, you queer, stop calling me a crypto-Nazi, or I'll sock you in the goddamn face and you'll stay plastered. Let the author of *Myra Breckinridge* go back to his pornography and stop making allusions of Nazism to somebody who was in the infantry in the last war." I thought they were about to come to blows and struggled to break the many wires tying me to my anchor desk in order to place myself between them. Then I realized how unnecessary my concern was: Buckley's arm had been broken in a yachting accident and was in a sling. Vidal was by nature combative only in words. Off-camera, however, seconds of Vidal, waiting in the wings, appeared ready to get physical. Paul Newman, the actor, seemed about to engage Buckley but was stopped cold by Buckley's riposte: "Does Mr. Vidal always have his friends do his fighting for him?" The incident passed into a footnote in the darker parts of convention history.

In the ensuing campaign I spent time with both candidates in turn. Nixon was relaxed, safe and sterile. Humphrey was outright heroic. He emerged from Chicago 16 percentage points behind Nixon in the Gallup poll. The early part of his effort to fight his way back was sabotaged by busloads of youthful hecklers who followed him about trying to keep him from being heard. On the small screen a couple of hundred saboteurs looked like an uprising of millions. A disenchanted and losing party did not attract funds, and lack of money kept Humphrey from getting to the public via television. But he was a great politician and speaker—"200 words a minute, gusting up to 300," said his friend Walter Heller—and a great human, and it began to come across. From 16 points behind in the September Gallup poll, Hubert closed to within 8 points behind in late October, then to 2 points behind in early November. On election night we stayed on the air all night and into the next morning. I was the first network anchor to declare Nixon had won, by a fraction of 1 percent.

A sour, wrenching, bloody year eased up at the end, helped by the success of three astronauts going to the moon and orbiting about it—a promise that we would soon be able to land on it. A few days before the inauguration of the new President, I phoned the White House from ABC, five blocks away, and left a casual message that, if Johnson had a moment sometime in the next few days, I would like to drop by and say goodbye to the outgoing President. To my surprise a call came back in five minutes telling me to come on over now.

The President was leaving the Oval Office as I was ushered into the inner hall. He had just decorated the astronauts in front of cameras, and he led me into the cubicle adjoining the office. There he and George Christian, who was also present, had scotch; I had bourbon. Johnson looked good and was in an expansive mood. He lectured me on how he never wanted to be President, and

I could check it with Senator Dick Russell of Georgia and Governor John Connally of Texas, with whom he had discussed it many times. He was pushed into running for Vice President on Kennedy's ticket; Philip Graham, publisher of *The Washington Post,* had written him an acceptance statement to nudge him into it. From that he went easily into a lecture on how he had wanted to quit four years before, and how Lady Bird had kept urging him to, and had once put a memo on his bedside table reminding him of his promise to do so. He didn't do it till a new President was coming on because it was unseemly for boys to be dying in Vietnam while their Commander in Chief was quitting.

I had expected to make a brief goodbye, but an hour passed. So I stood to leave. He said, "You are too damned commercial. You've got the quotes you want. Now you want to go. Sit down and be sociable." We each had our third drink. Then Lady Bird phoned down, and he gave me the phone. She said for us to come up and have dinner. So we went up. We stopped off in the Lincoln bedroom to take the moist cloths off a bust of Johnson being done by a famous sculptor, then went to the dining room where Lady Bird waited with a Dr. Wayne, a friend from the Mayo Clinic. Dr. Wayne said grace. While we were eating, the phone rang. The President took it, then handed it to Lady Bird. It was Hubert. She told him to come on up and at least have dessert. He came. I was surprised at how fine he looked, coming out of fiery political battle, and how vigorously he consumed peach ice cream.

Drink, food and fatigue caused Johnson's eyes to begin fluttering, and finally he left us and went to bed. Lady Bird and the doctor got up and went off to talk. Humphrey and I lingered on, conversing at the table. He was sure that, if the campaign had lasted a week more, he would have had a tight win; two weeks more, a comfortable majority. I mused that perhaps his career mistake was leaving the Senate and joining the Johnson ticket in 1964. He said firmly that there had been a mistake, but that was not it. The mistake, he said, was Johnson's withdrawal. He was sure that he and Johnson together would have bulldozed out a victory, and, in 1972, with Vietnam somehow out of the way, he could have run and won on his own. Think of it, he said, nearly a generation of liberal-minded government; it would have driven the editorial writers of *The Wall Street Journal* crazy. When we stood to leave, I reached over to the side table and picked up a couple of books of matches bearing the stately White House logo. "I guess I won't have a chance to get more of these soon," I said. Hubert said, "Come to think of it, neither will I," and he scooped up a handful of matchbooks, and we went out, looking like two kids who had just emptied the cookie jar.

A few days later I anchored ABC's reportage of the inauguration, our cameras dwelling at one point on the Johnson family departing Andrews Air Force base in Air Force One. Later Mrs. Johnson recounted their arrival home. Marine chauffeurs who had dealt carefully with the President were less concerned about the ex-President. They dumped all the Johnson luggage on the grass and left. Lady Bird said to her daughter, "I guess it's midnight, and we've all turned into pumpkins."

A good many books have been written much later about the youth rebellions of the sixties. Many are lyrical about the spirit of the youth and the wholesome changes forced on a stagnated America. That is because they are written by those same youths become middle-aged. They attribute the Civil Rights successes to the activists. In fact, those successes were due to a bevy of middle-aged Blacks, mainly preachers, a rigorously honest Chief Justice, and the heart and skill of an out-sized Texas politician. True, some youths joined. All praise and love are due the three who were murdered in Philadelphia, Mississippi. But the wish was made fact by people of considerable maturity. Other results, like the rise of feminism and the ecological movement, are claimed largely by the false argument of *post hoc, ergo propter hoc.*

The real changes wrought by the Children's Crusade of the time were negatives. Contrary to claims, they did not shorten the Vietnam War; it went on more bloodily than before for nearly five more years. I believe that, had they not presented the enemy with a picture of America crumbling with violent dissension, the negotiations might have succeeded, the Mekong River development could have begun and South Vietnam would now be one of the Asian Tigers growing prosperous and strong. They did not bestow a more liberal cast on American life; they ensured the election of Richard Nixon, and through Reagan and Bush a generation of conservative government wholly opposed to their aims. It speaks well of the American spirit that the nation survived the most self-centered and indulgent of its generations so far.

CHAPTER SEVENTY-TWO

President Jekyll

ABC had early acquired a very good, if compact, staff of reporters, but it lacked, despite long searches, a strong anchorman and a first-class producer for its main evening news program. It now found a producer in Av Westin who had worked with me at CBS, and a promising anchor in a young Canadian named Peter Jennings. Peter had everything—a fine voice, made interesting with an English accent, and looks that caused a popular magazine to list him as one of the handsomest men in America—everything but authority. In Canada he had been more a news reader in the BBC tradition than a news reporter. After a couple of years he asked to be relieved of the star role at ABC in order to go out and learn to dig news right out of the mines. He chose a complex assignment, the Middle East, and in several years became an authority. He would later return and in time become the highest-rated anchorman in the U.S. Meanwhile, ABC needed an anchorman for now.

During my year off, Sheehan came to my home and asked me to take a shot at it. I felt that the job called for a more showmanly quality than I possessed and said no. I suggested Frank Reynolds, our outstanding White House correspondent, and he was given the job. Now at the end of the election year, 1968, Sheehan again asked me to do it. I would co-anchor from Washington with Reynolds in New York. Also I would do a commentary on the news at the end of each day. I could not resist the offer.

My new eminence was coeval with the new Nixon Administration. I sought to establish contact. I was as surprised as anyone when the new President chose as his closest adviser on foreign affairs a dry, Germanic academic who spoke in a doomlike monotone, and even more taken aback when the academic turned out to be, once in the public eye, a witty celebrity who squired beautiful ladies about and was a magnet for news photographers. I knew Henry Kissinger from one of my discussion programs and now sent him a note requesting a meeting. He invited me to his office in the basement of the White House for a chat. After awhile the phone on his desk rang and he took it. His manner was so deferential that I knew who it was. He interrupted only to say, "Mr. Smith is here," then "Yes sir. Right away." And he said to me, "The President wants me in his office and would like for you to come along." In a corridor outside, we passed another surprising Nixon appointee, my old friend and Bennie's schoolmate from the London School of Economics, Daniel Patrick Moynihan, standing in his doorway in stocking feet. "Come see us sometime," he said. "We have no news but come anyhow."

When we entered the Oval Office, I thought for a moment that the new President had constructed a new office in a different place from that of the previous President; only the oval shape was the same. The great carpet displaying the Presidential seal in Johnson's office was in strong primary colors. Nixon's was in quiet tones. The drapes were drawn against the afternoon sun, making the room degrees darker than I had ever seen it. There was silence, hush; the wire service machines Johnson kept clattering under glass on the side were gone, as were the three TV monitors whose logos had been screwed off to keep it a secret that the First American watched the news on Japanese sets. Johnson had not seemed to have much use for the desk. He sat the visitor down in a chair or on the sofa to get in a nose-to-nose mode. Nixon remained seated behind the desk. Johnson offered whiskey or Dr. Pepper. Nixon offered nothing; an attendant brought in a cup of decaffeinated coffee unasked and placed it in front of me.

Nixon looked studiedly calm, as though just arisen from a nap, showered, shaved and powdered. I remarked how well and relaxed he appeared. He said that it was important that Americans see their Commander in Chief rested and calm. It created confidence in his capacity for making decisions. Kissinger broke in and said, "Mr. Smith has a suggestion." I was puzzled for a moment, then remembered that on the way up I had suggested that Nixon needed a spokesman on Capitol Hill. His previous defender, the formidable Senator Ev Dirksen, he of the mighty echo-chamber voice and irresistible persona, had died and left a yawning gap where a warrior was needed. On the Hill, challenges were, as always, incessant, and now were going unanswered.

Upon Kissinger's revelation that I had a proposal, Nixon said—this is not precise but reconstructed from notes—"Suggestions, ideas. That is what we need and will cultivate. My administration will be a listening administration. It is as important to listen as to communicate," and there followed a lecture on the theme of listening, during which I did it and he didn't. He told me he neither read the papers nor watched TV, but had aides prepare a daily summary of what these reported, and in which TV news was favored over print news at a ratio of 60 to 40. In at least one respect he was in a class with Churchill and Johnson: a conversation was a monologue.

But I was pleased that he was forthcoming. It was clear early on in his resurrection that getting along with the media was a deliberate new policy. At an early White House dinner with bureau chiefs as principal guests, he presented the Medal of Freedom, the highest civilian award, to three "senior" journalists, Arthur Krock of *The New York Times;* David Lawrence, founder and columnist of *U.S. News and World Report,* and Eddie Folliard, retired White House correspondent of *The Washington Post*. At the annual Gridiron dinner, at which reporters produce skits mocking politicians with song and dance, the new President asked for fifteen minutes to put on his own unique show. It happened that both Nixon and his Vice President, Spiro Agnew, were passably good pianists. At two pianos on stage they played duets. They would begin each popular song together, but after a few bars, Agnew would drift off into "Sewanee River." Nixon would then stop and turn to him and say, "No, Spiro, the election is over." The point was that Agnew had become so addicted to the

"Southern strategy" that won them the election that he could not control his fingers. The performance won Nixon the first roaring applause, and I believe the last, that reporters ever gave him.

I was not sure how I regarded the new President. I felt a touch of distrust, typical of the liberal reporting community, toward one who had earned the sobriquet "Tricky Dick." Yet most of my personal encounters with him had been pleasant to me and seemed to be to him, too. My introducing him to Martin Luther King in Ghana was, I think, felt by him to be an opening to a segment of voters he had not previously approached. After his famous "kitchen debate" with Khrushchev at an exhibition of American products in Moscow in 1959, CBS had offered him a half-hour of air time to tell his story, and I was assigned to squire him through the mysteries of producing a documentary effort. When my son was wounded in Vietnam, plain citizen Nixon sent me a compassionate note.

Now I think he decided to pay me particular attention because of a small embarrassment I had dealt him on national television. He had agreed to a one-hour interview in prime time with reporters from the three networks. It took place in Los Angeles. We—John Chancellor, Eric Sevareid and I—agreed that each of us should be allowed two uninterrupted follow-ups to each question we put, in order to pin down a politician known to be elusive. By lot, I was first. My question (this from notes) was, "The Tonkin Gulf Resolution empowered President Johnson to make war in Indochina. Congress has just revoked the Resolution. Absent it, what is the legal justification for our continuing to fight in Vietnam?" This, from a reporter generally sympathetic to his inherited predicament in Asia, seemed to jar him. He responded with a lecture on remaining faithful to allies and friends. My follow-up was, "Yes, I know the moral argument. But what is the *legal* basis for our continuing in Vietnam?" Again, hems and haws. I broke in with my last follow-up: "I know and understand, sir, but what I don't know is, what is the *legal* justification for our being in Vietnam now that the Tonkin Resolution is dead?" He pawed at an answer for a moment but was much relieved when another questioner changed the subject.

A few days later in Washington I was invited to the Marine barracks for an occasion. I was introduced to another guest, Charles Colson, who was the President's lawyer and general troubleshooter. Colson said to me, "You have caused me more trouble than all the rest of the press together." I said, "Why, I've never met you before; how can that be?" He said, "You remember the interview with Nixon the other night? Well, not one minute after it was over, my phone rang off the hook here in Washington. It was the President, calling from L.A. He said to me, 'What the hell is the legal basis for our being in Vietnam?'"

After that the President occasionally phoned me at home to discuss, confirm or dissent from commentaries I had made the day before. Our paths merged in other ways. When Tulane University organized a banquet to honor some of its sons in Congress, with me as master of ceremonies, Nixon showed up uninvited and won New Orleans votes for the rest of History by remembering Tulane's glory moment in 1932, when its football team played in the Rose Bowl. The inveterate football fan from California and the White House described it play by play.

During Nixon's terms in office Bennie and I were occasionally invited to the White House for dinners. Again, the old problem of seduction by invitation arose to worry me. I know of no solution to the problem but intestinal fortitude in the reporter.

The idea of journalism is to find and transmit information that enlightens and interests the public. Presidents originate or react importantly to much of that information, so access to a President can be of immense journalistic value, both for background information and as a source of scoops. When I reported Nixon's economic conversion, quoting him as saying "Now I am a Keynesian too," it was copied in every newspaper and has found a place in dozens of books. Once, after an interview, I regretted having inadequate time to bring up other subjects. He asked what others I had in mind. I said, China, and added that it seemed folly not to recognize China and make use of her animus toward our Cold War foe, Russia. He said with some enthusiasm that I was right, and that he had plans to do something about it. My report on the topic was, I think, the first public hint that the Administration's move toward establishing relations with China was afoot.

I obtained invaluable insights into large events in foreign affairs. A few days before Nixon went to China, he invited me, as the only non-official present, to a small stag dinner for André Malraux, the author of *Man's Fate,* the fine novel about China in the 1920s, and now de Gaulle's Minister for Culture. Kissinger, Secretary of State William Rogers and Counsel Leonard Garment were others present. The excuse for inviting me was that I had been in the uprising of the French Maquis, of which Malraux was a leader in WW II, and was now seated on the other side of the high guest to engage him in conversation in French. The occasion provided me with a very good preview of what Nixon sought on the visit, based on Malraux's advice. Soon after, I was assigned to co-anchor the *ABC Evening News* from Moscow, when Nixon went there to sign some arms reduction agreements. The final ceremony was a cocktail reception for the Nixon party in the large and beautiful St. George's Hall in the Kremlin. We, the peasants, were allowed to line the walls and watch the great ones march the length of the hall to an enclosure, where they sipped drinks. At the close, they marched back, and this time the peasants broke ranks and moved in and surrounded the great ones. Nixon was talking with Brezhnev, and when I tapped him on the sleeve, he looked at me, then turned back to Brezhnev saying, "I want you to meet Mr. Smith." The encounter became, with an interpreter's help, an interview—very brief and predictable, but the only one on this occasion with the last Red Tsar to exercise sure control of the vast Soviet octopus before its death.

Perhaps the main reason our relationship prospered was that I favored much of what Nixon was doing. His surprising enlistment of Kissinger, a Nelson Rockefeller aide for foreign affairs, and Pat Moynihan, a Democrat for domestic ones, were hopeful moves. There were some inexcusable horrors— dressing up the White House guard in chocolate soldier, light operetta uniforms (abandoned later); nominating the gross Harrold Carswell to the Supreme Court (rejected by the Senate); attempting to gut the wonderful landmark Voting Rights Act (defeated)—all duly scorched in my commentaries. But on much else Nixon was, to my surprise, emphatically progressive. He set up education "advisory committees" in each Southern state, made up of local White and Black officers, and thereby brought about more voluntary desegregation of schools than any previous President. He spread his Labor Secretary's "Philadelphia Plan" to other cities, requiring the hiring of Black workers on federal construction projects. He created the Environmental Protection Agency, initiated the Clean Air Act of 1970, doubled the issuance of food stamps and fathered the all-volunteer Army.

However disruptive the thought, I felt that he handled the generation's horror, the Vietnam war, as well as anyone could have. The nation wanted out, if possible with victory but absolutely with some dignity. He had the paradoxical mission of negotiating with the enemy while steadily withdrawing the U.S. troops that induced the enemy to negotiate at all. He was able to keep the enemy sitting at the talk table only by ordering occasional violent punitive stabs like the Christmas bombing of Hanoi and the U.S. invasion of Cambodia. That incursion into Cambodia was too long in coming. Throughout the war, Communist troops concentrated just across the border in Cambodia would periodically assault U.S. positions three miles distant on the South Vietnam side, then retreat into Cambodia and safety before daylight. The Nixon incursion, greeted with student rage in the U.S., was shallow but purposeful in protecting our diminishing forces. He kept to his withdrawal schedule, steadily reducing the cost in lives and funds. The aim was to leave the war in the hands of the South Vietnamese Army but with a threat that U.S. bombers would return if the North Vietnamese broke the eventual peace agreement. Alas, when they did, Nixon's other side had taken control of him, terminating his leverage for getting Congress to support any action and leaving his career a ruin.

CHAPTER SEVENTY-THREE

The Tangled Web

Tom Wicker put it succinctly: Given the immense accretion of powers and duties in the Presidency due to a Depression and three wars, something like Watergate was a crisis waiting to happen. The President's staff, once a couple of roomsful of aides in the White House, was now a diverse crowd in several buildings with many seams through which his confidences might leak into print. All modern Presidents have been harried by leaks. Early on Nixon consulted LBJ and got this characteristic advice: "Listen to what the newsmen are saying. Find out who they talk about as specially bright or intelligent or profound, and fire him." But a sense of humor had never been Nixon's strong suit.

Something like Watergate might have happened to any President, but Nixon seemed particularly eligible. He was engaged in especially sensitive encounters, a total reversal of policy toward the Red Chinese that had to take into account their notorious sensitivities, the first hopeful arms cut negotiations with Russia, and the nearest chance yet for an end of the war in Vietnam. The publication of the secret Pentagon Papers had made him hypersensitive about keeping his plans to a narrow circle.

And he himself was caught up in a mysterious change of person. I had dealt for four years with the man dubbed the New Nixon, a Dr. Jekyll, always friendly and helpful, the one who played the piano for working reporters and gave medals to retired ones. During and after his second election, the old Nixon began taking over again and seemed comfortable in his skin. Once at a dinner, when my wife described the study she had built for me, oval in shape due to a terrain problem, he had casually remarked to me, "You can use my Oval Office if you like; I never use it." He referred to his preference for doing hard thinking by retreating to his lonely hideaway in the Old Executive Office Building next door, where in solitude he sat at a table in a corner and inscribed his thoughts and plans on a yellow legal pad with a silver Parker pen. Now, I was told, he spent more time in the hideaway, using the Oval Office mainly for formal meetings. Months passed with no Cabinet meeting or press conference. The rising young Governor of Georgia, James Earl Carter, complained for many when he said the President had become inaccessible even for the most urgent consultations about sharing federal funds, which Nixon had once been enthusiastic about. To everyone's surprise, Nixon did not go up to Capitol Hill to deliver his annual State of the Union address; he sent it up by courier for legislators to read, something that had not happened in recent times except when President Eisenhower was too ill to speak.

He granted rare private interviews that seemed to say something particular about himself to a couple of print reporters. To one he confessed to being disappointed at his own reaction to, after several squeakers, winning a landslide reelection. He got no lift from it, he said; he felt only a letdown. To another he said that he missed having to fight. The election appeared to have been too easy; his spirits rose only to battle. Now his subsequent actions suggested that he was indeed spoiling for a fight. He was taking no pains to avoid a gathering battle with Congress about his practice of impounding moneys appropriated by Congress. Past presidents had impounded—refused to spend—appropriated funds, but never on the Nixon scale. Senators warned him that they were preparing a bill to force his hand, and it would amount to a head-on constitutional collision. He made no move to assuage them. Then Mr. Hyde really showed his teeth when he faced his other favorite foe, the press. Early in 1973, when he and Kissinger finally got their cease-fire agreement with the North Vietnamese, he held his first press conference in a long time. He was truculent throughout and did not look the reporters in the eyes. He spoke of his winning "peace with honor" and added, "though I know that is a phrase you gag on." It was the first of a sparse, infrequent series of press conferences that could aptly be called carnivorous.

In the clarity of retrospect, Nixon's descent into hell seems a gentle decline at first, turning into a chute into the pit at the end, but with a couple of flat places on the way where he might have turned back. Aggravated by leaks of his plans, irritated by J. Edgar Hoover's refusal to have the FBI snoop for him, he allowed the creation of a few secret operatives, the leak seekers, the "plumbers," in the pay of officials of the White House and of Nixon's reelection offices. Among other exploits they entered the Democratic National Headquarters in the Watergate apartments at night to plant a listening device there, and were caught by police. A tough judge smelled a rat and left hanging the threat of severe sentences until they broke and admitted to being in the illegal service of the President's men. The judge, some hard-digging reporters and a Senate committee steadily wove a web around Nixon. Senator Sam Ervin characterized the waffling and lying with a quotation, from Sir Walter Scott: "O, what a tangled web we weave, When first we practise to deceive!" The discovery that the President had taped conversations proving the worst about him, and that the tapes were available, turned the web into a noose around his neck.

I have none of the instincts of an investigative reporter, having worked most of my life to be a contemplative reporter or commentator. I needed more enlightenment to comment fairly, so I sought it where I had occasionally found it before. I phoned Nixon's Chief of Staff, General Alexander Haig, and told him that I needed to know more about what I was commenting on; then I suggested that the President might need to talk with someone not on his staff, an outsider; thus we might both benefit from a chat, on or off the record. Haig responded that he thought it was a good idea. He said he would get back to me. The next day he phoned and said, "He doesn't want to talk to anybody. The answer is no."

Bennie and I had met Nixon's daughter Julie, wife of David Eisenhower, at a small private dinner at the White House, and we were much taken with her presence and beauty. She resembled the actress Jennifer Jones, but was, I thought, prettier. When she expressed interest, we described to her the house we had built on the Potomac. She said she would like to see it. So now we phoned and invited her and David to come to dinner. On a pleasant summer evening in June they came, and had not been inside the door five minutes before Julie asked, "What would *you* do?" I said I was glad she asked that question and gave her my full answer: "I would tell all, absolutely all. I would even say—if it were so—that my first reaction to hearing about the burglary was to dismiss it, to cover it up. It was too silly an incident to be allowed to endanger a Presidential election campaign, which was naturally my overwhelming preoccupation at the time. But now I see that little things can lead to serious ones, and you may be sure I will give orders that nothing like it ever be allowed to happen again." Julie said, "I agree." But husband David said, "I don't! If he yields that much, the media will tear him to shreds." I said, "After what has happened he is a candidate for some shredding anyhow. But I don't think Americans like to see their President impeached. I think they would let him go ahead and accomplish some of the things he has been working on with Russia and China."

David's view was consonant with a Nixon trait my attention had been called to on an earlier occasion. I have mentioned the small dinner the President gave for André Malraux just before his historic trip to China. At one point in that dinner, he asked Malraux about Mao Tse-tung's motivation. Malraux responded to the effect that Mao saw himself as a favorite of Destiny. He was predestined to triumph from his birth. Nixon listened intently, then said, "Is not that true of all great men—don't they all see that they are predestined to prevail—is it not true of your boss, de Gaulle?" And they talked for a while, Nixon's eyes fastened on the guest, about the French President's self-assurance at all times, based on de Gaulle's belief that he was specially chosen by Fate. After dinner, as we stood about chatting, William P. Rogers, Nixon's Secretary of State and close friend, as well as a long-time friend of mine, came over to me and said, "Did you hear the talk about Mao and de Gaulle?" I said it had struck me how intently the President talked and listened. "Well," said

Rogers, "he wasn't talking about Mao or de Gaulle. He was talking about Richard Nixon, the man of Destiny. Back in 1960, when he lost the election to Kennedy, he said to me, 'I don't give a damn what they say. I am going to be President of the United States!'" Now, in the Watergate crisis, Nixon could not humble himself to the swelling opposition. He was sure he was destined to win. He had but to fight on, as Mao or de Gaulle, two other men of Destiny, surely would have done.

His last months should have assured anyone that Destiny is an abstraction not to be counted on in real life. Fate, if it exists, is no clear-eyed, elemental force, but a kind of fitful flurry that readily yields right of way to arbitrary and capricious circumstances. By the end of 1973, the Watergate box score was against Nixon: twelve aides or former aides were convicted; six more, including two Cabinet secretaries, were indicted; and seven more were sure to be indicted for several of a number of misdeeds—perjury, burglary, illegal wiretapping, obstruction of justice, destruction of evidence, fraud, extortion, solicitation of illegal campaign contributions, subornation of perjury and illegal distribution of campaign literature, not to mention several forms of conspiracy to commit illegal acts, or the (not Watergate-related) forced resignation of Vice President Agnew.

Sometime after the dinner with David and Julie, my feeling that the nation could not stand much more of this, and that the people's business was not being attended to, induced me to speak out on our *ABC Evening News.* I did a commentary saying that Nixon should resign. For the good of the country he needed to fight his battle for his reputation on his own time. With the inflation roaring unattended, an energy crisis as the Arabs cut off oil shipments following a Mideast war, a political crisis of near constitutional proportions as Congress rebelled against impoundments and Nixon's practice of undertaking foreign policy initiatives without letting the legislature have any say—with all this, we must have a leader who was free to consult and to lead. Nixon, I said, should resign.

Nothing quite so forthright had been said on television. It produced a flood of phoned and written comments, almost all in agreement. The President's Press Secretary, Ron Ziegler, called and asked me to come and see him. I did. His heart did not seem to be in the task of trying to persuade me that I was wrong. I told him that I had expected to have some morning-after regrets following my commentary; instead I felt regret at not having said it sooner.

What restrained many others from making the same proposal was the problem of the succession. Nixon's Vice President, the former Governor of Maryland, Spiro Agnew, was deemed by many to be inferior. In the autumn of 1973, that judgment was confirmed. Agnew, while a heartbeat from the presidency, was found to be continuing to receive payoffs from contractors he had favored while Governor of Maryland. He was presented with a series of charges, accompanied by detailed evidence, that would have resulted in his being sent to prison if he had been convicted of them. It was agreed that he plead no contest to a minor charge and resign his high office. He did so on October 10, 1973. Nixon was enabled to nominate a successor. He chose Congressman Gerald Ford, his old friend. Ford was quickly confirmed by Congress. The action improved a sullen atmosphere but also made getting rid of Nixon more acceptable. He clung on into the summer of 1974, when the House Judiciary Committee voted to impeach him on three charges. Then, on August 8, 1974, Richard Nixon forestalled trial in the Senate by becoming the first American President to resign the office. Ford's ascension brought a nearly audible sigh of national relief.

I assumed Nixon would never speak to me again. Later, however, when I was writing and narrating the three-part documentary program for the Public Broadcasting System about the changing, growing Presidency, I dared to phone his office in San Clemente. To my surprise he agreed to an interview. We appeared at the villa overlooking the Pacific. Nixon looked surprisingly fit and talked freely about the changing nature of the office he had lost; but when we got around to how he lost it, he became terse and reluctant. Still, I was astonished at my friendly reception.

A year later, he had found San Clemente too remote and isolated—on my visit there it had reminded me somewhat of Citizen Kane's Xanadu—and moved to an apartment in Manhattan. From there one day, an aide phoned and invited me to dinner. Professor A. L. Rowse, the Oxford Elizabethan historian was present. Ray Price, Nixon's speechwriter and one of the better influences on him, made it a foursome. In the course of a talky, pleasant dinner, Professor Rowse asked whether Nixon had another book in the works. Nixon responded that he could think of nothing more to write about. I reminded him that Winston Churchill spent part of his years in political exile writing occasional essays for the newspapers about famous people he had met. At the end they were all brought together in a book titled *Great Contemporaries*. Nixon, I suggested, had crossed paths with more leaders than had the young Churchill; why not write his own estimate of important people of his time? A few months later I had a note from him saying that he had not only adopted the idea but had just about finished the book. It appeared under the title *Leaders*, and opened the way to his writing others, making the destroyed President one of the prolific political authors of the time.

I had one last encounter with his former number two. I was returning exhausted from Egypt and an interview with President Anwar el-Sadat. I changed planes at Heathrow in London, hoping no one talkative would be seated next to me. When the plane took off I dared to turn and look at my accidental neighbor, and it was ex–Vice President Spiro Agnew. He did want to talk. "The world has got my case all wrong," he said. "The media?" I asked. "Yes," and he began to talk. I held up my hand. "Write a book about it," I said. He said, "The world is not ready for it yet." "I will wait till it is," I said and nestled against a pillow and went to sleep.

CHAPTER SEVENTY-FOUR

Changing Times

The third quarter of the twentieth century was probably the most favorable period of that duration for the human animal since he became human. In those twenty-five years, roughly from the onset of the Marshall Plan in 1948 to the Arab oil embargo in 1973, subject regions in Africa won their freedom and enjoyed a brief period of interest by Western investors, before they were found to be bottomless pits. Former subject regions in Asia entered the phase of "take-off" that would see their economies soar farther and faster than those anywhere else. The defeated of WW II—Germany and Japan—joined the victors and enjoyed a rise in standards that they probably could not have improved upon very much had they won the war.

In Barbara Ward's metaphor, the U.S., which led the world's great leap upward, created an additional national economy equal in size to its prewar one, and piled it atop the other to create an all-time wonder wealth-producing machine. Several factors enhanced growth. The GI Bill provided a generation, larger than any before, financially equipped to contribute to enterprise—to get college educations or to found small businesses. As the only secure, "unbombable" lab and testing ground in WW II for Allied war technology, the U.S. had become the magnet for the world's best scientists. Many of them remained after the war and helped make America the year-after-year winner of more Nobel science prizes than any other nation. With no serious trade competition, the U.S. led an opening up of the world trade. A half-dozen "rounds" of negotiations by all trading nations (the "Kennedy Round" has been mentioned), all initiated by the U.S., saw barriers fall and world trade increase by 6 percent a year, swelling the wealth of all.

An important factor increasing America's wealth in this period was, at long last, the end of the economic consequences of the Civil War: The South was reintegrated into the nation. The personnel demands of WW II mixed Southern boys with those of the rest of the nation as nothing had done before. Air-conditioning, which was applied to homes only after the war, removed the large obstacle of climate for industries moving into the region. Eisenhower's highway program, plus air travel, made movement easy. In the century after the Civil War no President was elected directly from a Southern state. Since 1964, four have been elected from states of the Old Confederacy (Johnson, Carter, Bush and Clinton) and two from hitherto neglected California (Nixon and Reagan). Bringing these regions in amounted to adding two rich new nations to the prewar United States.

That was the period whose main events as seen by this writer have been reviewed up to now. That most fruitful quarter-century came to an end around 1973 and 1974. Those two years were rich with indicative events. Following a new Arab–Israeli war, the Arab countries embargoed oil to the industrial nations, then lifted the embargo but multiplied the price of oil. In 1979 they repeated the action, altogether raising the price of oil by 547 percent. The long period of cheap oil to fuel industry was over. When Nixon was reelected in 1972, our foreign oil bill for the year was $4 billion. When he resigned in 1974, it was $23 billion and in 1990 $61 billion. The cost of imported oil made up most of the gigantic American deficit in trade with the world. From now on the U.S. would have to compete by improving productivity, turning out more and better things than others, at lower cost.

Yet, when we needed productivity most, it failed us. To quote Steven Rattner of Lazard Frères, "After 1973, productivity growth went off a cliff." Output per man-hour had been growing by 3 percent a year. Now the rate of growth fell to 0.7 percent a year. The reason for the fall is still not fully understood, but one new factor may have had something to do with it: the necessary absorption of large numbers of less-trained newcomers into the workforce— women and Black Americans.

But compete we had to. For a quarter-century, American businesses had marketed their products less on a level playing field than on a lonely one. Now the prewar giants were back and more competitive than ever. Germany and Japan had regained their prewar industrial strength and were now exceeding it—wonderful examples of the advantage of having been utterly destroyed and therefore being able to restart from scratch, provided that your conqueror is a rich uncle anxious to help you do so.

About the most conspicuous sign of a change for the worse in the U.S. was a fall in the nation's ability to compete in world trade. For a century America enjoyed a nearly permanent surplus in trade with the world, selling it more than we bought from it. In 1974, our trade went into permanent and alarmingly deep deficit. By way of instant example, as I sit at my writing machine now, I casually pick up a table of trade data and see that in 1994, the Germans ran a mercantile trade surplus of $44 billion with the world, the Japanese a startling surplus of $120 billion, while the U.S., the one-time champion, recorded a *deficit* of $150 billion!

The great American dollar (which among other things had allowed Bennie and me to furnish a home in London with antiques we could not have approached when the quarter-century was over) had been holding the world together in an all-nourishing expansion of trade. During the war the U.S. had agreed to tie the dollar to ever-desirable gold; we would exchange any dollars foreigners acquired into gold at a permanently fixed rate on demand. After the war, the U.S. made these stable dollars universally available by generous gifts for recovery, by investment in foreign businesses, or in payment for the upkeep of American bases in foreign lands. That supply of absolutely solid money to work for probably did more than any one factor to bring about the amazingly swift recovery of the world from the most destructive war.

But now the value of the dollar began to fall. Arab oil sheiks insisted that all buyers pay for their oil in U.S. dollars. They accumulated Croesus-like fortunes in dollars. By mid-1974, they had acquired reserves of gold and dollars equal to $650 billion—that in contrast to America's own reserves of $15 billion in gold. Foreign banks and investors acquired use of these fortunes and speculated in dollars, depriving the currency of much of its attractive stability. A point was reached where foreigners could cash in their dollars for our gold and exhaust our gold hoard instantly. To hold onto our reserves, President Nixon had to cancel the arrangement and cut the dollar off from gold. The privileged position of Americans in world trade began to decline.

All the numbers that mattered suddenly moved in the wrong direction. The annual federal budget deficit, small when it was a deficit at all, grew humongous. Over a period of little more than a decade our national debt was multiplied by three, and from being the world's biggest creditor nation we became the world's biggest debtor nation.

What happened? Events having nothing to do with the nation's economy may have had some effect. Certainly, the first President having to resign and the first lost war—Nixon and Vietnam—had a depressing effect. But I believe another psychological fact was decisive.

For all its faults, America is the most successful effort in the still mysterious art of government in recent times. But success can be as corrupting as power. In the quarter-century after WW II we enjoyed our greatest period of success ever. The conviction gradually spread that U.S. superiority was just part of the natural order of things. We were simply superior. An indicative moment followed the visit of John Foster Dulles, Eisenhower's Secretary of State, to Premier Yoshida in Japan in 1954. When he returned he was asked what had transpired. Dulles said he had persuaded Yoshida to gear Japan's economy to producing for the poor nations, for the Japanese were incapable of producing sophisticated things salable in the U.S. market. The incident, with its innocent arrogance, was a small unnoticed milestone on the course that led to Japan's seizing huge chunks of U.S. market for the most sophisticated products.

Business fell into the mood of politics. American corporations that had become world leaders settled back into self-satisfaction and, in the fourth quarter of the century, found themselves losing out to foreign competitors. Xerox, one of America's most progressive companies, became a frightening example. Having virtually invented the modern office environment with its revolutionary copying machine, Xerox adopted an attitude of assured supremacy. So, Japanese producers moved in and captured one after another of the company's markets, until in the 1970s it was nearly forced out of business. Recently, the company woke up and has been fighting its way back.

In the 1980s, I risked becoming a Johnny-One-Note, hammering away in commentaries and lectures at the sudden decline in America's spirit and performance. I proposed that the one aspect of our problems we could do something about quickly and most beneficially was improving productivity, output per worker. Inside our industry organization, the National Association of Broadcasters, an owner of radio stations in Philadelphia named Jerry Lee heard. He had had similar thoughts and he approached me and proposed a national campaign, with me as on-camera spokesman. With a little financial support from the Association we prepared 15-, 30- and 60-second exhortations for business and labor to cooperate to get productivity up to its old speed again, and much else would follow. It was a mighty pro bono effort, carried on most radio and TV stations of the nation for several years. We dared to believe that we were part cause of a marked rise in productivity that occurred in the late 1980s. We were sober enough to know that the profitability of turning out more and better at lower cost was a greater spur.

As no nation since antique Rome has been sentenced to decline and fall by commentators more often than the U.S., a cautionary note should be added: the decline in America's fortunes in the mid-1970s was real, but it was also relative. The annual rate of *growth* in productivity fell, but the American economy remained the most productive in the world. Exports no longer paid for imports, but America remained the world's biggest exporter, selling the world more than any other. The dollar lost value, but with nothing better around, it remained the reserve currency for many. There was, in short, nothing terminal: decline was still susceptible to being reversed.

The auto industry recovered. So did U.S. dominance in chips and computing generally. Many other industries simply moved abroad to places with cheaper labor. But they left behind as permanent consequences of the 1970s downturn a generation of youths maturing into a job-scarce economy, large numbers of the middle-aged put permanently out of work by the decline plus the rise in mechanical productivity, and a majority of wage-earners who watched their incomes stagnate or fall under pressure to compete with a newly risen world.

The big downturn began during the time of the Nixon Administration and deepened in the time of Ford and his successors. Much of the history of the rest of the century is the story of a nation growing puzzled and irritated by this trend, and turning outright angry at leaders who seem not to understand what needs to be done, or who lack the will to do it.

1974-1979

CHAPTER SEVENTY-FIVE

Not a Lincoln

I resume the pattern of telling my story in terms of successive Presidents, for it is they whom I spent almost all my professional life watching, studying, researching, reporting and occasionally meeting. Those who served in the 1960s were marked, each of them, with clear flaws. But it must be said that they were figures with uncommon political talents and large abilities. John Kennedy set and maintained a tone of purpose that buoyed the spirit of the nation and still resonated decades later. Lyndon Johnson was the ablest legislator, manager of perverse human nature and translator of aims into action, since FDR. He failed only at the undoable, honoring a foreign commitment that two predecessors willed him and that some 80 percent of polled Americans and all but two voters in Congress, wanted him to honor—till they changed their minds. Richard Nixon's home accomplishments were commendable, and his foreign ones outstanding, particularly his breakthrough to China, which had the effect of diverting toward the Chinese much of Russia's military power previously available for bullying us.

The two leaders of the rest of the 1970s were of a different order: decent, good of heart, constructive in spirit; but neither brought grasp and imagination to the mysterious art and business of governing a polyglot, loose-strung, unpredictable nation at a time when the ground beneath it and all its assumptions were shifting, and its cushion of unique wealth was diminishing.

No previous President had quite the warm national welcome accorded our only appointed one. Gerald Ford was what was so badly needed at that moment. His first address was just right: the long nightmare was over. We had a leader whose words we could believe. One did not have to take them apart to look for a hidden lie. The rejoicing lasted thirty days. At the end of that period, on a vacant Sunday, he suddenly issued a pardon to Richard Nixon. He did not explain his action. Shortly afterward I had occasion to ask him why, and he said that he was shocked on assuming office to see how urgently our national economy needed attention. At his first press conference he hoped to concentrate the public's attention on our runaway inflation, but almost all the reporters' question were about Nixon and Watergate. In the parade of important visitors through his office, conversation always gravitated to Watergate and Nixon. He decided that he had to get Nixon off the agenda. Thus the sudden pardon. Events bore out his judgment. Almost at once questions and headlines switched to other matters. But I think most of the public was offended. Too many awkward questions were raised. Was it not unjust that Nixon's aides, who had obeyed and protected him, were still on trial and sure to be sent to prison? How do you pardon someone who has not yet been charged with anything? Many Americans suspected that there was a deal: the gift of the White House in return for the promise of a pardon. I personally feel sure that there was no basis for this suspicion. But the new President lost his original sheen and never regained it.

My relations with Ford were as good as relations between politicians and ever-critical reporters get. Though liberal in inclination, I was invited to address House Republicans at breakfasts when he was their leader. In the White House he enlisted me for a service I thoroughly enjoyed. Concerned that American athletes were losing events in the Olympics that they should have won, he set up a commission to find out why and what to do about it, and named me to it. The chairman, Gerald Zornow, president of Kodak, became ill, so I chaired most of its hearings, held in cities over the nation, and was thrilled to sit beside Rafer Johnson and Bill Toomey, gold medalists in the decathlon, and many other famous athletes. As one of our complaints was that athletes were rarely honored by Presidents, Ford invited the latest American medalists in the Winter Olympics to lunch at the White House. After a welcoming ceremony, he called me aside and said that he had urgent business, and would I take them to lunch in the White House mess? I was delighted but I got the impression that our lithe young guests, having been promised a president, were somewhat let down by the substitution of a news hack.

The main thing we discovered in my view was that, like wild roses born to blush unseen, potential athletes go undiscovered in our loose, neglectful system, which is tied to colleges. Probably fewer than 15 percent of Americans participate in regular competitive sports at one time. In Germany, the figure is 60 percent, for sports are tied to the community, with government providing facilities, and cities and towns and businesses and unions organizing teams and leagues of teams in all sports. But there was much else in our report.

When his term was a year old, Ford invited four reporters in for an appraisal. We met for lunch in a room I had never seen before, a solarium in the middle of the top floor, illuminated by a big skylight in the ceiling. There is no record of what was said, but I left with the impression that the President was displeased by my contribution. I indicated that he had done nothing to relieve us of a new curse, which came to be called "stagflation." We, all Western nations, were caught in a box with no exits. If we took the usual steps to fend off recession, we were wracked with a killing inflation. If we took the usual steps to fight inflation, we went into stagnation or recession. In fact, no one knew how to deal with this new curse and would not know until we discovered that the problem was not economic but moral, as will be argued later.

Though in the end it was futile, Ford's most promising act to my mind was bringing Nelson Rockefeller, just resigned as four-term Governor of New York, to Washington to be Vice President. Rockefeller had become my favorite politician. I think he was the favorite of most reporters, whether or not they admitted to having preferences. Had he been able to break the right-wing veto on moderate-to-liberal Republican nominations for the Presidency, he might have won any Presidential election except LBJ's landslide of 1964.

I don't think I was influenced by the fact that the Governor of New York gave super parties. Though not much of a party goer, I dared not miss these epics. One was at the Rockefeller mansion on 3,000 acres of Pocantico Hills overlooking the Hudson River north of New York City. On the winding road up to the mansion, wooded nooks were decorated with elaborate mobiles and sculptures, the most impressive of which was a Henry Moore on a putting green. Everyone of note was present, from Edward Teller, the daddy of the hydrogen bomb, to Carol Channing, creator of the musical comedy roles of Lorelei Lee and Dolly Levy; from Danny Kaye to Theodore White (left) and William Buckley (right). A second party brightened the sky of New York City from the Rainbow Room atop the skyscraper at Rockefeller Plaza. There I was thrilled to shake the big catcher's mitt of a hand belonging to Jack Dempsey and the birdlike slender one of Gloria Swanson, both of whom I had watched in childhood on the silvered screen of the theaters of Monroe, Louisiana. Bennie and I shared a table with a rising millionaire named H. Ross Perot and his wife. A last party occurred as Rockefeller ended his political career at the family estate on Foxhall Road in Washington, D.C. It was hot July and all were in shirt sleeves. A photographer caught a shot of him shaking my hand in one of his and holding my shoulder with his other. He said, "You and I have come a long, long way together." I would have been charmed but for feeling sure that a moment later he would whisper to his wife, "What is that guy's name? I can never remember."

No, I favored the Rock because he was clearly the right man for the times. I first met him in 1958 when I roped him into a panel discussion on CBS. He and his brothers were sponsoring groups of expert thinkers seeking ways to deal with the nation's problems, and he was full of innovative ideas. He had easy access to the best minds in the country and kept a staff of twenty or so (including Henry Kissinger) in almost permanent employ. No politician ever had such familiarity with the worlds of politics, finance, industry and art as Rockefeller. On his nomination to be Ford's Vice President he said to the House Judiciary Committee, "Nothing delights me so much as facing up to a complex public issue, with all its confusions, turmoil and intensity, and trying to pull together the human resources to deal with it." This, I felt, was precisely the attitude and talent the nation needed. Tied to these qualities was a personality created for political campaigning. "He is the biggest political hit on the streets of New York since Theodore Roosevelt," wrote a reporter of his first run for governor. His record was commensurate. Among his measurable acts were increasing New York's state university system from forty-two campuses to seventy-one, and building "four and a half miles of new highway a day" for twelve years.

It took Congress awhile to confirm him as Vice President, less because of objections than because of puzzlement. They had never dealt with a nominee for high office with a personal income of $80,000 a week. A Congressman said, "If you had run against Kennedy, he would have been the poor man's candidate." Another, observing a list of his family's holding on everything, said, "You are a walking congregation of conflicts of interest." As the hearings dragged on, I did a commentary suggesting that the nation, suffering from a row of incomplete Presidencies, badly needed a Vice President in place, and Congress should act or get off the pot. A couple of days later, they voted to confirm him. He sent me a note of thanks. I assured him that I had said it for us, not him, and it was an accident that Congress decided to act when it did.

On the eve of commencing to campaign for election, Ford ran into his party's stern right wing and had to ditch the Rock if he wanted the nomination. Rockefeller compliantly wrote Ford a note that he wished to withdraw from politics, letting Ford choose a different vice presidential candidate. This probably ended Ford's chances of winning the election and the nation's opportunity for first-rate leadership.

Probably Ford carried too much other weight to win a race anyhow. He represented the party whose last elected President and Vice President had been forced to resign for shady doings unprecedented in such high places, and his two-year-long administration was presiding over a clinging recession. In addition, Ford suffered from self-delivered wounds. For inexplicable reasons this strong athletic man was given to stumbling over and bumping into things. On his first trip to Europe as President he tripped and fell down the airplane ramp while cameras rolled. At a state dinner he toasted the President of Egypt "in honor of your people and their country, Israel." Years before, Lyndon Johnson had said of Congressman Ford's coordination, "He can't walk and chew gum at the same time." And, "He played too much football without a helmet." Now those remarks were remembered and acquired new currency. In an interview I asked him if these quips affected him, and he said, "Frankly, they hurt." But he had to live with them. The comedian Chevy Chase performed a series of hilarious TV skits in which he played the role of Ford, expertly tumbling over everything in the Oval Office. In defense, Ford tried self-deprecating remarks of his own. He said that he had authorized combat pay for secret servicemen assigned to protect him when playing golf. In a speech he mispronounced the word "integrate" three times, then said, "I promised Betty I would learn this speech backward, and I did." But his goof of the century happened in the most sensitive place and time. In the second campaign debate on foreign affairs, with the Democratic candidate Jimmy Carter, he said, "There is no Soviet domination of Eastern Europe, and there never will be under a Ford Administration." Speaking of Poland, Romania and Yugoslavia, he said, "Each of these countries is independent, autonomous; it has its own territorial integrity." How he stumbled into these incredibles has not been explained. In a few weeks, the voters decided that a man who insisted that wrong was right shouldn't be elected President.

CHAPTER SEVENTY-SIX

The Governor of the United States

For absence of excitement, Ford met his match in the election campaign of 1976. Hurting from its Eugene McCarthy (1968) and George McGovern (1972) debacles, the Democratic Party went outside all the usual channels and chose an altogether different kind of candidate. It is perhaps more accurate to say that the small percentages of voters who participated in primary elections favored by modest majorities a wholly new face with no scratches from unseemly political squabbles of the past—that of James Earl Carter, the peanut farmer who was a graduate of the Naval Academy, a nuclear engineer and a one-term Governor of the state of Georgia.

The Ford–Carter contest would have been an eye-glazer but for the torrent of humor it unleashed. The prospect that the U.S. was going into decline and fall like Rome was a favored theme of the time; my comment was, "We are doing ancient Rome one better. Rome had one Nero fiddling while the place burned. We've got two." *Time* magazine assembled an anthology of such remarks. Bill Moyers described the campaign in football terms: "Both sides punted a lot." Sander Vanocur saw the candidates as "two consenting adults performing unnatural acts in public." The choice, said Johnny Carson, is "between fear of the unknown and fear of the known." Early on a reporter said, "It looks like apathy is peaking too early." When Carter, in an excess of self-inculpation, admitted to an interviewer that he had occasionally "lusted in his heart after" women, a lady reporter published a note she sent him: "If you are called upon to list names lusted after, it would be helpful to my career and greatly appreciated if you could bring yourself to include mine." Carter's two assets, a squeaky clean record in politics and a grin that seemingly bared serried rows of enormous white teeth, lent weapons to commentators. One said, "With teeth like those you could eat a pineapple through a tennis racquet." Mort Sahl was inspired to misquote the born-again Democrat as saying, "Nobody's perfect. But sometimes I come darn close." And, "I pray a lot. But I have never prayed to win the Presidency. I don't want to take advantage of the relationship."

When the Carter–Mondale ticket won, I filled my commentary moment with this greeting:

> As is well known, James Earl Carter will be our first President in over a century directly out of the South, not sanitized like Woodrow Wilson of Virginia by years in New Jersey, or LBJ of Texas who inherited the job from a Northerner.
>
> As may or may not be known, the rest of the country likes to make jokes about Southerners, generally delivered in bad imitations of a Southern accent.
>
> Denominating the Carter ticket Grits and Fritz was the first kindly example. They're getting a little meaner now like: *Question:* Did you know Georgia had peanut butter for Thanksgiving this year? *Second question:* Why? *Answer:* Because they're sending their turkey to Washington.
>
> This being the season for all to advise the next President, I beg to add my bit: These cracks will continue, and get worse. Lyndon Johnson underwent a slow burn at being proposed for a new TV series called the *Beverly Hillbillies in the White House.*
>
> As one Southerner to another, Mr. Carter, shrug them off. Above all, don't develop a siege mentality: You few Georgians against the mighty Eastern Establishment Media. It will only sour relations. Remember the media are badly infiltrated—Cronkite, Brinkley and this one are all Southerners too.
>
> Keep your sense of humor even when the cracks begin to smell a little fishy and unfunny. Smile; from now on you are always on *Candid Camera.*

In addition to being Southern, Carter's rare feature in the highest office was that he was not really a politician. He had no long-constructed political base he could count on, no core constituency to fall back on in difficult times. He was a loner, a "man without a country" in politics. A majority of White

Americans voted against him. He won by a margin of the votes of Black Americans. But he could not be sure of their constancy. When he fired a Black in his Cabinet, Andrew Young (an ex–New Orleanian like this writer), they became thoroughly disenchanted with him. Though he had been Governor of Georgia, at one point when Presidential reelection time loomed, an opinion poll showed that Georgians favored Edward Kennedy over Carter for the Democratic nomination.

He relished his loner status and exhibited his differentness as President in small ways, like wearing a business suit—bought off the rack in a small-town department store—instead of formal dress for his inauguration, carrying his own suitbag and luggage when traveling, visiting with plain people instead of notables. He liked to do things himself. During his campaign I asked an aide for some views on subjects not yet addressed by Carter. Instead of an aide I was given an appointment to see Carter himself alone in a private room for an hour. I was flattered, but thought it not a wise disposition of time in his crammed campaign schedule. In office, he often liked to answer his own phone. Congressmen sometimes found it easier to phone the President than to phone his secretary and seek an appointment to talk to the President. Trying always to do more and more of everything led to overload. To keep in shape for the job, he jogged thirty miles a week. A result was that awful picture of the President of the United States collapsing in the arms of a Secret Service agent, to be carried inside prone and packed with ice to treat extreme hypothermia. He claimed to read three books a week, in addition to staff papers, and sometimes indicated an overload of information too.

The new President was an optical illusion. He was mild of manner and soft in speech, but inside he was fiercely ambitious and sure of his rightness, which was one reason why he liked things to be done by the one person he trusted, himself. He talked with congressmen but did not seem to listen. Congress was alienated. In an introspective moment of truth he was heard to say, "I treated Congress like the Georgia State Legislature. So they treated me like the Governor of Georgia." When things were going very wrong at the midpoint of his term, he organized an elaborate "reassessment." In groups he brought about 150 cognoscenti from various realms in American life to Camp David. There he presided over long seminars, often in jeans, sitting cross-legged on the floor, taking notes, endless notes. But the upshot seemed to bear no relation to their advice. He announced that he was making a "lifestyle change." He demanded the resignations of thirty-four cabinet members and aides. He restored most to their offices, but accepted the resignations of some of the most original thinkers and doers, like Joseph Califano and James Schlesinger. And he gave greater authority to the so-called Georgia Mafia, a small group of young campaign aides who were loyal but not very experienced in what this President needed most, knowing the ways through the thickets of federal government. One of the changes in lifestyle was apparently a renewal of relationships with the media. My wife and I and a couple of executives from ABC, with a trio from *The New York Times,* were invited to a quiet dinner with the President and Rosalynn Carter in the White House. At the table, Mr. Carter gave a little orientation speech. He had, he said, spent the past eighteen months with his nose to the grindstone, as it were, learning the Presidency. Now he felt he was ready, he said, and wanted to be more outgoing, to be more sociable, in particular to improve relations with us, the media. He was a very methodical, conscientious man.

His basic problem was one for which I know no solution. He was a master of detail. A very hard worker, he assembled all the facts about everything he needed to know. Typically, one occasion he sought to raise interest rates 1 percentage point to fight inflation. A Treasury expert present advised him that there had been no increase that big since 1921. The President promptly corrected the expert, telling him that there had been such a rise in 1933. The expert went back to the books and found that his President was right about this as about most details. But there was no clear sight to see where those details would lead. Where he needed an instinct for the jugular when dealing with problems and people, Carter had an instinct for the capillaries. There was, said one observer, no clear view of far horizons, no imagination, no sense of history. He lacked vision; or more commonly put, he could not see the forest for the trees.

It was a pity, for some of his promised ideas were outstanding. He proposed a "zero-based budget." I took that to mean that, since more and more of the budget was put by Congress on automatic pilot, with expenditures rising automatically every year and beyond control, Carter wanted the automatic controls off, with each spending item reconsidered on its merits and passed or rejected each year. Had this been done, much of the subsequent failure of the U.S. economy might have been avoided. Carter proposed to simplify our tax schedules, which he described as a sinful disgrace in their complexity and perverted purpose. Great—but he had neither the vision nor the clout to do it.

Yet that sense of self-rightness led him to steps that were landmark successes in a field in which he had no prior experience, foreign affairs. To my mind, the two outstanding world figures in the 1970s were Anwar el-Sadat, the President of Egypt, and Deng Hsiao-ping of China. Carter drew on each in turn to achieve remarkable results.

Sadat, who had been Nasser's Vice President and fellow officer, was far clearer-sighted and more realistic than his glamorous predecessor. He saw that Egypt's mortal enemy was not Israel but Egypt's own erupting population on limited resources. He wanted to end the romantic enmity and focus energies on the internal threat. In one of the great gestures of modern times, he flew to Israel and offered to make peace. The new Israeli Premier, Menachem Begin, was a rock hardliner, so little progress was made. (Begin was as hard to talk with as Sadat was easy. A conversation with the relentless Israeli was, I found, rather like crawling through barbed wire. A conversation with Sadat, on a patio of his plain ranch house in the desert, with the pyramids nearby, was one of journalism's pleasant experiences. It was the first time an Arab had public relations assets superior to Israel's.) So, Jimmy Carter invited the two to Washington. Though warned that they would not get along, he locked them up in Camp David until, after 13 days, they came out with an agreement. When Carter announced it before a joint session, Congress cheered him roundly for the first time. When execution of the agreement stalled, Carter, again disregarding warnings about putting his reputation on the line, flew to the Middle East and induced a further agreement that was successful. By this time, Sadat had expelled the Russians Nasser had brought in, and transformed the strongest of the Arab nations into a friend of the U.S.

In China, Mao Tse-tung had sought to revive his flagging revolution by artificial reinforcements. The "Great Leap Forward" sought to force-grow the economy, and failed. Then the "Cultural Revolution" aimed to inspire revolutionary zeal by punishing laggards, but these turned out to be most of the intelligent Chinese. When Mao died, the diminutive Deng, one of those who had been badly punished a decade earlier, achieved power. He sought to replicate the marvelous progress he saw being achieved by Japan and Taiwan by releasing peasants from command and letting a fairly free market move them. It worked well, and soon was tried in other fields. Carter decided to cultivate this promising figure with an exchange of state visits and a marked strengthening of relations. (In the U.S., Deng embarrassed the State Department by turning every expression, toast, local speech into an anti-Russian diatribe.) Carter was criticized by the Right for downgrading Taiwan and recognizing Beijing as capital of the only China. But the tradeoff was great. "I've got us a billion new friends," he said.

In the 1970s Russia went on a kind of stealthy geopolitical rampage around the globe, putting a brigade of the Red Army in Cuba, inducing Cubans to send their troops to win civil wars for the Communist side in Angola and Ethiopia, winning a *coup d'état* in South Yemen and launching a Red Army invasion of Afghanistan. There was breast-beating in America about Russia's gaining the advantage. Actually, Carter's wooing of Egypt and China were more important than anything Russia did in those years.

But another Third Worlder of the time, the Ayatollah Khomeini of Iran, led to Carter's undoing. Iran was seen by the U.S. as a kind of keystone in an arch of resistance to the Russians in the oil-rich and strategic Middle East. The

Shah of Iran was applying his oil income to sweeping his country posthaste from backwardness to Western modernity. But he was doing so in a way that mortally offended two vital units, the Moslem religious establishment and the rising educated middle classes. The mullahs, beneficiaries of inherited lands and charity, were the equivalent of the nation's welfare state, distributing largesse to the poor. When the Shah took their lands to redistribute in a land reform, he created an unforgiving enemy. He helped youth to education in universities all over the world, mainly in the U.S., but then denied them one thing all rising middle classes insist on, a share of power. In crisis, the two joined forces and sent the Shah packing. As he was identified with the U.S., and we were identified with Israel and with resented Western culture generally, the revolution became anti-American. It was dominated by the returned exile, the Ayatollah Ruhollah Khomeini, a narrow, shallow, embittered old holy man who was himself best described by the sobriquet he applied to America, "the great Satan." The U.S. Embassy was invaded and taken over and fifty-two employees locked up as hostages. Carter's inability to get them out—who could have?—was interpreted as one more failure of purpose. His standing in an opinion poll was 21 percent favorable, the lowest ever (Nixon at bottom was 24 percent, Truman 23 percent). I thought it unfair that his reputation should suffer because of Iran. But I thought the low rating was just, for the reason that this decent kindly man lacked the essential qualities to be President.

CHAPTER SEVENTY-SEVEN

Climacteric

I guess it is common experience, but at the time it seemed unique and personal to me: old age came on suddenly. I was a slimmish, tallish, youngish man ever busy pushing to get the measure of the next experience and get to a typewriter and organize it for publication or broadcast. At a point during the Carter Administration a concatenation of events caused me to do something I had not done for a long time—take a serious look in the mirror. The slim tall young man I thought I inhabited was not there. My hair was almost wholly white. Somehow a round little pot had been attached to my navel. I had had premonitions of this, but succeeding tailors had dealt with it over the years so that it came as a shock that my 33-inch waist now measured nearly 38. "By God!" I said to the alien figure in the mirror, "You're an *old* man!"

The years leading up to this shock I spent anchoring the *ABC Evening News*. For eighteen months I co-anchored the program with Frank Reynolds. I considered Reynolds, short physically but large with intelligence and having a fine voice and general carriage, to be the nearly ideal anchorman. It was I who persuaded the bosses to take Frank off the White House beat and make him anchor. Ratings, indicating the size of one's audience, are an unplumbed mystery, but I was thought by the decision makers to be the reason our ratings had risen when I was joined to him as co-anchor, and he was considered to be the reason they had reached an inadequate plateau and got stuck. He was removed, and Harry Reasoner was acquired at great expense from CBS to be my co-anchor. I then worked with Reasoner for almost five years.

Reasoner had been one of the reporters on CBS's breathtakingly successful magazine program, *60 Minutes*. He was best known for narrating some eloquently whimsical documentaries, of which one named *Doors* was the most famous, simply a pictorial dissertation on entrances and exits all over the world. His face was creased with lines that formed into a warm, wise smile. He made audiences comfortable. In reality he was something of a disappointment. Those highly perceptive narrations were the work of the writer Andy Rooney (who eventually dared to appear in person before cameras to read his own lines and became famous). On coming to ABC, Harry was given a weekly half-hour, called *The Reasoner Report,* in which to be whimsical. But without the right writer it failed to take off and died an early death. He did little writing himself, "as little as possible," he said to an interviewer in my presence. He was quite simply lazy. His warmth was all in his face. In fact, I found him rather cold. But though he drank regularly, even while on the air, his performance was always perfect and his image winning, which is generally what matters on television.

Ratings point by arduous ratings point, the ABC entertainment network had risen from poor third to a competitor for first. The news network had also improved but not fast enough. President Bill Sheehan was under pressure to get those ratings up. He called me in and said that he had decided to end the dual anchor and go with one person. I agreed, for I had always disliked having to nurse diplomatic relations with a co-host. But, Sheehan said, the one anchor would be Reasoner, and I would be doing the commentary. I said that was a mistake; whenever Harry went away for a couple of weeks' vacation, the ratings always went up a notch. But there was no argument. A lot of money had been paid to get Reasoner to leave CBS, and ABC had to try to get something out of the deal.

It didn't work. The ratings slipped. Sheehan reached for a more spectacular stratagem. Barbara Walters, the star interviewer for NBC's *Today* show was approached, offered a million dollars—the first to breach this 4-minute mile of broadcast news—and something NBC would not give her: the central role of co-anchor on the flagship evening news report. I liked Barbara and readily joined in speaking a message of greeting to her at a small dinner given by ABC news executives when she came over. But Reasoner was offended by the arrangement, since it suggested that he had failed. He refused to rehearse a new format with her. "I already know how to read a teleprompter," he said to me. He behaved like a peeved child on and off the air.

The first night, ratings were double what they had been before. There was national curiosity about the first female network anchor and the first million-dollar newsperson. The second and third nights the ratings fell below their previous norm. Barbara had a high-pitched voice, and when required by the on-air director to speed up it rose to the level of incomprehensibility. This, plus an anchorman who appeared to be on a diet of lemons, made the experiment impossible. Later, when ABC created a new magazine program titled *20/20,* she became the star hostess, succeeding brilliantly at what she did better than almost anyone, interviewing.

Sheehan was removed. I was saddened to see him go; whatever staffing decisions he felt he had to make, he remained a warm, considerate friend. Roone Arledge, the chief of the network's highly successful—long ahead of the rest of the network—sports department, was prevailed upon to take over News. I do not know whether they were an intended succession or not, but unhappy events promptly created a friction between us, the first of which involved my wife.

I have told that when I left CBS I hired a professional agent to inform and represent me, and that my choice proved a bad one. After I had been at ABC for a couple of years, Elmer Lower, then president of ABC News, emerged from a session with him and confirmed my own view, saying, "Can't you find someone else? This fellow is impossible." A light went on in my brain. My wife knew all there was to know about me. She already represented me in negotiations for lectures and other assignments outside the network, and was famously pleasant to work with. Would Lower mind his lawyers dealing with her? He did not mind, so she took over, relations smoothed, and my income nearly doubled in a year. Concerned to avoid giving the impression of being a pushy wife, Bennie never came near my office or the newsrooms, but dealt only with lawyers and executives in New York, in their offices, or over lunch. Still, the mere idea of a wife representing a husband seemed unnatural and threatening to a few underlings of unsure masculinity, and one of them must have gotten to the new president Arledge.

One of Bennie's duties was to fit my leaves from ABC with schedules for the *Evening News* and Presidential appearances, which I always anchored for the network. It was a juggling job made more difficult because ABC was institutionally reluctant to let me go, and I was a workaholic usually reluctant to leave. At the time, I had not had a vacation for a long time, though six weeks were owed me. Bennie worked out an opening for me to take one week off, then phoned to get ABC's agreement. Her message was relayed to Arledge by some middleman and was apparently dramatized in transmission as a threat to take me off the air. Late that night Arledge phoned, and Bennie took the phone. It should be emphasized that neither Bennie nor I had ever met or even seen him. Without preface he lit into her with a furious cussing out that left her no instant to protest, explain or comment. When I came in and saw her listening stunned and in tears, I grabbed the phone, but he had hung up. That night and all the next day I called repeatedly. I finally caught him at a network conference in Puerto Rico a day later, taught him new wrinkles in cussing out and demanded an explanation and an apology. I never got the explanation, but the apology came the same night in the form of a dozen roses for Bennie with a note from Arledge, "This is more my style."

The next encounter was clearly my doing. Arledge began trying out anchormen for the *Evening News* in a most extraordinary way. He put all five candidates on together every night. Reasoner would open the show, introducing a report. Then Barbara would appear to introduce a second report. Then Frank Reynolds, then Peter Jennings, then I would pop up in the box to introduce segments. I thought it ridiculous. So, apparently, did Garry Trudeau the comics artist who did several amusing strips about it, one ending with a voice emerging from the box to a watching Doonesbury, "I'm the only one left here. My name is Carlos; I work upstairs in the stockroom. Here are tonight's headlines." After a month I asked to be released from the competition. But, unfortunately, in a press conference I gave after a speech at the University of Kansas, someone asked what I thought of the new format, and I answered thoughtlessly that "it's a Punch and Judy show." The AP put it on the wire. Arledge phoned me before I left the campus and was furious. Relations never recovered.

He hired two new vice presidents. I went to see one to get acquainted. He was so deliberately unpleasant that I assumed I must have been the subject of some adverse discussion in the executive suites. The other new vice president came to see us in my home in Washington. He wore a dark suit and a grave countenance, giving me the impression of your friendly local undertaker come to guess the measure of a potential customer. His message was that ABC was prepared to offer me a new contract, but he could think of nothing they could give me to do.

It was at this point that I consulted a mirror and subtracted my birth date from the current date and found that I was 65! It happened when I was look-ing the other way. It seemed clear that I would no longer find any professional satisfaction in the new ABC News administration; the new bunch might even take some pleasure in competing to find ways to smite the once honored. Sam Donaldson suggested that the fatal visit of the underling to discourage me had not been Arledge's plan, but a subordinate's response to a casual complaint like that of Henry II about Becket, "Who will free me from this turbulent priest?" That was no consolation; I reminded Sam that the turbulent priest was assassi-nated. I had to get out.

But it was a sad decision for me. I felt that I should leave with some va-grant link to a craft I had practiced, indeed pioneered, for nearly a lifetime. Af-ter all I had brought ABC some awards in a period when they were scarce for the third network. Just recently, the show business fraternity, the Friars Club, had given a huge banquet, Johnny Carson presiding, to honor "the nation's outstanding newscasters" and their choices were Cronkite, Brinkley and me. So I phoned Leonard Goldenson, the president of ABC, told him my plans and my wish to keep some kind of contact. I cited the example of Paley nam-ing Murrow, then Cronkite, to the board of CBS, and wondered if anything of that nature was possible in my case. It was ridiculous of me to think of it. Gold-enson was a business lawyer for whom business was restricted to businessmen. A bad idea died a-borning.

So I wrote out my resignation and had it hand-delivered to Arledge in New York. His first reaction was to protest my decision. But I had already tacked a notice of my resignation on the bulletin board in the Washington newsroom to establish finality. My letter was tart of tongue but foresightful in predicting Arledge's success. In addition to his executive gifts he had a guaran-tee of something we had never had before, lots of the green stuff that makes things grow: money. He applied the latter to emulate Citizen Kane and hire some of the best from other networks, mainly David Brinkley from NBC and Diane Sawyer from CBS. His executive flair helped make triumphs of two he inherited: Ted Koppel was given a late-night half-hour that appeared to be a throwaway. By skill, intelligence and hard labor, Koppel made *Nightline,* as it was named, into a class program that bested movies and Johnny Carson in rat-ings. Peter Jennings was brought back from the foreign staff to become an-chorman of a much embellished evening news roundup that made him and ABC number one in the nation.

For me there were vicissitudes and uncertainties to come. But one thing was subject to my control. I got that waistline back to 34—well, 35—and kept it there.

1979 AND AFTER

CHAPTER SEVENTY-EIGHT

Mr. Wonderful

I had never had an age crisis. I was busy, and thirty, forty and fifty went by like so many telephone poles past a train window. Now I had to notice. A trip to the Social Security office to register for Medicare made clear what the clock said. But—I wanted to cry to the young lady behind the desk—I don't want those golden years advertised in your brochure; I like mine in natural color. I could not shake the feeling that I was on an upward curve in my line of endeavor, and my best work, such as it would be, was still ahead. I was relieved when some others indicated they thought so too. Several syndication producers proposed plans. To my surprise, Mr. John Bookhout, the president of Shell Oil in Houston, came to Washington and asked me to join his board of directors. I thought it over seriously and, on Arthur Goldberg's advice, said no. Business is best done by businessmen, and my small collection of talents does not include theirs. Then PBS asked me to narrate a series of documentaries on the changing Presidency titled *Every Four Years.* I agreed not only to narrate, but to write the whole thing, for I always found it difficult to speak other writers' lines. Much of it was done with me in the Oval Office and the Cabinet room as on-camera anchor sites, late at night when President Carter was not using them.

The assignment was barely completed when a rich plum fell in my lap. The League of Women Voters acquired the franchise for all Presidential debates in the election year 1980 and asked me to moderate them. As the President was a Democrat and sure to be the candidate again, the incumbent party had no debates; all primary season encounters were Republican.

The first of them, in New Hampshire, was a confusing melange of political flavors, with ten candidates answering our questions. I have only one recollection: I asked Ronald Reagan how he could hope to keep a promise to balance the budget in three years, while reducing revenues with the biggest tax cut ever, and at the same time greatly increasing spending on arms. I don't remember his answer, but the question stuck in my mind because it dominated the Reagan years, and the true answer was, it couldn't be done.

Only four candidates were left for the second debate. A new format was tried. I alone, no panel, would put a question, let the candidates bat it around till I felt it was used up, then throw out another. A *New York Times* editorial said it was the best format yet. Two of the candidates were right-wingers who spent most of the time ragging the liberal John Anderson. Reagan sat there, quietly studying the ceiling, letting them damage one another, till I said, "You are enjoying this too much, Governor; say something to the boys, even if it's only goodbye."

There were two left for the final primary debate in Houston, Reagan and George Bush. Recently in a speech, Bush had termed Reagan's plan to spend more and tax less "voodoo economics." I felt that at last he had provided me with the means to induce a good exchange of views. But in the couple of days since the speech Bush had read the polls. He was not going to get the nomination; Reagan had sewn it up. So Bush was positioning himself to be chosen as Reagan's number two on the ticket. Thus the only sage observation he ever, to my mind, made in his career died on the vine, and I presented the public two debaters awash in sterile agreement.

For a long while it appeared that the two chosen as candidates for the general election, Carter and Reagan, would not debate. Both seemed to think it would be a risk. But as opinion polls indicated the two were close in public favor, both felt a need to shake some voters loose, so they agreed to confront one another at just about the last moment. The place was Cleveland. Next day accounts said there was doubt about who won. I, in the referee's seat, did not agree. Carter was uptight and brittle. Reagan was relaxed and graceful. Carter insisted on separate rooms for the two, and total isolation before the bout. Reagan was indifferent, and he and his wife chatted freely with me until drawn into required confinement. When the two had to come out from behind curtains and stand at their podiums to let lights and sound be adjusted, Carter looked stonily into the distance. Reagan looked at him and finally left his podium, walked across the stage and shook hands.

In substance no new points were made, but tactics and manner were one-sided. The actor had it all the way. When Carter criticized Reagan, the actor displayed a tolerant smile and said, "There you go again"—a nothing, but so delivered that it seemed to melt the arrowheads on Carter's arrows. The decisive point and tactic were Reagan's question, aimed straight at the television audience at the end: "Are you better off now than you were four years ago?" With stagflation worse, its mystery not even plumbed, there was no doubt that the answer was no. Afterward, Carter disappeared behind the curtain and was gone. Reagan and wife came over and chatted with us. A well-known pollster opined, "It was a wash." I disagreed. That night Reagan won the debate and, as they say, put the election on ice.

The result, though expected, tried my faith in my political judgment. Until very late I did not believe that a movie actor—and not a distinguished one at that—could be elected President, or that the electorate would deem a septuagenarian (he would be 77 when he left office) vigorous enough for the strenuous demands of the job.

Reagan won with a warm, happy personality, in contrast to Carter's weak, gloomy one. And the time was ripe. After half a century the New Deal had run out of gas. The world and the problems had changed. The nation knew it and needed something different. The principle that a vice is nothing but a virtue carried to extremes was illustrated on every hand. In the 1930s it was urgent that labor be legislated more power to demand more and to redistribute wealth downward. That was virtue. But by 1980 that power had led to regular high rises in wages and benefits that fed inflation and ate up the very gains just won. That was vice. Because of debt, Chrysler was being bailed out by the tax-payers—we could not afford to let so many jobs be lost—at a time when Chrysler was negotiating more inflationary wage increases, deepening its debt. The nation was in the dumps and needed something new, one knew not what.

Reagan had an old/new offering. He felt he wanted the America of his happy boyhood in Illinois, just updated some, and said he knew how to get it. Reduce taxes, reduce spending, reduce regulations, get government on the road to atrophy and let the natural vigor of Americans, acting on market motivations, supply all the wealth and jobs needed.

I think he saw life as a movie, so I should be rather proud to have been one of the bad guys he overcame in that famous speech for Goldwater. Rich conservatives, thrilled by it, insisted that he run for Governor of California, which he did and served two rather successful terms. When he first announced for President, I was sent to Los Angeles to report. With a camera crew I joined a row of cars at rest outside a small ranch house on Sunset Boulevard across from the campus of the University of California at Los Angeles. I had planned just to follow, but an aide saw me and invited me into the house, where I sat awkwardly in the corner as Ronald and Nancy had a quiet breakfast. I thought relations might be touchy after our exchange regarding the speech, but he was friendly. Later in the campus auditorium I thought tempers might flare when he talked to students, whom I remembered as rebellious. But I was out of date. Students now studied or goofed off, but no longer rebelled. He thoroughly captivated them. I figured that he never really got angry. His rare outbursts were adjusted to movie takes on camera. From long practice, being and appearing a good guy had become normal.

He was a different kind of campaigner. It made you feel good just to be within the range of that cheery smile and those really funny quips. He met a problem by dismissing it with a factoid of his own. Energy problem? Well, he said, "There is more oil in our Alaska than there is in Saudi Arabia," so ridiculously wrong that you had to think he knew something you didn't. He declared to an audience that air pollution had been successfully dealt with just before the last leg of a flight back home had to be diverted from Los Angeles because a poisonous smog made landing chancy.

When he won and had been in office a while, I was invited to a large lunch at the White House. I had done a film at White House request on voluntarism by locals dealing with local problems—points of light, as Bush would later call them. Usually the White House rewarded people with a tie that had little cameos of Adam Smith on it. I was deemed unsuited to the Tories' hero so was sent a tie with cameos of De Tocqueville on it. At the lunch there were about twelve tables, each seating six or eight guests. A servant showed me to my table, and there it was on the place card next to mine: The President. He came in to applause, shook a few hands, then sat down. After a few personal inquiries he told a joke, which led to another. Soon, it became a performance, a stand-up comedy sitting down, and all at our table were roaring. One story was proclaimed his favorite. For posterity I record it, with the caution that it carries no hidden meaning; it is simply nicely silly.

A city man driving in the country noticed a chicken running along beside him. He knew chickens could not run 40 miles an hour, but this one did. When he sped up, the chicken did too, and went off ahead of him down a side road. He followed. He lost the chicken but found a farmer. He asked, "Did you see a chicken going lickety split out this road?" *Farmer:* "Yep." *City Man:* "He was going so fast he looked like he had three legs." *Farmer:* "Yep, he had three legs all right." *City Man:* "I wonder how he got three legs." *Farmer:* "He's got 'em cause that's how I breed 'em, with three legs." *City Man:* "How come?" *Farmer:* "Well, I love chicken, but only the drumstick. And my wife's the same, loves the drumstick. So when we lived alone it was just right, one drumstick each. But then her sister came to live with us, and she wouldn't eat nothing but the drumsticks. So I had to breed chickens with three legs." *City Man:* "That's very interesting. How do they taste?" *Farmer:* "I don't know. I can't catch 'em."

The Reagan Presidency went off as if scripted by someone who liked him. He swept his record tax cut and big arms bill through Congress with ease. (The negatives in our legislative system disappear when you are giving something away.) There was an awful recession, but it came early and was generally blamed on Carter or, closer to the mark, on Paul Volcker, the Carter-appointed Chairman of the Federal Reserve Board. Volcker did Reagan the favor of squeezing out inflation that was 13 percent when Reagan became President and had recently gone as high as 18 percent. When time came for his reelection, inflation was low, and people were spending their tax cut bonus and creating jobs. The price of this extraordinary cut in revenues, coupled with an extraordinary increase in spending, was a raging deficit in the federal budget.

Hitherto the biggest deficit had been $66 billion, one year in Ford's term. Under Reagan the deficit beat that figure every year and exceeded $200 billion twice. Eventually it would begin to eat us alive, but at that time, the voting public, itself on a private spending spree, seemed not to care.

Luck smiled on him equally in foreign affairs. During his second term the Soviet empire turned soft, and the end began. Reagan spokesmen claimed he caused it, with his arms program, his tenacity about installing new nuclear missiles in Europe despite rowdy pacifist demonstrations, his invasion of Grenada in the Caribbean (small as an island, said one, but large as an aircraft carrier, providing Cuban troops with a half-way house to Africa where they fought for the Soviet cause in Angola) and, above all, in his advocacy of the "Star Wars" program, which aimed to create an umbrella that supposedly would make the U.S. impervious to Soviet missiles. In my view, if one president caused success in the Cold War, it was Harry Truman; he put the containment policy in place, rescued Greece, saved Berlin, rebuilt the Allied world with the Marshall Plan, democratized Germany and Japan, recruited them as prosperous allies in the Cold War, formed NATO and made it clear that he would fight if necessary, as in Korea. But Reagan does deserve credit for his robust manner and acts, which restored America's faith in its power and the world's respect for the U.S., both badly shaken by Vietnam.

For me, the defining feature of the Reagan years was his cheerful unawareness of the giant problems he was creating in the attempt to fulfill his dream. His budget director, David Stockman, told an illuminating story. Reagan promised to cut government spending to the bone. Stockman sought to persuade him that cutting spending was not easy, and a tax rise might be necessary to stanch the budget hemorrhage. Stockman could not get his point through to his boss, till he had an idea: He made a multiple-choice game of it. He listed fifty spending areas and, next to each, boxes Reagan could tick off to nick spending, or whack it, or leave it alone. Next to each was a note on what the impact might be. The President enjoyed the game. He took his time over it, consulting experts on each item. Finally he returned the form completed. Stockman studied it, then advised Reagan he had added a deficit of $800 billion over five years to the national debt! Yet Reagan did not get the point. Soon after, it was suggested that there might have to be a tax increase to slow the debt hemorrhage. The President's fist slammed the table, and he said, "I don't want to hear any more talk about taxes! The problem is deficit spending!"

Congresswoman Pat Schroeder carved Reagan's epitaph in permanent stone by dubbing him the Teflon President because nothing unpleasant ever stuck to him. His term saw the national debt nearly triple, and swollen interest payments suck away capital needed for the nation's progress. The Teapot Dome scandals of the 1920s dirtified President Harding's name forever, but

384 1979 AND AFTER

the Savings and Loan scandals of the late 1980s, which cost the nation a multiple of Teapot Dome, did no apparent damage to Reagan. Nor did the escapades of his polluter-friendly environmental officers, one of whom was sent to prison. Reagan's Assistant Attorney General William Weld resigned in protest at what he called unethical conduct by Reagan's close friend and Attorney General, Ed Meese. Weld (soon to be elected Governor of Massachusetts) was granted a meeting with the President to propose that Meese be prosecuted. As Weld spoke, Reagan nodded off.

Reagan was master of the funny quip. I think it was from him that I first heard Hollywood described as the place where "the stars are in the sidewalks and the dirt is in the sky." It is fitting that two quips by opponents may best describe him and his works. Campaigning against him, Walter Mondale adapted an old saying, "It ain't what he don't know that bothers me; it's what he knows for sure that ain't so." In response to an argument that Reagan brought the nation prosperity, Senator Lloyd Bentsen of Texas said, "Give me authority to pass 200 billion dollars worth of hot checks a year, and I'll give you the illusion of prosperity." My own quip chanced out of a question period after I talked about solving some national problems to the Trial Lawyers of Northern California in the St. Francis Hotel in San Francisco. Someone shouted, "What do we do about earthquakes?" I said, "Find out where Ronald Reagan is and stay close to him."

CHAPTER SEVENTY-NINE

The Market Economy Strikes Back

Ronald Reagan was a fun President, always upbeat, witty, affirmative, clad in cushions of good humor that deprived life's slings and arrows of wounding force. He disarmed critics by likening them to the hippie flower-girl who said to her scruffy fellows, "I can't see how he got elected. Nobody I know voted for him." But that easy quality made him an easy man to underestimate. In fact, he belongs among the landmark Presidents. He assured himself of lasting influence on government by a unique means: he set in train a rise in the nation's debt from $994 billion when he came into office, to $4.4 trillion twelve years later, when a new Democratic President took over. With an inherited burden of that immensity, future Presidents would have considerable trouble funding expensive new social programs. But Reagan's terms were more noteworthy for the momentum he gave to one of the great shifts of modern history.

In the 1920s capitalism discredited itself by its mad race in the service of greed, which ended in a thundering collision with the trade cycle. In reaction, there was a worldwide shift toward socialism or its way stations of state intervention and central decision-making. The high points were probably the establishment of the New Deal in the U.S. and, delayed a decade by war, the postwar triumph of Labour in Britain. These were the two nations where most of the rulers of the liberated colonies of the world were educated, and whose trends they copied or miscopied.

Now in the 1980s a severe reaction against the reaction set in. A shift of tectonic force moved the world back toward capitalism—now known by the new name, the "market economy," which smelled less of dogma: Let not government but individual businesses decide what and how much to produce and at which price, as directed by what consumers will pay, and all else will fall into place. A freed economy will see the clutter of government-run social programs become marginal or cease to exist.

Probably the main cause of the shift back was that government interventionism, like most overage trends, ran to excess and was no longer working as intended. For example, Medicare, free health care for the elderly, and Medicaid, health care for the poor, went out of control, their costs soaring into outer space. Another cause was a combination of two factors. The unrelenting advances in technology, exported freely from the U.S., provided any fairly well-educated nation with instant means to produce salable things well. And the dismantling of barriers and the opening up of world trade, led by the U.S., provided a wide market to sell in. These two American creations, said Milton Friedman, made it "possible, to a greater extent than at any time in the world's history, for a company to locate anywhere, to use resources from anywhere to produce a product that can be sold anywhere." The consequence was intense competition. Socialism, intelligently applied, was good at distributing the benefits and burdens of society relatively fairly, but it was no great shakes at competing. The market economy, squeezing costs down to levels people would pay, seemed right for the changed demands.

Reagan did not start it. The spectacular Mrs. Thatcher, Britain's first female Prime Minister, was there five years earlier. She first took on and whipped the British trade unions that had become almighty and irresponsible even to the point of overthrowing their own Labour governments. Then she put up for sale many of the businesses Labour had nationalized. She started a trend. By 1993, the governments of fifty other countries had sold off to private owners more than $350 billion dollars' worth of their assets.

At the same time, Japan was forcing the pace. With the military outlet closed, the Japanese applied their fierce national concentration to commercial industry. They conscientiously acquired the most advanced technologies and improved on them, then launched massive invasions of newly opened world markets. Though the Japanese government protected them and smoothed their way abroad, the method and the motivation were those of privately owned enterprise.

To the rest of Asia, the Japanese message was, if we can do it, so can you. And Korea, Singapore and Taiwan took up the idea, soon to be followed by other hitherto backward peoples. In the decade of the 1980s, the national economies of East Asia—leaving out Japan—grew 60 percent. Japan's growth was 35 percent, and the U.S. figure was 19 percent. East Asia's share of the world output of wealth in 1967 was 8 percent. By 1987 it was 20 percent. By that latter year, the U.S. was doing 37 percent of its foreign trade with East Asia (including Japan) and only 20 percent with Europe. For America this meant that the formerly poor nations of Asia had become ferocious competitors, and our need to switch to a system geared to competing with them was urgent.

But if the socialistic trend demonstrated the limits of socialism, so the new trend revealed the limits of the market system. As described earlier, the poor, lacking the skill to supply or the funds to demand have no part in a supply-and-demand economy. Having spent a part of my adolescence in such a condition, I very much believe in government intervention to relieve it. The market economy tends to falter, also, at the top of the income scale. Captains of business, acting from the requisite motivations of self-gain, often find it more profitable to share out a market with other captains of business, in cartel fashion, than to compete for it. So, rules enacted and enforced from the center are often essential to achieve the benefits of the free market.

Another worrisome consequence of the market economy is that it inevitably gives the initiative, not to say the whip hand, in all aspects of life to the owners and managers, and they, inevitably, use it to benefit themselves. Beginning in the 1980s, business was freed of much regulation and allowed more leverage than it had possessed since the late 1920s. The rich grew markedly richer; middle incomes stagnated; the poor got poorer. As the great Depression was aggravated by maldistribution—excessive wealth to producers and not enough for customers to buy their products—this trend has to be a cause for concern.

To become "lean and mean," to face fierce foreign competition, American business developed ingenious new ways of cutting costs. The Reagan years saw American business units subjected to an epidemic of raids, buyouts to prevent raids, mergers, downsizings, sell-offs, restructurings, mass hirings of "temps" and part-timers, offshore-movings and out-sourcings. Some of these stratagems sought to cut back the many benefits—health care, pensions, paid holidays—given to employees in the half-century since the New Deal to keep them loyal. It was found, for example, that hiring two part-time or temporary workers without benefits was as productive as, but cheaper than, keeping on one high-seniority worker with all the benefits. Out-sourcing was another method: instead of all the trouble and expense of dealing with a high-paid employee, farm his function out to another company, leaner and meaner and more willing to force a cut in costs.

I find it too early to reach conclusions as to the success or failure of the shift of power away from the government and back to the market. So far it has worked wonders for U.S. manufacturers. Mainly by applying the factor highlighted in the first chapter of this story—displacing human labor with ever-improving, computer-guided machines—American manufacturing enjoyed a boom in productivity and profits in the early 1990s. For example, the Birmingham Steel Corporation, which in 1987 turned out 912 tons of steel per worker, by 1992 was turning out 1,335 tons per worker. Generally, productivity growth in all U.S. business in 1992 was 3.5 percent, which was above the average of past best years. American automakers regained some of their lost market. American chip makers regained their lost lead.

But the trade-offs were painful. In some seasons in that period, hardly a week passed without large corporations announcing the cutting back of jobs in packets of thousands and even tens of thousands. Fortune 500 companies reduced their payrolls from 16.2 million workers to 11.8 million between 1990 and mid-1993. Labor unions, strengthened in the Depression in order to provide a balance of economic power in industrial life, were weakened radically and that balance endangered.

Bigger lessons will eventually be drawn from this experience. For now, one can feel safe in drawing only one. Neither the free market nor government regulation should have its own exclusive way. We must have both. Finding the right mix, which will change from one time to another, is going to be one of our main problems for a long time to come.

In the midst of the great shift, a happy prospect was opened to me. *The Wall Street Journal* had grown into the most interesting newspaper in America. It detailed the news in less space and with better prose than the others. Its editorial pages were slap-in-your-face right wing, but they were also the most sharply argued and best written in the business.

A decision was made in the paper's inner councils to enter what to them was an entirely new field—television. They wanted to launch a news-type program written and produced in the *Journal's* style, and I was summoned for a conference. It was held in the *Journal* offices, in what appeared to be an editorial board room, around which all the heads of departments sat and scrutinized me with an intentness I had not undergone since the Rhodes Scholar trials half a century before. Most seemed to regard me with narrowed eyes. But a friendly voice whispered to Bennie at my side, "I have never seen all these guys in one room before." So they were clearly very interested. To my surprise the verdict was favorable. Bennie and the lawyer for Dow Jones, the parent company, negotiated a satisfactory agreement for me to do the show.

But when time came to sign, there was a surprise. The Dow Jones lawyer informed us that I was to sign, not with the *Journal* or with Dow Jones, but with a private TV production company which would be under contract to produce the program. While I was willing, and indeed would have been proud, to work for the *Journal,* I was altogether unwilling to sign my professional life away to a private TV producer whom I considered autocratic and inadequate. If the *Journal* was my boss, I could insist to the producer on the program's quality; if the producer was my boss, I could not.

For the first time in my experience I was being "out-sourced." Rather than having the trouble of taking on a new employee, dealing with a new union and new problems, Dow Jones contracted with an outside company that would hire me and liberate the *Journal* from all those problems. Having just broken free of producers and started a new career of writing and speaking to please myself, I said no. The deal and the plan fell through. But at least I had learned first-hand what "out-sourcing" meant.

CHAPTER EIGHTY

Man on the Flying Trapeze

When I first took up journalism, I looked on it as modest-paying, dubiously secure work, to be done almost as much for love as for money. To be sure to make a living, I made a point of learning to ply all the many forms of the reporting craft in order to be able to leap with some agility, as if on a trapeze, to another branch when the branch beneath me grew shaky. Thus, throughout my career, in addition to holding a steady job, I wrote books and magazine articles, lectured and wrote columns for newspapers. During my tenure at CBS,

I wrote *The Atlantic*'s "Letter from London" for a long while. While at ABC, I was the first columnist for the *Washingtonian* magazine. Every day that I appeared on television I also did a broadcast for radio. Once I even emceed a banquet, replacing an ailing Bob Hope. Doing commercials I considered entirely out of bounds, as being incompatible with journalism; I once, though broke, turned down a flat million dollars to do three weeks of commercials for a well-known insurance company.

I go back in chronology for a moment now to recount an adventure in a not closely related branch of the media that became a small but enjoyable extra career for me: the movies. Gore Vidal's play, *The Best Man*, after a long, successful run on the stage, was being translated to film. A casting director phoned me from Hollywood and said they needed someone to appear as a TV commentator covering a fictional Presidential convention. Would I be interested? I would, and flew out.

The film was being shot on location at the Los Angeles Forum where I had covered the nomination of John Kennedy for President in 1960. The story was strung around two competitors for their party's nomination for President: Henry Fonda, playing a liberal Adlai Stevenson–like character; and Cliff Robertson, a tough Nixon-like one. Both sought the endorsement of an Eisenhower-like sitting President, played by Lee Tracy.

I met Tracy in the makeup room early my first morning on location. He set about flattering me: he said that he had been given four pictures of graying men to choose how he wished to be made gray to play a President. One was Senator Dirksen, there were two others he did not know, and the fourth was me. He chose me. I flattered him right back: I told him that as a student at Oxford I had gone to London to see Robert Sherwood's antiwar drama, *Idiot's Delight,* on the stage. Tracy was the star and made an unforgettable entrance in an overcoat held together with a buckleless belt pulled tight in a knot, and with a broad collar turned rakishly up behind his head. I told him I left the theater, sought out a haberdasher near Piccadilly Circus and bought myself a thick overcoat with a big turnupable collar and a buckleless belt. I wore it throughout the war and it made me feel as gung-ho as if I'd had epaulets on my undershirt.

My role in the film was a reporter serving as a kind of Greek chorus. I appeared standing outside the Forum in a milling crowd, facing a TV camera and fiddling nervously with my tie. A fictional director was shown to signal me for action, and I put on my anchorman expression and proceeded to explain to the camera what was afoot in the competition about to come to a head inside the auditorium. The joy of stardom struck me immediately. When I did my long piece without missing a beat, the milling crowd, all extras, stood and applauded. Henry Fonda dropped by and secured my impression that Clark

Gable had better watch out. But I also came to know the exquisite sadness of failure: that performance ended up on the cutting-room floor. All of me that appeared for the public to see was a couple of bits done in an anchor booth inside the Forum.

But the incident seemed to attract the attention of other casting directors. Soon I was invited back to appear in other films. One was a fable called *The Man* about a Negro Senator who, by a train of accidents, becomes the first Black President. Another was *Nashville* about Western and country singers. In *The Pink Panther* I was given star billing, but then cut out when it had to be shortened for television. Still another of my cinematic endeavors was *The Pursuit of D. B. Cooper,* about the true story of the hunt for the man who hijacked an airplane, demanded and got a big ransom, then parachuted from the plane and was never seen again. Robert Duvall and Treat Williams were the stars. I co-starred with Robert Redford in *The Candidate,* I appearing for twenty seconds and he for two hours. I did not like their script for my character, so they allowed me to write my own, and later admitted that mine was better than theirs. In *Close Encounters of the Third Kind* I actually had to do some acting, displaying fright and amazement at the arrival on earth of a flying saucer. The combination of emotions was not hard; I had the same expression for both. Other forgettable roles were in *Network, The Best Little Whorehouse in Texas,* and the TV series *The Odd Couple.*

The most enjoyable film for me was titled *V* and was the story of an invasion of Earth by denizens of another planet. After circulating as a movie, it was turned into a TV series. I appeared at the beginning of each episode, sitting in a studio and reporting the course of the war between invaders and earthlings. I was allowed to dream up my own news events and performed such prodigies as bringing Arabs and Israelis and South African Whites and Blacks together in alliance against the aliens—a few years before they decided to try it themselves.

Working in movies was fun as an avocation, but there was very little money in it. When I left ABC, I had to do some hard thinking about income. Though I had been pretty high up in television news since it began, my departure from CBS and arrival in an ABC still working its way up caused me to fall between the cracks both in income and in acquiring a pension. Bennie and I faced the prospect of having either to sell our beloved home or to find a new way to make money. That hunt led increasingly to the lectern. Bennie did the agenting, and in the first year invitations for a large number of speeches were offered and accepted. I soon reached my saturation point of fifty-odd talks a year.

I was sorry to discover that in the 1980s the university and college lecture circuit was not what it used to be. Now when I visited a campus, looking forward to speaking to the students, mostly I found myself addressing adults from the community or potential financial supporters of the institution. However, new and more satisfying outlets were large public forums and corporate America. Most of my talks were for the annual meetings or conventions of businesses, like Honeywell, Epson, Prudential, Tandy, Manufacturers Hanover Bank, Merrill Lynch, foreign and domestic carmakers, Anheuser-Busch and Travelers Insurance. A plurality were in the traditional sites of conventions— Miami, Las Vegas, San Francisco. The rest were spread over places I had never been—from Salem, Massachusetts, to Bakersfield, California; from Marquette on Lake Superior to El Paso on the Rio Grande. It proved a wonderful way to meet people and see the country. I addressed IBM groups thirteen times in one year. I made the featured talk at IBM's annual conference for its customers in the U.S. government, held in Colonial Williamsburg, for four successive years. One year I took part of a summer to go on a cruise to China, Korea and Japan, all costs for me and my family paid for by lectures I did on board.

I had to believe the talks were successful from the numbers of invitations and repeat invitations over many years. Also I noticed that restless audiences fell to pindrop silence and listened intently. Question periods, which many sponsors hesitated to schedule for fear no one would speak up, were always lively. The lecturers' professional organization, the International Platform Association, gave me their Lowell Thomas Award. In some part I think my success lay in overcoming the journalist's illusion that lecturing is a side bar to the profession, to be done offhandedly between broadcasts or newspaper columns. As reporters are articulate in putting sentences after one another on the typewriter or in reading a teleprompter, they tend to assume that they have a natural ability to speak articulately from the lectern without special effort; then they are often disappointed to find themselves stumbling and groping when looking at a sea of upturned faces. I have seen Walter Cronkite, champion of ad-libbers, crisp and gung-ho before a camera, turn soft and fumbly before an audience. Sevareid, eloquent with his carefully composed script on a teleprompter, and Teddy White, smooth and almost lyrical on the printed page, have appeared gagging and halting at a lectern. I long ago decided to look upon each talk as a special occasion, a most important mission. I studied the nature of each separate audience and did research for that particular speech, wrote it out word for word, read it over on the airplane and again just before speaking—then left the text in the hotel room and talked entirely without text or notes.

Still, every lecture I made was really what I had been doing all my life. It was a commentary on current events, dolled up with speaker's artifices. To me it was more enjoyable than doing commentaries on TV, for it was before a live, reacting audience, with no textual compromises to accommodate producers or nervous executives. And I had an ample hour, not a few tight minutes. My new career as a lecturer became a full-time occupation and extended my life in journalism for thirteen crammed years after leaving the network.

CHAPTER EIGHTY-ONE

The Crazy Aunt in the Basement

The destruction of Hitler and Stalin and their works was a good century's work. Add to that the creation of the most productive economy since industry began, the achievement of paramountcy in the world-shaping sciences and the sealing up, well and truly begun, of the racial fault line in U.S. history, and you would guess it to be a record to make Americans content and rather proud. Quite the contrary: the world's rich and only remaining superpower entered the last decades of the century in a bleak mood. Discontent, insecurity, fear of the future were palpable. Jimmy Carter devoted a famous speech to the "malaise" afflicting America, but didn't seem to know what caused it or what to do about it. America, said a critic of Carter, finds itself between a marshmallow and a hard place. After that politicians steered clear of the subject of the people's unhappiness; they seemed to sense that if they sought the cause too closely, they would find out that Pogo of the comic strip was right: they were it. In 1992 George Bush and Bill Clinton waged a Presidential campaign in which they seemed determined not to mention the trouble at all—till the prickly billionaire, Ross Perot, entered the race declaring, "It's like the crazy aunt they keep locked up in the basement. Everybody knows she is there, but nobody talks about her." I devoted most of my lecture time in the 1980s (before Perot) to the crazy aunt because that is what hung heavy on people's minds and what they wanted to talk about.

Perot's crazy aunt was the yawning, ever-growing, enervating budget deficit. But what drove the lady mad and got her locked away was something deeper: the deficit was but one aspect of the curious loss of will in America's leaders, the chronic practice of dodging problems, and letting arrears accumulate, rather than facing them. Since the general downturn of things in the mid-1970s, civic courage seemed to have disappeared from the halls of power. With simple perfection, new President George Bush in 1989 said exactly what the trouble was *not* in his State of the Union address. About his plans to deal with the problems troubling the nation, he said, "We have lots of will, but no wallets." That was precisely the opposite of the case: the richest country had lots of wallets, but not a nano-ounce of will to deal with matters.

The most appalling manifestation of lost will was the explosion of violent crime in which people, mainly youths, murdered others as much for some primitive urge to kill as for profit or purpose. Americans, once shocked by TV pictures of killings in Northern Ireland or Beirut, now watched, also on TV, more murders in the streets of any big American city than occurred in those famous foreign homes of violence.

The response of the elected was either to look the other way or to offer remedies of dubious relevance. The easy availability of guns was surely a big factor. But any effort to change the status quo on gun control met with absence of political courage. In Britain, where controls applied, handguns killed 22 people in the year 1990; that same year, in America, they killed 10,567. The police were outgunned by the criminals and wanted action. But no serious move to control guns, as they are controlled strictly in all other modern nations, was undertaken—lest the gun lobby be offended. Poverty had something to do with it. But the number of Americans living below the poverty line, which had been drastically cut by Johnson's War on Poverty, rose in 1993 to the highest point since records were kept. Education had a great deal to do with it. But government in Washington could not bring itself to fully fund and update the one educational program already in place that promised good results, the Head Start program. The epidemic of illegal drugs had very much to do with it. But the drug problem was mainly one of demand: as long as rich demand existed in the U.S., traffickers would risk and kill to make fortunes by supplying it. And instead of funding a network of effective treatment centers, which had a pretty good record of success, government moneys were mainly directed to cutting supply. There were big showy drug busts on TV—as the supply went on growing. Joblessness was surely a cause: youths won't desist from crime when that's all there is, and when privates don't supply jobs, government must. But such programs could be paid for only by a government reasonably near solvency, and ours was not.

This is being written in the mid-1990s, with a hope that some of the preceding problems are belatedly being corrected; but at the time of writing, it is a true portrait of a people suffering from a seemingly nearly brain-dead government. The response of Congress and the White House to the street horrors has so far been big, bloated, crime bills that emphasize numbers—mainly mandating longer, tougher sentences by courts breaking under the case load, putting more criminals into prisons too stuffed to keep them there long.

There are other manifestations of the problem of defaulting leaders, but the clearest expression of it—the one most open to analysis, to being quantified and explained—was Perot's criterion: debt. The annual budget of a nation is an X-ray of its character, its values, what it considers comes first, second, last. The record of the federal budget toward the hundredth year told Americans they were suffering not from standard complaints about the usual inadequacies in politicians. The governance they received in the last quarter of the century had been markedly, unusually poor.

In the year of change, 1974, the budget deficit for the year was $4.7 billion, not a problem. In 1990, the deficit for the year was $279 billion, a very big problem. Our leaders did not lose control, they abandoned it. They knew what had to be done: a mix of spending cuts and tax rises. But they would not do it. It was not a financial or an economic problem, but a moral one.

Like cancer, the debt grew until mere interest on it was one of the biggest spending items in the budget. No use seeking money for education or infrastructure; it had to go to pay interest on monster debt created without purpose. Like hookworm, the parasite favored young hosts. Years of adult self-indulgence were to be paid for by the next generation, in the form of falling standards and all the turbulences, riots, race frictions and demoralizations that accompany falling standards.

Another numerical measure of failure is inflation. Pouring unrequited billions into the nation's bloodstream deprives money of its value. People stop saving when money loses value. Businesses desert the long term; they have to produce a profit in the next quarter. Inflation leads to the condition described by George Bush's Budget Director Richard Darman: "now-nowism, our collective short-sightedness, our obsession with the here and now, our reluctance to address the future." There is an impression that inflation is normal to life, a parasite one must learn to live with. In fact, inflation is abnormal. On the facing page are graphs that appeared in *The Economist* magazine (February 22, 1992): one shows the course of prices in the United States since 1820, while the other shows the same in Britain since 1660. Together, they make the point that in periods of disasters or great wars inflation is severe, but in the normal course of events prices tend to be kept within an acceptable range by the forces of competition and productivity. The disasters of WW II and its aftermath were surely over by 1974. Any spike of inflation after that had to be due to nothing but poor, thoughtless management of our affairs.

Neither elected branch of government was without sin. Presidents were as responsible for inertia as Congresses. By law the President begins the budgeting process, sending Congress his proposed budget for the coming fiscal year. Originally, the President's budget was a serious attempt at a national accounting. But under Reagan the process lost connection to reality and became a

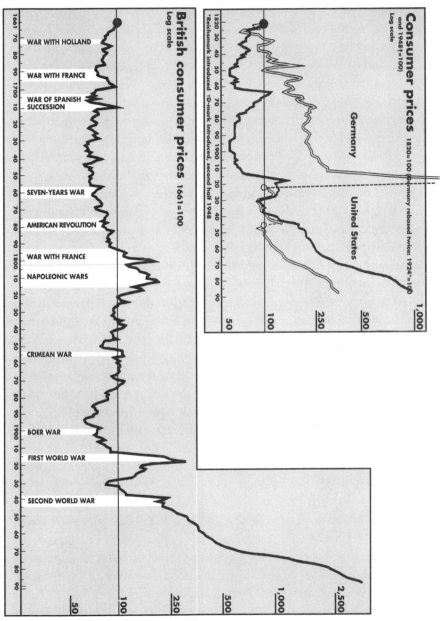

Consumer prices 1820=100 (Germany rebased twice: 1924* =100)
and 1948†=100)
Log scale

Germany

United States

1820 30 40 50 60 70 80 90 1900 10 20 30 40 50 60 70 80 90

50 100 250 500 1,000

*Reichsmark introduced †D-mark introduced, second half 1948

British consumer prices 1661=100
Log scale

1661 70 80 90 1700 10 20 30 40 50 60 70 80 90 1800 10 20 30 40 50 60 70 80 90 1900 10 20 30 40 50 60 70 80 90

WAR WITH HOLLAND

WAR WITH FRANCE

WAR OF SPANISH SUCCESSION

SEVEN-YEARS WAR

AMERICAN REVOLUTION

WAR WITH FRANCE

NAPOLEONIC WARS

CRIMEAN WAR

BOER WAR

FIRST WORLD WAR

SECOND WORLD WAR

50 100 250 500 1,000 2,500

political gesture, the more complex equivalent of a partisan bumper sticker. Reagan's budget director, David Stockman, has told how false numbers were pasted together by one Rosy Scenario, yielding an impossibly optimistic estimate of revenues. One year, the budget came back from the printer displaying, among the profusion of figures, a secretary's phone number that had been casually jotted down during discussions.

At the end of the budget process, the President in fact has the power of just less than two-thirds of Congress, thanks to the veto. President Reagan, who complained most about spending, applied the veto least. At one point he could have made constitutional history. Congress failed to pass essential legislation until the end of the year, then packed all bills and fundings into a single bloated bill and sent it to the President. As no one had read—could read—the mess, Solons freely injected it with pork for favored interests. Reagan displayed it on TV: a single piece of legislation consisting of a stack of paper 2 feet high and weighing 40 pounds. Had Reagan vetoed it and sent it back to Congress, he would have had the nation on his side, and probably the Supreme Court, too. By packing hundreds of bills into one, Congress effectively denied the President his constitutional right to weigh vetoing hundreds of individual bills on their own separate merits. It was a moment to display and overcome the moral poverty of Congress. But, ever good-humored, President Reagan grinned at the joke and signed the freak into law. The foremost foe of free lunches certified the biggest free lunch ever, and let the next generation pick up the tab.

The succeeding Presidency of George Bush was remarkable for skill and firmness in foreign affairs, deftly encouraging democratic forces in the dissolving U.S.S.R., and organizing nearly universal support for Desert Storm to prevent the world's richest oil resources from falling under control of a bloody-minded Iraqi dictator. But the Bushmen were a minus quantity in facing the problems that so troubled the American people. During Bush's campaign for the Presidency in 1988, *Newsweek* published a cover story titled "The Wimp Factor." It suggested that Bush might lose because of the public perception of him as being muddled and weak. The joke was told that what made the gangster John Gotti different from Bush was that the former had one conviction. The perception was heightened by Bush's thin, tinny voice and a personality that shrank with public exposure. "The camera diminishes him," said his wife to people surprised to learn that George Bush was in fact taller than the manly Ronald Reagan.

Stung by *Newsweek*, his handlers went to work thinking up tricks to make him appear strong. The most memorable of them was to steal a tough-guy expression from a Clint Eastwood movie for Bush to use in order to promise he wouldn't raise taxes. It was repeated in his every speech, uttered with an attempt at manly deliberation: "Read . . . My . . . Lips . . . No . . . New . . . Taxes." It was a ridiculous straitjacket to put himself in at a time when the utmost flexibility was needed in dealing with a mean national economy. Of course he had to break the pledge, but it lasted long enough to destroy the only real chance in those years to rehabilitate and liberate the crazy aunt.

That chance arose from an odd occasion. I was asked to make a kind of joint speech with Governor Mario Cuomo of New York to a business convention in Las Vegas. At one point I was asked from the floor how to induce Congress to deal with the budget deficit. I proposed a "Blue Ribbon Commission." I gave a brief history of such commissions from the Brownlow Commission, which enabled FDR to regain control of the New Deal, to the Greenspan Commission, which enabled Reagan to regain control of Social Security. They were bipartisan groups of widely respected "wise men" who would propose what all knew had to be done, but what no politician would dare recommend until the sages first said it was their idea. Cuomo listened intently to my answer but said nothing. In the next few weeks I heard him using my words to promote the idea of such a commission to people in authority. Congress was persuaded and formed the commission, headed by Robert Strauss and Drew Lewis. Ten of its twelve members were near agreement on a plan. Bush's budget director, Richard Darman, leaned toward agreeing.

Alas, some newspapers referred to the group as the Cuomo Commission, promoting a Democrat who might be Bush's opponent in a future election. He of the legible lips pronounced the Commission's proposals dead before arrival, liquidating the best chance in a decade to restore the basis for sound budgeting.

But over the long run it is hard to sustain pessimism about a nation with an almost obsessive dedication to civic rights. In the end the First Amendment will save us—the guarantee of freedom of speech. Few nations have a power so clearly and simply stated, and keep it so rustfree with use. As abuses accumulate, so does criticism. The demand for change grows irresistible. In the end, our powerfuls can achieve or keep power only by the votes of the people. One of my lectures on the neglected state of things ended with this:

> I never thought that I would derive inspiration from that famous entrepreneurial spirit from old Chicago, Alphonse Capone. But one of his maxims occurs to me now as applicable to our condition. Scarface Al once said, "You can get more with a kind word and a gun than you can with a kind word." Using ballots not bullets, let us make that our watchword.

I draw hope from the fact that a few years later the electorate began doing precisely that. In Congressional elections in 1992 and 1994, incumbents were decimated by barrages of ballots.

CHAPTER EIGHTY-TWO

Essay

Different writing people have different ways of propitiating the writing muse. Einstein may have done a little creative thinking on the back of that tram in Berne, but he put it into words sitting at a desk with a pen in his hand. Murrow did it pacing the room and smoking. I do it through my fingers. I place them on the keys of a writing machine in a typing mode, and after a moment thought begins to percolate and puff like a toy steam engine, and words begin to appear on the screen in sequence. As is said to happen in the case of ventriloquists, sometimes the instrument of one's trade takes over as master. So it is from time to time with me. Once not long ago I sat down to my machine to work on a lecture. I was tired of writing lectures and did not look forward to the long airplane trip to be undergone when the text was ready. I felt a mighty yearning to stay home and travel no farther than the outlying shrubs in Bennie's garden. But my fingers were in place, and these words soon appeared on the screen before me:

> I am 78 and witness to increasing small evidences that I shall not after all be exempt from mortality. As a writing man I feel I should leave something about my life in my own words. I begin, and we shall see how far I get.

By force of will, I got back to the lecture and finished it. But as soon as I returned home from the engagement, I was drawn to that paragraph as if magnetized, and spent a couple of days adding to it. Gradually I came to understand that my free will, left to wander unleashed, was telling me my leg-borne journalism days were near an end; the urge to sit still, meditate, summarize and integrate experience was not to be denied. I cut back gradually on speaking and spent more time studying old broadcasts and researching long-past events and writings. I never read the newspapers, I *study* them; I have filled shelves of loose-leaf books with notes on them—comments, notions, leads to be pursued. I now began to mine the notebooks. The words above became the first paragraph of this book. An editor persuaded me to delete it and start with the second paragraph, which now opens Chapter 1. But the absent paragraph finds a place in these concluding remarks, for had I not written it, I do not think I would have written the rest.

I wrote this story for the same reason that I rearranged Peter Rabbit's fate at age eight, and described the carnivorous herbivores at age eleven: I like to write. But I also hoped that the record might be of interest and even of use, as it covers the experience of a fairly educated and observant critic over a time period that the historian Robert D. Kaplan in *Balkan Ghosts* called "the most intensive seventy-five years in world history"—the span from 1914 and the outbreak of World War I until 1989 and the fall of the Berlin Wall.

My profession is called the first rough drafting of history. It can have a real utilitarian value. We have a better chance of avoiding error and doing something right if we know causes and effects of relevant past events. History may not tell us exactly what to do, but it is apt to widen and refine our options in ways not possible without some knowledge of what went before.

As a clear-cut illustration of the value of knowing history, Professor A. L. Rowse, the Oxford historian, cities the public lives of Winston Churchill and Neville Chamberlain. They were leaders in the same political party, the Conservatives, suggesting some similarity of outlook. They were of roughly the same social stratum and were moved by similar interests. Yet, when they surveyed the world of the late 1930s, they came to dramatically opposite conclusions. And one was proved by events to be completely right, and the other completely wrong.

The difference was, Rowse wrote, "Chamberlain simply did not know what to expect. Mr. Churchill knew very well. . . . But then he was a student of History; he had been there before." He not only knew history; he wrote it—thirty-two volumes of it! I have on my shelf a copy of what is probably Churchill's best work, his biography of his great ancestor, the Duke of Marlborough. It is precious because the author signed it for me. Though a main part of it deals with events in the early 1700s, it also describes with clarity an essentially similar strategic and political situation to the one Churchill as Prime Minister faced two centuries later.

America provides an even clearer illustration of the value of learning from History. It is the contrast in the behavior of two generations of Americans in the twentieth century. The generation that fought WW I went home, disenchanted and bitter, and pulled up the drawbridge behind it. The result was that, twenty-one years later, a second and worse world war arose from the neglected tinder of the first. But the generation that fought that second world war stayed where it had fought and assumed responsibility for what it had done. It not only participated in, but led, the organizing of the peace. The result was a stunning success, winning the Cold War and bringing our worst, tyrannical enemies into the circle of our best, democratized friends. We quite simply learned from history, with splendid consequences. It may not be an accident that the leader in this burst of creative statesmanship was our only recent President without a college education but with a deep self-education in history. "My debt to History," Harry Truman wrote in his memoirs (also precious: my copy of this, too, is autographed by the author), "cannot be calculated."

There are further favorable things to note about how our generation dealt with the worst war and its aftermath. Western Europe, hatchery of big wars, has been given more than half a century of peace—its longest respite from war ever. Unlike the post–WW I period there are no signs of, or preparations for, a coming breach; instead, impelled originally by the Marshall Plan, nations that have fought one another for centuries are busy with serious plans to cooperate and even unite.

Also, democracy enjoyed a new lease on life. After WW I, democratic institutions retreated to their turn-of-the-century confines in a cluster of nations, mostly on the shores of the North Atlantic. But since WW II, and especially since the winning of the Cold War, the democratic way has spread widely. Remarkably, we are experiencing the first years that all South America is ruled by governments freely elected by their peoples. For the first time that also applies to almost all of Europe. There may be regression by some countries, for it is a hard way to govern, but the opportunity for the spread of freedom has never been so great. Woodrow Wilson's suggestion that one purpose of our entry into a century of wars was to make the world "safe for democracy" no longer sounds ridiculous. It is not boastful but factual to state that this improvement is largely due to the spread of America's influence.

The record reflects favorably on the American temperament. For all its achievements, America retains a poor reputation for perseverance. We are thought, even among ourselves, to have an incurable need for instant gratification. We are seen, and see ourselves, as flighty, with attention spans too short for serious achievement. We are driven by short-term motives, are not up to long-term thought or activity.

If that reputation is just, how to account for the Cold War phenomenon? The whole American nation adopted a world policy of containment and clung to it through thick and thin, at every cost, for nearly half a century—until we prevailed. There are not many examples of stamina of purpose to match that.

I think that there is a message here for those who lead us. Given leadership of strong character, a clear, frank statement of the fix we are in and how we got there, sparing no bad news, and offered a credible set of proposals for getting out, Americans will by and large do what needs to be done and make the sacrifice entailed. That bit of wisdom is willed to the new generation that began to displace ours in the mid-1970s and had wholly displaced it by 1993 and the advent of the Clinton Administration.

Early returns on the Boomer generation's stewardship in the final quarter of the century leave much room for improvement. Poverty clings, and neither old wisdom nor fresh thought is applied to it. The hope that the civil rights laws of the 1960s would erase the color line has come under a shadow, seen most dramatically in the O. J. Simpson trial of 1995. Balancing the national accounts remains a promise, not a fact. Meanwhile the compounding clock is ticking, and the cost just of paying interest on that humongous debt is consuming ever more of our substance without purpose. We are laying on our children's children a burden that cannot be carried.

The quality of the government that must act on these matters has become deeply worrisome. Congress has sanitized the ways of corruption by calling its purchase price "campaign contributions." But Congress's actions often seem as nearly up for sale today as they were in the nineteenth century when such payments to elected officials by special interests were forthrightly called graft. Unless Congress is divorced from the special interests, it will be in no condition to deal with the national interest. What Carter called "malaise" in 1978 was rechristened a "funk" by Clinton in 1995, but it was the same disenchantment undealt with.

On top of these current problems, the new generation will see wholly new ones arise and demand attention. In my role as spear-carrier in the Depression–WW II–Cold War generation, I have sought in this narrative to suggest the main lines of causation of events in this century that will surely prevail into the next. As proposed in the opening chapter, the single persistent causal factor throughout—repeatedly destabilizing accepted ways, ever demanding new, painful adjustments—is the relentless and ever swifter advance in science and technology. Radical "improvements" in the instruments of mass killing made World War I an unprecedented horror that left a pacifist mindset in the world. The Depression, which brought to power in Germany and Japan the psychopaths who would exploit that mindset, was a consequence of technology's progress in turning out the goods of life too fast and copiously for the undercompensated consuming public to buy up (to be remedied in time not by trying to slow down technology but by taking measures to shift more wealth to consumers).

One effect of the Second World War was to make bigness essential to being a great power; only the big nations possessed the big backup industry and work force that world influence required. So the relatively small great powers of the prewar world—Britain, France, Germany and Japan—became mere satellites of the U.S., one of only two superpowers left after the war.

The relationship of the two superpowers was drastically affected by three further great technological advances. First, the atom bomb probably made a shooting war between the two impossible. If they were to fight, it would have to be on a "cold" basis, for they knew in their hearts that they would both be destroyed with doomsday weapons.

Their competition for what was the new military high ground produced the second great advance, the space industry, revolutionizing communication via satellites. The need to make and send complex and continuous computations far out to tiny capsules hastened the third great technological creation of the age, the modern computer. And the computer made sure that in the end the U.S. would prevail in the Cold War. Computer-aided production opened up avenues for creating and turning out far more effective products—and weapons—than were possible before. Russia had to adapt or fall behind hopelessly. But the computer could perform its magic only if all had access to free and true information. The Soviets could allow that only by dissolving their state. Thus did we watch a great empire collapse like a structure made of matchsticks, without a shot being fired.

At each stage new advances in technology set the parameters for action. But only the parameters. Within their limits the wisdom or folly of humans still determines success or failure. Politics remains the art of the possible, but leadership is the art of expanding what is possible.

It is easy to be pessimistic about the efforts so far of the malaised, funk-dipped new generation. But carping is a cop-out, an excuse for not settling down to find out what must be done and doing it. My experience, recorded in this book, makes me impatient for results, but also optimistic that results will come. There is momentum in our record for working things out. At the time the Depression seemed new, incomprehensible and unmanageable, until we found a handle to grasp. Once found, that handle—the Keynesian remedy—has been used to overcome without serious pain a dozen recessions since. Likewise the Cold War appeared beyond control, until George Kennan devised a concept that let us get a mental grip on it, George Marshall produced a plan, Dean Acheson created our first peacetime military alliance, and the whole people were inspired with a resolve to last it out. I expect the new generation will get a grip on its problems in much the same way, but I wish I could see more evidence of a will to do so than is now apparent.

Beyond these remarks, I have no clear idea of the shape of the future and its problems. John Maynard Keynes said, "The inevitable never happens. It is the unexpected always." In the end, no system or pattern will assure humans safe transit. Instead, all will depend on the ultimate duo: luck and the exercise of ancient virtues—intelligence, application, imagination, courage, character. It is a happy circumstance that the uncontrollable feature, luck, markedly improves when one works at the virtues.

CHAPTER EIGHTY-THREE

Judgment at Kalamazoo

Like fictional criminals, old men expecting soon to account to their Maker are drawn back to the scenes of past deeds. The attraction is the fugitive hope of running across some neglected scrap of debris that may tell something of themselves or their times.

The cotton fields that Ferriday and its railhead were founded to service have become increasingly planted with soybeans. Follow the harvester into them and a social epic unreels at your feet. In the fertile overgrown fields, you come upon one small sterile patch after another. These are the outlines of the bare foundations, all that is left of innumerable cabins, once the homes of families of five or a dozen Negroes who worked the fields. In a greater migration than the one that won the West, theirs to the North and to the West has in this century peopled Los Angeles and Chicago and every other city with new heroes and villains of the civic drama. The harvester that drove them out is operated from a cabin of another sort—a glassed-in, air-conditioned eyrie with stereophonic music to please its single driver as he accomplishes in a morning what whole tribes of Black families at the time of my birth took days to do.

The little town is now intimately tied into the great world. Its Chamber of Commerce issued a brochure: "Ferriday—Sportsman's Paradise." The claim is justified by two lakes, once elongated wetlands left over from the annual floods of the Mississippi (one still bears the name Old River), now sparkling blue jewels. In addition there is a state-conserved hunting area, a golf course, and "nearby airports from which New York or Los Angeles are readily reached." Heaven knows how, but a plain clapboard house where I was born remained, at last visit, in the middle of town. New is a museum of photos and relics of Ferriday's famous and once-famous, all their sins disremembered.

My childhood paradise, Monroe, not as far from Ferriday as it seemed in buggy days, has gained and lost with time. Where my brother's high school was once the summit of available education, the city now boasts a state university, in whose field house I was privileged to speak. The school I attended was, like much of America, torn down to accommodate new highways. A new one was officially desegregated but tending toward Black. The city made the national network news recently in a report on the problem of scanning children for firearms commonly being brought to classes. The Mayor, who once sent me a telegram, "When are you going to do something we can be proud of?" decided I had approximated his requirements sufficiently to make me the guest at a dinner in the civic center.

South of Ferriday, and very near my ancestors' plantation home at Lettsworth, the Corps of Engineers has, since I left Louisiana, constructed a long, high levee of pharaonic water barricades. These have virtually eliminated floods, allowing Ferriday's wetlands to settle as lovely lakes. When there is danger of flooding, the great gates are lifted, and the water pours away from the Mississippi, across lowlands, into the basin of the river of the lyric name Atchafalaya. These barricades, hugely expensive to maintain, hold New Orleans' fate like a hangman's noose. The river has been flirtatious with the Atchafalaya for centuries. Without the man-made barriers, it might of its own free will desert the present course and seek the shorter way to the Gulf, via the Atchafalaya. If economy and gravity ever have their way, New Orleans would find itself high and dry beside a large ditch of brackish water sucked up from the Gulf.

As ever, New Orleans seemed unworried by this or any peril. Mardi Gras has grown from about a half-dozen Krewes with parades to about thirty now. Bourbon Street remains site of Sodom and Gomorrah West, now answerable to the mob and the cops, not to down-at-the-heels impresarios of girly palaces as in my time. The visitor may experience the charm of evil without harm; watchful eyes make sure nobody gets rolled and hurts the tourist trade. For the nonvisitor, particularly the residents of poor neighborhoods where tourists do not go, safety is conditional. A recent investigation of an underpaid police force opened up horrors not equaled in any other big city. The police do not hunt the gangsters; they *are* the gangsters, carving up turf for purposes of exploiting the drug trade, and beating insensate any citizens who get in their way. The Mayor and a new Chief of Police promise reform. But they run up against the culture of ease, of turning a blind eye, of settling for the third rate, of taking pride in laxity, which leaves the hard day-by-day work of running things open to predators.

Uptown, some lovely old homes with those high ceilings and broad porches have been replaced by modern apartments, but there is so much grandeur left that it is still worth a ride on the world's biggest streetcars. Tulane has become a much finer educational instrument than in my youth, with curricula both wider and deeper. The physical plant serving that purpose has been built over my beloved playing fields. Big track now has a home in a large new stadium across town named after my old friend and mentor, Tad Gormley. Big football is played in the Louisiana Superdome, which looks like a giant pushbutton on the skyline.

Abroad, from thirty-one colleges Oxford has fattened to thirty-nine, some of the new ones bearing the names of contemporary millionaires, Wolfson, Nuffield, Templeton (the last a Connecticut Rhodes Scholar who defected to Britain and now bears the title and Christian name, Sir John). Oxford needed money. Education was becoming more expensive, and Mrs. Thatcher's government reduced subsidies. The University's operating head said in a notable speech that Oxford and all universities everywhere were suffering a fall of esteem in the minds of publics and governments. He said this was largely due to the rebellious outbursts of the 1960s exhibiting a generational spoliation and confusion of aim that the majority was no longer willing to pay for. The University and many of the colleges made public appeals for donations. I shall leave the reader to guess which grateful alumnus launched Merton's appeal in America. Ancient quadrangles were dug under to allow plumbing to be installed. No longer was personal cleanliness limited to what could be done with a tin of hot water in a crockery basin. No longer did nighttime stragglers in the quad have to fear that chamber pots might be emptied on them from high windows. The largest change and a historic improvement: women were accepted in colleges once reserved for men, and, true to the dire prophecies of misogynists, appeared on the way soon to dominate. By 1993, there were more female Rhodes Scholars from America than male. The new warden, or chief presiding officer, of Merton is for the first time in history a woman. After long lip service, majority rule is becoming reality in Oxford as in the rest of the Western world.

I think I liked London more than any city I have ever lived in. It is the best of all for walking, sight-seeing and window-shopping, as well as for living. Yet, I made but one return trip and wish to make no more. I went back to cover the funeral of Winston Churchill for ABC. It was an infinitely sad experience. One free night, I went out on the dark misty streets of London to my old neighborhood on the Regent's Park. I arrived at York Terrace to find my home at number 19 with the windows broken out and the doorway boarded up, our handsome door undoubtedly sold by the wrecker. The elegant row houses of the ancient Terrace were uneconomic and were being reorganized as flats to be rented out at an advantage. I felt so identified with that home that I was seized with a melancholy trance. I felt that I, not it, had been declared uneconomic. Bennie was gone, no trace. So were the children. Just a boarded-up shell where once a happy home had been. It became clear that I had died but was condemned to walk the earth and witness sights like these till some dark sin was expiated. I turned and fled from the scene. I took a plane to New York the next day, to be with my wife and family as soon as possible and to cling to them. I would never return to London.

My career and my life pretty closely bracketed Robert Kaplan's seventy-five most intensive years—our twentieth-century time of troubles, which is most clearly symbolized in Berlin. Indeed, the period was manifested in acts at either end of one street. At the far end of Unter den Linden, in August 1914, Kaiser Wilhelm appeared on the balcony of his palace to salute crowds cheering his invasion of Belgium. The old palace was reduced to rubble by bombers, but its facade is still there, encased, like a rare stone on a broach, by a new modern structure built around, and in support of, it—a display case to show the world the best symbol of a dreadfully wrong decision. Now, three quarters of a century later, I was at the near end of the same street, watching the Berlin Wall being transformed into the biggest source of paperweights on earth. This was the true end of the half century of Cold War.

It was an unanticipated return to Berlin. The Russians and the Germans were producing a monumental television documentary about the last days of the war. They sought witnesses to the final surrender of the Germans to the Russians at Karlshorst. They found surviving officers from Russia, Britain, France and Germany. But from America there was but one living remnant: me. Bennie and I were flown back, and I took part in a nostalgic but lively reenactment. The location, a school for German officers, had been made into a museum, which included a small shelf of books, in many languages, written about the surrender at the time. I was delighted to see that the only American book preserved was my friend Norman Corwin's great prose poem for CBS Radio in 1945, "On a Note of Triumph."

After I had done my bit before cameras at Karlshorst, we paid a visit to the place mentioned in the first lines of Corwin's work:

> *So they've given up.*
> *They're finally done in, and the rat is dead in an*
> *alley in back of the Wilhelmstrasse.*

The last previous time I had visited the place in back of the Wilhelmstrasse, the Chancellery was gone and the great area scraped clean and flat by the Russians. Now, fifty years after the dead rat had been removed, a complex of middle-class apartments had sprung up, with a children's playpen and a sandbox over what had been the bunker—a nice commonplace end of the story, with no clue that the killing in anger of 50 million humans was launched from there.

We went then to see the newest addition to Berlin's collection of military monuments, also commonplace but deeply impressive. It was an empty, neatly cobblestoned courtyard within the gray old German War Ministry in the Bendlerstrasse. There was nothing noteworthy but a place near a corner where fresh flowers are laid every morning. It is the spot where young Count von Stauffenberg was summarily executed with three co-conspirators hours after the bomb he carried and set off maimed but did not kill the rat in his headquarters. People entered the courtyard as they would a cathedral, speaking in whispers, a few genuflecting.

For our fiftieth wedding anniversary, Bennie and I were determined to do something special, but could not think what it would be. Nearly on the eve, we struck on it: revisit the place where our lives became one, and where we commenced the wonderful experience of living happily ever after. Soon we were on a plane to Zurich, then on the Schnellzug to Berne. We could have chosen no place so nearly untouched by time as the medieval city of the endless arcades and ornamented horse troughs. It was an expensive venture, the Swiss franc being much sought after on the currency exchanges, and the American dollar down in the dumps. It too was a ghostly visit, but with my girl attached to my arm, it was not traumatic as London had been. We found the room where we were married converted from a salle with curtains and ornaments to a bureaucrat's warren. We showed our marriage certificate to a Chef de Bureau, who glanced at the official's signature and said, "Oh, I recall the old fellow, retired and died several years ago." Everyone we asked about had died. The only surviving witness to our wedding, the retired English businessman (and wartime intelligence agent), our close friend Peter Jellinek, flew over from London to join us. On our wedding night plus fifty years, we dined in the Schweizerhof bar and grill, which seemed almost tomblike with no clutter of American reporters at the bar. Peter noted that he had never known us except together, and what did I do before? I told him I pretended to go to school, ran hurdles, traveled all over Europe, reported the news, as means of filling time till I found her. It was for her that I took a box of chocolates to kindergarten, with little Nancy Pugh as a stand-in.

One of the most gratifying of my revisitings was a return not to a place but to an issue. I went back to Birmingham, met the (Black) mayor, and made a commencement address at Samford University. But the remnant of the Civil

Rights Revolution that undid me at CBS had moved to another place, and I
followed it there. The law's delay had been long, but after twenty-two years it
arrived, on Wednesday, March 2, 1983, in Kalamazoo, Michigan. The two
worst beaten of the Birmingham Freedom Riders were suing the U.S. government. They were James Peck, who had required twenty-six stitches in his face,
and Walter Bergman, who had been crippled for life. It came out that the two
buttoned-down young FBI agents who visited me in my motel that terrible day
had been fully informed of the Klan's plan from the start. The FBI had a paid
informant in the leading circles of the Klan. But they and their bosses in Washington did nothing to warn the Riders, or otherwise fulfill the Constitution's
requirement to "insure domestic tranquility." The FBI's attitude, as they expressed it to me in a comment on the Freedom Riders, was, "They came looking for trouble, and they found it." Peck in New York and Bergman in
Michigan sued for damages. As the only nonparticipating witness, I did a de-
position for Peck and went to Kalamazoo to testify for Bergman.

The government was represented by two very young lawyers, a man and a
woman. At one point, they sought to question my civil conscience by asking:
since I was forewarned of the attack, why did I not alert the Birmingham police? I answered that all the evidence was, the Birmingham police knew about
it before I did; they were in at the creation. They sought to question my dis-
cernment by asking how I knew that the young men who approached me were
FBI agents. I said that they had shown me IDs with the words "Federal Bureau of Investigation" printed prominently on them, but that, of course, they
might have been fooling. There was a burst of laughter in the courtroom, my
cross-examiners at last joining in. Their young hearts were not in their assignment of defending wrong. Peck, then Bergman, won their suits. The courts
understood, as CBS had not, that truth is not somewhere equidistant between
right and wrong. As Jimmy Hoffa once said in an inspired moment, "Truth is
not between anything. Truth is where it's at." As I left the witness stand in
Kalamazoo, the judge said, "Have a good life, Mr. Smith." On the plane out,
Bennie thought that was the aptest remark. That, she said, was a good short
summary of what life's fitful fever is all about; and all things considered, we
were doing just fine.

INDEX

Note: HKS stands for Howard K. Smith